"It's hard to imagine a remembran[ce] [so] genial — so graceful, so immune to grudge, so seasoned throughout with the equally vivid recollections of his friends."

— JOHN LEONARD, *Newsday*

"Frightening, that if this book didn't exist, there would be no record of that particular time and climate — but it does and I loved it."

— BRUCE JAY FRIEDMAN

"Wakefield has written a kinder spirited *Moveable Feast* for his generation."

— *Publishers Weekly*

"A treasure, an open sesame into that golden age of youth when the possibilities seemed endless."

— JOHN GREGORY DUNNE

"This lovely, brimming book . . . tells anyone who was not there what it was like."

— *Boston Globe*

"A precious memoir, and one to be cherished."

— RABBI HAROLD KUSHNER

"This time trip with Wakefield proves fascinating, even poignant — a latter-day variation on Malcolm Cowley's look at the Jazz Age, *Exile's Return.*"

— *Hartford Courant*

NEW YORK
in the Fifties

DAN WAKEFIELD

HOUGHTON MIFFLIN / SEYMOUR LAWRENCE

BOSTON ▪ NEW YORK

For information about permission to reproduce selections from
this book, write to Permissions, Houghton Mifflin Company,
215 Park Avenue South, New York, New York 10003.

Library of Congress Cataloging-in-Publication Data
Wakefield, Dan.
New York in the fifties / Dan Wakefield.
p.   cm.
Includes index.
ISBN 0-395-51320-0 (cloth)
ISBN 0-395-66925-1 (pbk.)
1. Wakefield, Dan — Homes and haunts — New York (N.Y.)
2. Greenwich Village (New York, N.Y.) — Intellectual life — 20th century.
3. Greenwich Village (New York, N.Y.) — Social life and customs.
4. Novelists, American — 20th century — Biography.   5. Journalists —
United States — Biography.   I. Title.
PS3573.A413Z474   1992   91-46285
818'.5403 — dc20   CIP
[B]

Printed in the United States of America

AGM 10 9 8 7 6 5 4 3 2 1

Parts of this book have appeared in *GQ, Ploughshares,*
and *Columbia,* the magazine of Columbia University.

The author is grateful for permission to quote from previously published
works: Lines from "Dawn" by Federico García Lorca. Reprinted by permission of New Directions Publishing Corporation. Lines from the poetry
of May Swenson are reprinted by permission of the Literary Estate of May
Swenson. Excerpt from *Four Quartets,* copyright 1943 by T. S. Eliot and
renewed 1971 by Esme Valerie Eliot, reprinted by permission of Harcourt
Brace Jovanovich, Inc. Excerpt from "Recuerdo" by Edna St. Vincent Millay. From *Collected Poems,* Harper & Row. Copyright 1922, 1950 by Edna
St. Vincent Millay. Reprinted by permission of Elizabeth Barnett, literary
executor. Lines from the poem by Donald Cook are reprinted by permis-
sion of author. "Politics" by William Butler Yeats. Reprinted by permission of Macmillan Publishing Company from *The Poems of W. B. Yeats: A
New Edition,* edited by Richard J. Finneran. Copyright 1940 by Georgie
Yeats, renewed 1968 by Bertha Georgie Yeats, Michael Butler Yeats, and
Anne Yeats. "The Day Lady Died" by Frank O'Hara. From *Lunch Poems,*
copyright © 1964 by Frank O'Hara. Reprinted by permission of City
Lights Books.

To Sam Astrachan, Jane Wylie Genth,
Ivan Gold, Mike Standard,
Ted Steeg, and Helen Weaver

And to the memory of C. Wright Mills,
Robert Phelps, and May Swenson

Loved ones all, in New York
in the fifties, and beyond

There was a time when New York was everything to me: my mother, my mistress, my Mecca. . . . It persists, an indelible part of my young manhood, imbedded in the very core of my being.

— *Harvey Swados, "Nights in the Gardens of Brooklyn"*

Let us raise a standard to which the wise and the honest can repair. The event is in the hands of God.

— *George Washington to his troops, as quoted on the Washington Square arch*

tion for their contributions to it — and in many cases to my own life during that time. This book is theirs too: David Amram, Sam Astrachan, Ann Montgomery Brower, Brock Brower, William F. Buckley, Jr., William Cole, Dawn and Donald Cook, Joan Didion, Art d'Lugoff, Reverend Norman C. Eddy, Ed Fancher, Max Frankel, Jane Wylie Genth, Allen Ginsberg, Ivan Gold, Walter Goodman, Meg Greenfield, Ray Grist, Margot Hentoff, Nat Hentoff, Leslie Katz, Murray Kempton, Rabbi Harold Kushner, Richard Lingeman, Mary Ann McCoy, Marion Magid, Norman Mailer, David Markson, Gilbert Millstein, Mary Perot Nichols, Ned O'Gorman, Norman Podhoretz, Ned Polsky, Jane Richmond, Lynne Sharon Schwartz, Harvey Shapiro, Mike Standard, Ted Steeg, Bette Swados, Gay Talese, Calvin Trillin, Helen Tworkov, Kurt Vonnegut, Helen Weaver, and Dan Wolfe.

Thanks to dear writer friends who read and encouraged along the way: Sara Davidson, Ivan Gold, Marcie Hershman, Robert Manning, and Shaun O'Connell.

Thanks to DeWitt Henry, *Ploughshares,* and Emerson College for professional faith and support.

Acknowledgments

I wish to thank Sam Lawrence, who saw this book in me before I did, and whose faith and support have sustained not only this work but the literary heart of my career for more than twenty years.

Thanks to Art Cooper, whose interest and faith in my work over the years both as literary critic of *Newsweek* and editor of *GQ* have been a significant and greatly appreciated support.

Thanks to Lynn Nesbit, whose friendship, professional advice, and support in the past year have been an invaluable gift that improves "the quality of life."

Thanks to the superb Houghton Mifflin Company Library — headed by Guest Perry — a boon for authors. My special thanks to Amy Cohen-Rose, whose sensitivity, moral support, and professionalism were crucial to the completion of this book in the final months.

Thanks to Sarah Burnes of Houghton Mifflin for enthusiastic, expert assistance, and thanks to her and Alix Colow for gathering photographs. Thanks to Larry Cooper for editorial guidance, courtesy, and patience.

To Alice Olsen, for listening, believing, and holding my hand.

My gratitude goes to the friends and colleagues from New York in the fifties who gave me the gift of their time and memories, and evoked not only my feeling for that decade but also new apprecia-

Contents

Author's Note

In the 1950s, "Negro" was the accepted term of respect for the minority people who in the next decade would find both beauty and power in the word "black," which before then could have been taken as an insult. In the 1990s, "African American" is for many the preferred designation. In the 1950s, a definition of the word "girl" in my *American College Dictionary* (a standard reference book of the time, published by Harper's) was "2. a young unmarried woman." That usage was preferred by the young women I knew at the time, though their counterparts today would reject the term as disrespectful, or even demeaning, and prefer to be called women.

In using the terms "Negro" and "girl," I have tried to be faithful to the sound and speech of the 1950s. I do not intend any disrespect to current sensibilities by such usage.

INTRODUCTION

The "Silent Generation" Speaks Out

T HE DECADE I lived in New York was the heart of the 1950s. I arrived at Columbia the year that Dwight D. Eisenhower exchanged his presidency of the university for that of the United States. One of my early assignments as a reporter for the *Columbia Daily Spectator* was to photograph him at a campaign picnic before the homecoming game, and I captured a view of his famous bald dome bending over a piece of fried chicken. Despite opposition from the *Spectator* (most of us on the staff were "madly for Adlai"), Ike was elected, and he began an eight-year reign that marked the mood of the decade as one of benign middle-of-the-road Republicanism. The era was summed up in the comforting slogan so soothingly repeated by the solid majority of Americans, but — and this significant fact is forgotten — heard with teeth-grinding frustration by the rest: "I like Ike."

The autumn I left New York, for a Nieman fellowship in journalism at Harvard, John F. Kennedy was assassinated. If the charismatic young JFK's succession of Ike as president was seen as the end of an era, his death was a deeper, more tragic close to the innocence of the Eisenhower years. But these were endings, like the closing of great doors on the past, offering little or no vision of what was to come.

I got my first glimpse of the new era the following spring of 1964, when I returned to New York for the wedding brunch of a friend at the Plaza Hotel. I looked out the tall windows of the Edwardian Room and saw mounted police holding back a mob of unruly young people trying to get beyond traffic barricades to touch or glimpse a new pop music group from Liverpool who had come to appear on "The Ed Sullivan Show."

These English kid musicians, who were called by the odd name the Beatles, seemed in age, attire, manner, attitude, and music to be the polar opposite of the patriarchal Ike. Their arrival in New York represented the real changing of the guard, not just the political switch in style and rhetoric represented by JFK, but the real if belated beginning of the counterdecade — the anti-establishment, youth-on-the-loose, psychedelic sixties.

The time from Ike's election to the coming of the Beatles was a decade in which the taste, politics, mores, and culture of our society underwent a deep change, one that not only unleashed the tidal wave of the sixties but formed the patterns from which future decades would flow, shaping the way we live now in the closing years of what began as "the American century."

The sixties supposedly ushered in the era of change, revolt, and excitement, while the fifties have been dismissed as dull and boring, a time of quiet acquiescence to the status quo. My Columbia College classmate Rabbi Harold Kushner, author of *When Bad Things Happen to Good People* (a best seller of the eighties), articulated the feelings of many of us when he said in his address to the thirty-fifth reunion of the class of '55: "Ours is seen as a time when nothing happened — the Eisenhower years, the age of conformity, of passivity instead of passion, of panty raids instead of protest marches, the years of Levittown and *The Organization Man* and *The Lonely Crowd*. I think the time has come for us to look back in charity and ask ourselves: were the fifties really that dull and empty?"

In finding the strengths, virtues, and contributions of what he called "the last generation to trust our elders," Rabbi Kushner struck a chord in those of us who have long believed we were mistakenly stuck with the label of "the Silent Generation." In fact, I didn't know how strongly my friends from the fifties, many of them writers, felt about the inaccuracy of our generational dog tag and about the bad rap our decade was given until I began to ask them about it. I was pleased to find my own feelings affirmed, but I was surprised by the passion and eloquence with which these writers spoke of our time.

One of my friends when I lived in the Village was Meg Greenfield, who worked as a staff writer for *The Reporter* and is now the editorial page editor of the *Washington Post.* "I felt the Silent Generation thing was sort of a libel," she says. "Now it's simply become the accepted wisdom, but the fifties are a badly researched and badly reported time. There was more social action, and more sense than we're given credit for. Subsequent generations have politicized every emotion and believed it was happening to them for the first time. We experienced as much and understood more than we're given credit for. It didn't occur to you if you were having a problem with a boyfriend or with your family — all of us who left home and came to New York had a terrible struggle with our parents — to announce that it was the problem of the American political system and write articles denouncing something."

Max Frankel, who was my early idol and boss as editor of the *Spectator* when I went to Columbia in 1952 and now is executive editor of the *New York Times,* says without hesitation, "I thought the label 'Silent Generation' was dumb and inaccurate. When I was on the *Spectator,* we were noisy about not liking Ike and about upholding academic freedom and other issues we felt strongly about."

Marion Magid went to Barnard when I was at Columbia, but I didn't meet her until I was living in the Village, when she was writing critical pieces on the theater. She is now an associate editor of *Commentary,* which she has worked for as a writer and editor for many years. We met again recently in New York. "I don't believe the fifties was so namby-pamby as people later made it out to be," she says. "It was the last time it was possible to have a 'personal' life. There was a sense of discovery then, but later everything became so codified. Now relationships are mapped, there are pre-established attitudes. There's a sense that everything's been ransacked — every secret, ethnic and sexual. There's no more privacy. You meet and everyone exchanges credentials. We had more room to live the inner life."

Columnist Murray Kempton, who had already begun his career by the 1950s, says of my generation, "You were the country's younger brothers." Like many of my friends in New York, I regarded Murray as a wise older brother, and we would devour his iconoclastic column in the *New York Post*, which appeared three times a week. Murray now writes his column for *Newsday*. "When people came to America in those days," he says, "they wanted to know how we did it. It was like being in the Soviet Union in the thirties. We were the repository of every illusion of 'the better.' It was fun, and life was much clearer then. I was wildly patriotic. Of course, I was young then."

I'm aware that the passionate feelings my friends and I have about the decade when we came of age must in part be due to the fact that, as Kempton says, we were young. The day I called him to get together and talk about those years, he was writing a column on the death of Robert F. Wagner, Jr., the mayor of New York City who was first elected in 1953. Murray read me the line that became the lead of his piece: "If you live in New York long enough, what you thought was an age of lead will look like an age of gold."

I don't deny the nostalgia I feel, nor do I deny the darkness peculiar to the time and place I now celebrate. Almost everyone I reminisced with spoke about the heavy boozing without my bringing it up: "We drank too much," "How did we drink so much?" We abused our bodies with booze and lack of sleep, and inhaled packs of cigarettes as if they were oxygen. We cared nothing for diet or exercise. A few of us smoked pot, and many of us took the popular uppers of the time, on prescription from doctors or psychiatrists — Dexedrine and Dexamyl, those heart-shaped green and orange pills. But for all our excesses, which we often justified as "literary" in imitation of our Roaring Twenties idols, we somehow managed to survive and observe and create in an especially fruitful time.

I went to Columbia as a mid-semester sophomore transfer student in January of 1952 from Indiana University at Bloomington, leaving with excitement and relief the somnolent southern Indiana landscape of rolling hills and limestone quarries for the concrete canyons and skyscraping spires I had dreamed of while listening to Gordon Jenkins's mushy *Manhattan Towers,* a romantic anthem for many of my peers. I graduated from Columbia in 1955, lived for a while on the Upper West Side near Riverside Drive before moving on to what would be home in Greenwich Village (appropriate antithesis of what the Midwest means by "home"), until I said goodbye to New York in 1963.

I was lucky to learn from professors at Columbia whose work helped define the times, from the poet Mark Van Doren and the literary critic Lionel Trilling to C. Wright Mills, the rebel sociologist whose controversial books *White Collar* and *The Power Elite* delineated in disturbing strokes the new middle- and upper-class structure of America in the fifties.

Reporting on politics and culture for *The Nation,* I interviewed leaders and covered events that were shaping the period, from protests against civil defense air raid drills which were supposed to save New Yorkers from an A-bomb attack by sending them down to the subway, to Jack Kerouac's drunken reading from *On the Road* at a Village nightclub, which signaled the arrival of the Beat Generation. Writing about the Catholic Worker movement led me to live for a while in Spanish Harlem and write my first book, *Island in the City: The World of Spanish Harlem,* and I got involved in the grass-roots effort to help narcotics addicts and treat them as patients rather than criminals. For *Esquire,* I drew assignments to profile a spectrum of luminaries, dining (with notebook) in Harlem with Adam Clayton Powell, Jr., and at the New York Yacht Club with William F. Buckley, Jr.

My life and concerns were hardly limited to public figures and events, however. Like so many others of my time and place, I fell in love a hundred times, went into psychoanalysis, tried to write a novel, and listened to jazz musicians like Miles Davis and J. J. Johnson, going from glittery midtown music meccas like Birdland to crowded, smoky Village haunts like the Five Spot. I drank pints of arf 'n' arf and debated politics and books with James Baldwin and Michael Harrington at the White Horse Tavern; saw Jason Robards in *The Iceman Cometh* and Geraldine Page in *Summer and Smoke* at the Circle in the Square; and went with buddies and dates to the Amato Opera, a converted moviehouse with a single piano as orchestra, where music students carried cardboard elephants in the grand march of *Aïda,* all for whatever coins you could afford to put in the hat when it was passed.

This was a New York where you could go on a date to Louis' or the San Remo or the Grand Ticino in Greenwich Village and have a bottle of wine with your dinner for a little less than five bucks for the two of you. The subway was a dime and the Staten Island ferry a nickel. Four women college graduates who made no more than $50 a week from their magazine or publishing jobs could pitch in and rent a lovely furnished three-bedroom apartment on West End Avenue for $200 a month. Students could afford standing room at the Metropolitan Opera or one of the hit musicals on Broadway, like *Call Me Madam* with Ethel Merman. There was no cover or minimum charge to stand at the bar and hear Mingus at the Five Spot, in the Village. Carson McCullers read for free at Columbia and told how she wrote *The Heart Is a Lonely Hunter,* a novel that, along with *The Catcher in the Rye,* inspired my newly graduated generation.

I threw all-night parties with new friends who, like myself, had come from the hinterlands to make their fame and fortune and "find themselves" in the pulsing heart of the hip new world's hot center, with the ghosts of the recent past as guides. We quoted aloud Fitzgerald and Hemingway, Millay and e. e. cummings, as we drank the wine and burned at both ends the candle of early youth and bittersweet first disillusionment. We revived our faith with the incantations of Dylan Thomas, our secular poet-priest, whose chants we played at dawn on the Caedmon record that boomed the vow we took to "not go gentle into that good night."

If my generation was "silent," it was not in failure to speak out with our work, but in the sense of adopting a style that was not given to splash and spotlights. Max Frankel says, "We set out essentially to be spectators and reflectors on life. A dogged kind of centrism came out of this, and it was later confused with unfeelingness in the sixties, as if we didn't care enough for issues like the environment."

We had no desire to shout political slogans or march with banners, because we had seen the idealism of the radical thirties degenerate into the disillusionment of Stalinism and the backlash reaction of name-calling anticommunism. The naïve hope of salvation by politics seemed to have burned itself out in the thirties, replaced in the fifties too often by an equally naïve belief in salvation through psychoanalysis. My friends and I agreed with Hemingway's advice at the end of *Death in the Afternoon:* "Let those who want to save the world if you can get to see it clear and as a whole." Another of Papa's admonitions from the same book was reaffirmed for us in the fifties by James Baldwin in *Notes of a Native Son,* and it became a kind of creed: "The great thing, as Hemingway said, is to last and get your work done."

Ours was not the silence of timidity or apathy, but the kind James Joyce meant, in *Portrait of the Artist,* when he spoke of the young writer's vow as "silence, exile, and cunning." The "silence" of Joyce was not surrender; it simply meant not to blab or brag about your work. The "cunning" was finding a way to make a living and then doing it. The "exile" was the place far enough from the censure of home and middle-class convention to feel free enough to create. Our own chosen place of exile from middle America was not Europe but New York, where, like Paris in the twenties, you found your contemporary counterparts — allies, mentors, friends. Our fifties were far more exciting than the typical American experience because we were in New York, where people came to flee the average and find a group of like-minded souls. "We had our community, and there was stability and solidarity," Meg Greenfield says, recalling our group of writer friends, who were centered in the Village but also had connections on the Upper East and West sides.

There were actually many such communities in New York then, many of them interconnected. David Amram, the jazz musician and composer I used to hear play at the Five Spot, says, "There was a cross-pollination of music, painting, writing — an incredible world of painters, sculptors, musicians, writers, and actors, enough so we could be each other's fans. When I had concerts, painters would come, and I'd go play jazz at their art gallery openings, and I played piano while beats read their poetry. Kerouac asked Larry Rivers and me to be in the movie *Pull My Daisy,* with him and Allen Ginsberg."

Another community, which served as an intellectual and spiritual base for many young people who came to New York then, was the Catholic Worker movement in the Bowery, founded by Dorothy Day, an ex-bohemian who had turned, in the 1930s, from the lure of communism to a deeply felt Catholicism.

It was there that I met Mary Ann McCoy, who with two other young women had started a day care center for children in Spanish Harlem, and showed me the neighborhood that inspired my first book. Mary Ann now lives in a racially mixed neighborhood in

Brooklyn, where she's a community activist. "I associate the feeling of the Catholic Worker farm on Staten Island with our time, the fifties," she says. "There was a big oak tree and a cow mooing and the chapel was part of the barn. Mass was held every morning, and you celebrated the hours of the day. The people there had a commitment, and we gave up part of our personal life to care for the poor, like Dorothy Day. There was a balance there that the sixties didn't have. The sixties lacked a connection with the other things of life. What's ever come out of the sixties? What did it get us? I saw it as being one big party time."

The Catholic Worker also served as a community for a young poet named Ned O'Gorman, whom I used to see at Dorothy Day's Bowery mission and at the White Horse Tavern. Ned is now headmaster of the Storefront School for Children, which he founded in 1966 in Harlem.

"New York was safe then," he says, looking back on the time we were friends. "It was bouncing, almost like the whole of it was a little village where everybody knew everybody else. Literary life in New York had not yet become a commercial venture then. When Bill Clancy was editor of *Commonweal,* he used to have parties with serious young writers and priests, and you went because you were excited about a real intellectual life, not because you wanted to get in Suzy's column or get a book contract. I went to a literary party the other night and there was a mass of writers craning their necks to get photographed — it seems vulgar. I preferred the White Horse and the Catholic Worker to what passes for literary life in New York now."

There are, of course, new and different communities in New York now, with their own constituencies and their own contributions, but the city itself is not the same one we inhabited then and took for granted. I miss the people most of all, and some of them are gone forever. In January 1990 I went to a memorial service for one of my Village writer friends, Seymour Krim, and saw many familiar faces from the past. We'll be seeing each other again at similar gatherings, which will come with increasing frequency.

This book began as only a personal memoir, and it didn't feel right. I needed to hear other people's stories and impressions as well as my own, and when I went to New York on a short visit in the fall of 1990, I looked up some old friends. I had lunch with Dan Wolf, the cofounder and original editor of the *Village Voice*, at a Korean restaurant in midtown, met with Nat Hentoff at Bradley's bar in the Village, and called Gilbert Millstein to talk about his friendship with Jack Kerouac, which began when he reviewed *On the Road* in the *New York Times*. These conversations were so rich and gave such life to my own memory of the time that I started coming down more often and seeing more people. By the end of the year, I realized I wanted to spend more time in New York. My novelist friend Lynne Sharon Schwartz was looking for someone to sublet her studio apartment on West 96th Street for a few months, and I said I'd take it.

This book has become, I hope, a kind of community memoir as well as my own, and the effort to make it that, I think, is true to the spirit of the time and place, for we had a deep sense of community and comradeship then that was unique. I see now how important this was to all of us. Certainly I know how essential it was to me, and how precious it still is.

When I started this exploration, I had no idea how much there was to see and hear and remember. There could easily be ten or twelve books on aspects of New York in the fifties. There are huge, important subjects I haven't touched on at all, or only spoken of in passing. This book is in no way meant to be definitive, but only evocative, slanted to what were my own concerns and passions and those of my friends, who mostly had literary aspirations and were starting out. We were the newcomers, the people Carl Sandburg meant by the phrase "always the young strangers."

Even while it was all happening, I knew that the time and the place were special. I remember walking down Broadway in midtown and seeing people I identified as tourists and feeling sorry for them because they didn't live in New York! I felt privileged to be there, and now I feel proud as well, of the friends I had and the work we did and will continue to do for as long as we have the time and chance. Whatever we've done was shaped by the fortunate fact that we started out in the most exciting city of its era, a mecca that, like Paris in the twenties, exists now only in memory. Its naming now seems legendary: New York in the fifties.

ONE

To Grand Central Station

T HE ONLY WAY to go to New York from the rest of the country in 1952 was by train — I mean the only romantic, "literary" way. It was possible to fly, of course, but that was considered expensive and elite, even a little dangerous. My parents and I were the first on our block to travel by plane when we went to the New York World's Fair in 1939, and the neighbors all came to the airport to see us off, one of them warning my mother not to wear her good hat on the flight for fear "it might blow off up there." You could drive or hitchhike or take a bus, but all that seemed grubby and déclassé compared to going on the train, which popular songs, like "Blues in the Night," and poets and novelists from Walt Whitman to Thomas Wolfe had immortalized, invoking the whistle of the locomotive sounding in the dark as a signal of love, loss, and longing ("hear that lonesome whistle, whooee"), the pitch of our deepest hopes and dreams. The trains we took to New York are part of the dreams of my generation, a shared symbol of collective memory.

The train took you straight to the city's heart, to Penn Station or, better still, to the legendary Grand Central Station, whose name was the title of a radio drama I listened to faithfully on Saturday mornings in my family's kitchen. My friends and I were enthralled by the drama that began with the sounds of whistles, chugs, and escaping steam of the mighty trains that crossed the land, as the

deep voice of the announcer intoned each week these thrilling
words:

> As a bullet seeks its target, shining rails in every part of our great
> country are aimed at Grand Central Station, heart of the nation's
> greatest city. Drawn by the magnetic force, the fantastic metropolis,
> day and night great trains rush toward the Hudson River, sweep
> down its eastern bank for 140 miles, flash briefly past the long red
> row of tenement houses south of the 125th Street, dive with a roar
> into the two-and-a-half-mile tunnel which burrows beneath the
> glitter and swank of Park Avenue and then . . . [sound effects call
> for ESCAPING STEAM FROM LOCOMOTIVE] Grand Central
> Station . . . crossroads of a million private lives.

Whose blood could fail to be stirred by the prospect of such a
journey? Betty Bartelme, who became a book editor and now
teaches a course in the history of publishing at Hofstra College,
listened to "Grand Central Station" when she grew up in Iowa, and
she thought of the program — as if she were living out one of its
episodes — when she took a train called the Pacemaker to New
York from Chicago. She had just graduated from St. Catherine's
College in St. Paul, Minnesota, when she "went to New York to visit
a friend and never came back."

Grand Central also conjured up for Betty and me and our contemporaries the movie scenes of those classic meetings of soldiers
come home or about to embark, in either case embracing beneath
the great clock the girl of their dreams, the fur-coated fantasy of
glamour and love whose heart was worth fighting and dying to win.
It just wouldn't be the same at the Port Authority Bus Terminal.

The train stations of America's cities were not simply points of
arrival and departure, loading docks for people and baggage, but
awesome, vast cathedrals for the continent-crossing railways that
first connected us into one country. Union Station in Indianapolis
was the most impressive building in the city, its stained glass windows and high domed ceiling providing the closest thing we had to
Chartres. Travel was serious, mysterious, and fun, and the boarding of a train was an act, a decision, not to be taken lightly, for it

might well be the turning point of a life, just as it was in so many books and movies.

The trains themselves were nineteenth-century symbols of power, still potent because they were part of the stories we were raised on, part of the powerful sights and sounds of childhood. The Monon Railroad, which ran past the end of my backyard and on to Chicago, told the time for the whole neighborhood, the whistle of the 5:15 calling kids home for supper. Sometimes we put pennies on the track and collected them afterward as souvenirs, symbols of the power of the passing train.

David Amram put pennies on the track of the train whose station was only a mile from the farm he grew up on in Feasterville, Pennsylvania. He dreamed of someday taking his trumpet and going to New York on that train to play in a band; he would realize his dream as a jazz musician, composer, and conductor, playing with Charlie Mingus and later with his own groups. "It was a silver train called the Crusader," David remembers, "and it had a steam engine. I took it to New York in 1955."

The great cross-country trains had names, like proud ships, which added to the aura of adventure, the importance the traveler felt in making the journey. One I sometimes took to New York from Indianapolis was called the Spirit of St. Louis. That name reminded the passengers that, like Lindy crossing the Atlantic to Paris, we were part of a heritage of seekers, explorers, pioneers, taking a risk to move on, leave home, try the unknown.

The friends of my generation who came to New York still remember the names of the trains that took them, as well as the adventure of the journey. Meg Greenfield came from Seattle on the Empire Builder. She remembers how "the trains to college were full of all the kids from Seattle or Portland going to eastern schools. I also went sometimes on a train called the City of Portland. It was like a rolling party and marvelous fun — I mean, it was fun for us. It couldn't have been much fun for the other passengers."

When I went away to college at Columbia, my mother and father saw me off at Union Station with hugs and tears and promises to write, as if I were a soldier going to the front. In a way, that's how I felt, eager for action but a little afraid. Then I was greeted by a wonderful surprise: Mr. and Mrs. Evans Woollen were going to New York City on the same train.

I took this as confirmation of my fate, the best omen possible. They were not just the parents of my first high school girlfriend, Kithy Woollen, but also personages in their own right. Mr. Woollen was president of the Fletcher Trust bank in Indianapolis and a distinguished alumnus of Yale who always wore a three-piece suit with a gold watch chain across his vest, the symbol of solid, old-fashioned success and stability. I was awed and somewhat intimidated by him, but his wife, Lydia, was one of my favorite adults, a woman of charm and sharp wit, a kind of midwestern Katharine Hepburn, more soft and slow in speaking but possessing the same intensity of gaze. When I came to see her daughter, she would engage me in conversations about books I was reading and tell me of authors she admired, treating me as if my opinions were worthy of attention.

When they saw me on the train to New York, the Woollens invited me to dinner with them. The old cross-country trains boasted a dining car with a first-class menu and tables with linen cloths and polished silverware gleaming under lamplight, presided over by a staff of attentive colored (as they were called with respect then) waiters who served drinks and meals with a skill unmatched in the finest restaurants. There was also a club car with comfortable lounge chairs and cocktail tables for having a drink and a smoke and perhaps meeting a fellow passenger (*that* one, the mysterious blonde just lighting up a cigarette, who looks a bit like Ingrid Bergman in *Casablanca*), or reading a book and sipping a beer, as you watched the landscape and the past slip painlessly by through the window.

Leslie Katz, an author and the publisher of the Eakins Press, remembers the dining car of a B & O train called the Royal Blue, which he took the first time he went to New York from Baltimore: "They served the food on ceramic plates with pictures of railroad trains on them. I took that train at Christmas, and when you approached the Susquehanna, the conductor turned out the lights in the car and said, 'Now you can see the B & O Christmas tree.' And just then you passed this tree with colored lights."

When the maître d' grandly seated me and the Woollens at a table in the dining car and gave us menus to study, I tried to find a mod-est-priced meal among what seemed such luxurious choices, but be-fore I could make a selection, Mr. Woollen announced in a tone of finality (he tended to speak in ultimatums): "Dan, you'll have the steak." I'm sure he knew I never would have ordered the most ex-pensive dinner myself, but he wanted me to have it, I think, for sustenance and celebration on the eve of my new college career.

Mrs. Woollen asked me slyly, "Are you still WCTU or will you have a cocktail?" She knew I'd abstained throughout high school, and so made the joking reference to the Women's Christian Tem-perance Union, one of the "dry" lobbies for Prohibition that was now as outdated as raccoon coats, flapper styles, and other relics of the twenties. Proud to show I'd become a man of the world, I de-nied any allegiance to the WCTU and ordered a whiskey sour, sip-ping it with casual aplomb while Mr. and Mrs. Woollen enjoyed their own — a whiskey sour was *the* drink to have.

The Woollens toasted my going off to Columbia, which made me feel proud and relieved. I considered them the most sophisticated people I knew in Indianapolis, and their endorsement offset the recent lecture from my mother's cousins, Aunt Mary and Uncle Clayton, who had been summoned to warn me of the perils a young man faced going east to school. Such a questionable escapade was deemed especially dangerous at the liberal ("pinko" was the less po-lite designation) stronghold of Columbia, in alien New York City, particularly at this menacing time in history when our way of life was being threatened by godless communism, as Senator Joseph McCarthy and his followers were telling us all the time by exposing citizens they charged with being Reds in our very midst.

Aunt Mary Ridge was a member of the Indianapolis school board, and so was attuned to the ways in which the minds and val-ues of youth could be insidiously corrupted. Her pince-nez hung on a ribbon around her neck and lay over her ample bosom as she sat in our kitchen in silent support of tiny, gray Uncle Clayton, who quivered with age and emotion as he told me to "always remember what you learned in Sunday school, Danny, and the things your mother and father taught you, and don't be taken in by professors with funny ideas who don't believe in God, no matter how smart they are." I squirmed in discomfort, knowing these good people loved me and wanted to protect me, but wishing they would trust me and treat me like an adult.

That's how the Woollens were treating me at dinner on the train to New York.

We spoke of grand, sophisticated subjects, like the Broadway shows the Woollens were going to see on their trip. They had tickets for Henry Fonda in *Point of No Return,* a drama based on one of the novels by John P. Marquand about a burning issue of the day, the compromises of businessmen for their work. The Woollens would see other plays and musicals as well, but it was difficult to choose from the riches of a Broadway theater that also offered, in January 1952, Julie Harris in *I Am a Camera,* José Ferrer in *The Shrike,* Hume Cronin and Jessica Tandy in *The Four Poster,* Katherine Cornell in *The Constant Wife,* Audrey Hepburn in *Gigi,* Celeste Holm in *Anna Christie,* Barbara Bel Geddes in *The Moon Is Blue,* Uta Hagen in *Saint Joan,* and Laurence Olivier and Vivian Leigh in *Caesar and Cleopatra.* That did not even count the musicals, which included Gertrude Lawrence in *The King and I,* Phil Silvers in *Top Banana,* and Bert Lahr in *Two on the Aisle.*

As we discussed such exciting choices — ones I'd be able to make for myself by getting standing-room tickets while I was a student — I had the glorious feeling I was living a scene out of one of the novels of F. Scott Fitzgerald, my favorite author. The Woollens were the only people I knew in Indianapolis who might be in a Fitzgerald scene. Their oldest son, Evans Jr. (known as Chub), was following in Mr. Woollen's footsteps at Yale, and Kithy was already destined for Radcliffe. It was Mrs. Woollen who first recommended to me *The Far Side of Paradise,* the biography by Arthur Mizener that began the Fitzgerald revival of the fifties.

Sometimes fiction endorses and reaffirms experience, as it did then in the dining car with the Woollens. I knew I was feeling the kind of emotion described in *Gatsby* when Nick Carraway recalls with nostalgia going home from New York on the train in college at Christmastime:

> When we pulled out into the winter night and the real
> snow, our snow, began to stretch out beside us and twinkle

against the windows, and the dim lights of small Wisconsin stations moved by, a sharp wild brace came suddenly into the air. We drew in deep breaths of it as we walked back from dinner through the cold vestibules, unutterably aware of our identity with this country for one strange hour, before we melted indistinguishably into it again.

That's my Middle West — not the wheat or the prairies or the lost Swede towns, but the thrilling returning trains of my youth.

Now I was riding on one of those mythical trains, and as I "walked back from dinner through the cold vestibules," I realized I was on the journey because of two teachers, one of whom I had not yet met.

A young English instructor at Indiana University named Rexmond Cochrane had taken me under his wing, encouraged my writing, even urged me to enlarge my education by continuing it in some other part of the country, so I could learn what the world was like away from the familiar turf on which I'd grown up. Perhaps he instinctively knew that was what I wanted to hear, for I felt like an exile in Indiana, having retreated there in shame after starting out at Northwestern University, just outside Chicago in Evanston, and then running back home after being rejected across the board during fraternity rush week.

Fraternities were the stamp of approval for young men growing up in the Midwest in the fifties, and seemed a matter of life-shaping significance, as important to many people I knew as the choice of a college. I immediately understood how crucial it was for Scott Fitzgerald and his autobiographical hero Amory Blaine, in *This Side of Paradise,* to get into the right eating club at Princeton (I translated the Cottage Club as Princeton's version of Sigma Chi).

My fraternity rejection probably seared more deeply because I took it as judgment of my awful case of adolescent acne. It seemed a silent way for the world of beautiful people to which I aspired — the winners and leaders, prom queens and team captains — to give me the message affirming my own worst fears: you're ugly, no good, not wanted.

Back home again in Indiana, I pledged the Kappa Sigma fraternity at Bloomington, where I was known to friends and their older brothers and accepted in spite of my blemished face. But it only made me feel guilty for joining a system that I knew from my own painful experience hurt the people it rejected, made them feel like outcasts, ashamed and unwanted. On top of suffering the stupid physical punishment of hazing (beaten with polished wooden paddles by upperclassmen until bruised black-and-blue) and the inane indignities of Hell Week, I felt like a phony. I spent more time reading, especially novels, perhaps as a way of escaping the world I thought I had wanted but now found uncomfortable and silly. I was ripe for Rex Cochrane's encouragement to move on.

Tea with Mr. Cochrane and his welcoming wife at their graduate student apartment stoked my growing excitement about books as I saw their own love of them. It was a love expressed not only in the abundance of volumes that lined the walls and grew in piles on tables and desks, or the way the Cochranes spoke about books and the stories and ideas in them, but also in how they handled them, with a kind of familiar affection that I'd seen before in the way good basketball players picked up and held a basketball. This was the opposite of the attitude toward books of some of my fraternity brothers — like Brick, the jock who had plucked a novel out of my arm once, held it up like a dirty sock, and said, "You really like that stuff, don't you?"

Mr. Cochrane loaned me his own precious underlined, annotated copy of one of his favorite books, Sherwood Anderson's *A Story Teller's Story,* and I felt I'd been given a trust, the temporary guardianship of a sacred text that was no mere relic but a tangible source of knowledge and power. No wonder the essay I read that semester that struck me so deeply it changed the course of my life, catapulting me on to Columbia, was called "Education by Books."

When I got back to my seat in one of the coaches after dinner with the Woollens on the train that night, I pulled out the anthology the essay was in so I could read it again, for inspiration as well as affirmation of the road I was now taking. The essay was neither a polemic nor a call to action, but a quietly reasoned, sweetly ironic argument for a college education consisting solely of four years of reading, discussing, and finally understanding the books that were "the acknowledged masterpieces of the past three thousand years:

masterpieces of poetry, of history, of fiction, of theology, of natural science, of political and economic theory" — from Homer, the Bible, and Herodotus, to Freud, Proust, and Einstein.

The author of the essay admitted that students who finished the prescribed reading of great books without the frills might not immediately be able to cope with some of the aspects of the world they entered: "The only thing, indeed, to be said in their favor was that they were educated. . . . They might not save the world. They might not change it. But they would always be able to see where its center was."

From what I knew, people who tried to save the world or even change it were likely to become fanatics, religious or political, like the intellectuals who became Communists in the thirties, or the Moral Rearmament zealots of the fifties who tried to make people confess their sexual sins in group meetings. (They did it to my own parents in our living room in Indianapolis!) But people who were able to truly see the world and know where its center was, those must be the people I admired, writers like Hemingway and Fitzgerald, and the poet Robert Frost, who wrote, "I'm waiting for the one-man revolution / The only one that's coming."

When I finished reading that essay the first time, I felt a quiet excitement of the kind that comes when you discover something — a work of art or literature — that speaks directly to you, that seems to be a response to questions you didn't even know you were asking until the answers appeared with such clarity and power, as if they were waiting for you all the time. The author of the essay was Mark Van Doren, identified as a Pulitzer Prize–winning poet who was also a professor of English at Columbia.

Mark Van Doren. His name seemed to rise up off the page like an Indian smoke signal of the intellect or a Jack Armstrong secret code from the unconscious to guide me to his classroom. I knew without further explanation that somehow I was going to go to Columbia to study with Mark Van Doren.

Besides the lure of Van Doren, Columbia had the virtue of being in the heart of New York City, the place where everything important happened first, before the rest of the country was ready for it. The books, plays, and paintings, the very ideas that would inform, entertain, and inspire the nation and the world, were created in that single power-packed place. Now that I was no longer tied to mid-western collegiate fraternity standards — the ones that turned me down and out — now that I was free, as Rex Cochrane said, to go anywhere, it seemed not only natural but inevitable to go to the most exciting place of all.

Other generations had and would have other meccas: the literary "hub of the universe" in Boston, for midwesterners like William Dean Howells, had passed; the Hollywood of Stephen Spielberg was yet to come. Generations soon to follow would be lured by Los Angeles as the home of moviemaking and the popular music and record business; or drawn to San Francisco for laid-back, sophisticated culture and Love; or seduced by Seattle's natural beauty and clean air. In the fifties, though, New York had no real rival for youth who wanted to be at the creative — and creating — center of the American dream.

"There was early talk of San Francisco," Meg Greenfield recalls. "That was the only place that was competition for New York then, but San Francisco didn't have anything like the draw of it — we all thought New York was the only place you could possibly live."

Joan Didion, the novelist who grew up in Sacramento, says, "I always thought I'd go to New York. I just didn't know how I'd go about it." Mary Perot Nichols, from suburban Philadelphia, who became a reporter and columnist for the *Village Voice*, recalls, "I had an English teacher who'd been in publishing in New York, and she turned me on to it. I thought I'd be in publishing, or a writer for *The New Yorker*. From high school on, I wanted to live in New York."

For some, the desire to live in New York came even earlier. Leslie Katz was twelve years old when he came back home to Baltimore after visiting a friend in New York City whom he'd met at summer camp. He told his father, "That's where I want to live. There's just nothing like it."

Richard Lingeman, executive editor of *The Nation* and biographer of Theodore Dreiser, listened to the Gordon Jenkins album *Manhattan Towers* when he was going to high school in Crawfordsville, Indiana. After he went to New York on his high school senior trip and stayed at the Hotel Piccadilly in Times Square, "I imagined someday sitting in my own Manhattan tower."

Calvin Trillin, the author and *New Yorker* staff writer who came to New York from Kansas City via Yale ("because my father read *Stover at Yale* and wanted me to go there"), says, "The immigrant saga of the fifties was *My Sister Eileen* — which became the Broadway musical *Wonderful Town* — rather than the *Daily Forward*. It was people coming in from the Midwest instead of from Europe."

The siren songs of movies and musicals about New York sometimes served as the immediate inspiration of someone's pilgrimage. Ann Montgomery, who became a model for the Ford Agency, took a semester off from Miami University in Oxford, Ohio, and borrowed $50 from a friend to go to New York because "I'd come as a teenager and my uncle always got us theater tickets to musicals, and I believed them all — I thought everyone in New York was living a version of *Wonderful Town.*"

Ann was asked to share an apartment with some other girls who had gone to Miami, and shortly afterward she met a boy one of them dated. "Howie" Hayes, the son of a Baptist minister from North Carolina, reminded her that not all the young people migrated to New York from the Midwest; lots of eager southerners came too. This minister's son became the editor of *Esquire* and a mentor to many of the fifties generation — including Ann's future husband, the writer Brock Brower.

As a teenager, the novelist David Markson used to come down with his high school friends from Albany to go to Yankee Stadium, Ebbets Field, or the Polo Grounds, and after the games they would eat bowls of spaghetti near Times Square before going home. David returned on the GI Bill to go to graduate school at Columbia in January 1951, and "the minute I got here," he says, "I knew I wasn't ever going to leave New York. I've always been shocked by the people who came, looked, and didn't stay."

New York was also a mecca for those who grew up in the city itself, and the young people from other boroughs experienced the same thrill of discovery as we outlanders did on first coming into its heart, Manhattan. Bruce Jay Friedman "grew up in the Bronx next to Yankee Stadium, and went to college at the University of Missouri, but when people in Missouri or in the Air Force asked where I lived, I'd say New York as if to say, Where else on God's earth would a person live?"

If many of my friends first arrived in New York on those trains with impressive names, some came to Manhattan on the subway from the Bronx or Brooklyn or Queens. Marion Magid lived at home with her parents in the Bronx when she went to Barnard. "Our journey was to go from the Bronx to Manhattan," she says. "You discovered the city. Going to Manhattan was going to another world." The editor and critic Norman Podhoretz, who came out of Brooklyn to graduate from Columbia in 1950, explains that "when you came from Brooklyn you didn't consider yourself a New Yorker — that was only people in Manhattan. Manhattan meant New York. My attraction to it started early. I was eleven or twelve when I went to the Loew's Paramount for Frank Sinatra's solo appearance with Benny Goodman's band."

Lynne Sharon Schwartz, who went from Brooklyn to Barnard in 1956, wrote in her novel *Leaving Brooklyn* of the first time her heroine "ventured on the subway from Brooklyn to Park Avenue in mythic Manhattan, a mere river away, though it felt like another planet. . . . Even the sky seemed a better blue, a more sophisticated blue."

Some of us hitchhiked from our hometowns, and some took advantage of a popular mode of free transportation, the driveaway service: you got to where you were going at no charge by delivering someone's car to a prearranged destination. My friend Ted Steeg (known as "the Horse" for his speed, strength, and reliability, the guy you could count on) went to my high school in Indianapolis, graduated from Wabash College in Crawfordsville, Indiana, and wanted to come to New York when he got home from the Army in January 1955. He looked in the classified ads of the *Indianapolis Star* for a car to deliver to New York City, where he was going to study at Columbia on the GI Bill. He still remembers the journey. "I'd never been east of the Ohio, and when I came up the Jersey Turnpike I saw the skyline in the distance. It was night and the sky was lit up. I saw the Statue of Liberty — at first I didn't know what she was, she was turned the other way, but then I recognized her, and I got a lump in my throat. That and the skyline were thrilling."

Joan Didion, from Sacramento, opened the window of the bus she took from Idlewild (later Kennedy) Airport to Manhattan to get a glimpse of the skyline, but all she could see was the "wastes of Queens" and signs that said MIDTOWN TUNNEL THIS WAY. There was a sudden summer shower, which seemed exotic and remarkable to her because she was from the West, where there was no summer rain. She was a junior at Berkeley when she flew to New York that June of 1955 to be a college guest editor at *Mademoiselle*. She remembers it as her first trip on a plane. She recounted, in *Slouching Towards Bethlehem*, that the temporary terminal at Idlewild smelled of mildew, and some instinct, "programmed" by all the songs, movies, and stories she knew of New York, told her things would never be the same again.

On the train I took, after the great steak dinner in the dining car, I read until the overhead lights went out and then put down the anthology with Van Doren's essay in it on the seat beside me. I pressed my face against the darkened window, watching the scattered lights of isolated farmhouses shining like beacons across the fields as we moved through the land I could love perhaps for the first time now that I was leaving it.

The next morning I woke to the bright winter sunlight reflecting on steel and glass skyscrapers packed in a proud, upreaching outline, the one my friend Ted was thrilled to see from the Jersey Turnpike at night, the one my future professor and mentor, C. Wright Mills, pointed at one morning when we crossed the George Washington Bridge and said with a challenge in his voice, "Take *that* one, boy!"

TWO

Lions and Cubs on Morningside Heights

LIONS

WHEN NEW YORKERS said "train" it meant the subway. As in Duke Ellington's "Take the A Train," you took the train to go downtown to Greenwich Village or uptown to Columbia, on Morningside Heights. I took the IRT line to the local stop at 116th and Broadway and got off there to go to college. Crash and toot of congested traffic, underground earthquaking rush of the subway, faces black, yellow, and swarthy, voices speaking in foreign tongues, made the place seem as alien as Rangoon, yet I felt at home, sensing it was where I should be.

Columbia bore no resemblance to the idyllic, pastoral campuses of the movies, or the ones I knew in the Midwest, where ivy-clad buildings were set on rolling hills with ancient elms, and chapel bells tolled the slow passage of time. The quad of dormitories and classroom buildings that made up Columbia College was set in the gritty heart of the city, and the catalogue boasted, "New York is our laboratory." I loved it. What could be more removed from the rah-rah frat-house collegiate life I had fled?

Because I was a transfer student, I had to make up required courses I had missed, but my faculty advisor allowed me, as a reward, to take the elective Introduction to Poetry course of Mark

Van Doren my first semester. The morning that began a new term — and for me a whole new life — I went for breakfast at the drugstore my roommates recommended on Amsterdam Avenue (the eastern boundary of the campus, opposite Broadway), squeezing into a packed counter of students crying orders to the friendly pharmacist, Mr. Zipper, who reminded me of a plump Groucho Marx. I picked out something soft and sweet called a French cruller, a doughnut fancier than any I'd dunked in Hoosierdom, and washed it down with sugar-and-cream-laden coffee, hoping to dispel the butterflies I felt before going to meet for the first time the teacher whose words drew me halfway across the country.

Van Doren had become a prototype of the American author-scholar-sage as college professor. Winner of the Pulitzer Prize for his *Collected Poems* in 1940, he had influenced such gifted students as John Berryman and Louis Simpson (as well as young renegade poets still to be heard from, like Allen Ginsberg and Lawrence Ferlinghetti), the critics Maxwell Geismar and Lionel Trilling, the editors Robert Giroux and Clifton Fadiman, and the novelist Herbert Gold. He appeared in Whittaker Chambers's political autobiography, *Witness,* and in Thomas Merton's spiritual autobiography, *The Seven Storey Mountain.* After getting an A in Van Doren's course on Shakespeare, a football player named Jack Kerouac quit the Columbia team to spend more time studying literature. Before his retirement at the end of the decade, Van Doren would be described by *Newsweek* as "a living legend."

When I saw Van Doren in class that morning for the first time, his hair was gray and I had no idea of his age (fifty-eight), which was anyway irrelevant for he didn't seem old but ageless, like the visage of one of the presidents on Mount Rushmore. His face had that craggy granite look of being hewn or chiseled by hard-won experience and knowledge, but it wasn't grim or set in a stare of stony, locked-away wisdom. His eyes gave off a love of his work (which included the students seated before him) and the world, and he had a playful and wry sense of humor. To Allen Tate he was "the scholarly looking poet who always looks as if . . . he were going to say grace, but says instead damn."

The Noble Voice was the title Van Doren gave one of his books, and it was also an apt description of his own way of speaking — mellow, thoughtful, dignified without being formal. His voice was familiar to radio fans across the country, who heard him discuss great works of literature on "Invitation to Learning." Van Doren retained a flat midwestern accent (he was the fourth of five sons of an Illinois country doctor) that made me feel at home. He wasn't afraid to sound his *r*'s, and he spoke at a measured, leisurely pace, letting the words come out without being clipped at the end or hurried along like the New York traffic. He anglicized foreign words when he pronounced them, speaking of *Don Quixote* as "Quicks-ott," with the *x* sounding, rather than in the Spanish manner of "Key-ho-tay." He said with a wry smile that if we followed that style, we would have to call the capital of France "Paree," and he preferred plain "Paris."

Hearing that plain midwestern accent, as well as the plain thinking behind it, bolstered my confidence, proving that people from the hinterlands could make it in East Coast literary circles. It gave me courage to speak to some of my new classmates, jostling down the steps of Hamilton Hall after a lecture.

"Hey, Van Doren's great, huh?" I said.

One of them shrugged, and in a nasal New Yorkese said, "I dunno, he's a little too midwestuhn."

"Yeah, that's it!" I blurted out.

It was not just the familiar accent that made it easier to knock at the door of Van Doren's office and introduce myself later that semester. It was also the kindness in the older man's eyes, in his whole demeanor.

"May I come in?"

"Please."

Professor Van Doren greeted me as a fellow midwesterner and fellow lover of words and stories. I told him about the impact of reading his essay "Education by Books" and mentioned that a friend of mine from high school, John Sigler, had been one of his student hosts when he gave a reading at Dartmouth. Van Doren said he wished he'd known: "I would have told him you were a student of mine."

I left his office in Hamilton Hall not only feeling welcomed and acknowledged but somehow made safe in that alien place, intimidating city and sophisticated college. I had the reassuring sense that because such a man was here, no deep-down harm could come to me, no malevolence invade the grace of his plain goodness.

A student whose poetry Van Doren had encouraged (this was four years before I met him myself) came running into the office of the Columbia English department saying, "I just saw the light!" Most of the professors there thought the student's claim of a visionary experience meant he had finally cracked. The only one who wanted to hear about it was Mark Van Doren. More than forty-five years later, that former student, Allen Ginsberg, tells me, "At Columbia I found nourishment from Van Doren — spiritual nourishment. He had a spiritual gift."

Van Doren's kindness to students did not equal sentimentality, or excuse sloth. One morning in his poetry class he called on a student who confessed he had failed to read the assigned poem. Van Doren's face transformed, tightening, turning a deep and outraged red, and the voice, still measured and controlled, but stern as that of a ship's captain charging mutiny, ordered the student to leave the room. In the breath-held silence that followed, the hapless, hangdog fellow fumbled together his books and fled .

I downed a cold chocolate milk at Chock Full O' Nuts on Broadway to calm my anxiety after class, for I hadn't read the assignment myself, and I wondered what I'd have done if he'd called on me. From then on I was always prepared, but I wondered more deeply if the anger of this good man was an aberration or a part of his personality, a necessary component of being a great professor. I knew I'd learn the answer; Van Doren would teach me.

A hush of respect and excitement came over Van Doren's Narrative Art class when he said he was going to take time out from the great books we were studying to discuss a story written by one of our own classmates, Ivan Gold. Heads turned to Ivan, who slumped down in his seat just in front of me as Van Doren explained to the class that Mr. Gold's story, "A Change of Air," which had won the fiction price of the student literary magazine, *The Columbia Review,* was worthy of our attention.

The story was about a promiscuous young woman from the Lower East Side who voluntarily engaged in sex with members of a teenage gang. She was so traumatized she was sent to a mental hospital, saw a psychiatrist, and eventually returned to her neighborhood a transformed person who politely refused to have sex with any of the old gang. "That must have been one hell of a psychiatrist," one of the boys remarked with wonder.

Van Doren wanted to know what the force or power of change was behind this story. He educed or drew out of us (for that was his method of education) the realization that this new force in the world was psychiatry, which now was our accepted system for effecting change, just as in the writers of the past we had studied, like Homer, Dante, and the authors of the Bible, God was the source of transformation in people's lives.

Through our own classmate's story of a teenage sexual trauma, Van Doren taught us something not only about writing and literature but also about one of the major shifts in modern man's understanding of himself and his world, a shift just being recognized and acknowledged in my own generation.

"I didn't know what the story was about until Van Doren told me in class that day," Ivan Gold says. "I thought it was about these guys pissing away their time, but he showed me it was about the girl, and what changed her."

Ivan later learned that Van Doren had sent the story to an editor he knew at *New World Writing*, a prestigious literary periodical of the day, where it was published at the end of that year, 1953.

"Jesus was the most ruthless of men," Van Doren said in a tone as hard as a struck bell, and I came to tingling attention. The modern image of Jesus, Van Doren said, was of a man almost unrelated to the one described in the New Testament as a strong and stern leader, ruthless in following his conception of truth and iron in his will. "He was not," Van Doren said, "an easy man to follow. He was certainly not like our ministers now who try to be one of the crowd and take a drink at a cocktail party to prove it, or tell an off-color joke. That seems to be their approach today." The professor paused for a moment, and then he said, "Maybe that's why we hate them so much."

I remembered Van Doren's anger at the student who hadn't done his homework, and I realized it was no aberration but that Van Do-

ren, too, was ruthless in his teaching, and respected those who demanded the most of the people they led. I quoted some of his comments on Jesus in an article I wrote a few years later in *The Nation*,
"Slick Paper Christianity," and sent Van Doren a copy. I enclosed it
with a letter in which I acknowledged the gift of his teaching, and
recalled the New York student's saying he was "too midwestuhn."
He wrote back thanking me for telling him of the student's judgment: "I was afraid I had changed."

I waited until my junior year to take a course with Lionel Trilling,
fearing I wasn't yet up to the intellectual level of this professor, who
was described by his peers as "the most intelligent man of his generation" and "the intellectuals' conscience." *The Liberal Imagination*,
Trilling's book of essays published in 1950 which dealt not only with
literature but also with Freud, Kinsey, and American society, had
became a touchstone of the decade. I was equally impressed with
his novel, *The Middle of the Journey,* especially when I learned the
main character was based on his former classmate Whittaker Chambers, the controversial ex-Communist.

Trilling himself was as elegant as his prose. He looked the part of
the aristocratic critic as he stood before us at the front of the class
in his three-piece suit, his hair already a distinguished gray at forty-
eight. He had the darkest circles under his eyes I had ever seen, so
dark they reminded me of the shiners produced by a well-placed
punch in a street fight. I assumed these circles were results of the
deep study he engaged in, the heavy-duty intellectual battles.

Professor Trilling took a significant drag on the cigarette he inevitably held, sometimes gesturing with it like a wand, sometimes
holding it poised just beyond his lips, like people did in the old
movies of New York high life, where all the men seemed to wear
only tuxedos or dressing gowns and subsisted entirely on caviar and
champagne. Twin streams of smoke flowed from his nostrils, like
an underlining of his words.

"We shall not read any criticism of the work of the poets we are
going to study this semester," he announced. "We shall only read
the work itself — *all* the poems written by Wordsworth, Keats, and
Yeats."

There were intakes of breath as we absorbed the shock of hearing that our most distinguished literary critic wasn't going to assign us any criticism. When Trilling said we were going to read all the poems of Wordsworth, Keats, and Yeats, he didn't mean just once. "Until you have read a poem at least a dozen times," he explained, "you haven't even begun to get acquainted with it, much less to know what it means."

Ideas became as real as stories in the poetry of Yeats, as I learned to read it in Trilling's class, and by the end of the term I had other lines of verse running through my mind than the ones that I brought to college from childhood. "Little Orphan Annie came to our house to stay / To wash the cups and saucers and brush the crumbs away" had been replaced with Crazy Jane's "Wrap that foul body up / In as foul a rag / I carry the sun in a golden cup / The moon in a silver bag." The comforting time "When the frost is on the punkin / And the fodder's in the shock" was supplanted by the soul-shaking vision of a world in which — as I recited to myself in the roar of the hurtling IRT express and in the early morning hours in the dorm after studying Marx and Freud, Kierkegaard and Nietzsche, in our course in Contemporary Civilization — "Turning and turning in the widening gyre / The falcon cannot hear the falconer."

If Van Doren's course introduced me to poetry, Trilling instilled it in me, making it part of my consciousness, accessible for the rest of my life. Though the two teachers were different in style and manner — Harold Kushner describes Van Doren as "the populist" and Trilling "the aristocrat" — their approach to teaching was much the same. It made sense when I learned years later that Trilling had been Van Doren's student. It wouldn't have occurred to me in college, for both men looked to my youthful eyes like contemporaries; I assumed the great men of our faculty all sprang from the womb as full professors.

The only undergraduates who were barred from studying with Trilling, Van Doren, and the other stars of that golden age of Columbia's English department were the Barnard students. Women were not yet first-class citizens in academia, and college classes were segregated according to sex — though on isolated occasions a Columbia boy brought a girl to sit in on a popular professor's class like a date.

Marion Magid, who was a student at Barnard in the fifties, says, "We weren't allowed to take the famous Columbia courses — in retrospect, it's the only thing I feel resentful about. You never questioned that Trilling was for the boys and you were a girl, so you had to make do. Barnard was its own little world on the other side of Broadway. One was aware that high-class thinking was going on across the street."

Lynne Sharon Schwartz — who would write a brilliant novel, *Disturbances in the Field,* which followed the lives of three Barnard students through middle age — says that as a student she didn't take any courses with Van Doren or Trilling because "I felt that was for the men. I felt very cut off from all that, what was going on across the street." She believes that Barnard's hiring of two young working writers as faculty members — Robert Pack, a poet, and the novelist George P. Elliot — helped nurture a creative "outburst" in fiction among Barnard students of the late fifties, whose literary ranks included Lynne herself, novelists Rosellen Brown, Joyce Johnson, and the late Norma Klein, poet Judy Sherwin, and dance critic Tobi Tobias.

Though Trilling's donnish manner made some people think him aloof, he was always accessible and supportive of his students, especially the aspiring writers. On a spring day in 1953, Trilling walked in the park along the Hudson River below the campus, holding the hand of his four-year-old son, James, and talking with his student Ivan Gold. Ivan was going to graduate in June, and wondered, if his goal in life was to write fiction, whether he should go to grad school for an M.A. in literature, which would also get him a draft deferment from service during the ongoing Korean War (or "conflict," as it was called), or whether he should go ahead into the Army. Trilling admitted that he, too, wanted most of all to be a fiction writer, and said he regarded the literary criticism he did as secondary to the novel and short stories he had written. He didn't see academic life as the best route to Ivan's goal. "If you want to write, Mr. Gold," he said, "stay away from graduate school."

Ivan took the advice and was drafted after graduation. "Trilling was right, of course, the way those guys [our Columbia professors] always were," he says, looking back nearly forty years later. "After I got back from the Army and living in Japan, I did go to graduate school on the GI Bill for a while, but I couldn't hack it."

Ned O'Gorman, who met Van Doren and Trilling while he was a graduate student at Columbia in the fifties, says, "I sent Mark Van Doren every poem I ever wrote, and he sent me a postcard or letter the next day with his comments. Lionel met my adopted son, Ricky, at the Aspen Institute, and I have a picture of him cutting a watermelon with him. Trilling didn't know how to cut a watermelon, and he's cutting it the wrong way. It's a picture I treasure. Those men were surrogate fathers for many of us."

When Sam Astrachan was a junior at Columbia and his father died, Trilling got him a scholarship that lasted until graduation. When Sam showed Trilling part of his first novel, the professor got his student into Yaddo, the writers' colony, to finish it, and then sent the book to another former student, Robert Giroux, who published Astrachan's *An End to Dying* at Farrar, Straus.

In a letter Sam Astrachan wrote me last year from his home in Gordes, in the south of France, he said of Trilling, "When he died, I felt I had lost a father."

Van Doren and Trilling were more to us than lions.

The young lion of Columbia's faculty in the fifties was a brash, dynamic sociologist up from Texas, C. Wright Mills, who had made a name for himself beyond the academy with a provocative new book on the American middle class called *White Collar,* and was working on a similar but even more controversial critique of the upper classes called *The Power Elite.* If Mark Van Doren and Lionel Trilling epitomized in their personal style and the thrust of their work the best of traditional values, C. Wright Mills was a harbinger of the anti-establishment future.

Impossible to picture in the confinement of a three-piece suit — he even rebelled against wearing a tie — Mills roared down to Columbia on the BMW motorcycle he drove from his house in Rockland County, outfitted in work boots, helmet, flannel shirt, and heavy-duty corduroys. His broad chest was crisscrossed with canvas straps of duffel bags bearing books, a canteen, and packages of the prepared food he took on camping trips, which he heated up in his office to save time. He looked like a guerrilla warrior ready to do battle, and in a way he was.

I first became interested in Mills when my classmate Mike Naver pointed out to me an ad for *White Collar* that was part of an enticement for joining the Book Find Club, and I signed up to get Mills's work as a bonus. *White Collar* moved and excited me, as it had so many readers who, I'd heard, wrote letters to the author, responding to the issues he raised and also seeking his advice on problems, for the book seemed to address the deep discontent people felt about their jobs and their circumscribed futures. With its sharp critique of the growing impersonality of white-collar work, it touched my own typical fifties fear, shared by many of my fellow students, that we'd lockstep into some automated, sterile future. But the very articulation of the fear raised hope that we might transcend it.

I was eager to see the author of this powerful work in action in the classroom, but I had to get his permission to take his seminar, which was limited to "qualified" students. I waited for my quarry in the cold, cheerless lobby of Hamilton Hall, ambushed Mills on the way to the elevator, and squeezed in beside him. Riding in an elevator with Mills felt like riding in a Volkswagen with an elephant, not so much because of his size — he was a little over six feet tall and weighed two hundred pounds — but because of a sense of restlessness and ready-to-burst energy about him.

Mills fired the requisite questions at me in a rather aggressive, discouraging tone, and I'm sure my answers made obvious my lack of academic qualifications for the course, which I compensated for with enthusiasm. I trotted out my credentials as a journalist and threw in my admiration for *White Collar*. When the elevator ejected the crowd at his floor, Mills glanced back at me and said simply, "O.K."

Mills at thirty-eight was an exhilarating teacher. He stalked the room or pounded his fist on the table to emphasize a point, surprising us with ideas that seemed utopian, except he was so convinced of their practicality you couldn't dismiss them as mere theory. He shocked us out of our torpor by challenging each of us to build our own house, as he had done himself. He even insisted that, if he applied himself, any man could build his own *car* — a feat not even

Mills performed, though he made an intensive study of German engines and loved to tinker with them.

Mills urged us, as part of a new generation coming of age, to abandon the cities, which he felt were already hopelessly dehumanizing, and set up small, self-governing units around the country. His vision of communities where people could develop crafts and skills and work with their hands was in some way acted out in the communes of the sixties, though the drug culture would have been completely foreign to Mills. The yearning for such an independent and self-sufficient way of life that Mills expressed in the fifties was part of the message that so excited his audience.

Inspired by his challenge to think for ourselves, I tried an experiment in his course. Instead of cranking out the usual dry précis of one of the heavyweight books we read each week, I let my imagination go to town, comparing Ortega y Gasset's *Revolt of the Masses* with a Hemingway story.

When Mills handed back the papers, he scanned the classroom and asked with sly curiosity, "Which one is Wakefield?"

I took a deep breath and held up my hand.

"See me after class," he said.

In his office, I waited in suspense while Mills sat behind the desk, stoked up his pipe, and looked me over. Finally he asked what had made me write a paper comparing Ortega and Hemingway. I confessed I was bored by simply recounting the contents of the book in précis form.

"My God, I'm bored too, reading the damn things," he said, and we both laughed.

He told me to "do some more," continue to experiment. I started going to his office after class to talk about the latest paper, and these discussions broadened into friendly inquiries about my plans and goals, and even — to my flattered surprise — a sharing of his own work and concerns. I think he felt a bond with me because of our similar backgrounds as middle-class boys from the hinterlands who made it to the intellectual center, New York. I told him how my admiration for *White Collar* had inspired me to take his course, and he said what the book meant to him personally.

"I met a woman at a cocktail party who really understands me," he said. "She told me, 'I know you, Mills. I've read *White Collar* and

I know what it's all about.' I asked her to tell me, and she said, 'That's the story of a Texas boy who came to New York.'" Mills paused, frowning, and then broke into a giant grin and said, "My God, she was right." As he later wrote, *White Collar* was "a task primarily motivated by the desire to articulate my own experience in New York City since 1945."

I was glad to learn that Mills was more interested in the personal vision than in polls and statistics. He thought of himself as a writer rather than a sociologist, and attributed an almost magical power to the process of writing. Hadn't it brought him, with academic whistle-stops along the way, out of Texas to New York City and national prominence? He proudly explained how he managed to escape a teaching post in the farmlands of Maryland, proclaiming in his booming tone, "I wrote my way out of there!"

When I confessed I wanted to write novels someday, Mills said he had a friend named Harvey Swados who'd just finished his first novel, to be published in the coming year.

"Oh yes," I said, "it's called *Out Went the Candle.*"

"How did you know that?" Mills asked.

In a recent issue of *New World Writing*, I'd read a short story by Swados called "The Dancer," an allegory of a favorite fifties theme: a pure artist selling out to crass commercialism and dying as a result. The short author's bio mentioned his forthcoming novel. I said I was eager to read it.

"Would you like to meet Harvey?" Mills asked.

That was like asking me, ten years before, if I'd like to meet Blanchard or Davis, the stars of the Army football team.

The following week, I took the bus for the short trip up the Hudson to Rockland County, and Mills picked me up at the Nyack station in a well-worn but sporty red MG convertible. He drove me to his comfortable old frame house, which had floor-to-floor ceiling bookcases he had built in. He introduced me to his wife, Ruth, a tall blond, welcoming woman who immediately put me at ease. She had a zest and humor that matched Mills's, as well as a formidable, if unassuming, intellect.

Harvey Swados and his wife, Bette, arrived with a bottle of wine and a bubbling cheerfulness. Harvey and Mills were colleagues as well as neighbors, reading each other's manuscripts and offering criticism, advice, and support. Harvey was a "promising young writer" of short stories that dramatized concerns such as Mills addressed in *White Collar,* like the threat to individual freedom from new technology and corporate conformity.

The two couples took me in, making me feel a part of their good-humored camaraderie rather than like a mere student who was ignorant of their worldly wisdom. I needn't have worried about keeping up with their intellectual allusions; the evening turned on Mills's display of his latest motorcycle equipment, which he'd ordered from a magazine. Harvey ribbed him about that, saying it reminded him of a kid mailing in boxtops. Enjoying the kidding, Mills with jocular pride got out his new crash helmet, and to show how effective it was, he put it on and banged his head against the living room wall, sending us into hilarious laughter.

Mills became a friend whose help and guidance would see me through the early years in New York. Columbia had not only provided me with an education but a new family as well, in the city I'd adopted as home.

CUBS

If the real lions of Columbia were its star professors, I sensed very soon that some of my fellow students were future lions. They had come to the university to excel, to learn at the feet of great men in order to aim for greatness themselves, or at least to ascend to the highest ranks in their field. The college was a training ground for ambitious and talented cubs, especially those who would find careers in the media, whose national headquarters were based in New York — which, after all, was our laboratory. In 1952, the year I arrived at Columbia, the editor of the student newspaper was Max Frankel, who eventually became executive editor of the *New York Times;* the editor of the literary magazine was Robert Gottlieb, the future editor of *The New Yorker;* and the editor of the college yearbook was Roone Arledge, who years later became president of ABC News.

Some undergraduates already had a leonine aura about them, an air not of arrogance but of mission, as if they were ready to stride from the classroom to the IRT downtown local and take their places in New York, which was the world. I was awed most of all by Frankel, who was not just editor of the *Spectator* but also served as campus correspondent for the *New York Times*. I was further impressed because he was the first student I knew who always seemed to be wearing a suit. It was usually dark, worn with a white shirt and dark tie, and I took it as a symbol of the dignity of his office, a kind of uniform for those who bore the honor of representing the stately *Times*.

As a cub reporter when he was a senior, I didn't get to know Frankel well, but found him to be a serious, soft-spoken man whose intensity about his job did not prevent him from being gracious to a newcomer from the wilds of the Midwest. I immediately assumed — and reported this back to my high school journalism teacher — this man would someday be editor of the *Times*.

In his office, now forty years later, Frankel tells me how he got his start as campus correspondent for the *Times*. His friend Dave Wise, from the High School of Music and Art in Manhattan, worked on *Spec* and landed the job of Columbia correspondent for the *New York Herald Tribune*. The year after Frankel came and started working on *Spec*, the prized job of *Times* correspondent, then held by Nancy Edwards, opened up.

Wise saw Max at the *Spectator* office and said, "Now I have to decide whether to shift to the *Times* or stay at the *Tribune*." The two young men walked across Broadway to Prexy's (home of "the Hamburger with the College Education"), where they sat at the counter and talked it through over coffee.

"We doped it all out very dispassionately," Max recalls. "We decided a young man could move faster on the *Trib* at that time. We both wanted to go the political-journalism route, covering City Hall, then Albany, then Washington and national politics. Dave decided to stay at the *Trib*, so later he whispered in Nancy Edwards's ear about me being the best person to replace her. She'd been at the Graduate School of Journalism and was going to work on the *Times*'s society page — the opening women got in those days. She told the *Times* she had this great candidate for campus correspondent, but their jaws fell open when she said I was only a sophomore. Why shouldn't they hire someone from the journalism school? She said, 'This guy spends all day at *Spectator,* he knows all the stories coming in — you're getting fifty reporters instead of one.' They hired me."

Going out for *Spec* was my own entrée into the life of Columbia, and soon I was covering stories I'd never seen in Indiana, from crew races at Cornell to Broadway and TV actresses, who would appear in the Lions' Den, the dorm restaurant, to be crowned queen of some prom or other. " 'That ain't Dagmar,' said a confused Columbia man" was the lead of my first story, quoting a student who stumbled into the wrong coronation while looking for the famously buxom blonde who was one of the first celebrities created by television.

I elbowed my way through the homecoming crowd on assignment from *Spec* to get photos of Ike, on leave from the presidency of Columbia to run for the U.S. presidency. He was making a campaign stop at this pregame picnic lunch by the football field, and I snapped my Rolleiflex as he gnawed fried chicken with the faculty and tried to smile.

Homespun Ike never seemed comfortable at intellectual Columbia. "Dammit, what good are exceptional physicists . . . exceptional anything, unless they are exceptional Americans?" he fumed, questioning a university scholar. In the rah-rah fifties rhetoric he helped create, Eisenhower urged Columbia to become "a more effective and productive member of the American national team." He surely felt even more out of tune with Columbia's student body that fall, when the *Spectator* published a front-page editorial supporting Adlai Stevenson for president and described the Eisenhower campaign as "the Great Disenchantment."

As I worked more for *Spec,* I got to be friends with Max Frankel's successor as editor, a hard-driving newsman named Jerry Landauer, who seemed to be born with journalistic genes. Jerry was a lean and muscular man with a blond crew cut who reminded me of a student version of a *Front Page* reporter. He was literally a dashing figure, popping up wherever a story was breaking on campus with pencil poised, tie loosened, ready to fire the right question with the speed and accuracy of a bullet. Reporting came naturally to Jerry, but he sweated over the writing, fiercely rubbing his bristling hair while he composed sentences behind a typewriter or sat up late consuming black coffee at the counter of Chock Full O' Nuts on Broadway.

"Dammit, Danny! I wish I could write like you," Jerry said, throwing an arm around my shoulder and shaking his head as we hurried to the V & T Pizzeria on Amsterdam. He was the only college friend who called me Danny, the childhood name I wanted to leave behind in Indiana, but from Jerry I didn't mind it. How could I complain when he praised me like that?

"But Jerry," I always replied, "you're the best damn reporter. I never ask the right questions like you."

"Ah, to hell with it, Danny. You can *write*."

This exchange continued throughout our long friendship. Jerry went on to become an investigative reporter in Washington for the *Wall Street Journal,* and I'd go down there on assignments for *The Nation, Esquire,* and *The Atlantic,* in the sixties and seventies, and sleep on his living room couch. I wasn't surprised when he broke a top story by rooting in a wastebasket in a Senate hearing room after everyone had left, finding on a wadded scrap of paper a witness's doodles that provided the clue to hidden corruption.

Judah L. Berger, called Joe, had Jerry's intensity but wasn't as totally focused on journalism and *Spec,* even though he became its managing editor. He saw the study of history as a key to understanding what made things, and even people, tick — the way some of us looked to literature or psychology for clues to the human condition, and hoped to find answers to our own. Joe's favorite course was a class in American history taught by Lee Benson, a lively young instructor who was writing a book on a mundane topic he presented with the passion of high drama, as if it held the mystery and meaning of the universe: *Merchants, Farmers, and Railroads.*

Joe Berger was fascinated by Benson's obsession with his subject. "Railroads," Joe said, leaning forward, his eyes wide with amusement and awe. "Imagine, Wake-o, everything working out the way it has because of railroads!"

Who was the glamorous girl with Sam Astrachan, our fledgling novelist who paced Broadway late at night with his hands clasped behind his back? Sam was standing outside the College Inn restaurant on Broadway one early February evening in 1955 with this tall, attractive girl who had shiny black hair, bright red lipstick, and a long black coat with a fur collar. Sam, in his customary black suit and white shirt with no tie, was smiling more broadly than usual, and invited me to come to the West End Bar & Grill and have a drink with him and "Zelda."

She was really Jane Richmond, and she could have passed for a twenties flapper that night. She loved the legend surrounding Zelda and Scott Fitzgerald, our generation's idols of literary glamour and doom. Jane had published a story in *Focus,* the Barnard literary magazine (the undergraduate women's counterpart to *The Columbia Review,* as the *Barnard Bulletin* was their *Spectator*). Gender segregation of publications, as well as classrooms, was taken for granted; the problem was, Jane told us, there was no equivalent of Columbia's humor magazine. She and her friends wanted to start their own, a Barnard version of *Jester.* "We want to call it *Shvester,*" she said. "It's Yiddish for 'sister.' "

We agreed it was a great idea, but it never came to be.

"I was a literary girl, a writing major," Jane says, looking back. She won the Elizabeth Janeway Writing Prize when she graduated, started writing for the satirical television show of the sixties, "That Was the Week That Was," wrote scripts for "Kate and Allie," and continued her lifelong love of writing short stories, which have appeared in *The New Yorker* and other magazines.

Though Barnard girls were segregated from Columbia's undergraduate classes and publications, they were welcomed at the West End, whose notorious allure was unintentionally enhanced by Diana Trilling, Lionel's wife and herself a literary critic. Mrs. Trilling immortalized the place in a *Partisan Review* piece as "that dim waystation of undergraduate debauchery on Morningside Heights." She compared it unfavorably to the "well-lighted" Stewart Cafeteria, a popular literary hangout in *her* day.

With a horseshoe-shaped bar, a steam table offering stews and other student bargains, plus wooden booths and a jukebox, the West End was the all-purpose off-campus hangout for Columbia and Barnard. It provided a respite from academia as a place to go for drinks, dates, and fun, and also served as a haven where students could moan about their troubles over a beer. When the threat of being drafted to fight in Korea struck Columbia men at the start of the decade, they knew where to go for comfort. The editors of

Spec reported: "Rumors that the college ranks would be depleted by the end of the year [1951] caused many to lose faith and many more to find solace in the West End."

The West End owed its literary rep to Ginsberg, Kerouac, and other beats who frequented the place in the forties, and some of them reappeared in our own time. Jane Richmond saw Kerouac there just after *On the Road* came out and she was a senior at Barnard. "He loved women with dark hair," she says. "He'd look at me and say, 'You Greek girl? Why you all look like that?' " She had also met Ginsberg, "one of the sweetest people I've ever known. He told someone I always looked like I was wearing a big picture hat."

Ginsberg got the right image for Jane — a sense of largesse, bigness of spirit, a celebratory air. Her smile, her ability to make you laugh, her very presence, lit up the time and place.

I didn't meet Ginsberg at the West End back then, but I knew about him. He was a personage on the Columbia scene, a mixture of mystery and legend even before the publication of *Howl* had made him famous. A rumor buzzed among literature students that he'd been the inspiration for the brilliant, troubled student in Lionel Trilling's short story "Of This Time, of That Place," though Trilling later denied the character was based on any real people.

No one denied that Ginsberg had been suspended from the college and spent time at the Columbia Presbyterian Psychiatric Institute: "The people here see more visions in one day than I do in a year," he wrote his student friend Jack Kerouac. Both Trilling and Mark Van Doren testified for Ginsberg when he was brought to trial for possession of stolen goods. He had gotten mixed up with friends who pulled a robbery and stored the loot at his apartment; Van Doren told him he had to choose between criminals and society ("Some of us here have been thinking that it might be a good thing for you to hear the clank of iron"). Ginsberg was later cleared of the charge.

Besides such notorious escapades, Ginsberg was known for his talent as a poet, and was even recognized as such by Norman Podhoretz, a fellow student who became his literary arch-rival. "What I remember about him was his virtuosity with metrical forms," Podhoretz recalls. "I remember him writing something in heroic couplets, and he wrote in other traditional forms, so when he busted loose it was not as if he couldn't write conventional verse. He was more like an abstract painter who was good at figurative stuff."

Ginsberg was starting to read Whitman then, and felt at odds with the prevailing academic attitude toward poetry. "When I was at Columbia," he says, "Shelley was considered a jerk, Whitman 'an awkward prole,' and William Carlos Williams wasn't in the running." Ginsberg felt alienated from the faculty in other ways was well: "I told Trilling I smoked grass and he was horrified. He thought it was a nineteenth-century disease."

My friends and I at Columbia in the fifties would have been as shocked. "I was surprised by the beats coming out of Columbia," Max Frankel says. "That was a side of the college I never knew, and it was just a few years before me. We were such innocents. There wasn't any dope around, and a beer party was a big thing."

Because we were serious students who hit the books not out of a sense of duty but from a driving curiosity to find answers, to understand, didn't mean we spent all our time holed up in the library. "New York is our laboratory" was a jocular toast, as we winked knowingly and clinked glasses of draft beer at the San Remo in the Village, swilling it to give us the courage to pick up the wistful girls at another table whose long hair and sandals we hoped were signs of bohemian belief in free love (it more likely indicated a sophisticated disdain for college boys).

New York was not just our laboratory but our theater, our art museum, our opera house. It was one thing to take a music appreciation course — students at any college did that — but quite another to have the music of great professionals performed live. Mike Naver got us standing-room tickets for *Don Giovanni* at the Metropolitan Opera (the old one, on 39th and Broadway), and we looked over the massive, gilt-embellished tiers of boxes under jeweled chandeliers. This was the real thing.

New tastes burst inside me like music when I went to my first French restaurant, a modest place with red-checked tablecloths in the West 50s called the Café Brittany, where students and young office workers could afford to take a date for dinner. Continental cuisine had not made its way to the cities of the plains back then; I had known of no French food in Indianapolis. The Mandarin Inn, with chop suey, and the Italian Village, with the first post–World War II pizza, had been our exotic foreign restaurants.

What knocked me out in the Brittany was not so much the sauces and the tender flesh of coq au vin (so different from the chicken I knew, fried to a crisp) but the revelation — to a boy who had grown up eating vegetables condemned to death by midwestern ritual boiling rites — that green beans could actually have a taste.

That sense of bursting open, of blooming, accompanied all these excursions into the city. Here was the source, the living experience of books now lifting off the page, as after art appreciation classes I went for the first time with Columbia friends to the Museum of Modern Art. I was overwhelmed, shaken up, and turned around by Picasso's stark, howling *Guernica,* with arms that seemed to stretch from the canvas into my heart and mind.

I loved New York and Columbia, and was stricken when I had to stay out the fall semester of my junior year, but grateful I was alive to return after a car wreck in August 1953 put me in the South Chicago Community Hospital with a broken and dislocated fifth cervical vertebra. I was in traction for three months, and read the Greek tragedies and Dos Passos's *U.S.A.* with the aid of a pair of refracting glasses, as well as letters and copies of *Spectator* from my friends back at Columbia. I went home in a body cast and eagerly returned to Morningside Heights in a neck brace for the spring semester of 1954.

I took to smoking little cigars called Between the Acts, which came in a red and white tin, and making forays to Greenwich Village with Malcolm Barbour, whom I got to know in a writing class. My image of Englishmen was of stiff, tea-drinking gentlemen, but Barbour was a rumpled, irreverent, beer-drinking Brit, a regular guy whose humor was simply funneled through an accent. We became good friends, comparing rejection slips, reading each other's stories, dreaming of beautiful girls.

Once, while drinking our beers in a booth of the San Remo and speaking of the stories we wanted to write and the sex we wanted to have (our ongoing obsessions), our privacy was suddenly invaded by a wild man who looked like a bum, waving sheets of paper at us with poems he had written. He wanted to sell them, for either a dime or a quarter apiece (the price was negotiable). We got rid of him as quickly as possible and laughed as he left. A long-haired woman on her way back from the bar saw us laughing and said reproachfully, "That's Bodenheim."

"Bodenheim?" Barbour asked me as the woman moved on. "Who the hell's Bodenheim?" I didn't know either, and we watched as the poor man went to other tables and booths, trying to sell his wares. Most everyone seemed to know him, and some greeted him kindly, but no one that night bought any poems. In our undergraduate giddiness, Barbour and I thought the name itself was funny: "Was that *Bodenheim?*" "Don't you know *Bodenheim?*" I later learned, to my shame, that the man we were mocking had been a well-known poet in the twenties, one whose work Mark Van Doren had published in *The Nation*.

When I lived in the Village, I saw Bodenheim again on other nights in the San Remo, a favorite hangout of his and a source of sales. He always made me uncomfortable, not only out of guilt because I had thought him a wino pretending to be a real poet, but also because he *was* a real poet, one whose work had been recognized and acclaimed, and this was the end to which he had come. I liked to think justice triumphed, especially in literature — that serious artists who didn't sell out would somehow be rewarded or saved. I knew all the tragic stories of poets' lifelong struggles and early deaths, but I never had seen a poet whose presence proved that not all literary stories had a good ending, that refusing to sell out could lead in old age to selling one's work in a bar for spare change.

I ran into Malcolm Barbour in Los Angeles in 1976, when I was working on the television series I created, "James at 15," and he was working for a production company. In 1989 I saw his name listed as coproducer of "Cops," a docudrama series. I still remember a story he wrote in college about a penniless young artist in love with a beautiful dancer in Paris. I can picture the girl, with her long blond hair, walking in her black ballet shoes over the fallen wet leaves of the streets along the Left Bank.

Abruptly and with no fanfare, my college life ended in February 1955, an anticlimactic finish that came out of season because I lost a semester — and almost my life — after the car crash the summer before my senior year began. When I passed my last exam — in, of all things, geology (still using New York as our laboratory, we studied rock layers of the Palisades on the Hudson) — my college career was over. Of course, I could attend the graduation of the class of '55 in June; otherwise, I'd get my diploma in the mail, which seemed even more unreal, as if I'd simply sent away for it from a catalogue.

No longer in college and not yet launched on a job, I felt in limbo, like a man without a country. I rationalized that I still had business at Columbia, or at least the excuse of one last semi-official tie: I'd submitted a short story to that year's fiction contest of *The Columbia Review*, giving it to Sam Astrachan, who was now one of the editors. I nurtured hopes of a prize, or at least publication, which I thought might seem like my own graduation from Columbia.

Sam called me a week or so after the semester break to tell me my story had come in second, but the winning story was so long it would take up the whole issue, so no others would be published. He invited me to the West End for a beer, my consolation prize. He understood how I felt and was sympathetic without being condescending, as if we were both grown literary men who could take such blows in our stride as we moved ahead to create the next work. He led me on one of his long walks down Broadway, and I clasped my hands behind my back as he did, feeling like an accepted member of the writing fraternity. It was in that time of my defeat and his compassion that we really became friends.

Now that I was leaving, I began to think with nostalgia of the friends I had made at Columbia, guys I had gotten to know from *Spec* and the dorms and classes, and then from the literary life of the college. I realized most of them were Jews. In fact, the only exceptions were the Englishman Barbour and Mike Naver, who I thought at first was Jewish because he came from New York and most of the other guys from the city were Jews. It was not until I knew him more than a year that I learned Nave's roots were Italian Catholic.

At the high school I went to in Indianapolis, Jews were a definite minority and stayed within their own social structure, except for several Jewish boys and girls who each year, by some unspoken and unconscious social mechanism, became part of the In group of thirty or so kids who were the athletes and leaders of the class. I was good friends with Ferdie and Ads in high school, the Jewish boy and girl who were part of the In gang of my own class of '50 (in fact, I'd been madly in love with Ads), but I knew next to nothing about their religious or cultural heritage.

At Columbia *I* felt like the minority kid as a WASP from the Midwest, something of an oddity who was anyway accepted and befriended by these Jewish students from New York. I was flattered when Joe Berger took me home for a *Shabat* dinner with his Orthodox parents in the Bronx, and for the first time in my life I perched a yarmulke on the back of my head (terrified that it might fall off and be regarded as a sign of disrespect), listened to prayers in Hebrew, and ate chicken soup with matzoh balls. Riding back on the rocking subway, Joe and I spoke not of our cultural differences but the common problem we shared that cut deeper than the rituals of religion and ethnic roots: being the only child of doting parents.

I admired the savvy and intelligence of New York Jews, and envied their early, ingrained love of learning and unashamed respect for literature, music, and the arts. I also appreciated the kind of compassion I got from these friends, as demonstrated by Sam Astrachan in my time of disappointment. I identified with Jews as outsiders, since part of me always felt that way myself, despite all my efforts to be In. The kid born with an urge to write, which means a tendency and talent to observe, almost by definition is outside the society he sees and describes. I felt more kin than alien to my new Jewish friends. Perhaps most important of all, I was grateful to them for accepting and befriending me, the WASP outsider from the sticks.

Harold Kushner, in his reunion address to the class of '55, observed that "half of us were bright Jewish kids from Brooklyn and Queens who wanted Columbia to help us transcend our parochial origins and gain admission to the greater American scene . . . and the other half of us were high school hotshots from the Midwest who hoped that Columbia would teach us to pass for New York Jewish intellectuals."

Marion Magid, who came to Barnard from the Bronx and whose parents were immigrant Russian Jews, believes that "the cultural encounter of Jews and *goyim,* New York and Midwest, was the great experience of the fifties in New York."

On her first day at Barnard, at a tea for incoming freshmen, Marion met a student who came from the Midwest and had gone to an Episcopal boarding school. "She'd never seen a Jew before," Marion recalls. "There was a mutual fascination between us. She'd recite the names of her relatives — American names — and I'd give her back names of my relatives from Russian Jewry. It was a fructifying encounter, a much more crucial kind than the European-American encounter. Now it's become a syndrome, a reigning cliché, like Woody Allen and Diane Keaton. You can't live it now without knowing you're some kind of social phenomenon, but then it was unmapped terrain. It was like embarking on a voyage of discovery."

This cultural voyage of discovery led me to a real voyage to Israel shortly after college, where I sent dispatches to *The Nation* and traveled the country from Eilat to Haifa, working on *kibbutzim* as a shepherd, a hay pitcher, and a fruit picker. I talked late into the night with a couple my own age who lived on a *kibbutz* near the Dead Sea, hearing the husband's explanation of coming to Israel as a reaction to his sense of isolation as a Jew when he walked through the Christmas-lit streets of Manhattan, knowing he was outside all that. Yes, I said, for I too had felt outside, and I felt a kinship with this young guy, and his country.

On one of my walks down Broadway with Sam Astrachan after he had told me my story failed to get *The Columbia Review* prize, I said something rueful and self-deprecating that he especially appreciated. It made him laugh, and he stopped walking and put his arm around my shoulder with brotherly affection.

"Wakefield," he said, "you're a Jew."

I smiled, feeling proud and elated. The illumination from a streetlight on one side and the glow from the plate glass window of a Rikers late-night restaurant on the other made a pool of light where we stood in the middle of the sidewalk. There was a warmth about the moment, a festive aura. I felt, at last, I had graduated.

THREE

Getting Started

FIRST JOBS

I COULDN'T GET past the receptionists. When I went on my job search after college, the receptionists who barred my way from interviews at New York's great newspapers blended together into one gorgon-like image: a grim woman with a beehive hairdo wearing cat's-eye glasses studded with rhinestones, her red lips pursed in disapproval and rejection. Clutching the manila envelope of clippings I had published in my summer jobs at the *Indianapolis Star* and the *Grand Rapids Press,* I slunk away in dejection. I'd thought this would be a snap.

After all, one of my stories in the *Press* had drawn the managing editor himself out of his office to make a rare appearance in the city room. The legendary M. M. "Crow" Kesterson (it was whispered that his initials stood for Montmorency Maximilian, but one did not address him as such), who wore a neatly pointed gray mustache and sleeve garters, à la the editors from the golden age of journalism, shook my hand as he praised the lead of my feature on a woman who planted rosebushes in her garden that multiplied into more rosebushes. My opening sentence was "A rosebush is a rosebush is a rosebush in the garden of Mrs. Henry Frampton of 2245 Euclid Avenue." As he grasped my hand firmly in his own, Kesterson said,

"Congratulations. You are the first person to ever get Gertrude Stein into the pages of the *Grand Rapids Press*."

How could I fail to make it in New York?

Now I had another question. How could I hope to land a job if I couldn't even get past the receptionists? In desperation, I called home — not my parents but my favorite high school teachers. Jean Grubb, the journalism teacher who got me my first professional job, as our high school sports correspondent for the *Indianapolis Star*, had no contacts in New York. Nor did my first boss at the *Star*, the talented Corky Lamm, who had tried to crash the gates of New York journalism fresh out of college but ended up with a dull job at an insurance company and retreated back home to Indiana. I tried Dorothy Peterson, the history teacher whom so many in my class had looked to for guidance beyond the classroom. Miss Peterson had a friend from her own college days at DePauw who, she said, was in the newspaper business in New York. She would call him and suggest that he see me, at least to give me advice, if not a job.

For the first time, I got beyond a receptionist. In fact, I landed in the inner sanctum itself. The man behind the enormous desk was absorbed in reading my story of the multiplying rosebushes. The only sound in the plushly carpeted room was the muted stutter of a Dow Jones stock ticker, which looked like a small telegraph key inside an elegant bell jar with a gold base, set on a corner of the long desk. Miss Peterson's friend had not only agreed to see me but was actually interested in reading the clippings in the now dog-eared manila envelope I clutched to my chest like a life preserver. The man was Barney Kilgore, publisher of the *Wall Street Journal*.

Kilgore swiveled in his chair toward me, looked up from the clipping, and said, "Did you write this?"

I said I had.

"And the others too?"

He held up the manila envelope.

"Yes, sir," I said.

Kilgore's head jerked sideways in a twitching motion, a nervous tic that was one of the idiosyncrasies for which, I learned, he was famous. He was more justly famous as the brilliant journalist who became publisher of the *Wall Street Journal* at age thirty-nine and, with the acquisition of regional printing plants, was credited by *Time* with transforming a "dull financial sheet" into "one of the best U.S. newspapers."

I had heard that Kilgore was also renowned for making conscious use of his Hoosier background. He tried to pass himself off as a hick, wearing loud, hand-painted ties with unmatching shirts, and suit jackets that didn't go with the pants. It was said that Kilgore believed this approach disarmed his sophisticated New York competitors and gave him an edge in whatever he was doing, which was usually successful.

A friend on the *Journal* told me Kilgore once showed up in the city room without warning, and a new cub reporter handed him a story to take down to the printer, thinking Kilgore was a copy boy, one of those aging fellows in cast-off clothes who was lucky to get a job, roughly equivalent to a messenger. As well as dressing the part of a bumpkin, Kilgore spoke in a country-boy lingo, with a twang that made Will Rogers sound almost British by comparison.

"You're from Indiana," Kilgore said to me with approval. "You'll do all right in New York." His head yanked into a tic and he added, "Some of these New York fellas, they don't do so good here."

Kilgore explained that as publisher of the *Journal* he no longer got to do any "real" newspaper work, and that was what he loved most of all — getting his hands smeared with printer's ink and putting out a paper, in the old-time tradition of William Allen White and the great country editors. To remedy this, he had just bought his hometown weekly in Princeton, New Jersey, where he could do all the tinkering and puttering in the pressroom, or anyplace he wanted, without union restrictions. He offered me a job as reporter on the *Princeton Packet*, "New Jersey's Oldest Weekly," at the princely salary of $70 a week.

I was thrilled at the offer — my first full-time job in the postcollegiate, real world. The drawback was I'd have to live in suburban Princeton, a college and commuting town, rather than the one place in the world I wanted to be, New York City. But at least I was less than an hour away by train, and I could come up every weekend to be in the city and breathe the air that would keep my spirit alive. I accepted Kilgore's offer with thanks and gratitude. It was, after all, the only one I had, and I felt Barney Kilgore was a good guy even with his idiosyncrasies, which included (in my current view) not only

e, but just as Marion Magid, at Barnard, discovered that "Trill-
was for the boys" at Columbia, so was Leavis only for the boys
ambridge.

went there *for* Leavis, but they didn't let women be tutored by
," Meg explains. "You had to go to a women's college." She did,
ever, meet and become friends with some of the American boys
were studying with Leavis, like Robert Gottlieb, Norman Pod-
tz, and Daniel Ellsberg. "When I came back from Europe to
in New York, Bob Gottlieb called and said there was a woman
re he was working at Simon and Schuster — he'd just started
e — who was helping set up a Volunteers for Stevenson head-
rters, and there were lots of openings. I was given a volunteer
filing cards. If you were minimally intelligent and diligent, you
e valuable. I went to my boss after several weeks and said I no-
d that on some of the cards the word 'Negro' was written in big
rs beside the name. I wasn't an expert in these matters — I was
a grad school dropout — but I felt this was not the right thing
o. I said, 'If I were to come in here and find "Jew" written beside
name, I'd be upset.' Well, this nice sort of socialite lady said,
u're absolutely right, dear. Make all new cards for these people,
instead of "Negro," just put a capital *N* beside their names.' I
uld have known right then Adlai didn't have a chance.

was later promoted to a paying job as director of research,
siding over the clipping files. My first regular job was filing clip-
gs for *The Reporter*. I got my job there not just because of my
erience filing for the Stevenson volunteers, but because Claire
ling, the *Reporter*'s foreign correspondent who I met in Rome,
te to the managing editor, saying something like, 'This young
man hasn't done anything yet, but she'll be good.' While I did
filing at *The Reporter*, I worked on an article about Nixon. It took
about six months to write and was called 'The Prose of Richard
on.'" This brilliant satirical piece got her promoted to staff
ter.

ost of my friends and I lucked out in the first jobs we got. Even
ey didn't lead to something better, most were entertaining. Ann
ntgomery was hired through an employment agency as a recep-
ist for the New York City Anti-Crime Commission: "We kept
k of which restaurants the Mafia people went to eat in."

his twitch and his Hoosier mannerisms but also his Indiana Republican politics. Whatever our differences, I knew he would treat me
fairly and well, and he did.

When I told C. Wright Mills I'd taken a job on a weekly paper in
Princeton, he puffed on his pipe, shrugged, and said, "Small-town
stuff. You'll be back."

He was right, of course. I came back sooner than even I had
hoped, courtesy of a job offer from Mills himself. In the meantime,
I was proud and relieved to tell my parents I had not only graduated from college — I had a job.

As I found out, getting your first job in New York wasn't easy, and
some of us realized the challenge while still in college and wisely
planned ahead. Because of my injury from the auto accident, I was
not eligible for the draft, but other young male college graduates
faced two years of military service that further complicated their
career plans. Max Frankel, the ace Columbia correspondent for the
New York Times, was hired by the paper when he graduated, but the
draft was hanging over him.

"I was terrified that if I left for two years in the Army, no one at
the *Times* would remember me when I got back," Frankel says. "But
there was a law that if you had a job for one year and you were
drafted, they had to take you back when you returned from the
service. I went to my draft board and got a year's deferment to get
an M.A. in political science, then asked the *Times* if I could have my
two days off in the middle of the week — I could take a full load of
five courses by going to class on Tuesday and Wednesday."

When Max returned from two years of Army service, a guaran-
teed job at the *Times* was waiting, and his first assignment was police
reporter. "My first year I was in the police shack, hanging out with
guys who only covered cops. I rode around with these guys who
had guns in their glove compartment and talked rough cop talk.
The newspaper scene in New York then was vibrant. It was hotly
competitive, with papers of every conceivable stripe, from the
World-Telegram, which was sucking up to the establishment, to the
Hearst papers, the *Mirror* and the *American.* The *Daily News* was a
terrific tabloid, and we also had the liberal *Post.* There was very little
TV then."

Few of us planned our careers so well ahead. If we had no pre-vious experience or connections, we turned to family or friends. Just as I got my job with the aid of my high school history teacher, the future novelist Bruce Jay Friedman got his through what he calls "the Bronx mothers' Mafia." After a hard day of making the rounds of employment agencies when he came home from the Air Force in 1953, Bruce had dinner with his mother at the House of Chan in Manhattan. "We were having those drinks everybody used to have then, the ones with the orange slice and the cherry, when my mother spotted this woman she knew from the neighborhood sitting at the bar. My mother invited her over to our table and intro-duced me. She said, 'This is my son, and he wants to get started in writing.' This other Bronx mother nods and says, 'My son-in-law works for Magazine Management Company. He'd love to meet your son, maybe he could help him.'

"I started in 1953 with Magazine Management and stayed until 1965, but I never did get formally offered the job. I was given my own magazine to edit — *Swank,* a tepid harbinger of what girlie magazines were to become — then I was put in charge of four other magazines the company owned, called *Male, Man's World, Men,* and *True Action.*"

Joan Didion knew she wanted to be a writer and live in New York after her stint as a guest editor at *Mademoiselle,* the summer after her junior year at Berkeley. When she returned to the University of California, she entered a *Vogue* magazine contest for college seniors, which would bring her back to New York if she won it, and she did.

"The prize was your choice of a two-week trip to Paris," Joan recalls, "or a thousand dollars in cash and an interview for a job at *Vogue.* I took the money and the interview. The day I was inter-viewed I had a fever of a hundred two, but I got the job. I wrote promotional copy, merchandising copy — the kind that was sent to stores as advertising support. I'd sit there and think up things to write, like '*Vogue* says pink.' I threatened to quit and take the job of college editor of *Mademoiselle,* so then *Vogue* put me in the features department, mainly writing captions. I didn't get to write any arti-cles until some writer who was assigned to do a piece on jealousy didn't come in with it, and it was already on the cover. I wrote the

piece and they liked it enough to give me a byli[ne?] of the deal. This piece turned out to be popu[lar?] others like it."

When the future novelist and screenwriter J[ohn Dunne?] got out of the Army in September 1956, he w[ent to?] try to get a job on a magazine. The problem [was I'd?] never published anything, and I didn't even w[ork on a?] paper or literary magazine at Princeton. I wan[ted to write in?] the sense that I wanted *to have written.* I had a [title?] and a completely plotted-out novel about a m[ovie director. I'd?] never met a movie director and I hadn't the re[motest idea what?] one did. I didn't actually write. I would sit an[d jot?] down ideas, and I had the title and the first line[. It was?] called *Not the Macedonian,* and the opening line w[as 'I am not?] Alexander the Great.'"

Unlike Joan Didion (his future wife), John Du[nne hadn't won any?] magazine contests, and unlike me, he had no m[agazine clip-?]pings, so he used his imagination. "I went to the [news-?]stand in Times Square," he remembers, "an[d bought a Colorado?] Springs newspaper. I'd been stationed at Fort C[arson,?] and I remembered the paper from Colorado S[prings, so I cut out?] bylines. I got back issues and cut out stories and [made a port-?]folio. I figured the paper was far enough away [that no one could?] check. I went to an employment agency and the[y sent me out.?] It was a horrendous moment. But the portfoli[o got me a job?] through another agency, at a magazine called *I[ndustrial Design.* It?] was an artsy-craftsy publication on East 50th Stre[et, near St.?] Patrick's. I got a job as a writer — never having [written before —?] based on this spurious portfolio. I was getting $[70 a week, and when?] you crossed from $70 to $100 a week, that was [cutting the?] mustard. I began writing articles the magazine lik[ed.?] By '59 I had a *real* portfolio of stories, and I went [to *Time* maga-?]zine."

Meg Greenfield had some help in getting her [start in New?] York from friends she'd met in England and Italy [after graduating?] from Smith. She had gone to study at Cambridg[e with one of?] the leading literary critics of the day, F. R. Lea[vis.?]

There were also just plain lousy jobs, ones that were not what they promised. After graduating from Barnard, Jane Richmond was thrilled to work in an office that purported to be a literary agency, but it turned out to be more like a sweatshop. "There were forty women in a room rewriting people's novels," Jane remembers. "I was rewriting a book by a woman who had been a rumrunner during Prohibition. A lot of the writers were black girls who had been English majors and couldn't get a job in publishing. So the man who owned this agency said he was a great liberal by hiring them. He charged the clients fees for rewriting their work, and then I learned he never even sent the manuscripts out to publishers, but for another fee published the books himself. It was really a vanity press posing as a literary agency. He used to pay us in coins, and had us hold our hands out like supplicants, then he would break these packages of coins into our waiting hands. When I told him I was quitting he was furious, and he actually told me, 'You'll never work in New York again.' "

I felt that my friends were savoring the daily challenge and adventure of Manhattan — not to speak of the nightly romance — while I was trudging the tree-lined, somnolent streets of suburban Princeton, covering sewer commission meetings and the local police courts (traffic violations were the hottest crimes) and ferreting out the latest rezoning ordinances of the town council, returning at night to the flocked-wallpaper prison of my nook in Mrs. Mulford's roominghouse. I took the commuter train from Princeton Junction into New York every weekend to stay with my friend Ted Steeg and his roommates on West 92nd Street, and made romantic forays with them into the Village or to the jazz clubs on West 52nd Street.

We used to come back and drink until dawn, reciting the purplish sentimental poem by the radical journalist of the twenties John Reed, chanting together with dramatic fun (yet feeling a tingle at the same time) his hymn to New York: "Who that has known thee but shall burn / In exile till he come again / To do thy bitter will, O stern / Moon of the tides of men!" We called New York the Stern Moon, as in, "Wakefield, when you returning to the Stern Moon?"

After only four months in New Jersey — it seemed like four years — a letter came from C. Wright Mills, offering me a job. I let out a yelp of joy. Mills wrote that he'd been given a grant to hire a researcher for a new book he was writing on American intellectuals, and he'd like me to have the position. It meant taking a pay cut from the $70 a week I was making on the *Packet* to $60, and the job would last only six months, but those concerns seemed petty compared to the chance to get back to New York and immerse myself in literature and politics instead of deliberations of the town sewer commission. I gave Barney Kilgore notice enough to hire a replacement, and we parted with respect, if not rapport. I was on my way back to the Stern Moon.

I didn't have to look for a place to live in Manhattan, but moved right in with the group of guys I'd been staying with when I came up on weekends from my exile. There were three of them sharing a one-bedroom apartment at 312 West 92nd Street, and they looked on adding a fourth roommate not as overcrowding but as a chance to lower the overhead. The rent was $120, and adding another body meant each paid only $30 a month instead of $40. Three single beds were crammed into the one bedroom, dormitory style, and one person slept on the living room couch on a rotating basis.

We discovered a covey of girls, just graduated from Wells College in Aurora, New York, who shared an apartment not far away, on West End Avenue. They split four ways what seemed to us the extravagant rent of $200 for a roomy, nicely furnished two-bedroom apartment with high-ceilinged living room and dining room, paying shares from salaries of $40 to $50 a week earned from working on magazines and teaching school. We met through my high school friend Jane Adler, who had also gone to Wells, and I introduced the girls to the guys in our gang.

A series of "exchange" parties and dinners ensued, and we learned to love the more ambitious dinner dish of the West End Avenue girls, the famous tuna noodle casserole, held together with Campbell's cream of mushroom soup. Our only complaint, which we kept a secret, was what seemed to us the skimpiness of the portions they served, and we took to stuffing ourselves with Ritz crackers before arriving for one of their meals. All of us became friends, and two couples became husbands and wives, and lived happily ever after. (Only in the fifties.)

Other apartments of young guys and gals new to New York were meeting and mating in similar fashion. Like many young women during their first days in the city, Ann Montgomery had lived at a women's residence when she arrived: "My father, a classics professor at Miami University in Ohio, arranged for me to stay at the Parnassus Girls' Club at 112th and Broadway, knowing I'd be safe and have at least two meals a day." But soon she met some friends from her college who were sharing an apartment on West 95th Street and were looking for another roommate: "There were five of us, and I think we each paid $60 a month," Ann recalls. "We used to have pajama parties. The boys in the apartment upstairs would come down in their pajamas and we'd all drink beer, then the boys would go upstairs again. The exciting part was that we were in our nightgowns and the boys in their pajamas. One of the boys married one of the girls."

Just as young women fresh off the train stayed first at women's clubs, young men sometimes spent their first nights, as Richard Lingeman did, at the YMCA. "I stayed at the Sloane House Y on 34th Street. It was a huge place, with strange people — I have this memory of men speaking desperately on the phone. Then I got into an apartment with six or eight other guys on York Avenue, and after that moved to West 13th in the Village where I shared an apartment with Chris Lehmann-Haupt."

Not everyone found comradeship when starting out in the city. John Gregory Dunne says, "I first lived in a roominghouse at 43 East 75th Street that was populated by every failure in New York. A guy who had failed the New York Bar exam twice, and failed a third time while he was there, was typical. There were four people to a room, but it had a fancy address in a good-looking townhouse between Madison and Park. Eating was on the honor system. There was a big refrigerator and pantry and a price list — a Ritz cracker was four cents, with peanut butter it went up to seven cents. A glass of milk was a dime. I was accused of cheating on kitchen privileges, so after that I never ate anything there."

Most of us did a lot of moving around with what now seems remarkable ease, the ease that comes with the freedom of youth. That's what strikes Meg Greenfield when she recalls coming back from Europe to live in New York in 1955: "I was moved from my first apartment on 11th Street to a better one on 10th Street by

Kenneth Koch, the poet, and his wife, Janice, who were pals of mine. We had been to some dinner with poets and painters, and we came back late with their baby's English perambulator to move all my things in — I remember crossing Hudson Street with that perambulator. It was late at night and people were staring at us. We were able to move all my earthy goods in two loads of their baby carriage. Can you imagine that? And we didn't have other baggage, either."

Bruce Jay Friedman remembers: "When I got out of the Air Force in '53, I moved to New York with my wife, Ginger, who I met when I was stationed in St. Louis, and we found an apartment on West 57th. Like a lot of New Yorkers, we bragged about the building where we lived in terms of what well-known people lived there. In our building we had Betty Clooney, sister of Rosemary, and Julia Meade, a TV hostess of the time. Also, we went to the same pizza place on Ninth Avenue as Patty Duke. She was nine years old then, but we were proud of the fact that we went to the same place for pizza."

There was a sense that because you lived in New York, you were part of "the scene" and had some connection with famous people — actors, writers, politicians, piano players. They were your neighbors in the biggest small town in the world. I remember riding in a cab up Park Avenue after a snowstorm and seeing a woman at the curb waving to get a ride going the other way. As we got closer, I saw it was Eleanor Roosevelt. I smiled and waved to her, and she smiled and waved back. I felt that I knew her. We were both New Yorkers.

LIVING BY THE PEN

The puffs of smoke from the pipe of C. Wright Mills as he paced back and forth in his study, thinking aloud, reminded me of steam from an engine, for his mind in high gear seemed like a dynamo. The exciting part of my job with Mills was not the research work I did in Columbia's Butler Library that summer of 1955 when I moved back to New York from Princeton, but the day every week or so I went up to his house near Nyack, reporting and discussing my findings. I'd listen as Mills roamed his rustic, sunlit study filled with books and file cabinets, asking me questions and commenting on what I'd found in my research.

When the classes he taught resumed in the fall, I moved my notes and typewriter into Mills's office in Hamilton Hall and worked out of there. But his real office was at home. The Columbia office simply contained old student papers, files of finished projects, a hot plate for warming up soup, and an electric espresso machine — this utilitarian gear was all he desired in that room. Neither his stomach nor his mind operated with its usual gargantuan appetite at the college office, and our talks there were disjointed and disappointing. Mills always seemed subdued when he came in, spoke very little, and stalked off to class. He would usually burst back into the room tired and out of sorts, as he had that day when he slammed down his books and said, referring to his students, "Who *are* these guys?"

He told me about attending a party of Columbia graduate students in sociology, which he found maddening. "I simply sat in a chair in a corner," he said, "and one by one these guys would come up to me, sort of like approaching the pariah — curiosity stuff. They were working on their Ph.D.s, and after they'd introduced themselves I'd ask, 'What are you working on?' It would always be something like, 'The Impact of Work-Play Relationships Among Lower Income Families on the South Side of the Block on 112th Street Between Amsterdam and Broadway.' Then I would ask —" Mills paused, leaned forward, and in his most contemptuous voice, boomed, "*Why?*" Obviously, these people weren't "taking it big."

Mills was not only a boss but a friend and advisor, taking a fatherly interest in my personal welfare as well as guiding my research. "Now Dan," he counseled me, "you're not married, and you're probably not eating well with those other guys. If none of you can really cook" — he didn't count spaghetti and cornmeal mush as real food — "you must get one of your girls to come over every Sunday night and cook you up a big stew that will last a week. You bottle it up in seven Mason jars, and then you have a good healthy meal instead of that bachelor stuff." This was, of course, in the days when it was assumed that men couldn't cook and women could, and should, though Mills himself was soon to take up the culinary arts, applying himself in the kitchen with the same enthusiasm he brought to everything else he did. When I came to a lunch he'd prepared in his cooking days and praised the fresh bread, he said, "My God, man, don't you bake your own bread?"

Mills was full of advice that was often valuable and always entertaining, including what books I should read. He thrust James Agee's *Let Us Now Praise Famous Men* on me when it was out of print and known only to a small, ardent coterie. It seems forgotten, now that Agee's lyric work on sharecroppers is regarded as a classic, that Mills was one of the few who reviewed it admiringly after it was published, writing an incisive essay of praise in Dwight Macdonald's magazine *Politics*. "You want to write journalism? Take *that* one, boy!" Mills said as he plucked the book from his shelf and pushed it toward me.

Mills introduced me to the Homestead, a restaurant that was famous for serving the biggest pieces of beef at the best prices anywhere in New York City. It was over in the meat-packing district, on the western fringe of Greenwich Village, and supposedly its proximity to the fresh meat coming in accounted for the great deals the popular, plain-style restaurant could give its customers. Mills was known to go there and after the meal say to the waiter, "I'll have the same thing again." He'd eat a second helping of everything, including the sirloin steak, and pie for dessert. He practiced what he preached.

As it turned out, the journalist in Princeton, New Jersey, who became my most important mentor and launched my career as a writer was not my drawling, down-home fellow Hoosier Barney Kilgore but a fast-talking, hip intellectual described at the time by William F. Buckley, Jr., as "Murray Kempton, pinup boy of the bohemian left, who writes an impressionistic column for the *New York Post*." I was thrilled to learn that Kempton lived in Princeton with his wife and four young children, for I'd read his column during my Columbia days, and he'd become my idol.

Kempton's fans were a cult, a rabid band who realized nobody anywhere was writing this kind of elegant, ironic, iconoclastic prose about the passing scene in New York and America — and in a *newspaper*. H. L. Mencken, from Kempton's hometown of Baltimore, was probably the closest model. His liberal views were never orthodox; in fact, he and Buckley became fast friends as fellow intellectual raconteurs who sometimes seemed to be the only people who could comprehend their esoteric conversations. It wasn't Murray's politics that made the blood of his followers race, but his novelistic perception of current events and figures. For a nickel I got to read a new column by a journalistic Proust that was hot off the press three afternoons a week.

Kempton's first book was published the season I went to work in Princeton, and I seized the opportunity to review it for the *Packet* on the grounds that he was a local man, a point I stressed in my lead, which ran: "Murray Kempton of Edgerstoune Road and also the *New York Post* has written a book that was published last week called *Part of Our Time: Some Monuments and Ruins of the Nineteen Thirties.*"

The book was a series of essaylike portraits of leading political and literary figures who were shaped by "the myth of our time" in the thirties, like Whittaker Chambers and Alger Hiss, and it was the first thing I read that gave me a sense of the passion and excitement of what had always seemed to me a drab and dreary decade, the hangover after the Roaring Twenties.

But the book was more than the sum of its parts or the political or historical significance of its subject. It was a young person's book, a book that stirred the blood and caught the imagination of my friends and me, who not only read it but memorized parts and recited them aloud, as we had memorized the poetry of Yeats and Millay and that other dreamer in the guise of a journalist who brought ideas alive, John Reed. We took Kempton's words as wisdom, coming not from some graybeard but a journalistic genius in his prime, who had seen into the heart of things and understood them for us. We called *Part of Our Time* "the Good Book." It was our bible.

I can see Bill Chapman, the twenty-two-year-old copy boy who years later would be a foreign correspondent for the *Washington Post,* pacing the paint-peeling living room on West 92nd Street as we recited from Kempton's book and drank Chianti. I still remember these words: "Each of us lives with a sword over his head. There are those who can ignore its shadow and those who cannot. Those who cannot are the ones who make the special myth of their time."

Another passage switched on like a light in my mind for years afterward, in times of crisis far from New York, reminding me of the eerie power of Kempton's prose to predict the inner feelings of our futures: "There were new endeavors and fresh disasters, for they are the way of life, and the art of life is to save enough of yourself from each disaster to be able to go on in something like your old image."

In my review for the *Princeton Packet* I tried to sound like a critic, not just a fan. The next morning, after the paper came out, the landlady in my roominghouse shouted up the stairs that someone wanted to talk to me on the telephone. It was Murray Kempton, calling to thank me.

"You really dug the book," he said, then hastened to explain he meant "dug" in the sense of "understood," not just in its other sense, "liked." I dug what he was telling me — in both senses of the word. He invited me to come by sometime and have a beer. I was there that afternoon.

Kempton had reddish hair in a crew cut like Mills's, but unlike Mills he was strictly Ivy League straight in dress and appearance. No motorcycle gear for Murray: rep tie, tweed jacket, and cordovan shoes. He noticed other people's clothes as well. When I introduced him to the literary agent James Oliver Brown, he complimented Jim on his English shoes. Once when I showed up in Murray's office at the *Post* wearing a raggedy sport shirt and corduroys in need of a press, he looked at me with a grimace and said, "You look like something out of Judge Horowitz's court." That judge sat on juvenile delinquency cases.

Murray discussed books, baseball, and politics with equal fascination and interweaved them all, if you could only see the pattern. He knew the details of everything, from Shoeless Joe Jackson's batting average the year *before* the World Series to Thomas Jefferson's reading preferences *after* he left the presidency. While we were both covering the Teamsters Union convention in Miami that elected Jimmy Hoffa president, I found Murray in his hotel room poring over what he said was the key to understanding this whole damn thing — Robie Macauley's new introduction to Ford Madox Ford's novel *Parade's End*.

Once I had lunch with Murray and with Marion Magid, whom I

thought of as one of the most brilliant and witty people I knew in New York. Even she sometimes felt daunted by the rush of Murray's conversational connections and allusions. "After lunch with Murray," she told me, "my mind is so tired I feel like I have to lie down for an hour." We ate at Le Moal, a fancy East Side French restaurant near the office of Marion's magazine where many of its editors dined, and Murray dubbed it "the *Commentary* commissary." That consonance reminded him of the time he was having lunch at an Italian restaurant during the McCarthy era. As the diners discussed who was now an anti-Communist and who had become an *anti*-anti-Communist, the waiter came. A jaded reporter, despairing of getting everyone's latest affiliation straight, tossed aside his menu and said, "I'll have an anti-antipasto."

Toward the end of the summer of my work for Mills in 1955, I began to read about the case of a Negro boy from Chicago named Emmet Till, who was murdered in Mississippi for the crime of whistling at a white woman. The trial, scheduled to take place in the little town of Sumner, in the Mississippi Delta, promised to be one of those turning points in our history, a classic American courthouse drama like the Scopes trial, and I ached to go down and write about it. But not only did I need money to get there; I had to have credentials. I needed an assignment, and yet I hadn't published anything in a magazine and so had no contacts. I called Murray Kempton.

Murray was to cover the story for the *Post*, and he'd also been asked to do a piece for *The Nation,* which he didn't feel he could or should write in addition. He picked up the phone and told the editor of *The Nation* that he ought to let a young guy named Dan Wakefield do the story for him. Completely on Murray's recommendation, *The Nation* gave me a letter of introduction as credentials and the bus fare for the trip (I think it amounted to forty bucks).

When I got the assignment, a line came into my head by John Reed, who wrote somewhere that when he knew he was going on one of his first foreign stories, it was like "being on the edge of a beautiful dream." I was there. The dream was not just the story, and not just the nightmare of Emmet Till's death, but the opportunity of being on the scene to transcribe in my own words a meaningful moment in American history, and the promise of doing it again in other places, for other big stories.

On the bus that took me to Sumner ("A Good Place to Raise a Boy," a sign just outside town proclaimed with what seemed now a dark irony), I purposely sat next to a Negro woman, as if to show my comradeship. She smiled and asked me, "Are you a young lawyer?"

"No, ma'am," I said. "I'm a reporter, from New York."

It was on that trip that I first felt justified in identifying New York as my home. I went around the racially tense town in the Delta — even knocking on people's doors to interview them about the controversial case that was making headlines — proudly identifying myself as a reporter for *The Nation,* "in New York." It was hardly a way to win favor. Just being a reporter from up north was enough to get me taken for a ride by two sheriff's deputies, who dropped me in the middle of nowhere so I had to walk back to town in the gathering dark. I was lucky a ride was all they gave me.

I felt no fear because I was young and naïve, and also because Murray Kempton was there, to introduce me to the other reporters and make sure I knew what was going on. He saw to it that I had a room in town, and that I got out of there when the other reporters left for a motel in the bigger, less tense city of Greenville to write their stories, so I wouldn't be the lone Yankee in Sumner after the trial.

The trial in the small, sweltering, segregated courtroom was indeed classic, with the murdered boy's uncle, an aged Negro field hand named Moses Wright, testifying against Roy Bryant and J. W. Milam, the two white men accused of the brutal murder. Their acquittal was a foregone conclusion of white supremacy ruling over law. The drama set the stage for the conflict to come, the struggle for civil rights in the South, in which Mose Wright was only the first of the long-oppressed people of his race to stand up, in the face of threats and against the whole weight of tradition and power in the region, and proclaim the right to the freedom they were supposed to have received the century before.

I sat up all night writing so that I could file my report at Western Union the next morning, to make the deadline. I finished at dawn. The lead of my piece summed up my perception of the trial and the situation we were now to observe as it went through its struggle to change in the decade to come: "The crowds are gone and this Delta town is back to its silent, solid life that is based on cotton and the proposition that a whole race of men was created to pick it."

The Nation ran the story, "Justice in Sumner," with my byline, and suddenly I was a published writer in a national magazine. I bought up all the copies at the local newsstand and passed them out like cigars — this, in fact, was a birth. The editors and, more important, the publisher of *The Nation* liked the piece and wanted me to come in and meet them and talk about doing more work.

The offices of *The Nation* were at 333 Sixth Avenue, at the corner of West 4th Street in the heart of Greenwich Village. There was nothing colorful, however, about the dreary old building that housed the magazine. You took a rickety freight elevator to the fourth floor and saw an elderly telephone operator at one of those old-fashioned switchboards with wires that plugged into little sockets to connect calls, the kind you see in black-and-white movies from the thirties and forties. The operator also acted as receptionist, and you waited until she finished answering and connecting calls to say who it was you wanted to see.

The editor in chief was Carey McWilliams, a liberal journalist who had written a well-respected book called *Factories in the Field,* an account of migrant workers in California. Carey's working-editor garb was a gray cardigan sweater he buttoned halfway up his white shirt with tie; his jacket hung on a coatrack by his desk. He always had on those shoes specially formed for the feet, which reminded me of the kind Frankenstein wore — one *Nation* contributor, Norman Thomas di Giovanni, called them space shoes. Norman, in fact, called Carey "Space Shoes" or "Space" or "Old Space," a nickname that made me giggle and seemed so suitable I couldn't help using it for McWilliams myself, though we never said it in front of him.

Norman was the only *Nation* writer I knew who was, like me, under thirty — the rest of the staff seemed to be over forty or even fifty, which was ancient to us. Norman was an Italian-American anarchist from Boston with an Oberlin College degree who was working on a book about Sacco and Vanzetti. I stayed on his cot in a cold-water flat in the North End when I visited Boston, and he slept on a blanket on my floor when he came to New York.

We were both young and crazy for literature and experience, and to us Carey McWilliams, with his space shoes, buttoned-up cardigan, and thinning black hair slicked straight back from his pale forehead, seemed like the ultimate square. The image was reinforced by what we regarded as his sober, right-thinking, well-meaning, unexciting editorials. McWilliams seemed like the safe, predictable liberal, the person who believed in all the correct causes but without any passion or fire.

At least Norman — or Di G, as he was known — could charm Carey, as he could almost anyone, with his wild-man Italian enthusiasm, which he played with great élan. Carey and I simply never hit it off; we worked together and maintained a polite manner toward each other, but really felt no rapport.

After a pleasant but somewhat strained talk with McWilliams when I returned from Mississippi, I was taken in to meet the new publisher of *The Nation,* a ruggedly handsome, intellectually rough-around-the-edges man named George Kirstein. He looked as if he might have stepped out of an *Esquire* ad, with his sharp suit and tie, brilliantly shined shoes, well-coifed hair, and strong tanned face, weathered from the sailing he did on his yacht. George was direct, irreverent, sometimes impolite, and enjoyed a good laugh, a big drink, and a hearty meal.

In the hushed, serious atmosphere of the magazine, which had the dank aura of one of those cobwebby storerooms lived in by spinster sisters preserving the ancient family archives (the remains of the 1930s radical left wing), Kirstein seemed as colorful and refreshing as the playboy of the Western world. He was a wealthy man whose Boston family had made a fortune (Filene's department store was among their businesses) and given generously to good works and culture. George was a Harvard graduate who served on the National Labor Relations Board during World War II, and who injected a needed transfusion of money into the ailing *Nation* when he became publisher, the year I wrote my first article.

Kirstein suffered what seemed to me an unnecessary intellectual inferiority complex because of his two artistically prodigal siblings, the New York City Ballet director Lincoln Kirstein and the literary biographer Minna Curtiss, who had written a book on Proust. George's public image was that of the crass businessman among the *artistes,* which I think he cultivated in self-defense, yet I found his the most original mind at *The Nation.* McWilliams had the reputation of the brilliant liberal editor, yet to me his ideas often seemed recycled or geared to special causes of the magazine designed to spur bulk sales to a particular union or pressure group. It was George who wanted to try something new all the time — including me, which of course was one of the reasons I liked him.

"We could use a young guy like you," he said when I met him. His office was in the one bright room at the end of the floor, with windows that offered a view of the surrounding commercial and apartment buildings of the Village. He tamped his pipe and said he'd like me to do some more on-the-scene reporting, to provide something current among the long-range think pieces on politics, economics, public policy, and the arts that were the principal fare of the magazine.

Not surprisingly, this struck me as a wise and perceptive policy. A year or so later, when I had an offer to write for another publication, Kirstein proposed a weekly retainer of $75 in return for my writing two articles a month for *The Nation.* In the meantime, I was happy to free-lance for them at their going rate of $40 per article.

More than any other writer I knew, C. Wright Mills's friend and neighbor Harvey Swados embodied the search to live and do his work in a commercial world and maintain his commitment as an artist. Though a little more than a decade older than me and my generation, he served as a model for many of us, wrestling with problems we were just confronting or foresaw down the line as part of the struggle to live and write. He wrote most of his first novel, *Out Went the Candle,* on the commuter train to New York from his home in Valley Cottage, in Rockland County, while he worked in the office of Israel Bonds, writing publicity. After that experience he decided that a writer shouldn't have another job that drew on his ability to write, requiring him to use his craft for a lesser purpose than literature, which divided his mind — his very self — between art and commerce. That dilemma became a theme of his work and the subject of his novel *False Coin.*

Next he went in the opposite direction and got a laboring job, working on the assembly line at the Ford plant in Rockland County.

Out of that experience he drew the material for an insightful book of connected stories, *On the Line* — yet the job left him so exhausted, he found it hard to write in what time was left, so he gave up that route too. After that, he took a part-time position teaching writing at Sarah Lawrence. His teacher's salary, combined with grants, fellowships, journalistic assignments, and modest book advances, enabled him to support his wife and three children, in a home filled with books, talk, laughter, and music (Harvey played the piano and flute, his daughter Felice the harp) which I loved to visit.

Though I wasn't even considering starting a family, Harvey and his wife and children were the kind I'd have wanted. They showed me that family life was not only possible for a writer but could even be fulfilling, stimulating, and fun, with great books, Bach cantatas, and even a goat, which they kept in their yard in Valley Cottage and got milk from.

Harvey had an active social conscience as well as a creative imagination, and he loved to do journalism on the model of George Orwell, going down into a coal mine to write about what conditions were like, talking to the men on the assembly line at the Ford plant to explode "the Myth of the Happy Worker." He wrote essays and articles for magazines like *The Nation* and *Dissent* that paid little but adhered to his own principles — expressed in the title of his collection of some of those pieces, *A Radical's America* — and allowed him to get his message across without compromise. Few were as dedicated, or as pure in sticking to principle, as Harvey.

We all took different routes for survival, trying to write and make a living at the same time. The year Bruce Jay Friedman began working as a magazine editor, he published his first short story in *The New Yorker* ("Wonderful Golden Rule Days") and found time to write fiction after hours. He also helped many other young writers get their start or keep financially afloat by buying their stories for the men's adventure magazines he was running. "When I was in charge of the four magazines," Friedman says, "I needed thirty-six stories a month. I only had a staff of five or six, so I was dependent on an army of free-lancers. Someone recommended a guy called Mario Puzo, and I hired him on the basis of a novel he wrote, *The Dark Arena.* He thought my hiring him was the kindest thing anyone ever did, but I was just trying to make my own job easier by getting a good writer. He worked for me for five years while he was writing *The Godfather*. Mario probably wrote two billion words for me. I'd have an illustration done of some battle, and then enlarge it and show it to him. It would be some fictitious scene from World War II, because we'd run out of real battles and we couldn't just keep storming Anzio month after month. He wrote these novels we called book bonuses, and I was so enthusiastic about his work I put my own job on the line and demanded that our publisher break our salary cap of $500 per book bonus and pay Mario the unheard-of sum of $650. Mario thought it was fabulous. We've been friends ever since, and he still thanks me for that raise to $650."

Aspiring writers who had editorial jobs or even wrote unsigned pieces for magazines still wanted to have their own work published under their own name, and so they looked to the "little magazines" for outlets. "Before I got my first byline at *Vogue*," Joan Didion remembers, "I was sending things to other magazines. The first piece I ever published was about a quiz show I'd been on. I sent it to *The Reporter* first and got a nice note back, but they didn't take it. Then Noel Parmentel, who had written for *National Review*, sent it to *NR* and they published it. I got to know Frank Meyer, who was editor of *NR*'s back-of-the-book section, and began writing for him. *NR* started the writing careers of many people, like me, Renata Adler, John Leonard, Arlene Croce. All of us started writing our first freelance pieces for Frank Meyer."

Another person who got his start as a published writer at *National Review* was Joan's husband, John Dunne: "Joan and I had gotten to be good friends and often had dinner together. She was writing for *National Review*, and she was their young literary star. We were riding uptown in a cab one night and she said she'd been asked to do a piece for them on Edwin O'Connor's new book, *The Edge of Sadness*, and she didn't want to do it. I said I'd like to do it, and I wrote about growing up Irish Catholic in Hartford and *NR* published it. You got $25 for a review or a back-of-the-book piece. If you wrote for *NR* you were either a true believer in the conservative cause or a young person who wanted to get your stuff published.

"At the tag end of the fifties," John adds, "we all for the first time were beginning to get published. We'd made some connection — it didn't matter whether it was *The Nation* or *National Review* or *Time*."

Joan agrees: "Yes, it was like not being a freshman anymore."

There were those who didn't get published, of course, people who sometimes seemed as talented, if not more so, than those of us who did get our work in print. Some of them went back home to the Midwest, the South, or wherever else they had started from. Some stayed on in New York and found other means of expression and ways of making a living. The "starving artist" life lost its glamour after a few years, and people wanted, if not a little fame, at least a little fortune.

"I'm hungry," my friend Ted the Horse said one night at a party in the Village. At first I didn't understand, and suggested we go to Jim Atkins's hash house on Sheridan Square for eggs or pancakes.

"That's not what I mean," he said.

From the fierce look in his eye, I got it. He wanted to make some money. He was going to get what we called a real job. In preparation, he and I and his other friends read *The Organization Man*, which contained an appendix for the aid of those who wanted to be employed by big companies. It was titled "How to Cheat on Personality Tests." The first rule to remember in trying to decide the best answer to any psychological-test question was "I loved my mother and my father, but my father a little bit more." (The presumption was that anyone applying for a serious job in the business world was a man.)

Ted got a kick out of that and began to repeat it, making it a kind of refrain. The rest of us would join in, singing this key to success, jazzing it up, riffing on it as we went along, slapping our knees, clapping, as if this were some great tribal chant or hip new beat from the world of bop: "I-love-my-mother-and-my-father — but-my-father-a-little-bit-more."

Ted landed a job at McGraw-Hill, in the media department, where he learned to make slide shows and films, and later went on to launch Steeg Productions, his own company, for which he wrote, produced, and directed prizewinning documentaries and films for business, which took him on shooting locations around the world. It was not the voyage of the *Pequod,* but it used his creative talent and earned him a good living.

■　■　■

I may not have had a regular salary, and my fees for *Nation* articles were modest — Calvin Trillin later reported that for his column that magazine paid "in the high two figures" — but I had some great fringe benefits. George Kirstein used to invite me to the penthouse he and his wife, Jane, kept at the One Fifth Avenue Hotel, for drinks and dinner with friends; or I'd go up to their house in Mamaroneck for lunch and a swim (he was the first person I knew who had a private swimming pool); or I'd watch the America's Cup races from his sailboat. His pool had those floating chairs with a hole cut out of the arm to hold a drink, and leaning back in one of those with a Bloody Mary, discussing world events with George, I felt like the Negro boy in Philip Roth's *Goodbye, Columbus* when he looks at a library book of Gauguin paintings and says, "Ain't that the fuckin life."

My connection with *The Nation* gave me a base to begin a shaky subsistence — but one I would not have traded for anything less free and glamorous — as a writer in New York, living hand-to-mouth on the kind of writing known in the trade as "pieces." Later, toward the darker end of my New York days, I came to think of them as pieces of myself. Some of them seemed torn out of me unwillingly, by the roots, or what macho fellows in those days referred to as the short hairs, as the pressures of paying the rent and producing article after article mounted to an unrelenting treadmill of production. At the beginning, though, each byline provided a shot of adrenelin, each assignment a challenge and a chance for exploration of the city and its mysteries, unveiling new places and people, sounds and scenes.

My English writer friend in the Village, Sarel Eimerl ("a seriously witty man," according to Bruce Jay Friedman), described our profession with the elegant phrase "living by the pen." He said it with a certain irony, as we calculated such mundane problems as how to pay the gas bill. The exciting thing was that I was getting published, and a world of stories was out there waiting. Again the words of John Reed came to mind: it was like being "on the edge of a beautiful dream."

FOUR

Miracle in the Bowery

THE ONLY TIME I'd been to the Bowery was to drink at Mc-Sorley's, a saloon known for its cheap beer, sawdust on the floor, and the fact that it didn't allow women. It was a curiosity, the sort of lowlife place that college boys and other tourists could visit to feel they had gotten a taste of the infamous Bowery, whose name was synonymous with bums, men who huddled in doorways with bottles of rotgut wine in paper bags. The Bowery was still the symbol of poverty in a time of prosperity, a kind of sinkhole where people of all nationalities, even homegrown Americans, had fallen down. There was poverty, too, in the teeming streets of the Lower East Side, where the immigrants from Europe and their children were still struggling upward, and poverty in Harlem, where Negroes from the South and Puerto Ricans new to the mainland were trying to adapt and better themselves; but the Bowery was the bottom, and people who had descended to it were not expected to rise.

When my friend Sam Astrachan said he wanted to take me down there to meet a "character" I ought to write about, I assumed at first he meant a colorful Bowery bum. Now that he was about to be a published novelist, Sam was trying to help my budding career as a journalist. It was the summer of 1955, and after publishing my first story in *The Nation,* I was roaming the city in search of other subjects and doing research for C. Wright Mills the rest of the time.

I regarded New York not only as my new home, where I'd surely live the rest of my life (how could anyone of intelligence choose to live anyplace else?), but also as a fabulous source of stories, a bursting cornucopia of people and places to write about.

"So who is this character?" I asked Sam over the roar of the subway we took downtown.

"His name is Ammon Hennacy," Sam shouted back, "and he's written a book called *Autobiography of a Catholic Anarchist.*"

"How can he be both?" I wanted to know.

"Ask him," said Sam with a spreading smile.

I nodded, clutching the strap of the subway car as we rocketed underground. We emerged downtown, transferred to a bus, and walked through the sweltering streets until we came to a ramshackle building at 223 Chrystie Street, which was the headquarters of the Catholic Worker movement. In addition to putting out a newspaper that cost a penny, the Worker gave food and shelter to the poor, but instead of calling itself a mission, like other such institutions in the Bowery, it was called a hospitality house. Unlike most of the missions, the Catholic Worker house did not demand any declaration of faith or singing of hymns from the three hundred people it fed every day in its bread line; they only had to be hungry.

Ammon Hennacy greeted me and Sam, and pulled out chairs for us to sit with him around an old desk in a big room where a motley group of men and women went in and out. There was a shifting population of some fifty people who lived in the house at any given time — a "staff" of idealists and intellectuals committed to voluntary poverty who shared rooms, food, and clothes with winos and drifters who were admitted on a first-come, first-serve basis.

Hennacy himself was indeed a character. A gray-haired man with only a few teeth left in his mouth, he stood on street corners from Union Square to Broadway selling copies of the *Catholic Worker*, spoke to Quaker meetings (he called them "Quakes") and student groups at colleges — he told us he was going to talk to the Newman Club at Columbia, and then at Rutgers, before hitchhiking west.

Ammon had plenty of stories, and he loved to tell them: about the time he served in an Atlanta prison for refusing to register for the draft in 1917 on pacifist grounds, including seven months in solitary confinement for organizing a strike to protest the poor prison food; and about his arrest only a month before I met him, for protesting a civil defense air-raid drill. Along with a group from the Catholic Worker house, and other pacifists and protesters who believed that atomic war was not only wrong but impossible to defend against — that practice drills only lulled us into a false sense of security — Ammon had gone to City Hall Park and passed out antiwar leaflets instead of taking shelter when the sirens sounded.

What impressed me most of all was that Hennacy, as a teenage Ohio farm boy, had joined the IWW, the Industrial Workers of the World — he was a real live Wobbly, like those I'd read about in Dos Passos's *U.S.A.* and heard praised by C. Wright Mills as the only truly homegrown American radicals. As a Wobbly, Hennacy was an anarchist and considered himself a "non-church Christian," but he'd liked the *Catholic Worker* when a priest in Milwaukee gave him a copy in 1936, and Hennacy wrote for it for sixteen years before finally becoming a Catholic. He kept his anarchist-pacifist views, and annually picketed the White House at tax time, selling copies of the *Worker* as he walked back and forth on Pennsylvania Avenue.

The most surprising part of all this was that Hennacy conveyed it with a sense of delight and humor. There was nothing heavy or dour about him, but rather a feeling of joy and discovery. Murray Kempton later told me he'd invited Ammon to his home in Princeton, where he made a hit with the children by showing them how to catch and hold a garter snake in the backyard.

I asked Hennacy how he could be a Catholic and an anarchist at the same time, and he smiled and said I had to read his book to find out. It so happened he had some copies for sale, which he pulled out of a drawer, and I bought one.

Sam told Ammon he had a book of his own coming out, a novel.

"What do you call it?" Hennacy asked.

"*An End to Dying,*" Sam said with a certain dramatic tone.

"Well," said Ammon, squinting and rubbing his chin, "that might be all right."

We all burst out laughing.

Hennacy gave us copies of the latest *Catholic Worker* and introduced us to some of the people. There didn't seem to be much distinction between the ones who worked in the office or the kitchen and those who stood in the twice-daily bread lines. I learned that not all the people who lived in the rooms or ate the food of the Catholic Worker were Catholics, or workers. Some, who agreed with the aims of the movement, were pacifists or anarchists. Some were former monks. Some were alcoholics. Some were just hungry.

Ammon introduced us to a quietly imposing woman without makeup who wore her gray hair in a braid around her head, like a peasant or one of those strong midwestern farm women painted by Grant Wood. She was Dorothy Day, cofounder of the *Catholic Worker* and the guiding spirit of the movement. Dorothy greeted us politely, if reservedly and rather sternly, and let us see a copy of the first issue of the *Worker,* published on May Day of 1933, in the depths of the Great Depression. When I read the first editorial, one that she wrote, I had to sit down at once and copy it into my notebook. It said the paper would not be restricted to the people of any one religion or political belief, any one color of skin or cut of clothes, but that it was

> For those who are sitting on benches in the warm spring sunlight.
>
> For those who are huddling in shelters trying to escape the rain.
>
> For those who are walking the streets in the all but futile search for work.
>
> For those who think there is no hope for the future, no recognition of their plight.

I felt a tinge from the power of the words, and of the woman who wrote them. When I looked up, she was gone.

I was both surprised and impressed to learn that Dorothy Day, this stern, dedicated woman who some people already thought was a candidate for sainthood — a real movement for her canonization would start several decades later — had been a true bohemian free spirit in the 1920s, part of the glamorous life of Greenwich Village, where she hung out with Eugene O'Neill at a bar called the Hell Hole. Malcolm Cowley wrote in one of my favorite books of the time, a bible of twenties lore called *Exile's Return,* that all the gamblers in one of the Village bars that Dorothy frequented admired her because she could drink any one of them under the table.

As the twenties waned, Dorothy's concerns shifted from literature to politics, and she joined the IWW (a woman Wobbly!), served as an editor of *The Masses,* became a Catholic instead of a Communist, and reported on the hunger march in Washington in 1932, wondering what she could do to help the poor and homeless. She prayed, came home, and found Peter Maurin, a French peasant and migrant laborer who had a vision of helping the needy through hospitality houses (like the one on the Bowery), collective farms (like one that bore his name on Staten Island and supplied bread for the Chrystie Street house), round-table discussions, and a paper for the people in the street. Peter and Dorothy started the *Catholic Worker* in the kitchen of her apartment and sold the first issues themselves in Union Square.

The *Catholic Worker's* message of help and hope for the poor struck a deep response in Depression America, and circulation of the paper soared to 150,000 by 1936. But Dorothy would never compromise her pacifist principles, so she condemned both sides in the Spanish civil war and managed to alienate most politically conscious readers. As Dorothy put it in her autobiography *The Long Loneliness,* "Ours is indeed an unpopular front." A pacifist position in the patriotic tide that swept the country during World War II was even more unpopular, and circulation plummeted to a low of 30,000.

When I first saw the paper in the mid-fifties, it had climbed back to 65,000, despite its opposition to the war in Korea, which was vigorously supported by New York's Cardinal Spellman, who sprinkled holy water on the guns of the troops at Christmas. There were new controversial currents rising to the surface in the fifties that the *Worker* had caught, and it attracted a small but growing audience who found their own feelings expressed in the words and the woodcuts that illustrated them in this personal-sounding, radical paper that still cost only a penny a copy.

One of the paper's associate editors I met at the hospitality house was twenty-three-year-old Bob Steed, who had discovered the *Worker* when he saw the issue with a front-page illustration of Jesus embracing a Negro and a white worker, who are shaking hands. Steed sold copies of the *Catholic Worker* throughout the South before coming to live at Chrystie Street. When I first saw the paper that summer of 1955, it was (like Dorothy and Ammon and their friends) campaigning against nuclear testing, and protesting the "sham" of civil defense air-raid drills.

What drew me to the Catholic Worker movement, first as a journalist and then as a friend and sympathizer — a sort of idealistic fellow traveler — wasn't just the colorful personality of Ammon Hennacy, or Dorothy Day's bohemian-literary past, or even her eloquence or daily dedication to the poor. It was all those things perhaps, but more, a real mystique that called to young people of the fifties and drew them from all across the country, offering in the midst of the grim poverty of the Bowery something that all the glittering affluence around us lacked — a spirit, a purpose, a way of transcending self through service that those who came still vividly remember.

A young student from Boston, dissatisfied with his studies at Columbia Presbyterian Medical Center in New York, made his way to Chrystie Street in the spring of 1952 to look for Dorothy Day. He found her in a crowded room, enmeshed in a conversation with an obviously drunken woman, yet treating her as if she were a person of dignity and worth. When Dorothy saw the young man, she looked up and said, "Are you waiting to talk with one of us?"

Robert Coles became a volunteer and continued to see and listen to Dorothy Day for the rest of her life, after he became a doctor, psychiatrist, writer, and teacher. He recorded many conversations with her, which he used as a source for his memoir-biography *Dorothy Day: A Radical Devotion,* one of a growing number of books about her life and work that continue to stir interest decades after her death (a play was written about her too, and a movie on her life is now in the works).

When a young intellectual and writer from St. Louis named Michael Harrington found his way to Chrystie Street in 1951, he was told he could work there but couldn't be paid anything. He stayed for two years. In his later memoir, *Fragments of the Century,* he described Dorothy Day as severe yet serene, and thought she looked like a mystic out of a Dostoevsky novel. She was a presence, he wrote, the sort of person a stranger who had never heard of her would know was significant as soon as she entered a room. He counted himself as "one of hundreds of thousands who were influenced by her life."

An aspiring poet read a copy of the *Catholic Worker* while he was going to college at St. Michael's in Vermont, and he came down on a vacation in 1954, to seek out the hospitality house and volunteer. Ned O'Gorman, now the headmaster of the Storefront School in Harlem, which he founded in 1965, recalls his first visit to the hospitality house in the fifties: "I walked in wearing this expensive tweed jacket with my wallet in it, took off the jacket and threw it on a chair. The next thing I heard was Dorothy's voice: 'Who put this jacket on the chair? What a stupid thing to do, it'll be robbed.' I'd had these romantic notions, thinking, Oh, the poor, they go around with babushkas on, being noble. Dorothy and the Worker cured me of those illusions."

When he came to live in New York in 1955, to get a master's degree in English at Columbia, Ned became a regular at Chrystie Street, volunteering at the house and coming to Friday night sessions to join the discussions and sometimes read his own poetry.

Betty Bartelme, a young woman from Iowa who was beginning her career in New York in the early fifties by working on a Frick Collection catalogue, first heard about the Catholic Worker in a book she was reading. "It was a coming-of-age novel by Harry Sylvester, and there was a scene, a sort of set piece, that portrayed the Worker very romantically. I decided to go down and volunteer, but it wasn't at all romantic. I was greeted at the door by a rough-looking man named Smoky Joe, who I later learned had been a burglar, who lived there. He said, 'Whaddaya want?' It's a wonder I didn't turn right around and walk away.

"They were putting out the paper," Betty adds, "and I helped stuff envelopes with Dorothy Day and one of the editors, Tom Sullivan, and they asked me to come back."

Mary Ann McCoy worked for the telephone company and went to Ascension Church in Elmhurst, Queens, where the priest regularly sent her uncle with leftover food from the parish to the Catholic Worker house. One night her uncle came back from delivering the food with a copy of another autobiographical work by Dorothy Day, *From Union Square to Rome,* which he gave to his niece.

"It was just what I was looking for," Mary Ann recalls. "I was already a union steward in the telephone company. I was making $28 a week, and we went on strike for three months, and after that I was making $34 a week. My mother was a working-class girl and a staunch liberal Democrat who had empathy for the workers, and we were Catholics, so the Catholic Worker movement and what Dorothy Day was doing sounded just right." Mary Ann's eyes seem to get larger, as they always do when she makes an important point (I remember being struck by this forty years ago), and she adds, "And I wanted to have an interesting life!"

Mary Ann went to the Worker the first time she had a day off, and asked for Dorothy Day.

"She isn't here now," a man named Tony said.

Mary Ann felt like crying. "Oh, I came all the way here for nothing!" she said.

"Would you like to do some bookbinding?" Tony asked.

He brought some unbound copies of a book of Peter Maurin's essays and showed Mary Ann how to bind them. She spent several hours at the work, and when she finished, Tony said she could meet Dorothy Day if she came back on Friday night — Dorothy was going to speak on the Chinese revolution. Mary Ann took her friend Eileen, who also lived in Queens and worked at the telephone company, to the talk on Friday. A bunch of students from Columbia attacked Dorothy's views that night, and she stood her ground in an exciting debate.

"That was the beginning of the wonderful Friday nights at the Worker," Mary Ann says. "I heard Dorothy Day, there was Ned O'Gorman and other young poets who read from their work, Bayard Rustin and Dave Dellinger spoke on politics, there were talks on philosophy and literature, a whole series once on Paul Claudel. I was in heaven. To find out there were intellectuals, and discovering ideas — there was an exotic quality to that."

Yes. I knew.

Like any other newcomers who visited the place, Sam Astrachan and I were invited to attend a Friday night lecture, and we went, and returned again and again, sitting in an audience made up not only of people from the Bowery streets — they were no longer "bums," simply other people beside you listening to the same speaker — but also of eager young writers and intellectuals. After the lectures everyone filed down the squeaky, narrow stairs to the kitchen for coffee and conversation at long wooden tables. There were old and young, men and women, graduate students and Bowery denizens, eager to talk about the night's speech, whether it was given by a priest or a politician, a migrant worker or a Yeats scholar, and no one was squelched or snubbed or shushed; anyone could have a say.

There wasn't any magic that suddenly transformed skid row winos into intellectuals, but they listened, or pretended to listen, perhaps just appreciative of being included in the week's main social event and entertainment. Michael Harrington, whose young days at the Worker would later inform his landmark book *The Other America*, which inspired Lyndon Johnson's antipoverty program, recalled that the first talk he gave in the regular Friday night series was about Martin Buber's essays on communitarian socialism, to an audience that included "the somewhat perplexed refugees from the Bowery" as well as intellectual "adepts."

Some of the former winos and other "refugees" from the Bowery genuinely got caught up in the infectious intellectual excitement at the Worker. Tony, the tough guy who greeted Mary Ann McCoy at the door when she first came to Chrystie Street, had once sold pints of his blood for money to buy wine, a common practice of men in the Bowery. After a few years of living at the Worker, he sold a pint of blood to buy theater tickets for a play by García Lorca.

It was on Friday evenings that fall, after the talks at the Worker, that I met Mike Harrington, the wide-grinning guy from St. Louis who spoke of socialism with a midwestern twang, and Ned O'Gorman, a big, broad-shouldered graduate student who was bursting with poetry he loved to recite, whether it was Yeats's or his own. He would soon have his first book of verse published, *Night of the Hammer*. To my added surprise and delight I also met girls there, like Mary Ann McCoy, a vitally attractive Irish blonde from Queens, and Helen Russell, a tall, dark-haired former novice of a convent in California. The Mother Superior had discovered her playing Ravel's *Bolero* over and over, and said, "I know where you belong." She gave Helen the latest issue of the *Catholic Worker*. Helen read it and soon left the convent, took a bus to New York, and volunteered to work for Dorothy Day.

I was flattered to be asked to speak myself at one of the Friday night lectures, a few months after I first went there. I had just come back from the Emmet Till trial in Mississippi, and describing it to that very mixed audience in the backyard of the Chrystie Street house on a warm September evening was my first experience of public speaking, except for school and college. I could not have found a more polite and appreciative crowd, and it made me love the place all the more.

After the coffee session in the kitchen following the lectures, a group would usually gather to go to the White Horse Tavern. There the talk continued over pints of ale or beer, or the favored combination of arf 'n' arf, and soon everyone broke into songs of Irish rebellion, or love, or protest, folk songs joined and swelled by the Clancy Brothers or long-haired, blond Mary Travers, who also hung out in the back room of the Horse.

The radical spirit of the Catholic Worker did not just dissipate in talk and beer and folk songs, though. "I wanted to spread the word, so I took big stacks of the Catholic Worker back to my parish in Queens," Mary Ann McCoy recalls. "I'd stand outside the church after mass with the paper, but nobody would buy it, even for the price of a penny. This was the Cold War, remember — Senator McCarthy was hunting Reds, people were afraid. The little newsboys selling the *Brooklyn Tablet*, the paper of the diocese, took pity on me and slipped my copies of the *Catholic Worker* inside the *Tablet*, which was an archconservative paper."

The Catholic Worker caused controversy throughout the ranks of the faithful. Even though the pope sent a special blessing to all who were concerned with the movement, and some bishops and priests personally contributed to it, others forbade the paper from being sold at their churches. Catholics who were shocked at the pacifist-anarchist sentiments of the paper had even attacked people who sold it in the street.

"Our priest asked me to invite Tom Sullivan, one of the editors of the *Worker*, to speak at our parish," Mary Ann says, "but when I asked, Tom couldn't or didn't want to come to a conservative parish in Queens. Dorothy Day was listening and she said, 'I'll come.' She felt it was her duty to speak to everyone who asked, to spread the gospel message of the Catholic Worker."

"Well, the parish came out in droves to hear her. She spoke in defense of anarchism — she said you didn't need laws to be good. She said you should have a guest room in your house to take in someone who has no home, everyone who has a house should have this kind of hospitality room. Some people were impressed, others objected to her coming, thought she was a Red. Later there was a big argument about it at a meeting of the parish board. There was a man on the board who was a butcher in the neighborhood who once had been down and out on the Bowery, and he'd been fed by Dorothy and the Catholic Worker. He defended Dorothy, and when one of the other men objected to her coming to the parish, calling her a Red, the butcher wrestled the man to the floor."

Mary Ann was one of the group from Chrystie Street who had gone with Ammon Hennacy and Dorothy Day to City Hall Park to protest the air-raid drills, and all of them were thrown in jail. Betty Bartelme and some of the other Catholic Worker volunteers heard that the group had been arrested and went down to try to help get them out. "We couldn't get in to see them," Betty remembers, "but we could hear their voices call out to us. They said they were hungry, so we went to the Muni [the Municipal Cafeteria] on Canal Street and got sandwiches for them. Mary Ann McCoy was yelling out telephone numbers of friends to call to help raise bail. Another woman volunteer and I made phone calls from the jail, until one of the jailers said if we didn't get out he'd run us in as a couple of prostitutes. That night we ran all over town to try to raise money for bail. We managed to get enough together to get Dorothy out that day, but the others had to spend the night in jail."

The six protesters from the Catholic Worker and nineteen other pacifists who had been arrested for disobeying the New York State Emergency Defense Act were scheduled to appear for sentencing in December 1955 at a magistrate's court uptown. I went to court with Ammon Hennacy that morning. He had pleaded guilty and brought a canvas bag of books with him to read in jail. "If you don't take 'em with you," he told me, "you can bet they aren't going to give you any after you're in." He had packed a volume of poetry by Shelley, the stories of Tolstoy, a book on the Irish rebellion, and the Bible. With his books slung over his shoulder and a dark maroon stocking cap pulled down over his thick gray hair, Ammon was ready to go. I was proud to be with him.

What made me admire this snaggle-toothed old guy, with his cardboard picket signs and his hodgepodge of Catholic-anarchist beliefs, was his willingness to go against the grain, to challenge the conformity of the fifties. I found some notes I made at the time for an article I wanted to write on Ammon, and they convey the way I saw him as a symbol: "Far from the lonely crowd there lives an anti-organization man whose principal possessions are health and a vision."

The message of two best-selling books of the time, David Riesman's *The Lonely Crowd* and William H. Whyte's *The Organization Man,* was that our society was going to overwhelm the individual and make him (you and me!) part of an anonymous mass culture, blinding him to the evils around him, as well as to the passion and joy. Ammon's very existence was an antidote to that facelessness, proof that an individual could go his own way, follow his own lights, stick to his own unpopular course that he thought was right.

In court that morning, Judge Hyman Bushel read his sentence of a $25 fine or five days in prison, and Ammon stepped forward and asked permission to read a short statement. The judge nodded, and Hennacy pulled a folded piece of paper from his pocket and began to read: "As a Catholic, I twice refused to take part in air-raid drills in accordance with the practice of Saint Peter, who was arrested twice for speaking on the street, and he and all the Apostles said to the state that they should obey God rather than man. As an anarchist, I follow the practice of William Lloyd Garrison, the first American Christian anarchist . . ."

Hennacy concluded by saying that as a matter of principle he would not pay the fine but was willing to go to jail. Judge Bushel nodded and then announced he was suspending the sentences of the protesters. He talked at length about how he had been influenced in this decision by the many fine things he had heard about

Dorothy Day and the work she and her volunteers were doing down on Chrystie Street. Dorothy stood unmoving among those who faced the magistrate and listened in silence, expressionless.

Outside the courtroom, Ammon gave me his own summation of the proceedings. "You see," he said, "Dorothy swamped 'em with her spirituality."

Ammon was, as always, proud of Dorothy. He was also, I thought, a little disappointed that he didn't get to go to jail again. With his bag of books, he was all set. I went back home and rewrote my notes.

I used them as part of an article I'd been working on about the Catholic Worker movement that was published in *The Nation* under the title "Miracle in the Bowery." I was proud to give out copies to my friends at the Chrystie Street house, assuming they would be pleased to see this tribute to their cause. Most of them were, except for Dorothy Day. I was puzzled and disturbed. She not only didn't acknowledge the article, she didn't speak to me at all after it was published. She avoided me.

I asked my friends at the Worker what was wrong, and they told me Dorothy was angry that I'd quoted Malcolm Cowley, in *Exile's Return,* about her being able to drink the gamblers under the table at that Greenwich Village bar. I was shocked, because I considered it a great achievement for a woman to be able to drink heartier than a bunch of male barflies. Like most of my friends, I believed in the Hemingway outlook that being able to hold your liquor was a sign of character. I operated under the spell of that myth, living it out as I drank and came to rely on alcohol more and more. It would be another quarter century before I understood that Dorothy no longer saw the glamour in her drinking or wanted it advertised in that spirit because she saw every day the destruction alcohol had wrought in the lives of the men in the Bowery. As in so many other ways, she was ahead of her time.

Dorothy had similar feelings about the whole subject of her bohemian past, and I realize now that her wish to deny it — she went so far as to buy up copies of a novel she wrote before her conversion in order to destroy them — was not meant to cover up what she would later consider her sins, to make herself seem holier or purer in retrospect, but rather because she didn't want that behavior to serve as a model for other young people who might find it appealing.

"Dorothy was very protective of us," Betty Bartelme recalls. "She was very puritanical about sex. She told me once not to wear sleeveless blouses to the Worker because it tempted the men. You had to know her past experiences — living the bohemian life — to understand how she felt. We were all very innocent and she was not."

I was fearful that my gaffe of bringing up Dorothy's old drinking exploits in print might mean I wasn't welcome anymore on Chrystie Street, but it wasn't so. After my article came out and I returned from Israel as a correspondent for *The Nation*, I was invited to speak about the experience at one of the Friday night discussions. My friends at the Worker told me not to worry about their leader's displeasure. "That's just Dorothy," Mary Ann McCoy said with a shrug and a smile.

There were other sides of Dorothy too. "None of the books about her captured how Dorothy was so much fun to be with," Betty Bartelme says. "She was a terrible driver, and we used to go around with her in the car and she'd say the rosary out loud in traffic. We'd get to giggling in the back seat, and she'd turn around to shush us and almost run into a light pole, and we'd all get to laughing so hard we couldn't stop."

Dorothy liked to have a good time, but she didn't enjoy those worldly pleasures that violated her own principles. When Evelyn Waugh came to America in the early fifties, he wanted to meet Dorothy Day and see the Worker, and he invited her to dinner at the Chambord. Dorothy said her vow of poverty wouldn't allow her to go to such an expensive restaurant, and instead she took him to a homey place in Little Italy called Angelo's, on Mulberry Street. Waugh asked for the wine list, and of course there wasn't any — you just took the house red. It obviously wasn't the kind of dinner the elegant English novelist had in mind. Still, he must have been impressed with Dorothy and her work. After he wrote a piece for *Life* magazine about his travels in America, he instructed his agent to send a check to the mission house in the Bowery. The agent didn't know what the place was called, so the check was made out to "Dorothy Day's Soup Kitchen."

Some of Dorothy's old friends from her bohemian days still came around to see her at the Worker, becoming volunteers or contributing money, food, or clothing. Allen Tate donated an old seersucker jacket that Mike Harrington was later given from the common storeroom; even though it was several sizes too small for Mike, he wore it with pride because it once belonged to "an established poet."

"The Catholic Worker was such a *center*," Mary Ann says. "It was a magnet for intellectual life in New York and throughout the country. It was a newspaper, a center of activities for helping people, for working in communities."

That magnetic spirit drew people to its headquarters on Chrystie Street and sent them out again to spread the word of service and brotherhood to the poor and needy, *and* to practice it. "Our ideal," Mike Harrington wrote in retrospect, "was 'to see Christ in every man,' including the pathetic, shambling, shivering creature who would wander off in the streets with his pants caked with urine and his face scabbed with blood."

Mary Ann and her friend Eileen were "having a really great time" volunteering at the Catholic Worker, but at the same time they were growing dissatisfied and restless. "We were unhappy working at the telephone company, and we wanted our life to change," Mary Ann recalls.

One night when they were going back to Queens on the subway, Eileen said that she had taught religious instruction at a small church in East Harlem, the Parish of the Holy Agony. She loved the kids there, who were very poor, and often worried about how they were doing.

"Let's go," Mary Ann said.

They started attending mass at Holy Agony, on East 103rd Street, and afterward they gave a class for the kids, and then they'd pack lunches and take them on picnics to Wards Island.

"We got drawn into the life of the kids," Mary Ann explains. "Someone would say they needed to go to a clinic, and we'd take them. We were spending more and more time up there in the neighborhood, and we needed a base. There was a store empty on the corner of First Avenue and 101st Street, and we decided to rent it and make it a center for the kids. We quit our jobs, and Helen Russell, who we met on Friday nights at the Catholic Worker, joined us, and we all moved into an apartment at 321 East 100th Street.

We paid the rent, as well as the rent for the store, by taking turns doing temporary jobs.

"Dorothy suggested we take the kids to the Catholic Worker farm on Staten Island. They'd set up a big tent and the kids would be fed. Word of what we were doing got around the neighborhood and people started helping us. Numbers runners offered to drive us to the Staten Island ferry. Eileen wrote articles about the kids for the *Catholic Worker,* and people donated food and clothes."

It was perhaps the first day care center for children.

"Dorothy's ideas were so basic," Mary Ann says. "Land and food. She believed in property and had the foresight to buy that farm on Staten Island. There was a tranquility at the farm — I remember sitting by a big oak tree, and a cow mooing. The chapel was part of the barn, and mass was held every morning. You celebrated nature and the hours of the day. We'd say to the kids, 'Let's give thanks for the cows, and the milk the cows give.'

"There was a rhythm in the whole operation. We had haystacks and corn and people growing vegetables. Whole wheat bread was baked fresh every day. People took that food to the hungry men on the Bowery."

Moving to East Harlem and devoting themselves to the children of the neighborhood was "part of this whole dimension of life we saw at the Catholic Worker, and in Dorothy Day," Mary Ann says. "It goes with spirituality, an example of something higher than yourself."

The rhythms and cycles Mary Ann McCoy saw in the operation of the Catholic Worker seem to move through time as well, from the fifties to the nineties, from Staten Island to the Bowery to Harlem and throughout the country, in the pages of newspapers and books written by people who worked and lived or even just visited Chrystie Street.

Ned O'Gorman says, forty years later, "The Catholic Worker wasn't just a circle or even just a movement — it was a sensibility, a vision."

We are eating pancakes in the kitchen of the Storefront School in Harlem. Ned has on a pair of old jeans and a plaid shirt over a white shirt, with the sleeves of both rolled up, which is the way this headmaster dresses for work. He teaches each class in the school at least once a week and knows the names of all 104 students. This morning he begins a history class the way our old professor Mark Van Doren often began his classes, with a question: "What is an unjust man?" Later, one little boy says he never heard of Hitler, and Ned rolls his eyes toward the ceiling and says, "Holy mazackers!"

After class, kids surround Ned in the hall, and he hugs a few of them and looks above the head of a boy to say, "These are the most divine children in the universe." When we go down to the kitchen, a mother is waiting to get some advice about a job, and a young man from the neighborhood needs a check to give a lawyer for a case that is pending, and someone else wants the loan of a ten, and a pint-size kid wants to know the name of the God of the Iraqis ("Allah," says Ned, and the boy writes it down in his notebook, asking how it's spelled), and Ned tastes the chicken cooking for lunch before settling down to his breakfast. Our own talk goes back to the Catholic Worker, and Ned says, "Dorothy's influence was profound. I sometimes think I'm here in some way because I soaked up her vision of the human family."

Mary Ann married, moved to Brooklyn, and raised two children. She lives in the Lefferts Manor–Prospect Park neighborhood, which is mainly black and West Indian now. When whites started moving out in the early sixties, "a little band of people stuck when others left, restored deserted stores and old ghetto houses. We formed an organization of homeowners, had our own security patrol, tore down dead trees and put in new trees and planted flowers. We taught classes and started food co-ops, and people from all-white neighborhoods came and said, 'Why do all the interesting things happen in the worst neighborhoods?' "

Having dinner with Mary Ann McCoy DeWeese at Slade's restaurant in Brooklyn Heights in 1991, I remember the time she invited me to have dinner with her and Eileen and Helen on 100th Street in East Harlem one winter night thirty-five years before. I had met the girls at a Friday night discussion at the Catholic Worker and seen Mary Ann and Eileen again when I went to the sentencing of the air raid protesters. I was fascinated that three attractive white girls would be living in a neighborhood that was largely Negro and Puerto Rican, on a street the *New York Times,* in an article on slums, had called "the worst block in the city." I thought I could write an article about it — and see more of Mary Ann, whom I had a crush on.

I took the IRT to 96th Street, and then a crosstown bus through Central Park to Third Avenue. I walked up Third, which was brightly lit, to 100th Street, which was dark. I passed a trash-strewn vacant lot and found a building like most of the others, marked 321. The door was patched with raw board where glass had been, and I pushed my way through and went up the stairs. There were voices in Spanish and sounds of frying; an odor that conjured up dead cats possessed the stairway. At the third-floor front apartment the girls greeted me.

We had roast beef, bread, and wine, and talked of the civil defense trial and Dorothy Day and the Catholic Worker. A small boy came in carrying a plate, and with lowered eyes said, "For my mother." The girls piled it high with roast beef and bread, and the boy backed away, watching the strange feast with wonder.

I left late, and the street was alive with talk and music. A group of teenage boys huddled in a doorway, harmonizing on a rock 'n' roll song. The rhythm of a tambourine came from a storefront Pentecostal church's nightly revival. Older men played cards on a crate in the light from a barbershop window. At the end of the block a policeman twirled his nightstick.

After several more trips to the neighborhood, I decided it was far too rich and complex to be dealt with in a magazine article. I had found the subject of my first book. I didn't want to be a phony outsider who simply came to snoop, but a part of the life of the place I was writing about — in the way Mary Ann and the other girls were part of it in their own work. When the time came to begin the book, I would move to the neighborhood.

My crush on Mary Ann did not develop into the passionate romance I briefly fantasized, but became a lifelong friendship. Once in the beginning I took her home from a play, and in the hallway of her tenement I kissed her good night, and continued to hold her, not wanting to leave or let go, and she said in a plaintive voice I can still hear, "What do you want?"

We later laughed about her question, pretending the answer was obvious, yet I realize in retrospect she knew more than I did about my tangled, about-to-burst feelings that night. I wanted a woman's love but wasn't ready for it, and I also wanted something else, something more, something I couldn't name but had instinctively come to this turbulent neighborhood to find — some connection beyond my ego-self, beyond the self that began around that time to go prone five days a week on an analyst's couch, something Mary Ann had connected to through her work with the children, something all of us young seekers had sensed in the air of those Friday night meetings at the Catholic Worker, something Dorothy Day knew and possessed and somehow conveyed a sense of to others. It was precious, elusive, unexpected, like the sudden sweetness of the harmony from the teenagers singing in the darkened doorway on East 100th Street the first night I went to the neighborhood. A chord struck and something opened: a flower, a door, a chapter.

FIVE

In Spanish Harlem

ORANGES AND REDS, purples and yellows — tropical colors flashed against the tenement grime of gray, on shirts of men playing dominoes outside *bodegas* and swirling skirts the women flaunted in the night. Long strung flags of washing — white, green, aqua, pink — unfurled against brown slabs of buildings that bordered the junk-glittered vacant lots. High pitch and sensuous rhythm of Latin music blasted from radios, and pointed black shoes scraped time in the streets. This was East Harlem, the Spanish part, another island within the Island, a transplant of vital new blood and dreams from Puerto Rico, the biggest newcomer influx of the fifties.

East Harlem was like an archeology of immigration, a history of America in one concentrated area. When central Harlem, or just plain Harlem, whose center point is 135th Street and Lenox Avenue, had become known as a Negro community by 1910, the area from Fifth Avenue to the East River, known as East Harlem, was still all white, with a population of Russian Jews, Irish, and Italians, and it was not until after World War I that Puerto Ricans began to move in, giving the name Harlem the new adjective "Spanish." Puerto Ricans were followed by Negroes, and the polyglot nature of the neighborhood was still in evidence when I was there in 1957. Although most of my neighbors on 100th and 101st streets spoke Spanish, I woke one morning to the musical lilt of an Irish brogue and looked out my window to see a white-haired, crippled man holding his upturned battered hat as he sang "My Wild Irish Rose." Puerto Rican women leaned out their windows and flung down coins he hobbled to collect.

If my story of Spanish Harlem were an official one, it would begin with Muñoz Marín, then governor of Puerto Rico, but you already know it begins with Mary Ann McCoy. By the time I moved to East Harlem in the early spring of 1957, Mary Ann was already married, but I was lucky journalistically, if not romantically, for she still lived in the neighborhood and ran the day care center with the other Catholic Worker girls. They all helped me find an apartment to rent at 331 East 100th Street.

I had gotten a contract from a publisher to write my book, with what was then a standard advance against royalties for a first effort: the grand sum of $1,000. Half the advance, minus a 10 percent agent's fee, gave me a stake of $450 to get me through the project. It's a good thing I wanted to write about a poor neighborhood in Harlem rather than the high life of what was then known as the International Set (they were not yet jet-propelled) on the French Riviera.

I gave up my half of the apartment I shared at 10th and Bleecker with Ted "the Horse" Steeg and brought my clothes, pots, pans, and typewriter up from the Village. My new roommates were cock-roaches, and George Orwell was my literary mentor; he'd been down and out in Paris and London, and now I was following the same path in New York's premier slum, purposely going to live in the place so I could write about it authentically.

I wanted to gain the trust of the people in the neighborhood in order to get them to talk to me, and I felt I had to prove I was not just another uncaring outsider come to exploit them. Mary Ann and the Catholic Worker girls had found that even when they operated the storefront day care center for the kids, they weren't really trusted until they moved onto the block.

I was studying Spanish, and although I could speak only stray phrases with an unlikely Hoosier twang, I got so I could understand some of the language when I heard it spoken, even in the quick, clipped accent of the Puerto Ricans. It also helped the whole enter-prise when I found a Grove Press paperback of García Lorca's *Poet in New York,* with English translations by Ben Bellitt on facing pages. Besides improving my Spanish, the book supplied inspiration through the poet's vision of Harlem in passages I read: "The first on the street know the truth in their bones; / for these, neither Eden, nor passions unleafing" ("Dawn"); and "the boys lay inert on the cross of a yawn and stretched muscle" ("The King of Harlem"). With sirens and screams and sometimes gunshots waking me in the night to the sight of cockroaches skittering across a paint-peeling wall, this great lyric poetry helped me to see the mystery and beauty of where I was and what I was trying to do.

Roaming out from my base, I went in search of stories and immediately bumped into the biggest, most obvious one, the problem you couldn't go down the block without running up against — drugs. Heroin was spreading like a plague.

I learned that just a year before I moved to the neighborhood, a group of local people had gotten together to try to do something about it and formed a committee that met once a week in the back of the Family Center of the East Harlem Protestant Parish on East 100th Street, the very block where I was living. The parish was composed of three storefront churches in the neighborhood that were begun by a group of young men and women who had graduated from Union Theological Seminary after World War II, most of them veterans of the war. I was suspicious of a Protestant group of what seemed like missionaries to the slums, thinking all Protestants of the time were like Norman Vincent Peale, whom I considered a glad-handing country-club type of Christian, a pusher of easy steps to salvation.

I was prepared not to like the Reverend Norman C. Eddy, but since he, his wife Peg, who was also a minister, and their three children were now my neighbors, and since Norm was one of the founders and leaders of the neighborhood committee to help narcotics addicts, I was resigned to meeting the man. I expected, if not a glad-hander who would try to recruit me for Jesus, then some kind of long-faced missionary who'd warn me darkly of the wages of sin.

Norm laughed when I later told him I had feared he might try to save me from atheism the way I assumed he tried to save addicts from drugs. Norm was an open, vital man with an easy laugh and a sense of the ridiculous as well as the divine, and I had to admire him in spite of my prejudice against preachers, especially Protestants, because he wasn't preaching his message so much as living it. He was a much-respected and familiar figure on 100th Street, a tall man in his late thirties with a crop of hair that even before he moved to East Harlem had turned prematurely, totally white. He wore a gray shirt with a white collar and a smile that seemed to come spontaneously from a sense of genuine joy.

After I got to know him, Norm explained that one of the reasons he was drawn to working with narcotics addicts was that they were forced to grapple with the deepest questions of existence. "Those are the ones — the Big Questions — I am most interested in," Norm said. I added when I wrote about him: "And whom could Norman Eddy talk to within, say, the congregation of the Marble Collegiate Church?" That was the church of Norman Vincent Peale, my symbol of gray flannel Christianity.

The postwar world of middle-class complacency was just what Norm Eddy had fled. He came from a well-to-do family in Hartford, went to Yale, joined the ambulance corps of the American Field Service in World War II, and served as an ambulance driver at the battle of El Alamein, and in Syria and Italy. Once, in the desert, literally on the road to Damascus, he had an experience of "the spirit" — like a vision or visitation of the power, truth, and beauty of God — that changed his life and set him on a path that led to Union Seminary, the ministry, East Harlem and the Family Center on East 100th Street.

In the barren back room of the center, folding chairs and benches formed a circle beneath fluorescent lights that were still wound with red, green, and yellow crepe-paper left over from the canteen dances for neighborhood kids on Friday nights. The first hour of the meetings was for addicts and their families to come and talk with a volunteer psychologist in a sort of group therapy; during the second hour, anyone in the neighborhood could come and hear a speaker talk about narcotics. Doctors, sociologists, jazz musicians, cops, social workers — all came and gave their views and had them challenged in discussions that were angry, funny, and tough.

At my first meeting I saw Louis Leon, known as Pee-Wee, the young Puerto Rican who had gone to Norm Eddy the year before I moved to East Harlem and asked his help, and out of that was born the narcotics committee and its ongoing work. Pee-Wee was a big, heavyset man who grew up on 100th Street, and by the end of high school he had seen most of his friends get hooked on heroin. When I met him, at age twenty-one, he told me there were thirty-six guys in his high school class, and though he had lost track of some, he knew of only three who were "out doing something": himself (he was working in construction), an engineer, and an airplane pilot. The rest, he said, were scattered in jails and hospitals from New York to the Federal Narcotics Facility in Lexington, Kentucky.

Pee-Wee had spent the summer after high school trying to get his friends who were addicted to go to Riverside Hospital, on North Brother Island in the East River, the only facility for treating addicts under the age of twenty-one. Anyone below that age could be sent there by voluntarily petitioning a magistrate — or be assigned for treatment as part or all of a criminal sentence. An addict over twenty-one had nowhere to go for medical treatment unless he went to Lexington. The alternative was jail: an addict could apply to the Department of Correction to be sent to the prison on Rikers Island or to the Women's House of Detention in order to be locked up so he or she couldn't get drugs; this meant going cold turkey, a torturous process. Pee-Wee Leon didn't have much luck persuading his friends to voluntarily commit themselves to this agony, nor did he know of any alternative. In desperation, he went to his minister.

Sitting in the tiny backyard garden of the house where he lives now, on 105th Street in East Harlem, five blocks from where he lived when I met him more than thirty years ago, Norm recalls that time when the young man from his church asked for help. "Pee-Wee was one of our church's youth group who I knew very well. He loved people, and he saw his friends throwing away their lives on heroin. He came to me totally discouraged and said, 'What are we going to do?'" Norm pauses a moment, then laughs. "Like all good Americans, we formed a committee."

Norm and Pee-Wee asked two women from the neighborhood to join them, one whose daughter was addicted and one who worked as a secretary for the parish, whom I called in my book Maria Flores. Maria was simply concerned with the spread of drugs among people she knew.

"We decided we'd educate ourselves and others," Norm recalls, "and we sent the word out. We got seventy-five to a hundred people coming to meetings just to hear about different aspects of the problem. Heroin had been a very hush-hush subject, something people didn't discuss, so there were a lot of myths about it, and people hid their fears and problems, not wanting others to think they were addicted or had an addict in their family. Bringing it out in the open gave people a chance to learn and ask questions and share their concerns. We got people from the police department to come, and doctors and psychologists. We got Bill Dufty, who had just collaborated with Billie Holiday in writing her autobiography, *Lady Sings the Blues*."

I remember meeting Dufty at the *New York Post*, where he worked as a reporter, and Murray Kempton introduced me to him as the most intelligent man he knew. I sometimes sat in Murray's office while he and Dufty, who I thought looked like the youthful, journalistic Orson Welles of *Citizen Kane*, held elliptical conversations about New York politics interspersed with references to history and literature, rendered in hip talk so obscure I could barely follow it. But I found it immensely enjoyable, rather like a verbal Charlie Mingus concert. I got to know Dufty's flamboyant wife, Maely, at meetings and fund-raising events of the narcotics committee.

The first hour of the committee meetings, when addicts and families could talk and get information in what now might be called a support group, began with the serenity prayer used by Alcoholics Anonymous. The group was led by Ramon Muñoz. Ramon had been through the treatment program at Lexington and was one of the few who had managed to stay off drugs after coming back to the old neighborhood. I got permission to sit in on these sessions myself, where I played the journalistic role of fly on the wall, just listening and taking notes. I knew that strangers, especially from the press, were usually not allowed into such private sessions, and I felt privileged to be there.

Word spread that addicts who wanted to kick the habit could receive help in getting to Lexington. Norm Eddy had the forms to fill out, and sometimes the committee would provide bus fare. The problem was that it took several weeks before an applicant found out he was accepted. During this waiting period, the addict would often start using again and lose the desire to stop.

One night I watched a nervous young man, who tried to cover his broken English by speaking quickly, tell the committee, "I wanna go K.Y." He explained that he had only a six-month habit now, and he wanted to kick before it got any worse. Ramon recommended he go to Rikers for thirty days and kick his habit while he awaited word from Lexington. A discussion followed, with other addicts also urging the young man to commit himself to Rikers, and from there go straight to Kentucky, so he'd stay clean and out of trouble. By the end of the meeting, the young man had disappeared; he never showed up again.

An official from the prison on Rikers Island came one night to talk to the committee and answer questions, and one of the neighborhood boys who'd been there asked why addicts who went to kick their habit cold turkey were put on hard labor four or five days after they arrived, when they were often still sick from the process of withdrawal. The Rikers official explained that "many of you fellows come back again and again, sometimes two and three times a year. Well, we instituted that hard labor so you wouldn't get the idea we were running a country club out there."

Long, hard, bitter laughter burst from the audience.

Another night I heard some people at the committee meeting talk about going to visit one of the teenage boys from East 100th Street who was at Riverside Hospital, and I asked if I could go along. The next day we took a subway to 134th Street, where we boarded a ferry for North Brother Island, a small patch of land about ten minutes away. Standing in the spray of the deck with my new neighbors from East Harlem, it struck me that New York City had a ferry ride for everyone. My literary friends in Greenwich Village took the Staten Island ferry in imitation of Edna St. Vincent Millay, reciting her lines from "Recuerdo": "We were very tired / We were very merry / We went back and forth / All night on the ferry." Immigrants from Europe took the ferry from Ellis Island to the streets of New York, and tourists whose ancestors had made that trip in a former generation took a ferry to the Statue of Liberty, reciting in homage the verse of Emma Lazarus: "Give me your tired, your poor / Your huddled masses yearning to breathe free." On North Brother Island, teenagers were trying to breathe free of the enslavement of heroin.

We visited Julio in the detoxification ward, and he led us out to the solarium to talk. This was his second trip to Riverside: the first was on assignment from a judge, after being arrested for possession of heroin; this time was voluntary, after taking an overdose of some "strong stuff." He'd been told it was pure heroin but didn't believe it, and he took too much and OD'd. But now he had already kicked and was eager to get back to the streets. On his first visit here, he had stayed fifty-two days and twice tried to escape, once by swimming ("I was busted in the river"), once when he was just about to dive in. This time they wanted to keep him for a standard program of six months, but he said he didn't need it, he would never get hooked again. He said if that happened he wouldn't go back to jail or the hospital, he would just OD: "That's the only way out for a junkie." It was part of the lore, based on painful experience in the neighborhood: "Once a junkie, always a junkie."

On the wall of the bright solarium was scrawled in pencil JUN-KIES' PLACE, and under it was sketched a lopsided cross. Below that, someone had drawn a coat of arms with an addict's "works" (needle, syringe, and belt) on a field of chipping green plaster. Just beyond, the arc of big windows gave a sweeping, sun-washed view of the New York City skyline. I tried to see it from this vantage, through the eyes of a Puerto Rican kid hooked on heroin rather than from the starry-eyed perception of a young midwesterner out to fulfill his dreams. The soaring buildings seemed then not so inspiring as haughty and teasing, as if to say, "You can see us, but you can't reach us." It gave me a chill. I had a sense of the fractured, fragmented views Manhattan represented to its millions, the kind of shifting, kaleidoscopic experience Dos Passos tried to capture in his early novel *Manhattan Transfer*.

Riverside Hospital, at least, was a tangible indication of the city's awareness of the suffering of a whole segment of its population, a human response to the heroin epidemic that swept New York after World War II, especially among young people in the slums. At the time I visited Riverside, three fourths of the adolescent addicts lived in 15 percent of the city's census tracts — the poorest, most overcrowded and dilapidated areas of New York. Riverside was the only hospital in the world used exclusively for treating juvenile addicts, and the only *community* hospital of any kind in the country for the treatment of narcotics addiction.

The shame of addiction was felt deeply in East Harlem, but the committee's stand that addiction itself was not a crime but a sickness brought more people out and into open discussions. One night after a meeting, I listened to Pee-Wee and Maria debate the question that was argued so often in the neighborhood, the conundrum of cause and effect.

Pee-Wee said addiction wasn't caused by conditions of the neighborhood or society, but teenagers started "because it's a kick." They go from smoking pot to snorting coke to skin-popping heroin and end up mainlining. Maria disagreed. She said kids got on dope because of the miserable conditions, family problems, lack of a home. She believed the cause was often psychological: "Some of these kids that get hooked, they do it for punishment."

We had started walking down 100th Street, and we came to the corner of Second Avenue, where we stopped under a streetlight. Pee-Wee smiled and shook his head. "Listen, Maria. When you're flyin' through the air at ninety miles an hour and grabbin' hunks of cheese off the moon, that's no punishment."

I didn't learn about drugs just from going to committee meetings. One night while I was having dinner with Norm and Peg Eddy at their apartment, a well-known figure from the neighborhood burst in whom I'll call Boppo Cruz. He was a junkie who had been to prison twice for robbery, to get money to buy heroin, and now he was selling it. Norm had helped him when he wanted to kick on two occasions in the past few years, but he was using again, and high the night he came in as we were finishing dinner.

Boppo was a handsome, brown-skinned man of twenty-seven, sharply dressed in slacks, sport coat, and button-down shirt and sporting a natty leather cap. Norm introduced us, and Boppo turned and asked me what I was doing there, looking straight at me, or through me, the question flung down like a challenge. I knew I couldn't lie or hedge the truth, sensing he'd pick up on it at once. I said I was writing a book about the neighborhood. He asked if I'd written anything else — a pro wanting to know if he was talking to a pro — and I said I'd written articles for *The Nation*. He nodded, as if accepting my credentials, and pulled up a chair to join us for dinner.

Watching him eat in his hyper, exaggerated state of awareness, I kept thinking Boppo would drop something. He seemed to be moving in a dream, or under water, but at very high velocity. When he finished eating, he pushed his plate away and paced around the kitchen as he talked, seeming to bounce off the walls as he jerked back from them and turned, pacing the other way again. He said he was working the Upper West Side now, but he told Norm to keep a kid named Tony, from 100th Street, away from him. The kid was just back from Riverside, and he was still weak and Boppo could hook him — he snapped his fingers — like *that*. Norm told Boppo that people looked up to him, that he had a responsibility.

Boppo took a deep breath and began to speak in a resonant voice: "No man is an island, entire of itself; every man is a piece of the continent, a part of the main . . . any man's death diminishes me, because I am involved in mankind; and therefore never send to know for whom the bell tolls; it tolls for thee." He paused, then said quietly, "John Donne. I know that crap."

As if he'd finished a performance, he left the room. Norm got up to walk him to the door, and I followed. Boppo yanked his cap down on his head, turned to us, and said with a condescending smile, "If you hear of anything to do to make a living besides narcotics that isn't dull, let me know."

Eventually Boppo did find something more fascinating than narcotics. A few years after the night I met him, he fell in love. He tried to stop using, cut way down on his habit, and went to Norm to ask for help to get completely clean before he got married. Norm drove him up to Trail's End, a cabin the parish owned in upstate New York, and there he kicked what was left of his habit and came back down to be married in City Hall. He took straight jobs, fathered a child, but fell back to using drugs and then selling them again to support his habit, and his wife divorced him.

"He loved his wife, and the day he was divorced was the last shot of heroin he ever took," Norm tells me years later. "He finally made

Ike was happy to leave the presidency of Columbia University to become President of the United States. (*Columbia University, Columbiana Collection*)

Professor Mark Van Doren, a Pulitzer Prize–winning poet, inspired generations of students, from Thomas Merton and Whittaker Chambers to Allen Ginsberg and Jack Kerouac. (*Drawing by Harvey Dinnerstein*)

Dan Wakefield made a precarious "living by the pen," covering politics, jazz, and the literary beat for *The Nation* and other magazines. (*Fred W. McDarrah*)

Novelist Sam Astrachan (*left*) visited his Columbia friend and fellow novelist David Markson in Mexico before going to live in the south of France. (*Elaine Markson*)

A story by Ivan Gold won the *Columbia Review* fiction prize and was published in *New World Writing* while he was still an undergraduate. (*Charles Marowitz*)

Sociologist C. Wright Mills's books *White Collar* and *The Power Elite* shook up the status quo and set the stage for the New Left of the sixties. (*Yaroslava Mills*)

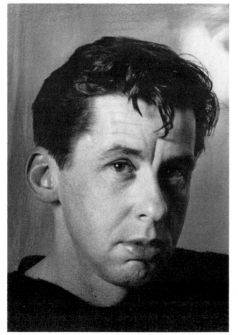

Above: No man in a gray flannel suit, Mills roared into Columbia on his motorcycle like an intellectual guerrilla warrior. (*Yaroslava Mills*)

Left: Novelist, essayist, critic, and editor, Robert Phelps was literary friend and guru to countless writers who, like Dan Wakefield, adopted him as "Uncle Bobby." (*Rosemarie Beck*)

Right: Editor and critic Marion Magid went to Barnard from the Bronx and discovered "the cultural encounter of Jews and goyim, New York and the Midwest." (*Gert Berliner*)

Dylan Thomas served as secular priest of a generation who chanted his poetry at the White Horse Tavern, where he had his last drink before dying at nearby St. Vincent's Hospital. (*Tal Jones/Time Magazine*)

Above: May Swenson, who came to New York from Utah, worked at New Directions publishing house by day, and wrote and read her poetry at night. (*Fred W. McDarrah*)
Below: Reverend Norman Eddy of the East Harlem Protestant Parish was honored by a Puerto Rican club on East 100th Street for his pastoral work in the neighborhood. At his side is his wife, Reverend Margaret Eddy. (*Sheldon Brody*)

Dorothy Day, cofounder and guiding spirit of the Catholic Worker, protested the war in Korea with anarchist Ammon Hennacy, who is holding the picket sign. (*Mottke Weissman*)

Michael Harrington, the "all-American" socialist, would use his experience at the Catholic Worker to write *The Other America*, which inspired the Johnson administration's anti-poverty program. (*Courtesy Stephanie Harrington*)

a commitment never to use again. He did get to drinking, though, and developed a disease related to alcohol. He died just before turning forty."

A few survived, like the man known as Doctor Joe. He managed to kick heroin by turning to booze, and felt it was his mission to "share the truth" with others. A number of addicts were able to get off heroin only to become alcoholics, but that was considered an improvement, a step up from hell, because it didn't put you in jail. Doctor Joe met junkies from the neighborhood who got off the ferry from Rikers or Riverside, took them right to a bar, and got them drunk, believing this course was better because it was legal. In the process of carrying out what he saw as his mission, he too became an alcoholic, went into a tailspin, and Peg Eddy found him passed out in the hallway of a building on 101st Street. She got him into an alcoholism program at Metropolitan Hospital, and he kicked that habit too.

"Joe later converted to Pentecostalism," Norm says, "and became a deacon in his church, and now works for the parks department." He is one of the few former addicts from the old narcotics committee days who is still alive, clean, and doing well.

Norm had been pastor of the storefront church on 100th Street, but he was spending so much of his time on the issue of narcotics — visiting addicts at Riverside and in prisons, going to court with guys who were arrested, helping them get jobs when they got out, counseling their families — that he decided to make that his full-time ministry. The committee got some unexpected outside help from several foundations and, in 1958, opened its own storefront office.

Looking back today on the influence of the committee's work, Norm says, "At the end of five years we had file folders on more than two thousand addicts we had seen and tried to help. Of that whole number there were only eight people we knew about who had stayed off drugs for more than a year. So I think it's fair to say we had *no* influence.

"We'd been doing commendable work," Norm adds, "but we failed to see the methods of helping an addict become a 'new man' or 'new woman' — the kind of transformation some of them found in Pentecostalism. I still run into people we knew in the days of the committee who say, 'You helped me go to a hospital and get a job and then I found a new life in the Pentecostal church.' What I began to see was that I've been a guide, a signpost, pointing people in a direction. The important thing was that we touched the lives of two thousand people, and some were touched by the spirit of God. We were only a step in a long path. We were also a clear Christian witness in demonstrating we cared."

Next to the Veteran Bar & Grill on First Avenue, around the corner from where I was living, was a boarded-up storefront painted black and decorated with silver handprints. There was no name on the door, but anyone in the neighborhood could tell you this was the clubhouse of a teenage gang called the Conservatives. The name had nothing to do with politics, but indicated a change of activity and purpose, from engaging in streetfights with rival gangs to holding dances, playing pool, and looking for jobs, with the help of an adult director, Ramon Diaz. In its own parlance, the gang had given up "bopping" and "gone social."

Teenage gangs were enmeshed in the culture of New York in the fifties, becoming part of the city's popular mythology with the runaway success of *West Side Story,* which translated the story of Romeo and Juliet to that of Maria and Tony, a Puerto Rican girl and an Italian boy, and the rival ethnic gangs of Sharks and Jets.

Guns and drugs proliferated in the tenement districts after World War II, and both were used by the burgeoning gangs, in a revival of the neighborhood gang tradition that began with the first Irish immigrants in the early nineteenth century. There was no tradition of gangs in Puerto Rico, but the kids picked it up in New York, part of their assimilation into life on the mainland.

It was when they decided to give up guns and street fighting that the Conservatives had changed their name. Before that they were known as the Enchanters, a gang that was formed right after the war. By the early fifties they had a total of seven "divisions" in East Harlem, grouped according to age — from nine to twenty, you moved up through the ranks from Tiny Tots to Mighty Mites, Juniors, and Seniors. The Enchanters spread to the Bronx, Brooklyn, and across the river to Hoboken, New Jersey. Their branch in lower

Manhattan was still one of the most active fighting gangs in the city when the East Harlem group went social in 1957. The change was not born out of idealism or a sudden transfusion of social responsibility, but simply because most of their leaders were dead or in jail. The new rules were no drugs or guns, and the members put their fingerprints in silver paint on the clubhouse door as a symbol that they would never have to be fingerprinted by the police.

I went to club nights of pool playing and rock 'n' roll harmonizing and dances, with girls in toreador pants, high heels, and tight sweaters, and boys in sport shirts and turbans wrapped around their heads, with a piece of costume jewelry from home pinned at the front like a headlight — the headgear was that summer's fad. They played Fats Domino and Latin records, danced the merengue, and during slow, romantic numbers the ministers there as chaperones patrolled the floor to make sure couples were doing the Fish and not the Grind. In both dances, the boy and girl mashed torsos together, but in the Fish, the feet had to be moving, which supposedly made it less provocative.

When dances ended on Saturday nights the music kept pulsing in the streets, from radios and records and from groups of teenage boys who gathered in doorways to harmonize, hoping to become pop groups and grow rich and famous, the new way up from the old neighborhood. The Conservatives had their own singing group, the Persuaders, and from doorways you heard their crooning, as their heads leaned together in concentration and they focused on a chorus of "Doo-wah, doo-wah, doo-wah," which sounded like a keening, plaintive lament.

One afternoon when I was hanging around the clubhouse, I met a young man I thought was a new boy, but he turned out to be a veteran of the old fighting gang, the Enchanters. He was about to be discharged from the U.S. Army after a hitch of peacetime service. Louie Melendez (the name I used when I wrote about him) was a small, fine-featured Puerto Rican with smooth, light skin and a thin mustache that made him look even younger than he was, like a pubescent boy who was trying to prove himself a man. He had an assurance about him, though, as he gave advice to Victor, a current member of the Conservatives, and told war stories — not of the Army but of the old gang.

"Right after World War Two," Louie told Victor, "I remember I was just a little kid and guns first started showing up in the open. At first it was a real big deal. A guy would pull a gun in the street and everyone out on the block would scatter. Maybe it wasn't even loaded, maybe you couldn't hit a thing with it — all you had to do was pull a gun. Then people got used to 'em, and after a while it got so a guy pulled a gun and another guy would just stand there and ask him, 'Well, you going to use that or not? You better use it or put it away.' "

When I told Louie later that I was a writer, he said he'd considered writing a book about the neighborhood himself, but nobody'd believe it. He said the guys at his own Army base wouldn't believe what it was like growing up in East Harlem. "You know, they say the Army makes a man of you, all the stuff you see and have to take. But those guys haven't seen anything. I say 100th Street makes a man of you."

That summer of 1957 the manhood of the Conservatives was tested in their first trial of staying social when bopping gangs came into the neighborhood. Norm Eddy was called on to act as mediator one hot Friday night when two rival gangs whose members had guns came onto 100th Street to fight, and warfare was averted. That Sunday he gave a sermon on "Jesus and His Gang" at the storefront church on 100th Street, where many of the new Conservatives and their parents attended services. Norm asked them to show "a special kind of courage" to resist getting involved in the gang fighting, even though it might mean being called a punk. But he knew it wasn't easy: "When a club comes into the neighborhood with their pieces, it's hard." Despite temptation, the Conservatives got through the tough hot months and kept to their social, nonviolent course.

At the end of the summer, after spending half a year in the neighborhood meeting people, taking notes, and going to every kind of event — from narcotics committee meetings to prayer meetings, gang-sponsored dances to political rallies — I moved back down to the Village to do the actual writing of my book. I was excited about it and felt a sense of responsibility, not only to the literary standards I aspired to, but also to the people I had met and come to care about. They trusted me by letting me into their apartments and their lives and telling me their stories, and now it was up to me to tell the world, or at least that small segment of it that was willing to listen.

I sat at a massive old office desk in the living room of the apartment I shared again with Ted the Horse, at 10th and Bleecker, smoking cigarettes and drinking coffee as I stared out the window and back at my notes, trying to conjure up the feel and sound and smell of the world I had entered for a while as a visitor.

Sam Astrachan came up from Fort Dix one weekend and I showed him the first chapter, walking nervously around the block while he read, wondering what his novelist's eye would see in my account of coming up with a planeload of migrants from San Juan on the cheapest flight to New York, which was bumpy and nerve-racking because for that price the cabin wasn't pressurized. Evidently Sam was pleased, for when I returned to the apartment, the cigarette was dangling more loosely than usual from the corner of his mouth because he was smiling.

"With this beginning, you can go anywhere," he said. He held out his hand to shake and I took it, holding his always perspiring palm for a moment in relief and gratitude.

More specific encouragement came when *Harper's Magazine* and *Commentary* took chapters to publish from the manuscript in progress, but when I finished I was still dissatisfied with the personal introduction, which I felt was crucial to the book, and I went down to Princeton one Saturday and gave it to Murray Kempton to read. He sipped a beer, then put down the pages and said, "Take out of the introduction everything that didn't happen to you while you were living in the neighborhood." In a single stroke, the self-righteous rhetoric and pompous generalizations were eliminated. It was the best one sentence of editorial advice I ever got.

Like all the young writers I knew, I was under the influence of Hemingway, and I wanted to make the book as honest and spare as his own first book of stories, *In Our Time.* He had interspersed the stories with brief impressionistic scenes from his own time, and so I wrote brief scenes from the neighborhood that I set between each chapter. I wanted to call the book *In Spanish Harlem,* in emulation of Hemingway's book and his uncompromising spirit, but the publisher thought it sounded too stark. I didn't agree, but I came up with something more colorful, which at least *they* liked better. After all, I rationalized, hadn't Carson McCullers, at the suggestion of the same publisher, changed the title of her first novel from *The Mutes* to *The Heart Is a Lonely Hunter?*

Waking up in the middle of the night, I wondered if this was the first indication of the dread process we all feared, the fifties version of Faustus — selling out. The novelist Herbert Gold, feeling he had to defend the publication of his short stories in *Playboy,* used to say, "I'm not selling out, I'm buying in." It made me nervous — I was writing for *Playboy* myself. Murray Kempton wrote a column lamenting the fact that Mike Wallace was going national, warning that Wallace wouldn't be able to do the same kind of tough, intelligent interviews he did on his New York TV show. The devil comes not with obvious lures, Kempton cautioned, but the offer of a bigger audience.

When *Island in the City: The World of Spanish Harlem* was published in the spring of 1959, Harrison Salisbury wrote in the *New York Times:* "To read Mr. Wakefield's book is to walk into Spanish Harlem and suddenly share its life, its problems and its tragedies." That was everything I'd hoped someone would say. The kind words cushioned the blow of the advance sale of only two thousand. (That was proof I hadn't sold out!) Like the authors I knew with disappointing book sales, which included almost all the ones I knew, I was comforted by recalling that James Agee's *Let Us Now Praise Famous Men* sold only five hundred copies when it was first published.

Though *Island in the City* never achieved that kind of fame, I was proud when it was republished in paperback in the sixties, and again in a hardcover library edition in the seventies. The greatest personal reward came from a few young men and women I met a decade or so later who said that reading the book had inspired them to go into social work or sociology in hopes of making a difference in the life of such neighborhoods. That eased the disappointment and guilt I'd begun to feel about the real utility of such a book — it hadn't improved the lives of the people I wrote about, but it helped my own career. That it led a few individuals to contribute something of their own lives made the whole enterprise seem more justified and justifiable.

Though I didn't stay on and live in East Harlem when I finished my work on the book, I kept going back up to see my new friends and sit in on meetings of the narcotics committee, sometimes helping out as a volunteer press aide and publicist for its causes. I really kept returning to the committee because I felt at home there and akin to the people — the addicts and those who were drawn to help them.

Later I read a book about addiction that Nat Hentoff recommended, *The Fantastic Lodge,* in which the author, herself an addict and writing under a pseudonym, said that everyone involved in narcotics, no matter which side of it — from judges to cops to junkies to pushers, as well as the social workers, ministers, nurses, and doctors who try to help — all are involved because "they have eyes." That, of course, would include people who choose to write about it.

According to that perceptive author, we who surrounded the addicts, whether with threats or help, were ourselves in some way addictive personalities drawn to drugs. Whether we actually used them or not, we were mesmerized by the subject, by the life-transforming power of the substances. Maybe this only meant that, like Norm Eddy, we were interested in the Big Questions. Whether we were on some level intellectual or emotional junkies or fellow travelers of dope I don't know — in my own case, I suspect it's true — but I do know I was comfortable with those people up at the narcotics committee and felt I was one of them, out on the edge, at some dangerous and real frontier of experience that was far removed from the men in the gray flannel suits, the country-club Christians, the organization men, the frightened herd that composed the lonely crowd.

It certainly wasn't some somber sense of good works that took me back to the narcotics committee, but the good times I had talking and going out after meetings for beers with friends like Norm Eddy, Pee-Wee, Maria, and Seymour Ostrow, the wry attorney who graduated from Yale Law School and chose to set up a practice in East Harlem instead of going to work for one of New York's prestigious downtown firms.

Sy was an anti—organization man who knew the language of the streets as well as of the courts and political clubhouses, and was always dressed in a three-piece suit with razor-creased pants and shoes shined to a high gloss. Once Maria Flores, looking over my scruffy clothes, gently suggested I try to dress a little more like Sy Ostrow. His tongue was even sharper than his outfits, as he proclaimed a cynical atheism while giving of his time and expert services to the work of the East Harlem Parish and the poor who needed representation against the System.

Like Norm Eddy, Sy possessed what Hemingway said was essential to any good writer, and I soon saw was also necessary for professionals working effectively in the city's deprived neighborhoods — a built-in shit detector. Sy most of all liked to mock the phony do-gooders who came to exploit the slums for quick headlines to promote their own careers and then disappeared: the lawyers who lost interest in cases that dropped out of the newspapers and who failed to show up in court to meet their clients; the political and religious vultures who sucked support from people in need and then were off making speeches when their help was needed in the streets.

Besides the mutual respect and friendship those of us who volunteered for the narcotics committee felt for one another, we believed we were playing a small part in making things happen, in changing the way things were, and there was a sense then that individuals working together could actually have some effect on the monstrous problems besetting the greatest city in the nation. In my very minor role as a free-lance press aide or publicist for the committee, I testified before a city hearing on addiction urging hospital beds for addicts, joined the picket line outside Metropolitan Hospital, and persuaded some reporter friends to come up and cover that protest, which helped bring about the opening of a ward for addicts at Metropolitan Hospital.

In a larger community effort the committee helped get the Metcalf-Volker bill passed in Albany, which recognized drug addiction as a disease rather than a crime and gave freedom to volunteer groups to treat addicts. We joined forces with other organizations throughout the city. Ed Fancher, publisher of the *Village Voice*, coordinated these different groups throughout New York, and there was a feeling of alliance, of the Village and East Harlem being able to work together and make something happen in far-off Albany.

A lot of new things were happening in East Harlem in the late fifties, and not only from the work of the narcotics committee. After the gang that went social, the Conservatives, got through the summer of 1957 without fighting, there seemed to be more opportunities for expression than the usual outlets of bopping and taking drugs. A wealthy downtown donor was sponsoring classes in the arts, with Geoffrey Holder teaching dance and a young painter from the neighborhood teaching art.

Louie Melendez, the former Enchanter, was home from the Army, and he introduced me to the artist friend he'd grown up with in the East River Housing Project. Ray Grist was a cool, handsome young guy with ramrod posture and a precise, distinct enunciation whose family came from St. Thomas in the Caribbean. He was teaching the art class and was eager to know about music, theater, and literature.

Louie, Ray, and I went out for beers, and they asked me what writers I liked. I started talking about Dostoevsky. Ray and Louie had never read his work but he sounded cool to them, and they wanted to know if I'd recommend something Dostoevsky wrote, and if they read it would I talk to them about it? The next thing I knew we had a reading group going, and to really introduce the guys to literature I invited them to come to the Village and I'd take them to the White Horse Tavern.

I introduced Ray and Louie to Sam Astrachan, who I knew was another great Dostoevsky fan, and the four of us drank pints of arf 'n' arf in the back room of the Horse and talked about the novel I'd assigned us all to read, *The Possessed*. We agreed that although it was, on the surface, a political novel, it was really about the human passions that underlay politics, the real stuff that made people tick, that drove them to action or madness. Louie asked how you pronounced the word "nihilist," and I said I thought it could either be "nee-hilist" or "ny-hilist."

"Man," Louie said, shaking his head in a show of appreciation, "them *ny*-hilists was really *on* to somethin'!"

We all broke up laughing and ordered more pints.

Like many young people caught up in the first excitement of

ideas and art, Ray and Louie wanted to start a newspaper. They got some money for printing from the East Harlem Protestant Parish and asked my help. I wrote an article and Ray solicited an editorial cartoon from Ted the Horse, who used to draw for his college paper. Ray wrote a short story, and other friends from the parish and the neighborhood contributed to the first issue of the *Edge,* which also proved to be the last. As Ray says now, looking back on our misguided effort, "It was supposed to be for the people of the neighborhood, but I think it was over everybody's head." We had made the mistake of addressing it to ourselves — we White Horse "ny-hilists" — rather than our intended audience.

Still, we had put out a newspaper, and it seemed part of the hopeful ferment of the time, along with the new "social" Conservatives, the victory of the protest that led to the addicts' ward at Metropolitan Hospital, the flow of people and ideas to and from Harlem. A talented novelist, Warren Miller, came up to the neighborhood, hung around the streets, and got out of it a novel that young people like Ray and Louie admired, and so did I, called *The Cool World.* There was talk of its being made into a play and a movie, and a few years later an excellent black-and-white film of it was made, directed by Shirley Clark and produced by Frederick Wiseman.

For a brief time it seemed that we, like the nihilists in Dostoevsky, were, as Louie put it, really *on* to somethin', and that these bright cool kids from East Harlem were going to be artists who spoke for their culture, as all of us contributed to the greater mainstream of the city. It was during that time, the spring of 1959, that I took James Baldwin up from the Village to meet Norm Eddy on 100th Street.

Baldwin had liked my book, wrote a blurb for it, and was curious about this white minister and his family I had written about who had come from the suburbs of Connecticut to live in East Harlem. He was also interested in the work of the narcotics committee and the whole subject of addiction. He had written a powerful short story, "Sonny's Blues," about a Negro jazz musician from Harlem who was an addict, that came out first in the summer 1957 issue of *Partisan Review.* Norm Eddy knew Baldwin's work and admired it, but he didn't want to talk literature; he wanted to talk about, well, what he always talked about, those Big Questions.

Baldwin and Norm hit it off right away, and I sat back and listened to their conversation with the rapt appreciation of a record producer who has brought together two musicians he admires and now gets to hear play together for the first time. They spoke freely and openly, and Norm said something I had never heard before when Baldwin asked why he had come to live in that neighborhood. Norm leaned forward with intense concentration and said it had nothing to do with saving souls or doing good or any of the stock assumptions people who visited (at least white people) often made. It might sound grandiose, Norm said, but the truth was, "I want to help create Plymouth Colony in East Harlem."

"Yes," Baldwin said immediately, "I understand."

Norm tells me many years later, "Baldwin was the first person I shared that vision with who knew what I was talking about."

It was a time of hope, of new beginnings, of colors mixing and complementing one another, as in the new abstract expressionist paintings being done in lofts down in the Bowery by Franz Kline, Willem de Kooning, and others, the same crowd of artist friends who gathered at the Five Spot after work to hear jazz groups. The musicians were sometimes of mixed colors, white David Amram playing with black Cecil Taylor or Charlie Mingus; black Sonny Rollins, who wrote "Freedom Suite" in 1958, hiring white guitarist Jim Hall in 1961 as part of a group that marked Rollins's return to public performance after a self-imposed exile. Although hiring a white musician drew criticism from some black activists, Rollins said, looking back years later, "I thought it was a healing symbol, and I didn't have any qualms about doing it." During this period Nat Hentoff and other friends in the Village collected money to help a talented young Negro poet who was short of the rent one month. The poet was married to a white girl then, and his name was still Jones (before he became Amiri Baraka).

It was not the racial millennium, understand. Miles Davis was busted outside Birdland, beaten, and taken to jail. Baldwin himself was beaten up at an Irish bar in the Village because he was sitting in a booth with two white friends, one of them a woman. So it was still a dangerous time for blacks, but there had been those exceptions, what seemed like lights going on, an offbeat, bebop kind of occasional, hopeful harmony.

It was a time when Norman Mailer and his second wife, Adele, went to rent parties in Harlem with their maid on Saturday nights and got to know her boyfriend, who couldn't read or write but had an enormous sophistication, and Mailer says, "That's where I got my understanding about hip and hipsters that led to my essay 'The White Negro.' That was a period I look back on with affection. Blacks and whites were moving toward one another. There was a marvelous sense of optimism."

These were the early days of the civil rights cause, and *The Nation* sent me south to cover school integration. I heard the stirring oratory of the young Reverend Martin Luther King and, shedding any pretense of objectivity, sang with the protesters, "Black and white together, we shall overcome." Up north among liberals I knew of all colors the goal was integration — not as it would later become, another kind of separation, when "Negroes" became "blacks" and wanted not just rights but power.

I am speaking of a time when Bayard Rustin, the scholarly black man with the Oxford accent who had worked with A. Philip Randolph of the AFL-CIO, studied with Gandhi, and advised Dr. King on nonviolence, let me in free to a benefit concert for the movement in New York because I was broke at the time. When I walked in and said, "Bayard, if it wasn't for you I wouldn't be here tonight," he threw back his head and laughed and said, "Oh, Dan, we are all here by the grace of God." Even though I didn't believe in those days, I felt a tremor of the eerie wonder of life.

It was four years before Baldwin would write *The Fire Next Time,* which shocked white liberals with the warning of the conflagration to come — and did come, as Baldwin predicted, in Watts and other city ghettos across the country. It was four years before I got into an awful argument with Baldwin over whether a teenage white girl could suffer as a black girl like his own sister had suffered, and in anger he said something that hung like a sword over all interracial friendships: "You're just like all the others." It meant, of course, the other whites, the ones who didn't understand. It meant: I thought you were different but I was fooled again, deluded again, you are one of Them after all.

Four years had gone by when I ran into Louie Melendez, in 1963, and we started by kidding about our old admiration for "them ny-hilists" in Dostoevsky, but before the evening was over it felt more like *we* were the nihilists. Louie told me he was working as a subcontractor. I assumed he meant a construction job, but he said he was dispensing drugs — not really a pusher, more like someone who simply was delivering packages of what had already been paid for.

I went with him to a run-down apartment on East 102nd Street, where a nervous young guy was eagerly waiting while his tough-looking teenage girlfriend lay on a bed. She was reading a comic book and chewing gum. The customer got out his works and asked Louie to fix him. Louie nodded but first went to a record player where a Modern Jazz Quartet LP was playing. I think it was "Cortege" from the album *No Sun in Venice*. Louie lifted the arm off the record and said, "John Lewis, you're too sad for me." Then he went to the waiting customer, who had already rolled up his sleeve.

I left New York that fall of 1963, and I don't think I went back to East Harlem until February 9, 1986, to attend a celebration of Norm Eddy's sixty-sixth birthday at the Church of the Resurrection, on East 101st Street. I'd renewed my friendship with Norm a few years before, when I let him know I'd returned to church in 1980, joining King's Chapel in Boston. Now I wanted to give him due credit for never having tried to recruit or convert me during my passionate atheistic years. On his birthday Norm spoke about "acts of prayer." I remembered with a jolt that when I first knew him and heard him say the Lord's Prayer, I used to substitute the words I learned from Hemingway's story "A Clean, Well-Lighted Place": "Our nada who art in nada, nada be thy name . . ."

There were two choirs at the birthday celebration, one from the church and one from a neighborhood drug rehabilitation center, and the sanctuary was full, with people from the neighborhood where Norm had lived and served for nearly forty years, and people from all across the country who had worked in his parish as volunteers, and a New York City councilwoman and representatives of religious and political groups from all around the city who had come to honor Norm and his vision and his work.

Norm spoke of the counseling and activism of the narcotics committee being a prelude to the sixties, of going to meet Martin Luther King in Montgomery, Alabama, in 1956, and being convinced he was the man to lead the nation in the civil rights struggle. It turned out King's driver was a former addict from 125th Street and Lenox Avenue, "in those days when addicts were all considered beyond hope," and this convinced Norm of King's trust in individuals to grow and change. That is the faith Norm lives by, and perhaps is why I and so many others have been drawn to him over the decades.

I had altogether lost track of Ray Grist, the aspiring painter, until Norm gave me his number in the spring of 1990. We meet at the Hunan Balcony restaurant on Broadway, and Ray is carrying a copy of a publication called *Jump,* subtitled "A Forum for New World Culture / A Voice for Us." As well as being a working artist whose paintings have been shown in Harlem galleries, Ray is the editor in chief of this paper. I say it looks very impressive, and he grins and says, "A little nicer than the *Edge.* Remember the *Edge*?"

I laugh and recall our high hopes for that long-forgotten publication. *Jump* already has a longer life. It was started by a group of black artists who called themselves the Pow Wow Group, who got together to talk about how to get their work shown, reviewed, and sold. *Jump* is part of that effort, listing galleries that show the work of black and Third World artists, and giving dates of exhibitions.

Ray says he has kept in touch with Norm Eddy over the years. "Norm and the other ministers of the East Harlem Protestant Parish nurtured us. They were very important to me — they woke up a whole intellectual curiosity. They asked questions like 'What is God?' and 'Do I have a social responsibility?'"

Ray remembers other people who came into the neighborhood back then: the donor who set up the art classes, the dancer Geoffrey Holder, Warren Miller and his novel *The Cool World.* We talk about our trips to the White Horse Tavern, and Ray speaks of meeting Sam Astrachan and James Baldwin there. "All these people gave us a sense of exposure to the world. We absorbed everything out there, and now we're putting it back as our experience, a new reality."

I ask if he's seen Louie Melendez lately, and that's a sore subject. Louie stayed with Ray awhile, going in on another big deal that didn't come off, one of the many he was trying to put together in later years, not with drugs but assorted high-risk business projects, like exporting fruit from the Caribbean in winter (a shipment was ruined by an early frost). These schemes seemed cursed and never quite materialized, and in the midst of a deal that started to fall apart, Louie, who was living on credit and Ray's hospitality, suddenly disappeared. I try on my own to track him down, but finally I'm told by someone from 100th Street that Louie left the country. He's living in Santo Domingo, they say, tending bar.

I think of our discussions about Dostoevsky, and the days when going from 100th Street in East Harlem to the White Horse Tavern in the Village to talk about nihilism seemed like the promise of some new sort of understanding that would make us triumphant and wise.

SIX

Home to the Village

RAISING A STANDARD

WHETHER I WAS coming back from Spanish Harlem or Indianapolis, Greenwich Village seemed like home. From the first time I saw it, as a student at Columbia, I was drawn to the place, entranced by it. You could tell the Village was special simply by looking at the map of Manhattan, where the ordered grid of avenues and streets went suddenly crooked, twisting and turning in an unruly whorl. Small lanes looped and stuck out at angles like so many secrets in a neighborhood where the regular compass of rules went defiantly, rebelliously awry.

Going to the Village for the first time in 1952 was like walking into a dream. It not only looked different from the rest of New York — small, cozy brick or frame houses on winding streets rather than skyscrapers looming above long avenues — it sounded different too. There was a quietness about the place, almost a hush, compared to the taxi-blasting traffic, street crowds, and vendors of Broadway, midtown, and Morningside Heights. The special quiet of the Village suggested creation rather than commerce and conveyed a tone of mystery. That aura was added to by the places hidden away like the prizes on a treasure hunt. On Patchin Place, e. e. cummings still lived and wrote his lowercase poetry. Chumley's, the restaurant-bar that began as a speakeasy in 1928, had never put its name on a sign outside, only a number on obscure Bedford Street. You opened the door to a warm room lit by a fireplace, where Village denizens drank and ate at wooden tables surrounded by a frieze of faded dust jackets on the walls, from books by the writers who frequented the place in the twenties and thirties. It was like walking into a wonderful secret and becoming part of it, taking your place in the play.

There was something of the same quality to Louis', off Sheridan Square, where you walked down a small flight of steps and drank at the bar or sat at a small table and ordered the house special of spaghetti and meatballs with tomato and lettuce salad for sixty-five cents (a bargain that held for a decade). That was the first meal I ate in the Village when Mike Naver, my Columbia classmate and native guide, took me downtown on the IRT. We sat at a window table, looking out through a soft rain in the Sunday dusk and watching the passersby, the real people who lived there, who might have been artists and writers, musicians and dancers, women with long hair and no makeup, men wearing sandals or boots and sometimes a beard. I imagined them writing and painting and making "free love," which meant you didn't have to be married or engaged or even pinned, like fraternity guys and sorority girls — you only had to want to do it. The thought of all this sex and art and poetry made me dizzy with fear and delight. I hoped Mike didn't notice my hands were shaking as I methodically cut my spaghetti with knife and fork as we did back home in Indiana, a place that felt as remote now as Mars.

Though the Village at first seemed exotically foreign, there was also something familiar about it, the way a remembered dream is familiar, a sense that I had some deeper connection to it than that of a mere tourist. I don't know if I consciously thought then, "I'll live here someday," but when I moved downtown in 1956, the act seemed not only obvious but inevitable: of course, where else in the world would I live?

The same thought occurred to many of my friends. Meg Greenfield, who became my neighbor on West 10th Street, says, "When I came back from Europe, it never occurred to me to live anyplace but the Village. I mean, where else would you live — in *Yorkville?*"

"I always wanted to live in the Village when I got to New York," Calvin Trillin says, "not because it was bohemian but because it was more like the United States than the rest of New York. You could see the sky, you knew your next-door neighbors, and it was informal — you didn't have to get dressed up. And that's why the original bohemians came, because it was more like home."

For some, of course, it seemed more like a nice place to visit. Jules Feiffer, whose hip cartoons of angst and analysis symbolized the Village of the fifties to readers of the *Village Voice* beginning in 1956, chose to live in the lower-key neighborhood of Brooklyn Heights. He explained that the Village made him tense, a sentiment that might have been spoken by one of his elongated cartoon figures on an analyst's couch.

For most of my friends, the authentic literary aura of the Village, not only in legend but in the flesh of famous neighbors, was lure enough to make it irresistible. The poet and editor Harvey Shapiro moved to Patchin Place in 1953, the little enclave of gray painted brick houses around a small courtyard with a gate at the entryway. "We had a room and a half right opposite e. e. cummings," Harvey remembers, "and I used to see him standing out at the gate with his sketchbook. He liked to draw and paint. He was one of the first poets to give readings of his work at colleges, and on spring nights, girls from Smith and Vassar would come into the courtyard and serenade him, or sometimes they'd shout up at his window, reciting lines from his poems: 'how do you like your blueeyed boy / Mister Death.'"

As if having cummings as a neighbor didn't provide enough atmosphere, Harvey had another literary star of the twenties in the apartment below, the novelist Djuna Barnes. "I was impressed," Harvey says, "because I'd read *Nightwood*. She wore a cape and carried a cane, and she used to knock the cane on her ceiling, which was our floor, to complain about the noise."

This enclave was threatened, Harvey recalls, when a new school was going to be built in the neighborhood. "They were either going to tear down Patchin Place or another site, called Rhinelander Gardens. All of us who lived in Patchin Place met in the cummings apartment, and e. e.'s wife, Marion, was one of the leaders of the campaign to save our street. We had petitions and signs we took all over the neighborhood, and I guess we worked harder than the people in Rhinelander Gardens, because that was torn down and Patchin Place was saved."

Later cummings himself was threatened with eviction by some bureaucratic zoning zealot who said there were not enough bathrooms in the apartment. A friend told Mary Perot Nichols, who wrote a story about it in the *Village Voice,* rallying support for the poet, and then Mary used her political clout: "I got to the housing commissioner, and I said if cummings was evicted I'd embarrass the Wagner administration — I'd really make it an issue. A deal was worked out whereby cummings got to stay in his apartment, but in return he had to go to City Hall and pose with Mayor Wagner, who of course got as much mileage out of it as he could, as the savior of the great poet." (Saving cummings's apartment was great, but even more impressive was that Mary Nichols's investigative reporting saved Washington Square from being destroyed by the highway Robert Moses tried to carve through the middle of it.)

I never met cummings, though I sometimes saw him walking around the neighborhood, and I learned that one of my friends had set some of cummings's works to music. This enhanced the already amazing reputation of John Rawlings, the first person I knew who actually lived in Greenwich Village.

Rawlings seemed the perfect prototype of the kind of youth who came to the Village from the provinces. He had gone to my high school in Indianapolis and moved down to Jones Street after graduating from Yale a few years before I got out of Columbia.

A bit of an oddball by virtue of his physical stature as well as his precocious talent as a writer, musician, and artist, John had the courage and wit to flaunt his fragile-looking frame of six feet seven or so bony inches by bounding in front of the crowds at Shortridge High School football and basketball games. As our most conspicuous cheerleader, he clowned it up as he reached higher and with greater gusto than anyone else in the whole city, to pull down laughs as well as yells for the Blue Devils.

He wrote and composed the music for an act in the Shortridge Vaudeville spoofing ancient Egypt, called "My Mummy Done Ptolemy," which earned him a trip to Hollywood during summer vacation to work on the screenplay for *Duel in the Sun,* a fifties hit movie with Jennifer Jones and Gregory Peck. At Yale he wrote music and poetry and graduated from the architecture school, then moved to Greenwich Village. Of course.

I had never been inside anyone's apartment in the Village until the time I visited Rawlings's place when I was still at Columbia. Before that, I had only seen what any tourist could see who had the price of that spaghetti and meatball special at Louis' bar, or a beer at Julius's, the popular hangout with cobwebs on the ceiling, or a ticket to the Circle in the Square Theatre to watch Jason Robards or Geraldine Page. Walking into Rawlings's apartment, you left the bourgeois world of home, with its overstuffed furniture and flocked walls, left the dull, predictable decor of dorm room bullfight posters and heavy, battered desks with wobbly stacks of books in corners. There was no clutter, and I automatically felt less encumbered myself as I entered a realm that was not especially large yet seemed to offer an abundance of space and light.

There was a Japanese tone in the spareness of white walls and the simple pallet on the floor. A circular shade made of tan paper enclosed the light bulb that hung from the ceiling. Instead of a desk, a plain pine door was set on two construction horses. The only decorative object was something else that hung from the ceiling, a contraption of many armatures that dangled from one another like a child's toy and moved slightly in the soft breeze from the window. John said it was a mobile, and was made by the friend from whom he sublet this apartment, a sculptor named Alexander Calder (I later met Sandy Calder at one of Rawlings's parties).

John was free to fling his long arms and legs wherever he pleased; there were no vases or table lamps to knock over, no gewgaws to scatter. The space was filled with talk of books, plays, movies, and poetry, talk of what Rawlings was doing now, which included not only his architectural drawings but also the work he'd begun at Yale of setting e. e. cummings's poems to music — with the sanction of the poet, who was now a friend and neighbor. John was also performing at a midtown nightclub, where he sang his own songs and accompanied himself on the piano, flailing his arms and fingers over the keyboard, accentuating his dramatic physique. He billed himself as the Playing Mantis.

Later John worked as a costume designer for Paul Taylor's dance company, and Taylor praised him in his autobiography, *Private Domain,* as "one of the few people I've ever really collaborated with. He has an uncanny grasp of what the emerging dance is trying to be." Once when Taylor showed Rawlings a new dance and asked what the performers should wear, John shielded his eyes in thought for a moment and murmured, "Bananas. I see bunches of large bananas." The dance turned out to be *From Sea to Shining Sea,* a title that came from Rawlings as well. Taylor was so pleased with his collaborator, whom he called "the seven footer" (Rawlings was so thin he *seemed* that tall), that he gave him "a smooch" on the nearest thing he could reach — his necktie.

I came away from my first visit with Rawlings as impressed with him as Paul Taylor would be. I loved the free and open feeling of his Village apartment, which seemed to inspire creative thought and activity, and I was in awe of Rawlings's invention of himself as a unique creative and performing artist defying all the pressures of conformity that the current era was famous for exerting.

Our generation in the fifties needed the Village and all it stood for as much as the artists, writers, and rebels of preceding generations — maybe even more. If the mood of the country was to force everyone to conform, to look and dress like the man in the gray flannel suit, surely it was all the more important to have at least one haven where people were not only allowed but expected to dress, speak, and behave differently from the herd. This was a time when a beard might be regarded as a sign of subversion, or at least raised suspicion about the character of the person who wore it. When the writer Sara Davidson went as a teenager to Disneyland in the fifties, she and her otherwise well-dressed date were turned away because he had a beard; a Disney official explained that this was a place for families.

All the more essential that somewhere in the land was a place where a beard was a badge of honor. Beyond the symbolic freedom it represented was the deeper freedom to create that writers and artists found in the atmosphere of the Village. I had no desire to grow a beard, but I wanted to write books. My friends and I who went to the Village in the fifties felt the creative tradition of the place as an inspiration. We wanted to tap the power of it, absorb the literary heritage reflected by those dust jackets around the walls of

Chumley's, from books written by people who had talked and drunk at the very tables where we now sat. Supposedly Fitzgerald and Hemingway had drunk — or had been drunk — there, and James Joyce was said to have spent several months at a corner table, writing part of *Ulysses* (in fact, Joyce never came to America).

Some of the 1920s crowd had already declared the Village dead, but generations of poets and painters had been saying that since it first became a bohemian center in the early 1900s. Floyd Dell, a writer friend of fellow Villager John Reed, thought the neighborhood had been ruined by becoming fashionable and commercialized during World War *One*. Yet even though earlier writers like Sinclair Lewis bemoaned the passing of the "real" Village before the First World War, it enjoyed its greatest heyday in the twenties, when Edna St. Vincent Millay was "burning the candle at both ends" and Eugene O'Neill was drinking Dorothy Day under the table at the Hell Hole while he recited Francis Thompson's poem "The Hound of Heaven." The Lost Generation's literary chronicler, Malcolm Cowley, declared that the "real" Village wasn't ruined by commercialism until after World War *Two*.

My own Village friend Michael Harrington arrived from St. Louis in 1949 to find the place still flourishing with other "voluntary exiles from the middle class." Discovering the "bohemia of talent" he had hoped for, Mike would later write in his autobiography, *Fragments of the Century*, "The Village didn't die till I got there." Happily, he found the bohemian party we had all dreamed about back in the Midwest was still in progress.

The party was going strong — with Harrington one of its welcoming hosts in the back room of the White Horse Tavern — when I moved to the Village in 1956. Though the editor of *Partisan Review*, William Phillips, had expressed the old, familiar lament for "the death of bohemia" in his magazine's symposium on "Our Country, Our Culture" in 1952, citing the demise of the cold-water flat and the rise of modern apartment buildings, where rents became too steep for artists and writers, I was able to find my own affordable foothold in the Village.

It wasn't easy. Reasonable rentals (forget about cheap) were still possible but damnably scarce, and apartment hunters, a fierce and ruthless breed, haunted the newsstands of Sheridan Square and over on Sixth Avenue and 8th Street for the earliest copies of the weeklies, the *Voice* and the *Villager,* and lined up at night to grab the next day's early edition of the *New York Times,* then dashed to a phone to try to make a deal, or be on the doorsteps of realtors or landlords at dawn.

With diligent effort I was able to grab a single room the shape of a cell (plus kitchenette and bath), with bars on the window, in a dilapidated building on Jones Street across from Rawlings's sublet. The rent was $70, only $15 more than the windowless basement on West 77th Street I lived in during my last semester at Columbia. The location, a few blocks from Sheridan Square, was great, but the jail-like ambience of the "studio" itself was so oppressive that my good friend Ted the Horse took one look around, assessed the apartment and my own black mood, left over from a broken love affair, and said, "Wake, you gotta get out of here."

We figured we could do better by sharing the rent on a bigger place, and gleefully grabbed a two-room apartment at the corner of 10th and Bleecker for $110 a month, a price neither of us could afford alone but which became a good deal when divided in half. It boasted a separate living room and bedroom, a kitchenette, and a standard-size bathroom. The building even had a self-service elevator, a feature so luxurious I was fearful that my friends who lived in five- and six-floor walk-ups would think I had sold out.

We were on the top floor of our six-story building and could climb to the roof for a view of the Village. The roof had no deck or railing, it was simply black tar paper, yet we took our friends or dates up there with drinks at night to see the lights of the city, feeling we owned it. We held our glasses out toward the city, chanting John Reed's purple poem that we parodied at the same time we felt its spell: "Who that has known thee but shall burn / In exile till he come again / To do thy bitter will, O stern / Moon of the tides of men!" We christened our new apartment "The Towers," the tag by which it was known for the next four years as new friends came and went, staying for weekends or weeks or a summer, joining the Village party that started half a century before.

If the gangly, offbeat genius John Rawlings might well have been voted my high school's Most Likely to Emigrate to Greenwich Village, my roommate Ted the Horse would surely be the last person anyone predicted to follow that route. He was not just a successful ladies' man and jock, but a natural leader (president of his high school class by a landslide) with a quick mind. Those who knew him in high school and at Wabash College in Indiana already were touting him as a future governor of the Hoosier state.

How did a guy like that get to Greenwich Village instead? By way of Japan.

The Horse was stationed there after serving in the Army in Korea, and like many young men of our generation who got a glimpse of Japanese culture for the first time, he began to question the assumptions of his own society, exchanging the memorized answers that brought approval at church and school for the *koans* posed by ancient masters that perhaps had no answers at all but whose contemplation might bring not simply knowledge but the ultimate prize, *satori*.

The enemies we defeated in World War II became the sages of youth in my generation, as the translated catchwords of their culture were not only spread by returning GIs like the Horse, but popularized by our principal literary seer, J. D. Salinger. His fictional Glass family of whiz kids added to the conversations at New York parties a question so popular it became a form of intellectual graffiti, which the Horse inscribed on the wall above our bathroom mirror on 10th Street: "What is the sound of one hand clapping?"

After his time in Japan, the Horse didn't want to settle down back home in Indiana; he didn't want to settle at all for the circumscribed, comfortable life laid out for him there, with the split-level home, the two-car garage, the 2.7 children, and the gold watch at retirement. He wanted to seek the answers to the big riddles, so he left the safe world behind and went to New York on the GI Bill to study at Columbia. He brought a batch of short stories he had started writing in Japan and got a job working on a live TV show (a "Max Liebman Special"), where he began to learn the skills that would enable him later to start his own film company. He explored the Village like a soldier on reconnaissance — questioning, searching, talking — and we ended up, when the bars closed at three in the morning, at Jim Atkins's hash house in Sheridan Square, wolfing down scrambled eggs and french fries. Downing the last of the steaming coffee, Ted the Horse would end the evening with the ritual question: "What is the sound of one hand clapping?"

Maybe Ivan Gold knew.

One of the writing stars of Columbia had just come back from Japan himself. He had stayed on after serving in Korea, to learn the Japanese language, tutor English, and continue the literary career he'd begun in college. He'd returned to his parents' apartment on the Lower East Side but soon moved to the Village. Even though it was just across town from the neighborhood where he grew up, the significance of leaving home and coming to the Village was as great for Ivan as it was for me and the Horse. I introduced Ivan to my roommate and they became friends.

My Columbia friends who were native New Yorkers were just as much exiles as my high school buddies from Indianapolis when they came to live in the Village. It was the same for Sam Astrachan from the Bronx, Sarel Eimerl from England, Meg Greenfield from Seattle, or anyone in the other shifting groups of friends who lived in that liberated zone below 14th Street. (That was the border; you didn't have to put on a tie or get dressed up unless you went north of it.) We made up only one of countless circles of young people with common interests and outlook, sharing the camaraderie of pioneers living where we did not by the accident of birth or marriage or corporate or military transfer, but by our own choice and declaration, as committed to it as Brigham Young when he said, "This is the place!"

I knew it for sure the day I looked up at the arch in Washington Square and for the first time read the words there. It was a quote from George Washington to his troops, but it seemed a slogan for those of us who had come to live in that neighborhood: "Let us raise a standard to which the wise and the honest can repair. The event is in the hands of God."

We all had a group identity (at least one, maybe more, some of them overlapping) within the larger identity of being Villagers. "I was part of a group of poets who lived in the Village and Brooklyn Heights," Harvey Shapiro recalls. "Jean Garrigue was *the* poet. I loved her poetry — we all did, and we all sort of gathered around her. There was May Swenson, Leslie Katz, Jane Mayhall, Ruth Hirshberger, and Arthur Gregor."

Calvin Trillin lived on Jane Street, and his own circle of friends had more of a journalistic bent: "I was part of a group of writers who played basketball at a court on Gansevoort Street. There was Victor Navasky, Christopher Lehmann-Haupt, Dick 'Swish' Lingeman — because he was from Indiana he was a good shot — and for a while LeRoi Jones played. We called the court the Field of Honor, and we had a banquet every year where we gave awards, like the Roy Cohn Award for the Most Improved Jewish Player."

Young mothers also had their own groups, with their own interests and outlook. "There were lots of mothers with children in the Village in the fifties," Mary Nichols says. "The group of mothers I was friends with used to sit in Washington Square Park and read Dostoevsky and sneer at what we called the Lamb Chop Set — they were also the Nylon Blouse Set — who lived on lower Fifth Avenue and were always talking about what they were going to have for dinner."

My friends and I wouldn't consider the Lamb Chop Set "real" Villagers, for they didn't share our bohemian outlook but simply liked the real estate. They were like our parents and friends back home, who didn't care about the same things we did.

The parents, friends, and neighbors we had left behind, whether on the Lower East Side or Indianapolis, in Mike Harrington's St. Louis or James Baldwin's Harlem, May Swenson's Utah or Robert Phelps's Ohio, were not really interested in trying to find out the answer to questions like "What is the sound of one hand clapping?" If asked, they'd probably tell you it was nothing at all. To us, it was everything.

Rejecting the answers we were given in childhood, turning our backs on our roots and religion, we searched in books and poems, on analysts' couches and lovers' beds, and most of all, inside those shrines of contemplation and conversation, our second homes any night we wished until three the next morning: the bars of the Village. Everyone had his or her favorite, but for writers, the one place where you could always find a friend, join a conversation, relax and feel you were part of a community was the White Horse.

TO THE TABLES AT THE WHITE HORSE

*"The birds did warble from every tree
The song they sang was old Ireland free"*

It was in the back room of the White Horse Tavern on Hudson Street that I learned and sang songs of Irish rebellion as if they were the anthems of my own and my friends' personal struggles. In a way they were, for I'd never been to Ireland and knew next to nothing of its history or politics except that it seemed to be in a continuous state of rebellion against oppression, and my friends and I identified with the Irish as underdogs battling the mighty British Empire. We regulars in the back room thought of ourselves as underdogs and rebels in Eisenhower's America, and so we lustily joined in the songs, sometimes led by the Clancy Brothers (they were real Irishmen and understood the whole thing), who made the White Horse their headquarters.

The Horse was like a social club or informal fraternity, and veterans took pride in telling something of the history of the place to novices. On one of my first visits a habitué volunteering as host showed me the table where Dylan Thomas, one of the legendary patrons, had his last drink (the shot that killed him?). My host then pointed out the window to St. Vincent's Hospital, up the street, and explained with hushed reverence that there the great Welsh poet was taken to die at age thirty-nine. The proximity of the tavern to the hospital seemed a real convenience, giving assurance to a newcomer that if he, too, were to drink himself to oblivion at one of these historic tables, an emergency room was not far away.

I was twenty-three at the time, and the whole thing seemed not only tragic but glamorous and wise, for life after forty sounded so far off as to seem superfluous, and most great poets died young anyway, didn't they? Whenever I could, I tried to get a seat at Dylan Thomas's "last table" and told the story to impress people new to the place, especially girls. Sometimes I took a date there and then back to my apartment to play her my Caedmon record of Thomas reciting his passionate poetry. As seductive as any record of Sinatra singing "In the Wee Small Hours" or even the sexy June Christy throatily crooning "Something Cool" was the poet himself telling us not to go gentle into that good night.

I always wondered how Thomas had discovered the White Horse in the first place, which before he came was mainly known as a long-shoremen's hangout and had no literary aura at all. An old-time Village friend told me the novelist David Markson, who wrote *Springer's Progress, The Ballad of Dingus Magee,* and *Wittgenstein's Mistress,* was the one who first brought the Welshman to the bar on Hudson Street, but Markson says it was the other way around — it was Thomas who took *him* to the White Horse.

"I was a graduate student at Columbia when Dylan Thomas gave a reading there in 1952," Markson remembers. "I went backstage because I wanted to see a real writer, up close and in the flesh. I don't know where I got the chutzpah, but I asked him if he wanted to have some drinks with a couple of would-be writers at the West End bar. He said he had to go to a party first, given by the critic William York Tyndall, who taught at Columbia, but he said, 'If you wait, I'll be out of there soon.' We didn't think he'd really come to drink with us, but he did.

"The next time I saw him I was supposed to meet him at a bar next door to the Chelsea Hotel, where he was staying, and he said, 'Let's go down to the White Horse.' I went there a number of times with him, and people would be sitting around staring at him — and then at me, wondering who the hell I was because I was with Dylan. People would be eight deep at the bar, all because Dylan Thomas was there."

John Malcolm Brinnin, the poet and teacher who escorted Thomas on his American reading tour and wrote about it in *Dylan Thomas in America,* says it was really the Scottish poet Ruthven Todd who introduced Thomas to the White Horse. Brinnin explains that "the British who came to New York liked the White Horse because it reminded them of a pub. Before Todd took Dylan to the Horse, I'd been trying to keep him in check, take him to places like the Blarney Stone, which wasn't all that interesting, didn't have a lot of people for him to talk to, but when he got to the White Horse it was all over."

Thomas's patronage of the White Horse is immortalized now on the bar's menu, which boasts, "Over 100 years old, the White Horse Tavern first found favor as the favorite watering hole of Welsh poet Dylan Thomas. (In fact, his final collapse came a few staggering steps from the front door.) The White Horse remains a fascinating collection of history, color, charm, and character . . ." There's a plaque on the wall now indicating the table where the poet had his last drink, but in the old days it was one of an insider's privileges to *know*, and reveal the sacred spot to newcomers.

The literary fame of the bar was enhanced soon after Thomas started drinking there, when one of the young novelists to emerge after World War II, Vance Bourjaily (*The End of My Life* was an influential novel of the period), organized a regular Sunday afternoon gathering of writers at the White Horse. One of them was Norman Mailer.

"The group didn't have a name," Mailer recalls, "but on any given Sunday we got together — probably twenty times or more. There was Vance, and me, Calder Willingham, John Aldridge, John Clellon Holmes, even Herman Wouk came a few times — he was the most successful author we knew. The only woman who was part of the group was Rosalind Drexler. She was a lady wrestler as well as a writer, and we were agog with the idea we had a woman wrestler in our group. It was like she was a creature from a carnival — we were scared stiff, knowing that if she wanted to she could throw any one of us across the room. She was bright, and she realized we'd come to gawk. In this quiet voice she told us we really didn't care about her writing, and she wasn't going to come anymore. The group finally petered out, I think because there were no themes, no literary discussion, no ongoing arguments. Vance was disappointed — he had more of the collegial spirit than I did."

The White Horse wasn't the only popular bar in the Village, of course. In those days people made the rounds, going to several bars for an evening's entertainment, but it seemed the Horse was on the route of everyone I knew, and usually served as the final stop, the high point of the evening.

Art d'Lugoff, who started the Village Gate nightclub, says, "I used to make the rounds of the bars — Julius's for those fat hamburgers on toast, then the San Remo, the Kettle of Fish, and the White Horse. Booze was a social thing. The bar scene wasn't just to get drunk. It was like the public square in a town or a sidewalk café in Paris — comradely meeting and talking."

The *Village Voice* columnist and reporter Mary Nichols also made the rounds. "When I still lived in East Harlem with the Swarthmore graduates in the el cheapo apartment, before I worked for the *Voice,* I took the El to the Village every night and went to the San Remo, where my friends hung out. We had a regular route, from the Remo to Minetta's to Louis' and then the White Horse."

David Amram, the musician who managed to cross comfortably between the worlds of writing and painting, frequented the Cedar Tavern. "I met de Kooning, Rivers, Kline, and Alfred Leslie there. The White Horse was all Dylan Thomas fans and people who liked writing. Also, I met the Clancy Brothers there and began playing Irish music, backing them up."

Ed Fancher, the cofounder and original publisher of the *Village Voice,* says, "There was a smaller bohemian world in the fifties — the writers were at the White Horse or the Remo, the artists were at the Cedar. There's nothing comparable today."

Most often when I went to the White Horse I was waved to a table by Mike Harrington, the author and activist who served as the informal host of an ongoing seminar on culture and politics, dispensing information and opinion interspersed with great anecdotes about left-wing labor leaders and colorful factional fights of political splinter groups that I could never keep straight, with exotic designations like Schactmanites, Sweezyites, Browderites, Musteites, and Cochranites, not to speak of Trotskyites, Socialist-Laborites, and "Yipsuls" (of the YPSL, or Young People's Socialist League).

The added charm and fascination of hearing all this radical political exotica from Mike Harrington was that in looks, voice, and manner he could have passed for an older version of Huck Finn, or even Jack Armstrong, the All-American Boy. This was the era in which McCarthyism had brought about the fear that anything left of the mainstream of politics or ideology was — that ugly word — un-American. But here was Mike, a lanky, straightforward guy with freckles, a boyish grin, and broomstraw hair, speaking in a strong Missouri twang, continuing in a time of conformity the great American tradition of questioning the status quo, caring about the underdog, challenging the powers that be. Had it not been for Mike's taking over the nearly moribund Socialist youth factions, forming the Young Socialist League in 1954 and leading with dignity and intelligence the Socialist movement in America until his death in 1989, it is hard to imagine that tradition surviving the fifties.

Mike lived and worked for a while at the Catholic Worker hospitality house, and the young idealists and intellectuals who were drawn to the place joined Mike's table at the Horse after the Friday night sessions on Chrystie Street. When he became the head of the YSL, the people who heard him speak and lead those meetings also followed him to the Horse.

One night Mike was engaged in a lively colloquy with a Yale professor named Robert Bone, who wrote for *Dissent* and shunned the Whiffenpoofs for the Clancy Brothers at the White Horse whenever he could escape New Haven. He and Mike were discussing the arcane factions of the Spanish civil war — as popular a topic here as the Irish rebellion — when they noticed that two young women none of us knew had appeared at the big table and seemed obviously in the dark.

It was not all that common for girls to show up at the Horse unless they were part of a group like the Catholic Worker or the YSL and knew the regulars, or were brought here on a date by a man; these young women were by themselves and new on the scene. Mike graciously asked what they did, and they said they were telephone operators. There was an uneasy silence as everyone tried to figure out how they happened to wander into this bar, and how we could make them feel at home, since attractive girls showing up in the back room was a happy and welcome event. What could they be told that would make them feel part of a discussion on the intricacies of the Spanish civil war? It was painfully clear the subject was about as familiar to them as nuclear physics.

Bob Bone suddenly brightened and broke the awkward silence: "Telephone operators! Why, telephone operators played a key role in the fighting in Barcelona during the Spanish civil war. Franco's troops were trying to cut off all communications, but the workers at the Barcelona telephone exchange kept the lines open in spite of being under attack." The men smiled with relief and approval, and the girls perked up, honored by this revelation of the noble behavior of their Catalonian sisters. Pints of arf 'n' arf were ordered for them, and soon the table broke into some song of Irish rebellion, which cut the tension altogether and allowed everyone to relax. (In the back room, after many pints of ale, the Irish rebellion and the Spanish civil war seemed to blend together in one grand battle of noble underdogs against tyrant oppressors, waged from the dawn of history, and any rousing song of freedom stood just as well for the brave lads of Spain or Ireland, either one — or for any of us who had left home to come to the Village.)

I was asked to write book reviews for *Commonweal,* the liberal Catholic magazine, when I drank with its editors in the back room of the Horse, where they sat at a table with Harrington or at one of their own, in a kind of continuous editorial meeting. I never knew exactly where the office of *Commonweal* was — somewhere downtown, I thought — but I considered the White Horse its true headquarters. It was there I met the editors Jim Finn, John Cogley, Wilfred "Bill" Sheed, and a friendly man described by the *Village Voice* writer Seymour Krim as "a tolerant and sympathetic book editor named Bill Clancy."

I could echo Krim's experience with Clancy, who, Krim said, "sensed I was not a native or orthodox critic but nevertheless brought out of me some of the best I could do because he had a taste for fullness of expression rather than the narrower, stricter conception of criticism then at its height." Krim felt that as a Jew, "even writing for a Roman Catholic magazine like *Commonweal* I literally had much more freedom of expression than in *Commentary.* . . . It took the life out of a young American-Jewish writer to do a piece for them."

As an unaffiliated WASP, I myself enjoyed a sense of freedom when I later began writing for both the Catholic and the Jewish magazines. The publication I would have felt stifled writing for in those days was the *Indianapolis Star!*

I'd been following the jazzy, electric prose of Seymour Krim in the *Voice;* he used his personal experience as material — often like raw wounds — to comment on the literature, culture, and politics of the time. Krim was an unsung father of what was later called the New Journalism, and his pieces from the fifties were collected at the end of the decade in *Views of a Nearsighted Cannoneer,* which had a real influence on other writers. He always worked out on the frontier of trends and lingo; he coined the term "radical chic" before Tom Wolfe made it famous, and his essay "Making It" preceded Podhoretz's book of that title. Krim's souped-up style was similar to Norman Mailer's nonfiction riffs, which were also appearing in the *Voice* in those days. In a foreword to *Cannoneer* Mailer wrote: "Krim in his odd honest garish sober grim surface is a child of our time. I think sometimes, as a matter of style, he is *the* child of our time, he is New York in the middle of the 20th century, a city man, his prose as brilliant upon occasion as the electronic beauty of our lights, his shifts and shatterings of mood as searching and true as the grinding wheels in a subway train. He has the guts of New York, old Krim."

I met Seymour Krim at the White Horse, in the most embarrassing "literary encounter" of my life, one that almost turned into a brawl. Surprisingly, for a bar of steadily drinking patrons, continually engaged in passionate discussions, there weren't many bad scenes, and only a few times I know of when fights were even threatened.

Murray Kempton had quoted something from Dostoevsky in his column in the *Post* that day, and I was holding forth on how great it was. Just as I was reaching a crescendo of praise, I heard a high, squeaky female voice screech from a few tables away: "I just can't *stand* Murray Kempton!"

When I heard the slur, a kind of calm, trancelike state came over me. I got up from my chair, took my nearly full pint, walked with deliberate steps to the table where the woman sat with several other people, raised my glass above her, and poured the contents over her head. As she screamed, I calmly walked back to my own table and took up the conversation as if nothing had happened. In my trance, I did not expect any further response. I somehow thought I had simply taken the only appropriate action called for under the circumstances.

I was surprised when two pairs of hands yanked me roughly from my seat. Two men who'd been sitting with the screecher had come to defend her honor. We started shouting at each other: "Why you goddam — who the hell do you think you are!" Then one of the men, a tall, intellectual-looking guy wearing horn-rims, grabbed me by the collar and said, "I know who you are, Wakefield. I've seen you around. I never thought you'd —" Now I grabbed his collar and demanded, "Who the hell are you?" When he told me he was Seymour Krim, I said, "No kidding? I read your stuff in the *Voice*," and he said, "Yeah? I read your stuff in *The Nation*." We were still gripping each other by the collar and snarling through our teeth. "Great piece you did on Bellevue," I said, and he said, "I dug the one you did on Kerouac," but everyone was watching and we couldn't release ourselves from our roles as ferocious antagonists. We both admitted later how relieved we were when a big waiter came over and broke us apart, which allowed us to sit down without losing face.

Krim became a friend in the Village whose work I read and enjoyed discussing over beers at the Horse, and over veal scaloppine at John's, a marvelous restaurant he introduced me to on East 10th Street. It was handy to Krim's dinky, book-erupting studio apartment on the same street where, to the everlasting amusement of his friends, he once entertained Paul Newman and Joanne Woodward by turning a couple of garbage cans upside down for them to sit on — the only seats in the place.

What Mailer described as Krim's "odd honest garish sober grim surface" was created in part by those thick black-rimmed glasses beneath a head of matted-down wavy black hair. He always seemed to be wearing the same black corduroy sport jacket with a thin tie, as if he were a hip diplomat of the literary fringe come to negotiate his ideas with you. Behind that formal surface was a healthy sense of humor that broke out in his prose as well as his conversation, in quirky, jazzy phrasings like the description of his friend Milton Klonsky, a legendary Village poet-genius of the forties, who Krim claimed had "an IQ that would stutter your butter."

I felt a bond with Krim because we had both known the urge and passion to write early on. He started publishing in high school — DeWitt Clinton in the Bronx — where he wrote for the school magazine, *The Magpie,* and coedited a more avant-garde mimeographed sheet called *expression* ("Man, were we swingingly lowercase back in 1939," he later said). We also shared a devotion to the Village, where Krim, a decade older than I, had moved in 1943 at age twenty-one, thrilled to find a "one-room bohemian fantasy on Cornelia Street." One of his literary heroes, James Agee, had lived on that street, and Krim as a high school student made a pilgrimage there to meet and interview him.

In an odd and unexpected way, Krim's love of the Village and his feeling for it as home saved him from a downward personal spiral that started in the summer of 1955, when he experienced what we called then a "crack-up" or "nervous breakdown." He describes in his unforgettable essay "The Insanity Bit" how he was handcuffed and taken to Bellevue, and sent from there to "a private laughing academy in Westchester," where he was given insulin shock treatments. A few months after his release he confessed to a psychologist a suicide attempt he'd planned but didn't carry out, and was dispatched "this time to another hedge-trimmed bin in Long Island," where "electric shock clubbed my good brain into needless unconsciousness" (as it did to some of the great Negro jazz musicians of the time, damaging or altogether destroying their ability, as in the case of Bud Powell).

When, after the battering of electric shock, the house psychiatrists battered at Krim's belief in his own powers of reason, intelligence, and talent — one of them wanted him to, Krim wrote, "accept my former life, which had produced some good work, as a lie to myself" — and tried to get him to "equate sanity with the current clichés of adjustment," he was almost, for the second time, "humbled, ashamed, willing to stand up before the class and repeat the middle-class credo of limited expressiveness." He might have been incarcerated for many more years, or come out so robbed of his beliefs that he wouldn't have written again, but the road to his recovery of confidence came when one of the house psychiatrists finally went too far. The shrink described Greenwich Village as a "psychotic community."

They might pin some label of nuttiness on *him*, but not the Village! When he heard that, he "saw with sudden clarity that *insanity* and *psychosis* can no longer be respected as meaningful definitions — but are used by limited individuals in positions of social power to describe ways of behaving and thinking that are alien, threatening, and *obscure* to them."

After that Krim wasn't taking any more. He argued for his "basic right to the insecurity of freedom," and with the help of a friend who "did the dirty infighting," got his release from the sanatorium. A year later he brought a woman psychiatrist friend to the San Remo, one of his favorite Village bars, and she told him with a straight face that it reminded her of "the admissions ward at Bellevue," where she had been an intern.

Krim felt the "incommunicable helplessness" of the gap between her and a well-known poet whom he'd had a drink with two weeks before at the Remo: "The poet was at home, or at least the heat was off there; while the psychiatrist felt alien and had made a contemptuous psycho-sociological generalization." Yet both the poet and the psychiatrist were "intelligent and honest human beings, each of whom contributed to my life."

To the benefit of all concerned — especially the fans of his work and the many writers, like myself, whom Krim gave so much help as a friend, editor, and reviewer — he remained at the Remo, the White Horse, and other such havens of the Village, never again to return to Bellevue.

> *"The birds did warble from every tree*
> *The song they sang was old Ireland free"*

If at Chumley's nostalgia-filled bar you saw book jackets and photographs of authors from the twenties, at the White Horse you saw in the flesh the writers of books you had read just a week or a year before. One night, through the haze of smoke in the back room, I recognized the face of an author I'd recently seen on a book, not on the back but filling the whole front cover.

What had struck me when I first saw the photo were the eyes. They were large and looked very wise, older than the face in which they were set. There was a sadness about them, but more than that, a power and strength that survived whatever blows — physical or psychic — had caused the deep shadows around them, giving them the bruised look of a fighter who'd been punched. It might, in fact, have been the face of a fighter, a young black man with a thin mustache who had boxed his way out of the ghetto. He had actually done just that, but with words rather than fists. I knew the name that was set in yellow letters across the top of the black-crowned head in the photograph: James Baldwin. His face stared up at me from the book of essays, *Notes of a Native Son,* on a rack of new paperbacks at the bookstore in Sheridan Square in 1958.

I picked up the book, flipped through the Autobiographical Notes at the beginning, and was as quickly transfixed by the writing as I had been by the eyes on the cover. The words, like the eyes, burned with a special intensity. Though I didn't spend money lightly on books, or on anything else in those days, and this was one of those large, expensive paperbacks priced at $1.25, I bought it and rushed back to my apartment to read it, alive with that heightened excitement of having discovered something so powerful I sensed it could change my own thinking and writing, my very life.

The direct simplicity of the prose, the radiant clarity of it, delivered a message I adopted as a creed. The final sentence of that blazing introduction was not about race relations or what was then called the Negro Question. It seemed to be about how I, as a young journalist aspiring to write novels, might try to conduct myself as a human being in a murderous and corrupting world: "I want to be an honest man and a good writer."

There was the author at the next table.

He was older than the face in the picture. The rather scraggly mustache was gone, and he looked more mature and self-assured. He was thirty-three at the time, and I was twenty-five, a gap that made him seem like a wise elder. His big, staring eyes were like a trademark, an appropriate symbol for the way his unrelenting gaze as a writer penetrated the walls and disguises of a whole social structure. The eyes seemed almost to protrude from his face in a look of unsparing inquiry. (Later, I was shocked to learn that as a child Baldwin had been told he was ugly, and believed it; I thought he was beautiful.) When he turned those eyes on me, I felt that he could see through me, into my mind, read my thoughts, and that I would never be able to avoid or even shade the truth in his presence.

One of the regulars introduced me. Jimmy, he was called, which surprised me. The diminutive didn't seem to suit his natural dignity, the way he held himself so straight, alert, giving his rather small frame a sense of the greater stature he had as a writer and as a man. There was an authority about him, not aggressiveness or pomposity but the earned authority of the Whitman line he quoted as the epigraph of *Giovanni's Room:* "I was the man, I suffered, I was there." You felt that authority in his prose, in the sureness of it, and in his own speech, so that his use of slang or idiom, which would have sounded pretentious or cute from anyone else, seemed right coming from Baldwin. He was the only man I've ever known who could call me "baby" without making me wince.

At the time I met him I was writing *Island in the City.* Baldwin had read some of my pieces in *The Nation* about the emerging civil rights struggle in the South, and he expressed an appreciative interest in my Spanish Harlem book, rather than the condescension or challenge that a black writer born in Harlem might well have presented to a white outsider presuming to report on that scene. He treated me not as an interloper but as a like-minded colleague, a fellow writer. In the same spirit, he also invited me to come by his apartment in the Village and have a drink some afternoon.

Baldwin lived on Horatio Street, in a high-ceilinged studio that was clean and sparsely furnished — all I remember is a couch and a hi-fi set, bare hardwood floors and tall windows. He always offered bourbon, my favorite drink at the time, and we would sip it with ice and talk about Harlem, the South, the racial madness, and politics, but mainly we talked about writing. After reading *Notes of a Native Son,* I had quickly devoured Baldwin's two published novels, *Go Tell It on the Mountain,* a powerhouse family drama of growing up black, and *Giovanni's Room,* about a middle-class American boy in Paris who discovers his homosexuality.

I showed Baldwin the pieces I was writing, and he read them and gave me encouragement, not always in an immediate way, with a "That's good" or "I like it," but sometimes in a later conversation on another subject, when his praise would surprise me. I went to him once full of enthusiasm for a book by John Reed I hadn't read before, praising Reed's prose and his compassion for the people he wrote about, and Baldwin turned those great eyes on me and said, "But that's *you.*"

Baldwin and I agreed in our literary preferences, and I loved hearing him extol the virtues of Henry James and deflate what he felt was the overblown literary reputation of the beat writers. He was especially disturbed by Kerouac's romantic portrayal of Negro life, and said once of such a passage in a Kerouac novel, raising his eyebrows with disdain, "He had better not read that from the stage of the Apollo Theater." Referring sardonically to their infatuation with Zen Buddhism and the teachings of D. T. Suzuki, Baldwin liked to refer to Ginsberg, Kerouac, and their followers as "the Suzuki Rhythm Boys."

Sometimes he passed on advice he had gotten from someone else and had adopted for himself. Once, he came back from giving a talk at Howard University extremely stirred by a conversation with a venerable Negro professor he admired on the faculty. The professor had told him always to keep in mind that the work of a writer was first of all to write — rather than to speak or picket or campaign for causes — and that his primary goal in life should be to end up with his own "shelf of books." Baldwin was constantly asked to lend his name and presence to civil rights and other causes he deeply believed in, and he was often torn by the question of how much time to devote to those endeavors. The counsel of the old Howard professor had seemed like a validation of his own wish to put writing first. In giving me the advice, he was reinforcing it for himself as he nodded, pointed a finger at my chest, and said, "Remember, baby. A shelf of books — a whole *shelf*."

Around five o'clock on those afternoons of our talks, the buzzer would sound and other friends would arrive. By eight a Village party of talk and music and drinking would be in full swing, and ended only when the host announced it was time for dinner. He would lead us across the street to El Faro, a Spanish restaurant, where he would commandeer a big table. Baldwin usually paid the bill with a personal check, and those who could afford it tossed in some money.

The talk was always good with Baldwin — he'd been a preacher as a teenager in Harlem, and he spoke in the cadence of biblical prose and with the clarity of a musical instrument, which matched the clarity of his writing. There was no more brilliant conversationalist, but the talk was not always intense and literary; it was often just fun. Baldwin had a delightful sense of humor and a joy that seemed to explode when his face cracked open in an enormous smile and hearty laughter. He could express mountainous irony with a slight upward shift of his eyes, as he did the night we were at a party and he excused himself to phone an editor who was trying to sign up his next book. "It seems I'm in a Madison Avenue price war," he explained, making that tilt of his eyes that spoke his disdain for the whole commercial literary machine.

When he told me the name of the editor he was calling, I winced and said I hoped he wouldn't sign with that man. He had done gratuitous harm to a friend of mine, and he didn't like me either. Baldwin beckoned me to the phone as he made the call and said to the editor, "Hello, this is Jimmy. I'm calling from a party in the Village. I'm here with my friend Dan Wakefield." He grinned, and I smiled back and raised my glass. It was a cold winter night and Baldwin was wearing one of those Russian-style fur hats — he had kept it on after we'd come inside — and he looked mischievous and happy, like a kid.

Unhappily, even in the Village Baldwin could not escape the reality of racial paranoia and hatred. One night he went to a bar down the street from the White Horse called the Paddock, where working people hung out, and sat drinking in a booth with Dick Bagley, the cameraman who shot *On the Bowery* and was one of the White Horse regulars, and two girls of their acquaintance. Some of the patrons were enraged at the sight of a white girl sitting next to a Negro, and they attacked Baldwin and Bagley, beating them brutally.

Baldwin later reminisced about that nightmare episode when he met up with Mike Harrington in Paris in 1963. Jimmy remembered squeezing himself into a ball under the bar as one of the men tried to kick him in the genitals. It was at that moment, Baldwin said, that he knew he would never be safe in white America.

Nor was it only blacks who experienced the violence of "neighbors" in the Village who regarded all bohemians as suspicious interlopers. The hostility toward all nonconformists was heightened during the McCarthy fervor of the fifties, when mostly Irish kids from the surrounding area made raids on the Horse, swinging fists and chairs, calling the regulars "Commies and faggots."

The White Horse was patronized by Irish longshoremen as well as bohemian writers and politicos, and one night Old Ernie, the owner, asked Mike Harrington if he couldn't have his friends sing their radical songs in French or German instead of English so the other customers wouldn't be able to understand the words and get upset.

Another night the Horse closed early, so Mike and his pals moved on to a bar around the corner. They were singing their labor songs when the trade union regulars who drank at the place took the sentiments the wrong way — and the White Horse guys were merely expressing their solidarity with the workers! When the union men threatened Mike and his friends, who they thought were Commies, the owner had to call the police, and the guys from the Horse escaped through the back door.

There was also a long history of hostility to the bohemians from the Italian residents, who made up the largest ethnic group of the Village. When Seymour Krim first moved to Cornelia Street with his girlfriend, he confessed that he was "scared of the Italian street-threat that used to psychically de-ball all us violin-souled Jewish boys who had fled downtown."

My Italian superintendent on Jones Street banged on my door one morning to yell at me for throwing a party for "beatniks" the previous night. I angrily shouted back that one of the guests was my minister friend from East Harlem, the *Reverend* Norman Eddy, and this quieted him down. What the super really hated me for was the doe-eyed girl he saw emerging from my place in the mornings. He had been her pal and protector when she had first moved in down the street, in another of his buildings, but he stopped speaking to her when he saw her coming from my place after spending the night.

In the ongoing war between the bohemians and beatniks and the locals — working-class Irish and Italians — sexual mores were often at the root of the hostility. As Mike Harrington observed in *Fragments of the Century,* when the neighborhood kids attacked the White Horse regulars as "faggots," the epithet expressed "their fury that we were always in the company of good-looking and liberated women while they drank in the patriotic virility of all-male groups."

The tension between bohemian beatniks and Italians had roots going back to the twenties, but in the fifties the conflict erupted politically when independent Democratic reformers in the Village battled Carmine De Sapio's Tammany Hall. I described it as a contest between "two different tribes" when I wrote about it for *Commentary.* The *New York Daily Mirror* called De Sapio's opposition "Village Commies, lefties, eggheads and beatniks." In fact, they were the first yuppies — a bunch of young lawyers and other professionals. One of their leaders was a young guy whom Mike Harrington judged at the time as "a diffident, somewhat lovable schlemiel" with a "retiring, modest manner." I also thought the man a nice, harmless nerd. His name was Ed Koch.

VILLAGE VOICES:
THE NEWSPAPER AND NORMAN

Brock Brower and Ann Montgomery each went to Europe after graduation from college (she to model for the Ford Agency, he on a Rhodes scholarship) and later met at the American Express office in Paris. They fell in love, got married, came to New York, and moved into a ground-floor apartment in the Village in 1956. Brock had just sold a verse play to *New World Writing* and was working as a first reader at the Viking Press, and Ann had a job in subsidiary rights at Farrar, Straus. "We became avid readers of the *Village Voice*," Brock says. "It defined the place for us."

It served that role for many residents of the Village from the time of its first appearance in 1955, and also for readers all over the country who, if they weren't lucky enough (or gutsy enough) to live there, could get a sense of it, a feel for it, in the pages of the *Voice*.

One of the powerful attractions of the new weekly newspaper for readers like this young Village couple was Norman Mailer's column. "My God!" Brock Brower says, some thirty-five years later. "My father had given me a copy of *The Naked and the Dead* as a Christmas present when I was sixteen, with the inscription, 'The opinions expressed by the author are not necessarily those of your father.' I loved it. And then we went to a party in the Village and Mailer was actually there, on view."

"He was cute and friendly," Ann remembers. Apparently, it was one of Mailer's better nights.

Mailer's fellow *Voice* columnist Mary Nichols says, "I liked the controversy Mailer stirred up at the *Voice*. I kept running into him there, of course. At the annual Christmas party he would always get drunk and punch somebody out. It was inevitable, part of the holiday ritual."

Mailer was part of the Village in the fifties and part of the *Voice*, helping define them both, even though he resigned from writing his column, some six months after it began, when his running disagreements with the editors came to a head over a typo: "nuisances" instead of "nuances." The column in which the typo appeared led to one of his most provocative and fruitful subjects, hip versus square, and the later publication of his controversial essay "The White Negro" in *Dissent*.

Even though he wasn't writing his column anymore, Mailer was still a presence in the pages of the *Voice* — he still wrote for the paper from time to time, and the paper always seemed to be writing about him — and in the Village. He was admired, attacked, scorned, loved, hated, lusted after.

When Millicent Brower, a witty and talented Villager who wrote for the *Voice*, did articles on "The Greenwich Village Girl" and "Those Village Men," based on interviews with the natives, there were comments in each about Norman Mailer. A man identified as "C.D., 40, advertising, Bleecker Street," said, "What I'm looking forward to is the return of the Bloomer Girl — all carrying hockey sticks to protect themselves from Norman Mailer." A woman from West 16th Street wrote to divide the "species" of Greenwich Village males into four categories, including "4. The Genius. You've got dozens of him working on your paper. Norman Mailer is not one of them. He's in category 2 [The Promising Young Man]."

Mailer, it seemed, was everywhere. Seymour Krim would later write a piece called "Ubiquitous Mailer and Monolithic Me," complaining he couldn't escape the shadow and presence and symbol of Mailer because of "his aggressive ubiquitousness in the literary-sexual-intellectual avant-garde."

To say Mailer invited controversy would be putting it mildly. He demanded it. In his first appearance in the *Voice*, under the heading "Quickly, a Column for Slow Readers," Mailer began by jabbing his audience: "Given your general animus to those more talented than yourselves, the only way I see myself becoming one of the cherished traditions of the Village is to be actively disliked each week."

He cast himself in the role of devil's advocate, which he advertised in case anyone missed it. In a column urging the Democrats to draft Ernest Hemingway for president in 1956, Mailer added a postscript: "One advantage of being a Village villain is that one is always certain of influencing events by arguing the opposite of what one really wants."

Still, this was a villain whom people sought out and befriended. Dan Wolf met him "at a party given by Jean Malaquais, whose course in modern literature I was taking at the New School." The New School for Social Research, in the Village, had the hottest faculty around when Dan went there after World War II on the GI Bill: Erich Fromm and Karen Horney taught psychology, Max Lerner taught American studies. Malaquais was a French intellectual whom Norman Mailer had met in Paris in 1948, after Malaquais translated *The Naked and the Dead*. Mailer dedicated *Barbary Shore* to Malaquais, and says of him now, "If I had any mentor, Malaquais would have been it. He's the most brilliant man I ever knew."

Malaquais invited a few of his students, including Dan Wolf, to the party at his house in Brooklyn Heights, and Mailer brought his first wife, Bea. "Of course I'd read *The Naked and the Dead*," Wolf says. "Mailer was then the most famous young American writer, though not yet the most colorful.

"We got to be close friends, and he wanted to come and live in Manhattan, so he found an apartment next to mine on First Avenue between 2nd and 3rd streets. My apartment was $16 a month, but Norman was affluent, so he could afford *two* cold-water flats, front to back. The flats went from street to rear and looked out on a wonderful old cemetery. It was the best view in New York.

"Mailer wanted to meet more bohemian types. There were still people left over from old bohemian days, and young people who'd been in the war, who saw the Village as an extension or a successor to Paris. The young people who came after the vets were not as literary as the older ones. And then came the beats, who were even less so."

Wolf's best friends at the time were Mailer and a fellow student at the New School who was studying psychology, Ed Fancher: "One day I said to Ed, 'The Village ought to have its own newspaper — we should start it.' He said, 'I'll think about it and let you know tomorrow.' I was surprised. I thought he'd just say yes, let's do it. But he did say yes the next day. That was the beginning. Then I went to Mailer, and without hesitation he said, 'Absolutely.' He put some of his own money in."

Ed Fancher, who became publisher of the *Voice* when Dan Wolf became editor, is a psychologist who practices Freudian analysis in the Village, where he still lives. "We needed money desperately," he recalls. "I borrowed $5,000 from the bank, put up a little stock I had, and my father guaranteed the stock. Mailer was one of the few people we knew who had money. He put up $5,000, so we launched a newspaper. We figured we'd break even by Christmas. That's how crazy we were — we just rented an office and thought it would work. When the *Voice* found itself in financial trouble, Mailer said, 'Let's go out with a bang. Let's have the most outrageous paper imaginable.' We just wanted to save the paper. Mailer thought we were too stodgy and middle class. Well, we were by today's standards, but that was thirty-five years ago."

Mailer was, as always, ahead of his time.

Harvey Shapiro, the first advertising manager and the poetry editor of the *Voice*, remembers his shock when Mailer bought a half-page advertisement in the paper in order to quote some of the worst reviews of *The Deer Park*. Under the heading "*The Deer Park* is getting nothing but RAVES" were pans from papers around the country: "sordid and crummy" (*Chicago Sun-Times*); "the year's worst snake pit in fiction" (*Cleveland News*); and "moronic mindlessness" (*New York Herald Tribune*).

"I knew Mailer and I saw him around the *Voice* at that time," Harvey says. "He was even delivering papers on occasion. One night we left the office together after he'd bought that ad, and I remember standing on a street corner with him and saying, 'Norman, writers don't act this way. It's not the dignified thing to do, it can only hurt you.' But I was wrong. Everything changed — and Mailer changed it!" Harvey shakes his head and says with a smile, "I was very fifties in the fifties."

So was I. I admired *The Deer Park* because, unlike Mailer's other work, it was controlled, honed, and spare — the opposite of the style of prose and life for which he was becoming famous. I couldn't share the blanket enthusiasm of Brock Brower, who admired Mailer so much he went on to write a major profile of him for *Life* magazine. Norman wasn't pleased with the piece, though, and shot off a telegram from Provincetown that included an offer Brower could and did refuse: "If you have any honor, come up this weekend, and bring your dear wife Ann for protection."

I didn't know Mailer personally, though I used to see him at those *Village Voice* parties and talked to him a few times at big social events over the years. As long as I was speaking with him one-on-one, Mailer was a gracious, pleasant, fascinating conversationalist, but as soon as a group of people gathered around to listen, his voice tended to rise, and his manner and opinions became more brash and pugnacious. Krim had a similar experience, finding that conversation with Mailer "immediately changed when we met in a group or anywhere in public where there were more than just the two of us; when that happened he assumed (and I didn't contest it) the central role. . . . There was usually a turning point in my presence (around the third drink?) when the showboat cowboy in Mailer would start to ride high, bucking and broncking."

That was long ago, however, and those who know him say Mailer has mellowed. His longtime debating foe and personal friend William F. Buckley tells me, "I knew Norman in his bellicose years. He's become quite avuncular now."

Mailer has agreed to talk with me about the fifties and suggests we meet at El Taquito, a small and funky Mexican restaurant on West 44th Street, convenient to the Actors' Studio, where he's been involved since the fifties and is now on the board of directors.

Over lunch he tells me about the old writers' group Vance Bourjaily started at the White Horse, and adds that "the *Voice* was more significant than anything else at the time in giving a sense of community to writers, but that first couple of years I felt its positions were not adventurous enough, then I left and that improved. Sometimes you get what you want by no longer being there — your ghost gets you farther than if you were still around.

"The *Voice* changed the nature of American journalism. People like Pete Hamill came out of it, and James Wolcott. Of course, Jimmy Breslin was an enormous influence on journalism too. Breslin and the *Voice* were big influences of the time."

When I remind him of Harvey Shapiro's cautioning him about the ad for *The Deer Park* in the *Voice*, Mailer says, "I realized when the book was turned down by Stanley Rinehart that the literary world was being run for the convenience of publishers and book reviewers. As a writer you were supposed to be a nice little boy, but that was good for them, not us. They told us it was a gentlemen's occupation, so we had to be nice. Well, I had the feeling of not looking back. I wrote a line once: 'Like a true killer, he never looked back.' In fact, I was killing part of my attitude, part of my slave mentality. It was analogous to Black Power — they wanted us to be nice and agreeable, which was nice for them, not for us. This later happened with Black Power and then the feminist movement. The end of the fifties represented 'more news to follow.' "

I tell Mailer that *The Deer Park* had been called "the most controversial novel of 1955," and Mailer smiles and says, "Isn't that unbelievable? Compare it now to *American Psycho*. Anything that dealt openly with sex was controversial back then. The issue of sex was the cutting edge of the new novel of exploration in the fifties. It was the way of going beyond the frontier."

I hadn't realized until recently that *The Deer Park* was turned down not only by Rinehart but also by Random House, Knopf, Scribner's, Harper & Row, Simon & Schuster, and Harcourt, Brace — before being bought by Putnam. Walter Minton, who was advertising manager as well as the son of the ailing president of the company, and a great fan of *The Naked and the Dead,* was responsible for taking on the novel. He paid its author the biggest advance in the firm's history, $10,000. Minton's instinct was justified when the novel sold more than fifty thousand copies in hardcover and rose to number six on the *New York Times* best-seller list.

Most novelists who had written a best seller, had their second book panned (as *Barbary Shore* was), and their third book rejected by seven publishers would have thrown in the towel, or thrown themselves off a cliff. Mailer dug in. He began writing the new personal journalism that brought him notoriety and a pair of Pulitzer prizes (*The Armies of the Night* and *The Executioner's Song*), and became the most famous writer in America.

And he did it alone. "I've always been a solitary, never found myself in groups," Mailer says. "I've felt it's bad practice for your work to join a group — what you gain in companionship you lose in the power to think independently. We were all finding our way in the fifties, and the Kerouac people acted as mentors for each other — there was a gang. Kerouac had Ginsberg, and Ginsberg had Kerouac and Burroughs. I was not part of that."

After lunch Mailer turns to go back to the Actors' Studio, and I see that he limps a little. He is wearing a short-sleeved shirt with gray stripes that hangs out over khaki pants. His hair is nearly white, and he has a bit of a spare tire. He seems small and vulnerable, but there is still that jauntiness about him. Seeing him go, what I think of is not the bluster or rhetoric I sometimes associate with him, but a gentler, more private side I learned about from Marion Magid.

"He's a tremendously sexy man," Marion has told me. "I'm part of the generation that had a crush on Mailer — like JFK in a way. He's fascinating in spite of everything. There's a deep sweetness in him, sort of like Sinatra — you love him anyway in spite of all the awful things he may have done. Once I was in a cab with Mailer, on the way back from a party at Norman Podhoretz's house. I told him I was getting married, and he started giving me advice, in a very nice way. He said, 'When one is married one fights. Be sure you fight for the right reasons and on the right ground.' There was a brotherly sweetness about him, and a kind of wisdom."

After lunch with Mailer I find myself taking the IRT down to Sheridan Square. Even though I'm staying on West 96th Street I keep gravitating back to the Village, especially after I've talked about the old days. I just go and walk around, or stop at the Peacock on Greenwich Avenue and have cappuccino. This is where I feel most at ease in New York. For seven years it was my home, and I felt surrounded by friends, some of whom were more than that, were more like family, the kind I chose and was chosen by rather than born with.

FAMILY

Shortly after I got to know him, I began to call Robert Phelps "Uncle Bobby." I met him at Yaddo, the writers' and artists' colony, where I'd gone in the summer of 1959 to try to start a novel. I didn't return to the Village with the beginning of a book, as I had hoped, but with something less tangible and in the long run more valuable: the beginning of my friendship with Phelps. Without it, I wonder if I would have survived the next half decade.

Robert was a boyish-looking man in his mid-thirties when I met him, usually dressed neatly but casually in corduroys, loafers, and a sweater or sweatshirt. Sometimes, to go to an office uptown, he would wrap himself in a sport coat and tie, but he always looked unnaturally confined in such a getup, like a kid who was forced to dress for Sunday school. With his curly, tousled hair and easy smile, Robert reminded me of a late-blooming graduate student. "He was young, and so he would be forever," his friend the novelist James Salter said in tribute many years later.

Robert had written a novel called *Heroes and Orators,* which Leslie Fiedler later praised as one of the unjustly neglected books of the fifties. I had never heard of it before I met Robert, and did not in fact learn about it from him but from another of his friends and admirers, Martha Murphy (now Martha Duffy, a senior editor of *Time*), who worked then at McDowell, Obolensky, the publisher of the book. She mailed me a copy with her own warm recommendation of it, as well as of its author, when I went to Yaddo. When I told Robert that our mutual friend Martha had sent me *Heroes and Orators,* he winced and waved his hands around in one of his typical gestures of impatient dismissal, saying, "Oh, that old novel. Never mind *that.*"

Robert later told me he'd had trouble writing the book, and the only way he got himself to finish it was to make a deal with David McDowell, the editor and publisher, to send him a chapter every month in return for a payment. When he finished the book, Robert was still dissatisfied. He wanted to take the manuscript back and rewrite it, but McDowell convinced him to go ahead and have it published — knowing, I suspect, that Robert would have spent the rest of his life rewriting and never been satisfied. In fact, it was the only novel Robert published. I'm sure its story of a young husband who discovers his homosexuality in a love affair with a handsome young man was simply too taboo for the time, especially as a first novel by an unknown writer. (Gore Vidal and James Baldwin had already established themselves as serious authors when they published their novels with homosexual themes — *The City and the Pillar* and *Giovanni's Room,* respectively.)

Robert was genuinely modest about his accomplishments, and again it was from someone else I learned that he had founded Grove Press, which became the most important avant-garde publisher in America. After publishing three books, Robert had sold the company to the son of a wealthy banker from Chicago, Barney Rosset.

Robert was no businessman, and couldn't tolerate the nine-to-five routine of office work, but in a part-time, free-lance (and very underpaid) way he was one of the most important editors of his time. He worked in this part-time manner for George Braziller as well as for McDowell, Obolensky, where his literary instincts contributed to the success of James Agee's posthumous novel, *A Death in the Family,* which won the Pulitzer Prize in fiction. It had been Robert's inspired idea to set at the beginning of the book a poetic essay of Agee's called "Knoxville, Summer, 1915." That lyrical piece established the mood and spirit of the story to come in such a stunning way that it really put the whole work on a different plane, a more universal level of experience.

Later Robert edited the *Letters of James Agee to Father Flye* (Agee's former teacher, mentor, and friend), edited the criticism of poet Louise Bogan, and encouraged the composer Ned Rorem to publish his diaries. His final piece of work was a longtime labor of love, editing the journals of Glenway Wescott, a literary light of the 1920s.

Robert became known as an expert on Colette and Cocteau, and would ingeniously piece together a marvelous "autobiography" of Colette from her own works called *Earthly Delights.* Pictures of Colette, Gertrude Stein, James Agee, and other writers crowded his walls like family portraits, as books and notebooks, clippings and diaries, swelled from desk and shelves in his Village apartments, first on West 13th and then on East 12th Street. Each place he lived in became a warm and cozy nest of literary treasures, the principal one being Robert himself.

"Oh, no one can do it like Scott Fitzgerald," he'd say. "The way that man could write, my God, he's like a, a" — Robert's face would burst into a smile of delight as he imagined the analogy — "like a *water spider*." And he'd fling his hands up, the fingers moving, tracing patterns in the air, demonstrating the delicacy of the prose he was describing.

He loved graceful language: "Oh, Dan'l, I'm afraid if I have any talent at writing at all it's a very *wooden* talent," he said with a slight wringing of his hands in dismissal. Sometimes he spoke of a novel he was working on and then would put aside, never to complete or publish it. I'm sure it was because his own standards were so high. He told me titles — *Available Light, The Silent Partner* — speaking of them as fondly as if they were the names of lovers, lovers perhaps so impossibly perfect as to finally be unattainable.

What most annoyed Robert and stirred his ire was generalization of any kind, prose as pronouncement, political hyperbole. He had no patience for politics, I think in part because its language was so purposely imprecise, and also because to him the subject was simply boring compared to literature; it had no beauty, no truth.

One of the times I saw Robert most angrily exercised was when we walked down West 4th Street talking about a recent *Partisan Review* article on taste in America, called "Masscult and Midcult," by Dwight Macdonald. It typified to Robert what he considered the grievous sins of sociological generalization. "Why can't that man tell me something *real*?" he moaned, waving his arms about in frustration. "Why can't he say —" Here Robert stopped, tapped himself vehemently on the chest, and declared, "I'm a middle-aged man and I can't sew a button on my shirt!"

That was specific, that was real, that was literature.

That's why Robert loved diaries, the kind of writing in which people recorded specific scenes, talk, impressions, dreams, desires. That's why he encouraged Rorem to publish his diaries, which became notorious as well as widely praised and read.

Friends flocked to Robert not only for literary advice and counsel but for personal aid and comfort. He was a kind of unassuming and unintentional guru whose wisdom and warmth drew people to him instinctively. When I introduced Robert to my friend Helen Weaver, she told me after that first meeting, "I want to take him home and put him on my mantle, like a household god."

One morning I rushed over to Robert's apartment and found

that he wasn't there at the moment, but met his wife, Rosemarie Beck, a painter who had come down from Woodstock, where she was living at the time. I introduced myself and said I was looking for Robert. Becky was a tall, striking woman with natural dignity and a straightforward manner that went directly to the point.

"Are you in trouble?" she asked me.

"How did you know?"

"People always come to Robert when they're in trouble," she said.

Yes, the instinct was automatic. I went to him for advice on everything from love to publishing. It was to Robert I turned in the most desperate of times, when toward the end of my long and dispiriting psychoanalysis, I found myself lying on the floor of the analyst's office in such a state of devastation I didn't think I could get out the door by myself, much less go home. The analyst asked me if I had a friend who would retrieve me. I gave him Robert's phone number, and he came right away.

"Look what you've done to him!" he said to the doctor in a white rage, pointing at me as I lay collapsed on the floor.

It was Robert Phelps, the writer, rather than my M.D. psychoanalyst, member of the New York Psychoanalytic Association, who took the responsibility for my life at that moment and got me safely home. Other friends in the Village also literally saved my life by staying with me through the nightmare ride of hallucinatory hell at the end of the analysis. (It was not alcoholic hallucination but an unleashing of the unconscious like a bad acid trip, and like an LSD experience, the hallucinations returned sometimes in flashes for years afterward, during periods of not using any alcoholic or chemical substances.) Ivan Gold and Robert and Alice Stewart and Jane Wylie would sit with me until dawn, holding and soothing me, giving me shelter, psychic as well as physical, seeing me through. Like my friend Seymour Krim, I found the people of the Village more sane and responsible than the professional psychoanalysts who told me only to go on talking and then put me out the door.

Robert saw me through less desperate hours as well, dispensing good advice and sometimes, at my urging, looking up planetary influences on the astrological chart he made for me. He was the first amateur astrologer I knew, and he mixed in the lore of signs and stars with his already perceptive insights into people and their mysterious behavior, which never ceased to fascinate him.

At heart Uncle Bobby was more practical than mystical, though, and in times of crisis his advice was admirably down-to-earth. When I went to him one day worried about my ability to meet an important magazine deadline after a drinking binge that left me weak, depressed, and with a mammoth hangover, he said, "Now, Dan'l, the first thing you want to do is get some decent food in you. Make yourself some scrambled eggs, soft scrambled eggs. Use lots of butter and milk, stir them *gently* . . ." He had a way of making everything, from the simplest cooking to the most intricate theories of fiction and poetry, sound intriguing, alluring. As I left with his instructions that day, both culinary and literary, Robert put a hand on my shoulder and repeated, "Gently, Dan'l. Treat yourself gently."

I thought of Robert and his words of advice long after I left the Village, waking on mornings many years later with pounding headaches and overall angst in Boston or Los Angeles or Iowa City, comforted by the memory of Robert's voice saying, *"Gently,* Dan'l . . ." I could not have been born with a better uncle.

Writers I knew in the Village didn't take vacations. That was for rich people who went to their summer houses or exotic islands, or for the folks back home in the Midwest, fishing trips with Mom and Dad in a rowboat under a hot sun on some anonymous lake — "drowning worms," as we used to call it in Indiana. Besides, the whole middle-class idea of "getting away from it all" was irrelevant if you were where you wanted to be in the first place — the Village. Everyone I knew went or wanted to go to Europe at some time or other, but that was not considered a vacation; it was part of one's work and life. Going to Paris and Spain was a holy pilgrimage, not tourism.

A vacation simply for the sake of recreation was not in our vocabulary, but it was all right to go on some literary mission: a stay at a writers' colony like Yaddo in Saratoga Springs, New York, or the MacDowell Colony in Peterborough, New Hampshire. It was also acceptable to go to the Bread Loaf Writers' Conference, in Middlebury, Vermont, and in 1958 I went there as a winner of the Bernard DeVoto fellowship.

Among my distinguished fellows at Bread Loaf were two women writers who became good friends when I returned to New York. May Swenson was a poet who lived a few blocks away from me on Perry Street, and the novelist Jane Mayhall lived with her husband, Leslie Katz, in Brooklyn Heights, which I thought of as a suburb of Greenwich Village, a quiet bedroom community where writers lived in reasonably priced apartments near a pleasant boardwalk with a view of the water.

May worked part-time as an editor at New Directions, another avant-garde publisher in the Village. She was from Logan, Utah, and she had a plain, straightforward western manner, speaking in a flat, spare voice almost without accent, sometimes punctuated by a smoker's hack and a raspy laugh. Her face was open, framed by short, straight brown hair with bangs, set with powerful, unflinching eyes. She was the only person I've ever met who made gum chewing seem a serious endeavor, a way of intensifying her concentration, which was focused on whatever you were saying — maybe even what you were thinking. The way that May looked at you, she seemed to be looking *into* you as well, not because she was prying but because she cared what was there. She was interested in truth, the truth of poetry, the kind she expressed in her work, which made her one of the most accomplished and influential poets of her time.

Though May's poetry was timeless, dealing with the age-old themes and questions, she also absorbed and articulated in her poems the special ethos of the place and time she was living in, New York in the fifties. I can think of no other poem that so eloquently put the questions that absorbed me and the people I knew then and there as "The Key to Everything."

So deeply did it go to the heart of our searches that I used to read it to girls I'd just met, when I brought them up to my apartment for the first time, attempting to establish intimacy with music (Miles Davis or the Modern Jazz Quartet in the background), booze (bourbon with ice and water, or Chianti out of the wicker-bound bottle), and poetry. "The Key to Everything" asked what all men and women seemed to be asking one another then, in the hope born of the Freudian promise of transformation:

Is there anything I can do
or has everything been done
or do
you prefer somebody else to do
it or don't
you trust me to do
it right or is it hopeless and no one can do
a thing or do
you suppose I don't
really want to do
it and am just saying that or don't
you hear me at all or what?

It was the new love poem of the postwar world, the fifties revision of the innocent, romantic verse of Edna St. Vincent Millay. May's poem "Mortal Surge" was like an eloquent primal scream, predating Allen Ginsberg's "Howl" and making that more famous poem seem to me journalistic in comparison. My own "howl" was best expressed by May's poem that opened with a recitation of exact inner feelings that articulated my own. The lines went through my mind as I walked the Village streets to meet a girl or an editor, hoping for love or publication: "We are eager / We pant / We whine like whips cutting the air."

I also saw reflected in May's verse the "unpoetic," real details of life in the city, as when in "Snow in New York" she reported, "I went to Rikers to blow my nose / in a napkin and drink coffee for its steam." Her words showed me better the pictures I saw every day. In "The Garden at St. John's," a church near where she lived in the Village, she imagines the rector's wife walking with her baby in that garden "of succulent green in the broil of the city," and sees in the sky "the surgical gleam of an airplane . . . ripping its way through the denim air." When I looked up from Village streets and saw an airplane, those lines would run through my mind like the words of a song. May knew I appreciated her poetry, and she not only admired my journalism but encouraged my fiction at a time before any of it was published. She was one of the few people I trusted enough to show the short stories I was writing, in between my articles for *The Nation,* and my first abortive attempt at a novel.

Sometimes I went to May's apartment for dinner, and other times I stopped by for coffee or a drink. She also invited me to parties on Perry Street — she threw the kind of Village parties that featured good talk with other good writers. Usually I saw there her friends Jane Mayhall, the novelist from Louisville (author of the now nearly unknown, brilliant coming-of-age novel *Cousin to Human*) who had gone to Black Mountain College, where she met her husband, Leslie Katz, the writer, art critic, and art collector from Baltimore who founded the Eakins Press. At May's I also met the poet and editor Harvey Shapiro, who later became editor of *The New York Times Book Review;* the art critic Hilton Kramer, now editor of *The New Criterion;* and the art writer and editor Elizabeth Pollet, ex-wife of the poet Delmore Schwartz.

During the years I knew May, she lived with a woman who was not just a roommate but a mate. I did not question this arrangement, nor did anyone I knew, nor did she speak of it directly, or need to do so. It was perfectly natural because it was May, and there was nothing about her that was not of the greatest dignity and integrity, from her poetry to her work as an editor to her personal life.

This was before "gay" had any other meaning besides "happy," and homosexual rights were not a political issue, perhaps because such rights weren't acknowledged or accepted in society at large but were part of the unspoken, understood freedom of the Village; that was one of the reasons I loved it. Though "straight" myself, I felt like a misfit in the middle America of the fifties, where even ideas that didn't conform to the mainstream were regarded as "queer." In the Village, people were free to think what they wanted and be who they were, without condemnation or suspicion by what was called "polite society." The term seemed especially ironic to me; by literal definition it should have been "rude society," since it meant the intrusive kind that probed with disapproval into people's private lives and opinions, from sexual to political.

I didn't think of May in terms of her sexual preference but simply as a poet, which was her most basic identity. (By the same token, it occurs to me that I never thought of Richard Wilbur primarily as a "married man," or of Anne Sexton as a "married woman" or "mother," but as poets — the rest was incidental, and not even relevant to their poetry.) Beyond that, I thought of May personally as an older sister, an idea that took specific form when her mate told me once that I reminded May of her younger brother, and said that was one of the reasons she felt especially close to me. I remember her friend's warm smile when she told me this, knowing, I think, that she was giving me the information as a gift. I received it as such and was proud.

There's a family feeling to the recollections of other Villagers of my time, a sense of closeness with neighbors and friends and even business people that comes from the feeling you are part of a common enterprise, a shared vision of the value of art and literature, of music and drama, of individuality and personal freedom.

Art d'Lugoff was one of the first advertisers in the *Village Voice* when he took out an ad for the first concert he put on, a midnight show in November 1955 (he was able to rent the theater at that hour for $25): "Art d'Lugoff presents Pete Seeger at the Circle in the Square."

"We had to turn people away," Art says, and he recalls the help he got from Lorraine Hansberry, the gifted black playwright whose drama *A Raisin in the Sun* would become a hit on Broadway starring Sidney Poitier. "Lorraine wrote my first leaflets, typed them up, and took them around to coffeehouses. I got to know her husband, Bob Nemiroff, at NYU. They became close friends of mine, and I worked with her at her in-laws' restaurant — called Potpourri, on Washington Place — now it's a hair salon. Lorraine and I waited and bused tables. Later she wrote *The Sign in Sidney Brustein's Window,* based on me — at least she told me I was part of a composite of the character. It was quite a thrill."

Art remembers that "Lorraine used to come to the Gate to hear Nina Simone. Those were interesting days." I went to the Village Gate myself to hear Nina Simone, and I met Lorraine Hansberry after sending her a fan letter. Some critic had attacked *A Raisin in the Sun* as being "propaganda," and it made me angry. I wrote to Hansberry saying I had learned in Lionel Trilling's class that "all art is propaganda," but in the best sense — of propagating values. I said her play was "propaganda for humanity and survival."

She called me up to thank me, and invited me to meet her and her husband, Bob Nemeroff, at the Limelight in Sheridan Square. I don't remember the words we spoke over our cappuccinos, but I remember the intensity of them, the sense of commitment and camaraderie, the feeling that we were part of the same grand effort of art and language to communicate, to break down barriers, to make people see one another as individuals, as we did in the Village, our home, where the arch above Washington Square said, "Let us raise a standard to which the wise and the honest can repair . . ."

May Swenson and Robert Phelps both died a few years back, and Lorraine died even earlier, when she was only in her thirties. Bob Nemiroff lovingly carried on her work by piecing together from her writing the play *To Be Young, Gifted, and Black,* which is performed all over the world. Just recently I read Bob's obit as well.

Mike Harrington thought the Village we knew — the last of the old bohemia — ended "the night a gawky kid named Bob Dylan showed up at the Horse in a floppy hat." Mike heard Dylan give an impromptu concert at McGowan's restaurant, at the urging of his journalistic champion, Robert Shelton of the *New York Times.* Mike said, "I heard the future and I didn't like it" (though he later gave a nod to Dylan's genius when he heard "Blowin' in the Wind").

In a way, Bob Dylan marked the dividing line between our generation and the one to come, though as Mike Harrington pointed out, Allen Ginsberg sounded the change earlier with "Howl," and Mike quoted Irving Howe's definition of the new sensibility as one that is impatient with coherence and wants literature to be "as unarguable as orgasm and as delicious as a lollipop."

Dylan represented the new "stutter style," as Harrington dubbed it, and Art d'Lugoff turned him down for a gig at the Village Gate: "Dylan auditioned for me, tried to interest me in his music. He was so influenced by Woody Guthrie — he didn't have much beyond that then. When he started writing his own songs he got interesting, but when he started out, my interest wasn't piqued."

Nat Hentoff says, "My wife and I used to see Dylan around the Village. She was captivated by him — not his music, but the way he looked, with that cap and all. I didn't take him seriously until Robert Shelton wrote about him in the *Times.* Then I did a profile of him in *The New Yorker,* and he told me he had run away from home when he was thirteen or fourteen to join a band, but after the piece came out I learned it never happened. He lied to me."

Maybe the Village of my generation went from the time Dylan Thomas came to the White Horse to the time Bob Dylan showed up that night in 1961 wearing his floppy hat. Maybe from the time of Floyd Dell and Edna Millay up through Malcolm Cowley to Mike Harrington and my own generation, everyone thinks "the real Village" is the one they knew, and declares it "dead" when a new wave of youth comes on the scene. It doesn't much matter, though, since the Village and what it means — the freedom and art and experimentation and promise of discovery and love — keep going on, drawing new hearts and faces to its winding, willful streets. Brock and Ann Brower tell me they just helped one of their daughters who is fresh out of college move into an apartment on Jones Street. It's next door to the building where I lived when I first came to the Village in 1956.

SEVEN

What Rough Beats?

I N JANUARY 1957, a couple of years after we graduated from Columbia, my novelist friend Sam Astrachan took me to a hip new
bar in the Village called Johnny Romero's. Romero's had a smol-
dering kind of illicit sexual excitement about it, for the place was
supposedly a rendezvous for white girls to meet black men. I went,
and returned many times later, motivated by curiosity and voyeur-
ism, as well as a sense of being on the inside of what was happening,
at a nerve center of the latest hip behavior patterns. Romero's
wasn't known as a literary bar, yet that first time I went there Sam
spotted a writer he knew at a table in the back and took me over to
meet him. He briefed me that the writer had gone to Columbia in
the forties, where he played on the football team until he dropped
out of college. He'd written a very good, Thomas Wolfe–like novel
that was published in 1950 called *The Town and the City*. His name
was Jack Kerouac.

Wearing a red-and-black-checked flannel shirt, with mussy hair
and a day's growth of beard, Kerouac seemed more lumberjack
than literary man as he gruffly offered to buy us a drink. He was
celebrating an advance he had gotten for another novel. We sat
down at a table with Kerouac and several of his friends, and Jack
talked in the rather grumpy, desultory way he had, evidently his
customary manner with people he'd just met. I took him to be a

heavily serious sort of person, one who seemed more weighed down than elated about the sale of his novel to Viking Press, a prestigious publisher of fiction.

I was in awe of anyone who wrote novels. My classmate Sam had published his first novel, *An End to Dying,* the year after graduation, and I regarded the journalistic pieces I was writing for *The Nation* as training, in the Hemingway tradition, for someday writing my own novel, a dream I'd finally realize thirteen years later with the publication of *Going All the Way.* I had no idea then that Kerouac had written four other novels, as yet unpublished, and that it had taken Viking six years to decide to accept the manuscript of the one we were celebrating, *On the Road.*

What most impressed me about Kerouac, though, was that he paid for our drinks by pulling a wad of bills from a money belt he wore around his waist that contained some of the cash from his $1,000 advance from the publisher (he received it in a series of installments of $100 a month). I had heard about money belts, perhaps on one of my boyhood radio serials like "Jack Armstrong," but I had never seen one before in real life, and it symbolized to me adventure and intrigue. If anyone had asked me then what Jack Kerouac was like, I would have said he was a moody guy who wore a money belt.

I forgot about Kerouac until the following September, when his name popped out at me from the pages of the *New York Times* one morning while I was having scrambled eggs and french fries for breakfast at Jim Atkins's hash house in Sheridan Square. The novel whose advance had bought me drinks at Johnny Romero's bar was hailed in the day's book review of September 5, 1957, in terms of praise I had never before seen lavished on a new work by a young and almost unknown author. *On the Road* was described not only as an "authentic work of art" and a "major novel" but, more important, as a "historic occasion."

I gulped my coffee, concentrating on this review that was the literary equivalent of "a star is born." The *Times* critic declared: "Just as, more than any other novel of the Twenties, *The Sun Also Rises* came to be regarded as the testament of the 'Lost Generation,' so it seems certain that *On the Road* will come to be known as that of the 'Beat Generation.' " I knew that the *New York Times* was "the newspaper of record," especially in the interpretation of literary matters to the public, so its own prediction of the book's historic status ("it seems certain . . .") automatically made it true. The book and the generation it celebrated were officially anointed.

Oddly enough, this crucial review was not written by the *Times*'s regular daily book critic. As a matter of fact, it was hard for me to imagine the conservative, establishment-oriented Orville Prescott finding any literary merit — much less historical significance — in Kerouac's work, or in the whole idea of a new generation of rootless young people smoking marijuana and driving to the Coast looking for kicks. But Prescott, the *Times*'s daily reviewer, didn't write this landmark notice that launched a book, its author, and a whole way of life to the level of a national industry, and changed the cultural course of our society.

The rave for *On the Road* and its author was written by a *Times* staff writer named Gilbert Millstein, whom I came to recognize later as a denizen of the Village — a friendly, sharp-minded man I saw around in bars like the San Remo and the Kettle of Fish, always ready to have a beer and engage in a good discussion of the latest novel, poetry volume, or jazz group. Was he given Kerouac's novel because he was an expert on the subject? I assumed that must be the case, since he wrote in his review, as if to explain and defend his role as the novel's critic, "This book requires exegesis and a detailing of background."

Millstein was, in fact, a logical person to provide such exegesis and background, for five years before, he had given a very favorable notice in *The New York Times Book Review* to a first novel called *Go,* which described the lifestyle of "the beats" and used the term in print for the first time. Then, at Millstein's suggestion, the novel's young author, John Clellon Holmes, had written an article, "This Is the Beat Generation," for *The New York Times Magazine* of November 16, 1952, which first defined this new phenomenon for the public: "The generation which went through the last war, or at least could get a drink easily once it was over, seems to possess a uniform, general quality which demands an adjective. It was John [*sic*] Kerouac, the author of a fine, neglected novel, *The Town and the City,* who finally came up with it. . . . One day he said, 'You know, this is really a *beat* generation.' "

Kerouac later recalled that day for *Village Voice* photographer Fred McDarrah: "John Clellon Holmes and I were sitting around trying to think up the meaning of the Lost Generation and the subsequent existentialism, and I said, 'You know, this is really a beat generation,' and he leapt up and said, 'That's it, that's right!' " It was one of those great moments in American literary history, like the time in Paris when Gertrude Stein said to Ernest Hemingway, "You are all a lost generation" and began the obsession with "generations" that became a national pastime.

That morning in Jim Atkins's beanery as I munched the last of my toast, I imagined the *Times* had assigned the review to Millstein because of his role as an expert on a subject that must have been of little or no interest to Orville Prescott. Maybe Prescott himself had recognized his own lack of interest and sympathy for the scene of the novel, and out of a sense of fairness passed it on. (I was very young.)

Long afterward, I heard and read that it happened because Prescott was on vacation, but as I looked back on the event, I wondered if anything so significant could have occurred simply by accident. There must be more to the story, I suspected, and decided to track it down. I found Millstein's name in the Manhattan phone book, thirty-three years after the event, and called him to ask about it. Sounding as friendly and interesting as he had been when he held forth back at the San Remo and the Kettle of Fish, Millstein explains that he didn't get the book to review because of his own expertise or by any design at all. Not only was Prescott off on vacation; Millstein was about to leave for his own.

"But before I left," he says, "I went up to the book review department to choose several books to take with me to read — the idea was I'd review them later, in good time. I looked through the pile and saw Kerouac's novel, and picked it because I'd heard about him from John Clellon Holmes. I wasn't looking for Kerouac's novel beforehand. I didn't even know it was coming out.

"When Prescott got back and read my review of *On the Road* he was enraged. He hated the book. He even hated to *look* at it. That was the end of me in daily book reviewing for the *Times*, though I did do some more for the Sunday *Book Review*."

Millstein had not only called the publication of *On the Road* a "historic occasion" but also cast its author as "the principal avatar" of "the generation Kerouac himself named years ago as 'beat.' " Millstein hadn't known Kerouac before reviewing his novel, but met him soon afterward: "I was enchanted by him. The only word for him was sweet. He was a sweet man and he loved his mother. That, of course, was literally true, you know.

"After my review came out, I used to go out with Jack on the Bowery, drinking in those bars. He would always end up dead drunk, passed out with his head on the table. We'd have to get a cab and somebody would take him home."

I ask Millstein if Kerouac appreciated what his review in the *Times* had done for him.

"Oh yes, and he made no bones about it, either. When he introduced me to people, he'd put an arm around me and say, 'This is Gilbert Millstein — he made me.' "

In the weeks that followed Millstein's review of *On the Road*, Kerouac was photographed, interviewed, enshrined, adored, and deplored, on television and in the press; overnight he became the hot new controversial antihero of the national media. A few months later I was covering his act myself when he opened at the Village Vanguard, reading his work to the accompaniment of a jazz piano player on a double bill with the J. J. Johnson Quartet.

The Vanguard was in my own neighborhood, on Seventh Avenue near Sheridan Square, and I sometimes went there to listen to jazz. When I passed the place I usually checked the pictures outside to see if there was any musician or group I wanted to catch. On a cold Friday night in December, the week before Christmas, I was on my way to a poetry reading (non-beat) at NYU when, outside the Vanguard, I saw a glossy photo of Kerouac. I decided to stop by later and watch the avatar in action, sensing at once I could get a good, ironic piece out of it for *The Nation*.

I didn't come as an objective reporter, much less an admirer, of Kerouac and his work or of the Beat Generation he seemed to have created, like Frankenstein's monster, with the publication of *On the Road*. Like many of my friends under thirty, I resented being labeled because of my age first as "silent" and suddenly as "beat," when my own life and work, like that of the writers I admired — James Baldwin and William Styron, J. D. Salinger and Carson

McCullers — had little in common with the life or literary style exemplified by what Seymour Krim called Kerouac's "non-stop gush."

We were what Krim rightly distinguished as "the writer writers," as opposed to the beat writers. Kerouac himself made a similar distinction when he called *The Town and the City* his "novel novel," as opposed to his later books, which were transcribed in the free-flowing style. With his usual flair for popularizing his friends' work, Allen Ginsberg christened Kerouac's method as "spontaneous bop prosody." Truman Capote coined the *mot* that became the accepted literary judgment of the time when he said that Kerouac's prose wasn't writing at all but "typing."

I tried to read *On the Road* and found it hard to take — embarrassing not only in what I considered the amateurish style or purposeful lack of it, but in what seemed to me the hokey, high school exuberance of these innocents abroad in their own land:

> "Man, wow, there's so many things to do, so many things to write! How to even *begin* to get it all down and without modified restraints and all hung-up on like literary inhibitions and grammatical fears. . . ."
> I took a big swig in the wild, lyrical, drizzling air of Nebraska. "Whooee, here we go!"
> I said to myself, "Wow, what'll *Denver* be like!"

Wow. Whooee. I figured Kerouac must regard me and my friends, the Village "writer writers," as "the arty types . . . all over America, sucking up its blood."

Some of the Columbia literary alums, a little closer to Kerouac's age than my own, were among his most adamant attackers. Herbert Gold wrote acidly in *The Nation* that *On the Road* was "proof of illness rather than a creation of art, a novel." Norman Podhoretz, the young critic and *Commentary* editor, called it "an inept imitation of Faulkner and Joyce done by a man who thinks all you have to do . . . is sit back and pour out anything that pops into your head." He suggested in an *Esquire* essay that the Beat Generation was "a conspiracy to overthrow civilization" and replace it with "the world of the adolescent street gang." Harvard grad John Updike later added a parody of the novel in *The New Yorker* called "On the Sidewalk," which portrayed Kerouac's characters as childish and ridiculous. My wry friend Marion Magid recalls her reaction back then to *On the Road:* "I found it boring. It was eventless, and besides, I was never interested in vehicles."

Still, if you were a New York writer you had to read, or at least try to read, *On the Road* in the fall of 1957, simply to be able to express your dislike of it with authority at the bars and coffeehouses where such things were discussed. "After that Millstein review in the *Times,*" Nat Hentoff recalls, "if you didn't read it, you were a square."

True to his genuinely liberal nature, Nat was my only writer friend in the Village who admits to enjoying the book when it came out. "I thought it was exciting because it was about a new scene," he says. "I'd known itinerants before, but not people like this. I wasn't sure this was the arrival of a whole new generation, though. I just thought it was about some interesting persons."

In *Advertisements for Myself,* published two years after *On the Road,* Norman Mailer evaluated his competitors for the crown of great novelist. He called Kerouac as a writer "pretentious as a rich whore" and "sentimental as a lollipop," though he granted Kerouac "a large talent." Looking back, Mailer now recalls a more personal reaction to *On the Road* when it came out: "I read it with a sinking heart. We were very competitive back then. I was thinking, Oh shit, this guy's done it. He was there, living it, and I was just an intellectual, writing about it.

"I enjoyed it more when I read it a few years ago, now that I was no longer competitive about it," Mailer says. "I felt I betrayed Kerouac — and so betrayed myself — when I was supposed to defend him on a TV show with Truman Capote. It was Capote's first time on TV, and he made his remark that became famous about Kerouac's work, that it isn't writing, it's typing, and that won the evening. If I was as wise then as I am now, I'd have defended Kerouac with all my ability. A half-assed defense is a form of self-treachery."

In Mailer's evaluation of Kerouac in *Advertisements for Myself,* he advised that "to judge his worth it is better to forget about him as a novelist and see him instead as an action painter or a bard." Perhaps it was as a bard that his freedom song appealed.

Richard Lingeman, now executive editor of *The Nation,* remembers how *On the Road* affected him when he was a student at Yale Law School. "There was a voice in it that called you. It was very seductive and had the effect of making me want to get away from the straight world. I don't know if *On the Road* decided me to quit law school, but it helped me develop a revulsion to that whole mindset, and the urge to be a writer came up in me — so that book was probably one of many influences. Anyway, I dropped out of law school and went back home to try to write a novel." Lingeman didn't finish that novel, but six months later he moved to New York and began his career as a writer and editor.

Why were so many of the rest of us so mad at Kerouac and his book? Perhaps others felt as I did, that Kerouac was not only giving our generation a bad name ("beat"), but by his antics he was also — a worse crime — giving writing and writers in general a bad name, making them look like the foolish clowns that the worst of our parochial hometown critics took us to be. Kerouac seemed to be playing right into the hands of the enemy — Time Inc. — giving them fodder for reams of copy decrying youth, writers, artists, iconoclasts, rebels; dismissing all the people I thought of as *real* writers and rebels in a clichéd generalization of a whole generation as "beat," which sounded tired and defeated (I thought of us as proud and *un*defeated), and worst of all, silly.

Kerouac later tried to claim that "beatific" was the real source of the meaning of "beat," but that didn't seem to jibe with drugs and indiscriminate sex. I felt a truer sense of the concept came not from Kerouac's Catholic boyhood, but rather the attitude Columbia's football coach Lou Little had summed up in explaining why Jack quit the team: "Kerouac is tired," he'd said. (When Mailer met Kerouac a decade later, he felt Jack "was tired, as indeed why should he not be, for he has traveled in a world where adrenalin devours the blood.")

That night at the Vanguard, Kerouac lived up to my worst expectations. Of course, just by appearing in the role of entertainer at a jazz nightclub, he was by my standards compromising himself as a serious writer. Reading poetry to jazz was one of the new fads associated with the beats, much ballyhooed by one of the practitioners, the elder statesman of the San Francisco avant-garde fringe, Kenneth Rexroth, who dubbed it "jazz-etry." Ivan Gold thought the term as pretentiously silly as the "art form" its fans proclaimed it to be, and suggested one night over beers at the Kettle of Fish that instead of "jazz-etry" they ought to call it "po-azz."

By whatever name, the whole thing sounded spurious to me, and a *novelist* reading his work to jazz accompaniment seemed even more transparently a show business rather than a literary enterprise. Something in Kerouac himself must have felt the same way — either that or it was stage fright — for he was drunk by the time he appeared on stage, dropping the papers he was trying to read from, slurring his words, swaying back and forth not in time to the rhythm of the music but simply as a man does when he is trying not to fall down.

Kerouac was wearing an open-neck sport shirt with gold threads that glistened in the dark and a pair of brown slacks. The outfit itself seemed buffoonish to me, for the "writer writers" I knew, even the Village rebels, wore a jacket and tie when they gave readings or took part in panel discussions. Seymour Krim, that lover of the avant-garde, always appeared in public wearing that black corduroy sport coat, along with the trademark thin tie. The Young Socialist leader Mike Harrington, even when he lived at the Catholic Worker's hospitality house in the Bowery, wore a jacket, no matter how threadbare, when speaking at a public meeting. Dan Wolf, the editor and cofounder of the *Village Voice,* who always had on a coat and tie, told me years later (still in coat and tie) that "being a bohemian didn't depend on how you dressed, it depended on the decisions you made."

Proclaiming your rebellion by the clothes you wore was one of the many factors that separated the traditional bohemians from the beats. The new attitude made clothing a statement of rebellion, a political act, as in Kenneth Rexroth's famous line from his poem on the death of Dylan Thomas: "You killed him, in your goddam Brooks Brothers suit."

Kerouac started off his set by reading a piece about his pal the bartender at the Cellar in San Francisco, one of the beats' hangouts. I looked toward Lou, the bartender at the Vanguard, to get his reaction. When Kerouac finished, Lou shook his head and said, "He won't make many bartender friends if he keeps on usin' *that.*"

I drifted from my stool at the bar to try to hear other reactions.

People who I guessed were leftovers from an uptown office party were shifting restlessly at their table and speaking under their breath while Kerouac read, until one man shushed the others into quiet and explained, "Some people like this stuff."

There was scattered, perfunctory applause when Kerouac finished, and I followed him to the room backstage where the trombone player J. J. Johnson and his sidemen were sitting around a table talking quietly — and soberly — at their break. Kerouac pulled up a chair to the edge of their group, but no one paid any attention to him until he asked Johnson, "What did you think of what I read?" Johnson, a dignified Negro from my hometown of Indianapolis, stared at the reeling writer a moment and asked politely if he had written it himself. Kerouac admitted he had, and after a pause Johnson said diplomatically, "It sounded very deep."

Kerouac complimented Johnson's trombone playing and said he had always wanted to play saxophone himself: "Man, I could really work with a tenor sax."

Johnson eyed him coolly and said, "You look more like a trumpet man to me."

That was all Kerouac got from the pros.

He returned to the spotlight to read a piece called "The Life of a Sixty-Year-Old Mexican Junkie," and I made my way to a corner table in the back, where some of his friends were sitting. There was in the author's corner, I would report, "one seaman, one poet, and one blonde." The blonde was Joyce Glassman, whom I knew from around the Village. She was a former Barnard girl who sometimes worked for publishers, and was writing a novel of her own. (*Come and Join the Dance* was published four years later; under her married name, Joyce Johnson, she published a fine memoir of Jack and the beats, in 1983, called *Minor Characters.*)

Joyce was Kerouac's current girlfriend, a fresh-looking young woman of twenty-two with a round, pale face of the smoothest white skin, framed with straight honey-colored hair that was set off dramatically by the standard beat women's outfit she wore: black sweater, black skirt, black stockings and shoes. Obviously uneasy about the evening's proceedings, she loyally defended Jack, explaining the he didn't really like this business of performing in a nightclub, but it might help the sales of *On the Road.* "If it gets back on the best-seller list," said the practical Joyce, "they may take it as a movie. If he sells it as a movie, he won't have to do *this* sort of thing anymore."

I had no sympathy, but went back home, around the corner to 10th and Bleecker, and wrote a low-key put-down of Kerouac's performance, ending by comparing it unfavorably to the reading I attended earlier in the evening over at NYU by one of my favorite poets, Richard Wilbur, whom I'd heard lecture the past summer at Bread Loaf in Vermont. I made the point that Wilbur, at thirty-six, was only a year older than Kerouac, but they were opposites in personal as well as literary style: Wilbur was a tall, blond, happily married husband and father who believed — in life as well as in art — in the virtue and power of what he called, in a poem that gave the title to one of his books, ceremony.

Sweating beneath the spotlights of a nightclub, Jack was "on the town," I wrote, while Wilbur was really the one who was "on the road, who has been all along." By that I meant the poet was on the same quest as the "writer writers" were, for a deeper understanding and the expression of it in language.

A few weeks later, Kenneth Rexroth came to New York for one of his jazz and poetry readings, and complained about my piece to George Kirstein, the publisher of *The Nation.* I wasn't surprised, since Rexroth was one of the principal champions of the beats, and besides, my article also made fun of his famous line accusing society of killing Dylan Thomas in a "goddam Brooks Brothers suit." If clothes could kill, I wondered, what genocide would be wreaked by Kerouac's gold-threaded shirt?

"Who is this Wakefield, anyway?" Rexroth demanded. "Some stuffy old guy who works for Time-Life?"

Kirstein said no, Wakefield was a young guy — I was twenty-five at the time — who eked out a living as a free-lancer and lived in the Village.

That didn't fit Rexroth's image, but he argued that anyway I *sounded* like some stuffy old guy who worked for Time-Life.

"Frankly," Kirstein told me over lunch, "I was beginning to feel uneasy, like maybe we were wrong to run a piece putting down the hero of this important new literary and social movement, the whole beat thing."

I started to defend my Kerouac piece when Kirstein smiled and held up his hand. "Mr. Rexroth was wearing one of those string ties — the kind of cowboy western thing like a shoelace — and he asked me, 'You know why I wear this string tie?' I said, 'No, Mr. Rexroth, why?' and he leaned across the table and said, with utter seriousness, 'That's my way of sayin' fuck 'em!' "

Kirstein, who was always elegantly clad in expensive-looking European suits, shook his head in disdain of an act of rebellion he considered so tepid, if not tacky. "I wasn't worried anymore about publishing your piece," he told me. "I figured you had the right fix on it."

It was anyway the general consensus on Kerouac's gig at the Vanguard. He closed after seven nights, a week before the scheduled finale.

I saw Kerouac at a couple of parties in the Village over the next few years, but kept my distance. He always seemed sulkily drunk and hostile, which his friends said was defensiveness, his self-protective reaction to the sudden onslaught of public praise and damnation brought on by *On the Road*. I'm sorry I missed the sweetness and playful sense of humor others saw him display. Bill Cole, the popular Knopf book publicist, watched Kerouac entertain at a party by holding his arms close to his sides and falling forward like a tree that was felled, catching himself the moment before he hit the floor. "He was like a kid, proud of his stunt, getting a kick out of entertaining everyone," Cole recalls.

The resident Village sociologist, Ned Polsky, was at the Riviera bar off Sheridan Square one night when Kerouac was proudly celebrating the purchase of a house for his mother in Florida; he said he was going down there soon to write.

"Jarvis Braun was there that night," Polsky remembers, "and when he heard about the house, he told Jack he'd been thinking of going to Florida himself, and he'd like to come and stay for a while. Now, Jarvis was supposedly the model for the hipster in Anatole Broyard's essay "Portrait of a Hipster" in *Partisan Review* — he was known for borrowing money and living off people, drifting from one person's place to another, eating their food and staying till he was kicked out. So when he announced his intention to come to visit at the new house Kerouac had bought for his mother, Jack suddenly stood up and recited a poem he composed on the spot, 'Jarvis Braun, Don't Come to Florida.' It was hilarious. He declaimed it to the whole bar and had everyone in stitches."

Maybe I missed Kerouac's playful side because I tended to avoid him at bars and parties after my put-down of his Vanguard performance came out in *The Nation*. I knew if he'd read it he wouldn't like it, and I didn't want to have a bad scene over it. When I did meet up with him face-to-face again five years later, I was assured beforehand that he was in a mellow mood and no longer hostile — at least not on that particular afternoon. The guarantee of Kerouac's new equanimity was given me by a young research psychologist down from Harvard, Timothy Leary, who had come to New York to dispense a new drug called psilocybin to creative artists as part of what he told me was a scientific experiment.

I met Leary at Allen Ginsberg's apartment in the East Village, where I had gone one snowy Sunday in January 1961 to interview the poet for an article I was writing on marijuana. I had been apprehensive about meeting Ginsberg, fearing he would have Kerouac's hostility to writers who weren't part of the beat scene or exhibit the kind of condescension with which some of the beats treated outsiders they regarded as squares. To my great surprise and relief, I found Ginsberg friendly, businesslike, and helpful. He gave me information from his own experience and from his files, making me feel welcome among the many friends and hangers-on who flopped or crashed or simply "fell by" (in the new hip lingo) his place in those days. He was like a practical saint who sheltered and fed the floating population who passed through his pad; every time I was there he was roasting chickens to feed whoever was hungry at the time.

When I got to his apartment, Allen introduced me to Dr. Leary, who looked like an eager fraternity alum among the more laid-back beats. When Leary heard I was a journalist writing about marijuana, he immediately wanted to tell me about psilocybin. Since Allen was on his way out to buy more chickens to feed the growing company assembled that afternoon — including a glowering Kerouac, whom I didn't approach — Leary suggested we tag along with Ginsberg and all stop for a beer at the corner bar.

Over our beers, Leary regaled me with stories of the wonders of psilocybin, offering to give me some to try for myself. It was a wonderful stimulant to creativity, he said, which was why he was so excited about trying it out on some of the poets and writers gathered at Ginsberg's that day. He was going to give them pencils and paper and see what they wrote after taking the drug — that's what I gathered was the essence of his "scientific experiment."

With his crew cut and bubbly manner, Leary seemed more like an overeager salesman than an experimenter seeking data. (Not long afterward, he was dismissed from Harvard and went on to independent guru-hood, as did his fellow researcher Richard Alpert, who later transformed himself into the best-selling holy man known as Ram Dass.) Leary sounded like a pitchman for a new cure-all elixir as he told me this drug not only stimulated creativity, it made people feel so good they lost their old hostility.

"You take Jack Kerouac," Leary said enthusiastically. "Now there's a guy who exhibited a lot of hostility, especially when he was drinking."

I said I knew. I'd seen him a couple of times around the Village when he seemed quite angry.

"Wait'll you talk to him today," Leary said with a grin. "You'll see for yourself — since he took the psilocybin he's been mild, calm, and very friendly."

I said I'd really like to see that, and Leary gulped down the rest of his beer and said, "Let's go," anxious to display the amiable new Kerouac.

Jack was standing by himself, staring out the window of Ginsberg's pad with what looked to me like the same sour, glowering expression I'd seen before. Still, I went up and introduced myself, smiling.

"Oh yeah," Jack said, looking me up and down with evident disdain. "Didn't you write a big, bad piece about me in *Commentary?*"

"No," I said, "it was in *The Nation.*"

"Aren't you a friend of Norman Podhoretz?" he asked accusingly. Podhoretz was one of the severest critics of Kerouac, Ginsberg, and the whole beat phenomenon.

"I don't know him very well personally, but I've written for his magazine," I said.

"Yeah, I know. You bastards are all alike," Kerouac said. "You know what I'd like to do?"

I didn't want to guess.

"I'd like to throw your ass out this window," he said.

Losing my faith in the calming powers of psilocybin, I stepped away from Kerouac. Just then Leary came up, laughing nervously, and handed Jack a pencil and a piece of paper. He asked him to write something, but Kerouac made a grunting sound and turned away.

Leary then explained to Kerouac that it was part of the deal — you got the psilocybin if you agreed to write something while under its influence. This was a scientific experiment to test the effect of the drug on creativity, remember? Kerouac seemed not to care. Then Leary suggested that if Jack wrote something, he would get another psilocybin pill. At that, Kerouac's interest returned, and he took the pencil and paper. He held the writing instruments but didn't seem to know what to do with them.

"Come on, Jack," Leary urged. "Write something in your bop prosody."

Leary laughed nervously again, and Kerouac methodically drew a straight line. Then he drew another one beside it. Leary looked on with rapt fascination as Kerouac drew more lines across the page. Then he turned the paper sideways and drew another set of lines, intersecting the first set. When he had accomplished that task he handed the paper to Leary, who made his nervous laugh again and rewarded Kerouac with a pill. Kerouac then went and lay down. Other people I noticed, were lying down too. It didn't look as if much writing was going to take place, bop prosody or otherwise. I figured the creative part of the scientific experiment was over, and I thanked Ginsberg for his hospitality and left.

Psilocybin not only failed to produce the creative effects Leary had predicted, but Kerouac later reported, in an article he wrote for the *Chicago Tribune* Sunday magazine, that the drug "stupefies the mind and hand for weeks on end." As his own life went down-hill and deeper into drink, Jack sometimes told friends that he be-lieved the psilocybin had had a more permanent damaging effect, that after taking it he "hadn't been right since."

It wasn't until I read his *Desolation Angels*, published in 1965, that

I felt a real sympathy for Kerouac and appreciated the dilemma he found himself in as an unexpected "avatar" as well as a writer. He lamented in that autobiographical novel that when he fled New York for Tangier after finishing the final revisions Viking Press wanted for *On the Road,* he found himself in William Burroughs's hotel room, in a scene that made him feel guilty as well as depressed:

> Just like in New York or Frisco or anywhere there they all are hunching around in marijuana smoke, talking, the cool girls with long thin legs in slacks, the men with goatees, all an enormous drag after all and at the time (1957) not even started yet officially with the name of "Beat Generation." To think that I had so much to do with it, too, in fact at that very moment the manuscript of *Road* was being lino-typed for imminent publication and I was already sick of the whole subject. . . . But all I could do was sit on the edge of the bed in despair like Lazarus listening to their awful "likes" and "like you know" and "wow crazy" and "a wig, man," "a real gas" — All this was about to sprout out all over America even down to High School level and be attributed in part to my doing!

I reviewed the book in *The Atlantic:* "If the Pulitzer Prize in fiction were given for the book that is most representative of American life, I would nominate *Desolation Angels.*" It didn't win, and I never heard from Kerouac, but I hope he read the piece and that it gave him some comfort and made up for the snide nature of my earlier review of his performance at the Vanguard. I, at least, was more mellow, not from psilocybin or any other drug, but maybe just from the benefit of a few more years, or because by then I had left New York, with all its pressures that Kerouac knew too well. He left the city himself, for Lowell, Massachusetts, his old hometown, and then for St. Petersburg, where he died in 1969 at the age of forty-seven, of hemorrhaging described by one biographer as "the classic drunkard's death."

As Seymour Krim wrote, in a tough appreciation on learning of Kerouac's premature passing, "He died lonely and isolated like a hunched old man at only 47 with a comicstrip beer belly and faded, gross, ex–good looks, full of slack-lipped mutterings about 'the New York Jewish literary Mafia.' " But Krim also revised his own earlier denigration of Kerouac's work. "It would not surprise me in the least," he wrote in "The Kerouac Legacy," "to have his brave and unbelligerently up-yours style become the most authentic prose record of our screwy neo-adolescent era, appreciated more as time makes its seeming eccentricities acceptable."

The pity is that Kerouac didn't live to enjoy his later celebrity (assuming a mellower age would have enabled him to savor it more than the jolt of early fame): the re-publication of his books, the growing number of books about him and his works, cult followings in new generations that listen to recordings of his readings, re-evaluations from some of his critics who came, admiringly if sometimes grudgingly, to acknowledge his special role.

Re-reading *On the Road,* I find the most poignant sentence describes the author's youthful faith in the American dream: "Somewhere along the line I knew there'd be girls, visions, everything; somewhere along the line the pearl would be handed to me." It was, but it turned out to be a bitter pill.

Things turned out quite differently for Allen Ginsberg.

It has been almost thirty years since I met Ginsberg. I decide to go to see him again, this time to get his reflections on the era he did so much to influence, in his role as poet and co-creator (with Kerouac) of the Beat Generation. I'm also curious to see how one of the original daddies of the beats is doing at an age that would have seemed inconceivable for a man whose name, work, and image symbolized youthful rebellion not only for the beats of the fifties but also for the hippies who followed in the psychedelic decade. Merely to state the statistic sounds shocking: Allen Ginsberg is sixty-five.

On the snowy Sunday I first went to see him in 1961, Ginsberg lived in a walk-up apartment on East 2nd Street on the Lower East Side; on the snowy day I go to meet him in 1991, he lives in a walk-up on East 12th Street in the same neighborhood. Going along the block of run-down buildings and seedy stores as I search for the right address, I think how much it looks like the scene where I first found Ginsberg thirty years before.

Back then, I'd been commissioned to write a serious, no-holds-barred report on marijuana. Pot, charge, tea, hemp, gage, grass, weed — it was moving from the back rooms of jazz bars and cold-water pads of hipsters in Harlem and the East Village, seeping through the walls of college dormitories and into middle-class consciousness.

"You've got to see Allen," said Helen Weaver, my girlfriend in the Village who was a hip editorial assistant at Farrar, Straus and knew everyone worth knowing, including Ginsberg. "Allen knows everything about it," she said, "and he keeps these incredible files."

Indeed, when I went to interview him, which I did several times, Allen opened a big file cabinet and pulled out reports for me to read on the medical, legal, and historical aspects of *Cannabis sativa*. He was eager to help anyone who would write objectively about this drug he believed should be legalized, offering facts and opinions and background information, all in a friendly, matter-of-fact manner. To my great relief, he did not use jargon or hip lingo ("Like, you know, I was uptight that he might jive me, but he was cool"), nor was he ever stoned when I talked with him, a possibility I'd also feared.

Explaining the role of marijuana to the poets of his own circle, he told me that "almost everyone has experimented with it and tried writing something on it. It's all part of their poetic — no, their metaphysical — education."

He was speaking of the writers identified with the beat movement, those who had come out of the San Francisco poetry renaissance of the fifties or lived where he did, in what was just beginning to be called the East Village, instead of the Lower East Side. The poets I knew and admired lived in the West Village, hung out at the White Horse, wrote rhymed and metered verse, and got their poetic and "metaphysical" education from bourbon and beer rather than pot. But Ginsberg and his friends wrote different kinds of poems, whose lack of rhyme and reverence were shocking to the sensibility of the times, poems like the one whose title summed up in a single syllable the whole attitude and style of the new social and literary ferment: "Howl."

This long diatribe of a poem had already made Allen Ginsberg famous (infamous, to many people) within a year or so after its publication. This was the year of Eisenhower's re-election, the capstone of America's complacency. Nothing could have seemed more out of tune with the times than that poetic shriek of pain and rebellion, which came in a stark, black and white paperback edition: *Howl and Other Poems*, published by City Lights Bookshop of San Francisco in its "Pocket Poets Series."

I remember when I first saw it at my drugstore-bookstore in Sheridan Square, in the winter of 1957. It didn't even look like a regular book of poetry. At first I thought it was some kind of offbeat political manifesto (the kind of thing a Dostoevsky character would have read and carried around with him in *The Possessed*), a small explosive of the mind to be hurled at the status quo. And it was.

"This poem has created a furor of praise or abuse whenever read or heard," wrote the elder statesman poet Richard Eberhart in an explication of "Howl" in *The New York Times Book Review* of September 2, 1956. Eberhart described Ginsberg's controversial verse as "a howl against everything in our mechanistic civilization which kills the spirit, assuming that the louder you shout the more likely you are to be heard. It lays bare the nerves of suffering and spiritual struggle. Its positive force and energy come from a redemptive quality of love, although it destructively catalogues evils of our time from physical deprivation to madness."

The "abuse" Eberhart mentioned came from leading literary critics like M. L. Rosenthal, poetry editor of *The Nation*, who howled against "Howl" as "the single-minded frenzy of a raving madwoman [*sic*]," and labeled Ginsberg the "poet of the new violence." Norman Podhoretz, in an essay in *Commentary* called "The Know-Nothing Bohemians," argued that "juvenile crime can be explained partly in terms of the same resentment against normal feeling and the attempt to cope with the world through intelligence that lies behind Kerouac and Ginsberg." The novelist Dan Jacobson, writing in *Commentary*, blasted "Howl" as "incoherent, frenzied, frantic, self-indulgent," and Herberg Gold dismissed it in *The Nation* as "blathering."

An even more threatening kind of criticism came a year after the poem appeared, when the publisher of *Howl and Other Poems*, poet and City Lights Bookshop owner Lawrence Ferlinghetti, was arrested in San Francisco, along with a clerk who sold the book to two policemen acting on orders from their captain. The alleged literary culprits were charged with obscenity, and the ensuing trial was covered by *Life* (with a photograph of the poet, described as "WILD-EYED SHOCKER Allen Ginsberg"), which helped make *Howl* a best seller. Judge W. J. Clayton Horn, however, found the poem was not without "even the slightest redeeming social importance," despite the fact that "coarse and vulgar language is used in treatment and sex acts are mentioned," as well as "unorthodox and controversial ideas."

The language and ideas in the poem (it speaks of "loveboys," copulation, and "whoring," madness and poverty, fixes and drugs, as well as illuminations, religion, and "the whole boatload of sensitive bullshit") have continued to cause controversy: as recently as 1988, "Howl" was prohibited by FCC regulation from being read on the radio until after midnight (perhaps before it is read on the air, the FCC should require the "warning" about it written by William Carlos Williams in his introduction to the first edition of *Howl:* "Hold back the edges of your gowns, Ladies, we are going through hell"). That same year, the beats' perennial critic Norman Podhoretz wrote in the *New York Post:* "In its glorification of madness, drugs, and homosexuality, and in its contempt and hatred for anything and everything generally deemed healthy, normal, or decent, Ginsberg's poem simultaneously foreshadowed and helped to propagate the values of the youth culture of the 1960s."

My own antipathy to the poem, when I read it in December 1957 (after hearing Jack Kerouac declaim Ginsberg's work as well as his own at the Village Vanguard), began with the very first line, where the poet states he has seen the best minds of his generation destroyed by madness. Another blow to our much-maligned generation! First we were "silent," and now we were not only "beat" but crazy!

My friend George P. Elliot, whose novel *Parktilden Village* skewered the middle-class mores of the time with the irony I admired, wrote an article in *The Nation* called "Who Is We?" complaining of Ginsberg's famous generalization in "Howl." Elliot noted with tongue in cheek that one of the best minds of *his* generation (the same as Ginsberg's) was a scientist friend who had not gone mad at all but was working in Toledo, Ohio.

But it was more than the matter of our generation's image that troubled my Village friends and me about "Howl" when it first came out. We shared an outlook I can best explain by conjuring up a particular evening in the spring of 1958, a year after I first read the poem. It was May 21, my birthday. The next day was the birthday of my fabulous new girlfriend Sharon, a sparkling, dark-eyed exile from Kansas City by way of Vassar. In the pale yellow light of a booth at the Cedar Tavern we exchanged presents.

I hardly ever went to the Cedar because it was a hangout for painters, not writers, but Sharon was a painter and she gravitated there in the way I was drawn to the White Horse. Being fellow refugees from the Midwest, liberated by eastern colleges, gave us a common bond, and sometimes it seemed we were male-female manifestations of the same spirit of rebellion and searching. When each of us drew from our laps the gifts we passed across the table at the same time, we started to laugh because both packages were the same shape and size. We tore open the separate wrappings to find inside each one the same slim volume with a gold jacket that said in plain black letters: CEREMONY. A BOOK OF POEMS BY RICHARD WILBUR.

The title poem of Wilbur's collection told us that when things looked orderly on the surface, "I think there are most tigers in the wood." Didn't we know this from our own experience? Isn't this what we had learned growing up in those orderly houses behind the deceptively neat white picket fences where our own families wept secret tears and tried to hide their pain? Wasn't the deepest anguish, the hardest truth, portrayed most convincingly in poems with form, like those of Yeats and Wilbur, and in traditional novels that provided a shape to hold our experience and understanding of coming of age, books like Styron's *Lie Down in Darkness*, Salinger's *Catcher in the Rye*, and Baldwin's *Go Tell It on the Mountain*?

What I couldn't see back in the fifties but now seems clear is that a major shift had taken place in the order of the world since World War II, and that out of it a new kind of shattered experience had been born — a rootless, drug-stoked, existential, kaleidoscopic assault on the soul by modern technology and its weapons. From it arose that rough beast of Yeats's poem "The Second Coming," which my friends and I quoted as a kind of testament — the rough beast that was "slouching towards Bethlehem to be born" (no accident that Joan Didion used that line in the title of her first book of essays).

Though the writers I admired were able to portray that "beast" within the boundaries of the literary forms that were handed down to us, it was also inevitable that writers would come along who found they needed to break the old forms to express themselves. I can see now that Kerouac's *On the Road* served as such a landmark, though I still don't get its artistic merits. It's easier for me to appreciate the rhythm and anger and pain poured out in Ginsberg's authentic "Howl" — and see, with the wisdom of hindsight, that nothing less than a howl would have done.

The defensive reactions of our fifties generation did not, of course, trouble the seething, rebellious hippies of the sixties, the flower children who rightly saw in Ginsberg a natural ally. He became their guru, and was so familiar a part of our cultural scene (posters of Ginsberg, with his black beard and glasses, decorated the walls of college dorms and coffeehouses across America) that by 1969 he was grudgingly acknowledged by his old adversary *Time* magazine as "a peculiar national treasure of sorts."

The literary establishment that once scorned Ginsberg's work enshrined him in the eighties as a member of the American Academy and Institute of Arts and Letters, and he has won the National Book Award and the National Arts Club gold medal. According to a solid 1989 biography by Barry Miles, he is "the most famous living poet on earth." (At first the claim seems extravagant, but I wonder who else can rival it, except perhaps Russia's Yevtushenko, a rebel of his own society's status quo and an innovator of its language.)

"The most famous living poet" is as unassuming and hospitable when he shows me in to his apartment in 1991 as he had been during his days as a beat rebel. The bushy black beard of the sixties posters is neatly trimmed now and mostly turned to gray, the black-rimmed glasses replaced with a pair of bifocals whose plastic frames are gray too. He wears a blue button-down shirt open at the neck, with a pair of khaki pants. He seems trim and as brisk in his movements as he had been thirty years before.

Ginsberg puts on a pot of water for tea. He points out, above the stove, a photograph of his poetic patron saint, Walt Whitman ("I Love Old Whitman So" he called an affectionate poem he wrote in 1984), and takes me on a quick tour of his apartment. He moved here in 1975 and gradually made it more of a permanent base than the places he had occupied on East 2nd Street, East 5th Street (where the water and heat were shut off and each tenant was given $100 to relocate), and East 10th Street (where junkies broke in and stole his typewriter). There are six small, neat rooms with white walls. Ginsberg stops to point out a reproduction of his favorite painting, Bellini's *Saint Francis in Ecstasy*.

"I love it because not only Saint Francis but also the animals and even the *trees* seem to be in this moment of ecstasy," Allen says. "But the ecstasy isn't some otherworldly experience, it's more like being awake, like the condition Zen calls 'ordinary mind.' "

We move on to his study, a room with bookshelves running from floor to ceiling along two walls. Several shelves are filled with his own books, including the many foreign editions "from Czech to Yugoslavian" (his poems have been translated into most languages, including Chinese and Serbo-Croatian). One section contains contemporary poetry, "from Auden to Zukovsky," and another section is all books of or about William Blake: "I decided to buy anything of Blake that became available that was under $100." (Allen's first vision, or "awakening," occurred when he was a student at Columbia, reading Blake's poem "Ah! Sun-Flower!")

There's a photograph in his study of the Venerable Chogyam Trungpa, Rinpoche, his Tibetan meditation teacher, which reminds Allen he's going next weekend to give a benefit reading in Ann Arbor to help raise money for a new Buddhist center there, which some friends of his are starting. On the door of the study is a leaflet that says "Stop the War," which at first I think is a souvenir from the Vietnam era but turns out to be a reference to the Persian Gulf War that ended only the previous month. Decades seem to mix and meld this morning in Ginsberg's apartment.

Against a wall in the study, the big file cabinet, from which he had drawn the documents about marijuana when I interviewed him thirty years ago, is the only piece of furniture I remember from the past.

In his bedroom there's a real bed instead of the mattresses strewn about the floor in his place I first visited on East 2nd Street. There had been a starkness to that flat, with peeling paint the only wall decoration, as opposed to the prints and photographs that give his current apartment a homey feeling, though hardly an air of luxury. The modesty of Ginsberg's lifestyle can be measured by the teasing of a friend who accused him of becoming a yuppie when, in the mid-1980s, he got a dish rack and an electric clock for the kitchen.

When we finish the apartment tour and sit at the kitchen table with tea and instant decaf coffee, Allen says he'd been going over some of his journals from the fifties, and I ask what he thinks the significance of that era is now.

"In the fifties, Kerouac and Burroughs and I saw that society had to change," he says. "There had to be a new vision, as in Yeats's 'A Vision,' in which there's a cyclical integration of history, what Yeats called an 'interchange of tinctures,' and the objective becomes subjective. It's like in Einstein's work, where the appearance of the universe depends on the observer, or when Blake says, 'The eye altering alters all.' We were on to that back then. None of us were Marxists — we'd already smoked a little tea, and in '51 we took some peyote. I'd had a visionary experience in '47, but it had nothing to do with drugs. It was a small *satori,* an experience of what Zen calls 'ordinary mind.' In the Zen Buddhist view there is a nontheistic awareness of that kind that in those days was excluded from conversation.

"Back in the forties that kind of spiritual liberation began, then in the fifties there was the 'liberation of the word' against censorship, ending with Henry Miller's books and Burroughs's *Naked Lunch* winning obscenity trials and not being banned anymore. Then in the sixties all this we had fought for became all-American and was influencing new generations."

When Ginsberg speaks of the fifties, during which he played such a major role, he speaks not of his own exploits or accomplishments but those of his friends, whom he sees as his mentors. "I'm basically a student of Kerouac. He and Burroughs were my teachers. I felt dumb compared to them. I was always a good student — I check out the wisdom of my elders."

Kerouac was only four years older than Ginsberg, but Allen regarded him as a literary and philosophical guide, and still defends him at every opportunity. He says when *On the Road* was published and its author branded a "know-nothing" by Norman Podhoretz, "Jack was seventeen years into Buddhist literature by then. He knew the Diamond Sutra, understood a great deal, and had written a six-hundred-page manuscript that still has never been published of his notes on reading the sutras. According to Gary Snyder [poet and student of Zen], who locked eyebrows with him on the subject in the fifties, Jack was sharp and spiritually well developed. He was no barbarian."

To try to persuade Podhoretz that he was wrong in his harsh and angry assessment of their work, Jack and Allen invited him to the Village after his article "The Know-Nothing Bohemians" appeared in *Partisan Review.*

As Norman Podhoretz remembers the event, it was Kerouac's girlfriend at the time, Joyce Glassman, who actually invited him to come to her place and have a drink with Jack and Allen. Podhoretz talked to me recently about the events of that evening. "When I got a call from Joyce Glassman, I thought it was a put-on. Then Allen got on the phone and said, 'Jack and I are just sitting around here. Why don't you come and see us?' It was on a Saturday night, and I was recently married and had two stepchildren, and lived on the Upper West Side. I decided, with misgivings, to go down to the Village and see them. I shaved and put on a jacket and tie. I got there around eight or nine o'clock. They were sitting around in this rather bleak apartment of Joyce's — Allen, Peter Orlovsky [Ginsberg's special friend in that era], and Kerouac. I'd hardly known Jack at Columbia. I'm not sure I even met him then.

"I felt that the whole point of the evening was to argue with me — they acted like writers who were hurt by a critic who'd been unfair. They made the point later, which Herb Gold also made to me, that the literary critics of the twenties *liked* writers, that those critics explained and defended the writers of their day, and now critics like me were attacking them. The other side of all this was they were trying to put me down — it felt like spiritual bullying. They talked about all kinds of glorious adventures I was deprived of, from sexual to chemical, by not seeing things their way."

Allen remembers it differently: "We were just trying to find out what was going on with him. We were trying to make friends. Podhoretz had never met Jack, and didn't know what a gentle manner he had."

That evening Podhoretz did, in fact, alter his view of Kerouac the man, if not the writer: "I finally said I had to split, and Jack walked with me to the subway. He was very cheery, very handsome in those days. To my surprise, I liked him."

There were, however, no further get-togethers between the beat writers and their most persistent and harshest critic, despite some later efforts by Ginsberg. "I write to Podhoretz every once in a while," Allen said. "In '82 I invited him to the Nairopa Institute in Denver. I thought he'd feel safe there. It was the twenty-fifth anniversary of *On the Road,* and we were going to have a symposium on the book and its impact. I thought, Why not invite Norman? Why not cover the spectrum of opinion? He didn't come, though. He was afraid of being attacked. I told him, 'No, it's a Buddhist scene,' but he wasn't persuaded."

The conflict between the two old Columbia literary men that began in the fifties continues through the years, a kind of literary-political version of the Muhammad Ali–Joe Frazier rivalry. I happen to like them both, perhaps because if they represent opposite ends of a spectrum, I find myself in the middle of it, with elements of each (and like each, a Columbia alum!).

I don't share the neo-conservative political views Norman has come to espouse in the past few decades, but part of me is at home in the suit and tie of tradition he wears, and respects his no-nonsense honesty in intellectual and personal matters. (When I saw him for the first time in twenty-five years, he seemed only slightly stockier and balder than he had been before, so I diplomatically said, "You look just the same." Without missing a beat, Norman said, "You look older.") I don't share Allen's appreciation of hallucinatory and other recreational drugs, yet I've given up the booze I once believed was part of my literary and personal identity and taken up meditational prayer and yoga, which I once dismissed as the kooky stuff that only beats and hippies — people like Allen Ginsberg — would indulge in.

After meeting with Allen and Norman again, I had a fantasy of bringing those two good men together, of sitting them down at my kitchen table to share in a common understanding of the powerful contributions of their intertwined past. But I suspect that scene will remain in the realm of fantasy; in the real world, each man keeps setting off sparks in the other.

When the Jack Kerouac Commemorative (a monument in the form of a mandala, with passages from his work cut into granite columns) was dedicated in the author's hometown of Lowell in June 1988, Podhoretz wrote in the *New York Post* that "Kerouac and Ginsberg once played a part in ruining a great many young people who were influenced by their 'distaste for normal life and common decency.'"

In an interview in *New Letters*, Ginsberg was asked to respond to the charge. Instead of attacking his old rival, Allen said he had come to think of Podhoretz as "a sort of sacred personage in my life, in a way; someone whose vision is so opposite from mine that it's provocative and interesting . . . so I should really respect him as one of the sacred personae in the drama of my own transitory existence."

When we talk in his kitchen, I ask Allen if that meant he's grown more mellow.

He smiles and asks, "Didn't it mention that I was on Ecstasy when I said that?"

I tell him the excerpt that I saw failed to mention it.

"Anyway, after I had made that statement, Norman said, 'You still don't understand me.'"

Ginsberg lays out on the table a book of his photographs published in Czechoslovakia called *Allen Ginsberg: Fotografier, 1947–87.* The main subject is Allen's favorite topic, his friends. Seeing the now famous shots of his Beat Generation buddies prompts him to talk of them again with pride as he points to their photographs in the book: "Burroughs just had his seventy-seventh birthday this year, and he's writing up a storm. He finished a trilogy, and now he's writing a new book whose protaganist is Jesus. He's breaking the God monopoly of the fundamentalists. He acted in the movie *Drugstore Cowboy*, you know. His great love is denouncing the government's war on drugs, which he says is just an excuse for having the police apparatus."

Ginsberg defends Burroughs's view, saying, "There's a spiritual war going on now for liberation of consciousness and expansion of consciousness, as opposed to another close-down. It's a different view of reality. We want liberation from the reign of alcohol and cigarettes and heroin.

"Do you know the statistics? Between 20,000 and 35,000 people a year die of hard drugs, 100,000 of alcohol, and 400,000 die of nicotine or related causes, like heart failure, high blood pressure, and so on. So our eccentric use of recreational drugs was healthier than the average insurance salesman's casualty list."

Allen smiles and takes another sip of his tea. "My own peers have led healthy lives," he says. "They seem to get stronger as they get older. Nobody I know died of an OD on junk, or committed suicide on acid, though some people did get freaked out on amphetamines. The big killer drug was booze, certainly in Kerouac's case. And the casualty list of academic poets on booze is enormous — John Berryman, Delmore Schwartz, and on and on."

Unlike the boozers, Ginsberg has lasted to enjoy the acceptance of his work by most of his peers, with the exception of his "sacred" adversary, Podhoretz. Some who didn't appreciate "Howl" and the attendant publicity of the beats came to appreciate Ginsberg's later work. The poet and editor Harvey Shapiro says, "I wasn't really interested in the beats. I wasn't convinced of Ginsberg's genius until 'Kaddish.' " "Kaddish," a long work dedicated to Allen's mother, Naomi, is described by the poet as "proem, narrative, lament, litany and fugue."

Now, Allen and Harvey Shapiro are on the board of PEN, the international writers' organization. "I see him around," Harvey says. "Once I gave a reading with him, M. L. Rosenthal, who was poetry editor of *The Nation,* and LeRoi Jones [before the black poet took the Muslim name Imamu Amiri Baraka] after the Eighth Street Bookstore burned down. You know, the Eighth Street Bookstore was *the* place for poets — I met other poets there, some poets even got their mail there, it was a real center for us. So we gave this reading to honor the store and the owner, to give him the desire to go on after the fire. What I mainly remember about the evening was that Allen improvised a poem, 'The Burning of the Eighth Street Bookstore.' It was really pretty good. Allen has a kind of ready-made rhetoric, like Milton, that enables him to do such things. He thought it was good too, and after the reading he ran around the audience to see if anyone had a tape recorder so he could save it, get a copy of it."

Ginsberg still plays to full houses on college campuses, and some of his poems — like "To Aunt Rose," a sympathetic lament for an aging woman — are now taught to high school students. He needs a secretary to keep track of his crowded schedule of teaching, writing, speaking, campaigning for political causes, and raising money for Buddhist centers and needy poets.

We finish our tea and coffee, and walk through the snow to lunch at Allen's favorite neighborhood restaurant, Christine's, an old-fashioned luncheonette on First Avenue between 13th and 14th streets. "It's an institution around here for hungry rock 'n' roll musicians," he says as we sit down at a table by a window. There are paintings by Larry Rivers on the walls, and a photograph of Ginsberg, and he says, "They want me to give them some manuscript pages to frame and put on the wall too."

I order what Allen has — barley soup and pirogi, Polish ravioli — and a man and woman from another table come over to introduce themselves, and say how much they like his work. When they leave, I tell Allen that all the literary people I talked with who knew him at Columbia — even Norman Podhoretz — have spoken with admiration of his mastery of poetic form when he was still a student. In typical fashion, he brushes off the praise.

"I never took it as a big thing, being an accomplished poet. After all, my father was a poet. It's like the family business." Louis Ginsberg was a high school English teacher and lyric poet whose verse was included in collections such as Louis Untermeyer's *Modern American and British Poetry.* He was known to recite Milton while the rest of the family read the Sunday paper.

Ginsberg saves his pride for the work of his friends. I think of a comment Murray Kempton made a few weeks before: "I never understood what Kerouac was about, but I loved Allen Ginsberg because he was Allen Ginsberg."

His early work that caused such controversy now seems part of the vitality of our common language as well as our social, cultural, and political history. If in "Howl" he foreshadowed the anger and anguish of the sixties, in some of the other poems of his first book, like "A Supermarket in California" ("What peaches and what penumbras!") and "Sunflower Sutra," he articulated the innocent joy and beauty that became the flower-child ethos: "We're not our skin of grime, we're not our dread bleak imageless locomotive, we're all beautiful golden sunflowers inside." In "America" he also gave us a way of seeing our postwar macho-victorious image as a nation with humor and irony, ending with his marvelously mocking pledge: "America, I put my queer shoulder to the wheel."

After lunch, Allen hails a cab and I ride with him to Union Square, where he keeps an office. We talk of the mystery of time, and growing older, and Allen says he recently took his aunt to dinner for her eighty-fifth birthday. "I asked her what she had learned by now, what life was all about, and she said, 'Life is a dream — it's all a dream.'" He looks out at the snow and smiles. "I believe it."

William Carlos Williams's tribute to Ginsberg, in the introduction to *Howl and Other Poems,* sounds more prophetic with the passing years: "Say what you will, he proves to us, in spite of the most debasing experiences that life can offer a man, the spirit of love survives to ennoble our lives if we have the wit and the courage and the faith — and the art! to persist."

The snow that silently slants past the windows of the cab I ride in with Allen Ginsberg in 1991 reminds me of another snowy scene I picture him in, from 1956, a scene described to me by Helen Weaver, the friend who introduced me to Allen. Helen graduated from Oberlin College and moved to New York, where she got an apartment in the Village and a job at Farrar, Straus. A striking young woman, she was tall and slim, with dark brown hair worn in bangs and cut straight across just above her shoulders. She could quote Henry James, read novels in French, and besides all that was a great cook. What literary man could resist her? (Not Jack Kerouac. Not me.)

It was a Sunday morning in late November 1956 when the buzzer rang in Helen's apartment on West 11th Street, across from the White Horse. Helen's roommate, also named Helen, went to the window and looked down into the courtyard to see who was there. The buzzer that released the lock on the door of the building was broken, and to let someone in you had to throw down a key inside a sock.

"Oh, it's Jack and Allen," Helen's roommate announced.

Kerouac and Ginsberg. With them were Peter Orlovsky and his brother, Lafcadio. Now Helen Weaver looked out to the courtyard and saw that all four guys carried sleeping bags and backpacks.

"In my memory it's snowing," Helen says, "and they are looking up at us through the snow. They were penniless and exhausted, hungry and cold, and, well" — Helen paused and laughed — "they were *beat*. There would be articles about the beats that year in *Mademoiselle* and the *Village Voice*. Jack and Allen were on the threshold of being discovered.

"Allen was setting this up for Jack," Helen explains of their arrival in the courtyard. "Allen had another place to stay himself, but Jack didn't, and Allen knew either Helen or I would take Jack in. He was right. Jack stayed with me from the word go. It was like a movie, the way everything proceeded as planned. Nothing like that had ever happened to me before. From the very first night he was with me — it wasn't even discussed, it was understood. As soon as Jack came in the door we locked eyeballs — and immediately started arguing. He took off his backpack and started showing me his books. He had manuscripts and a copy of his first novel, *The Town and the City,* and he handed it to me and said, 'This is like Thomas Wolfe.' He was very proud of that. I liked Thomas Wolfe, he was one of my favorites, but I was into Henry James at the time. Telling that to Jack was like waving a red flag in front of a bull, but the arguing wasn't acrimonious.

"It was almost impossible not to fall for Jack. Aside from looking like a movie star, he had this combination of innocence and humility — unfortunately he lost both — and wildness. All that was irresistible to me. So the others lined up their sleeping bags on the floor, and Jack stayed with me. He stayed until he went to Florida for Christmas to see his mother. While he was gone I read *The Town and the City.* That was his sweet side, and it renewed my love for him.

"He came back after New Year's. He was doing some editing and polishing —" Helen laughs. "I know it was supposed to be all spontaneous, but that's what he was doing then.

"I knew very early on that our relationship wasn't going to last. I was from Scarsdale, the sheltered life. Jack opened lots of doors for me. I loved him and was charmed by him. But I knew I couldn't handle the drinking, the crazy schedule, the inconsistency — he'd fall off a fire escape and not show up, and then arrive two days later.

"I was just going into analysis. I had a terrible analyst, one of those strict Freudians who said almost nothing. So he didn't say anything about Jack, but he exuded hostility toward him. When I finally told Jack to leave, I think my shrink was the only person who was pleased, though of course he said nothing. I suspected he was afraid I'd give my money to Jack instead of to him.

"I was a mass of ambivalence and anxiety at the time. I was the only one in the household who had to show up at a job every day in some kind of reasonable shape. It was a stressful situation for a little girl from Scarsdale with her own set of problems. One night Jack and his friend Lucien Carr came in late and were rampaging around, playing records at top volume, and I lost it completely and started beating on Jack and tore out a hunk of his hair — after that he said that was where his hair started falling out. Jack never hit me back. I can't imagine Jack ever hitting a woman. But after that, something just gave. I banished myself to my room and Jack left with Lucien and my roommate's dog.

"Shortly after that night, I sat down with Jack and said, 'This is not working.' But it was the fifties, you know, so I felt guilty and wrung my handkerchief. I thought I was a terrible person for throwing him out. I could see from the beginning Jack was going to be famous, he and Allen. I could also see he was going to drink himself to death. It was not a turn-on, ultimately."

Helen sighs and sits back in her chair. A waitress brings our cappuccinos. Helen has come to New York from her home in Connecticut to share her memories of Jack, and of the time she and I spent together in the Village. It's been thirty-four years since Jack and Allen, Peter and Lafcadio materialized in her courtyard on their way back from the Coast. It feels as if it might have been the day before.

We're sitting in the Peacock, a coffeehouse on Greenwich Avenue, not far from Helen's old apartment. It's the perfect place to evoke such memories, for its atmosphere is coffeehouse-timeless. It could just as well be the fifties, or for all I know the twenties. People are talking or musing or writing in notebooks as some smoke cigarettes or eat pastry or sip espresso at the heavy wooden tables with wire-back chairs, like the ones in old-fashioned drugstores, and no one hustles you out. It's warm and the Saturday autumn sunlight falls in the front windows in long beams where dust motes stir lazily. The place smells comfortably of coffee, chocolate, and dust.

Helen shows me some of the pages of her journal from the time she knew Jack, and one of the entries mentioned she had bought him a red-and-black-checked flannel shirt. It must have been the shirt he was wearing when I first met him at Johnny Romero's bar. The thought of it gives me an eerie feeling, the way everything seems connected. It doesn't make me jealous, though, as it would have back in 1960 when Helen was my girlfriend, several years after she'd known Jack. Hearing such loving details back then would have no doubt given me a fit.

When we finish our cappuccinos, we decide to walk to Washington Square as part of our nostalgia trip. At the corner of Sixth Avenue and 8th Street, Helen stops and says, "This is where the Howard Johnson's used to be, the one where Jack met Joyce Glassman [Johnson]. Allen arranged it because Jack needed a place to stay again after I'd kicked him out." Helen laughs. "When Jack needed a place to stay, Allen got busy. He called up all the girls he knew until he found one who agreed to meet Jack. He knew if he could just get the girl to meet Jack, then Jack would have a place to stay."

As we walk to Washington Square, Helen looks around and says, "You know, when I see the Village now, with the new buildings instead of places we knew and used to go to — like the supermarket where Louis' bar used to be — I have this feeling that what we see now is like a stage set, and the *real* Village is there underneath, just like it used to be."

We sit for a while in Washington Square Park, where we used to go on Sundays to hear the folksingers and mingle with the crowd, which always included people we knew. It was a community scene, like people in a small town gathering for a concert, but instead of a brass band we had guitar players, and we sang along with them, telling Michael to row the boat ashore or proclaiming this land is your land, this land is my land — with the arch over us, and Washington's words like a blessing: "Let us raise a standard to which the wise and the honest can repair . . ."

Helen and I reminisce for a while in the park and then decide to pay homage to another of our shrines, the White Horse. Helen injured her leg the week before while taking action photographs of a women's rights demonstration in Washington, D.C., and it's painful for her to walk on it very far, so we get a cab. Except for the injured leg, Helen is in excellent shape, for she does yoga and meditation practice every day.

Back in the fifties, I would not have been surprised to hear that Helen would become a photographer, writer, editor-publisher of a newsletter, sometime professional astrologer, and one of the finest American translators of books from the French. Her English version of *The Selected Writings of Antonin Artaud* was nominated for a National Book Award in translation, and of the fifty-some books of poetry, fiction, and nonfiction she has translated from the French for U.S. publishers, including works by Flaubert, Claudel, and Teilhard de Chardin, she is most proud of her translation of Philippe Ariès's *The Hour of Our Death,* a massive scholarly study of attitudes toward death in the Christian West.

Such accomplishments would not have surprised me, but I would not, though, have guessed the yoga, vegetarianism, and meditation. Helen and I used to sit at her kitchen table on West 13th Street and create fantasies of the future, but we never could have conjured up the scene that took place in the summer of 1987 when we met at a place called the Kripalu Center in Lenox, Massachusetts, where both of us had been before on retreats for health and fitness, and arranged to go at the same time to enjoy each other's company at silent vegetarian meals, in meditation and yoga classes. In the days when we stayed up until closing time at the White Horse, we'd have laughed ourselves to the floor at the very idea and then ordered another round of arf 'n' arf.

At the Horse now, we order a round of tea, mine iced, Helen's hot. The waitress is obliging, polite, at this obviously uncommon request. I look around and ask Helen if the place has shrunk — it looks so small, I think they must have cut the back room in half. But no, she assures me, it's just the same — one of the tricks of time.

Helen had come here to drink with Kerouac too, and when she speaks of him again, I say I'm sorry I had seen only his surly side.

"He was just like a child," Helen says. "He loved to play. If he was comfortable with people he knew and trusted, he was the life of the party. He had endless imagination — and that gorgeous Massachusetts accent, and his sweetness."

I say sweetness was exactly the word Gilbert Millstein used to describe Kerouac, and I tell Helen the story of how Millstein happened to review *On the Road* and then became friends with Jack.

"In a way, that review that made him famous ruined his life," Helen says. "He got creamed by the media, especially TV. He needed to be protected and sheltered, and instead he was baited, attacked — he aroused incredible hostility. Even now, they still want to tear him apart and prove beyond the shadow of a doubt he couldn't write — and the guy's been dead for twenty-one years! I went to Lowell last year and read his correspondence with John Clellon Holmes. Dan, it was beautiful. People try to portray Jack as this illiterate barbarian, but if you read those letters you see a different person. You hear the voices of two highly literate writers discussing their craft. Someone should publish those letters.

"Alcohol was his defense. He was phobic in crowds, shy and supersensitive. He was always open, taking in everything that happened. He felt his divine mission was to be like a recording angel and tell all that happened to him. I had no idea how good a writer he was until I read *Dr. Sax,* only this year. I think it's his best work, an American classic. Reading it made me feel ashamed that I was one of those people who put him down. We all owe him, at the very least, an apology. I want to write my own book about him, in part as a kind of atonement."

Helen and I leave the White Horse, and at the corner of Hudson she points across 11th Street to the building where she used to live — the one where Jack and Allen and their friends turned up that November Sunday morning in the courtyard on their way back from California and Mexico, on their way to fame. That's the morning it was snowing.

I can see the snow falling in the courtyard as the travelers with their backpacks and sleeping bags look up hopefully at the window — so tired, hungry, and — well, is there any other word than the one they were about to make famous, along with themselves, on their way to creating the myth of a generation?

They were beat.

EIGHT

Roses, Dreams, and Diaphragms

A ROMANTIC EDUCATION

THE THROATY LILT of sexy June Christy swinging out with "I'll Take Romance" seemed to me a companion song to Mel Torme's crooning "We'll Have Manhattan." A bright young man like Gay Talese came to live in New York because it was "the capital of newspapers," while for others it was the capital of commerce, the arts, entertainment, intellectual life — and for all of us it seemed the capital of love and romance, at least for America and perhaps the world. Though Paris held the title in the twenties, romantic as well as literary and artistic supremacy seemed to have shifted from the Seine to the Hudson in the fifties.

New York's romantic spirit was epitomized for me by a stately Negro lady named Mabel Mercer, who sat on a high stool beneath a single spotlight in a pitch-dark nightclub on the West Side called the By-Line Room and huskily sang-spoke sophisticated love songs like "Dancing on the Ceiling" and "My Funny Valentine." Couples crunched hands and mashed knees together beneath tiny tables as the chanteuse raised one hand from her lap in a single gesture of finale, declaring each day Valentine's Day or proclaiming Manhattan an isle of joy, just made for a girl and boy (as we males and females under thirty were known in those days).

Romance was everywhere in New York, even if you couldn't afford a nightclub cover charge. For a nickel you could ride the Staten Island ferry, reciting the famous lines of Edna St. Vincent Millay: "We were very tired / We were very merry / We went back and forth / All night on the ferry." Some grand Saturday nights we took our dates to the Amato Opera House, a converted movie theater where unemployed singers performed to the accompaniment of a piano, and we dropped coins into a hat that was passed between the acts. We went for beers to Chumley's, the former Village speakeasy with no sign on the door, which Richard Lingeman remembers as "a great place for sophisticates — you had to know where it was" on Bedford, one of the winding little streets of the Village.

This aura of romance and sophistication emanating from the island of Manhattan made many of our parents in the hinterlands fear for our bodies and souls when we announced our intentions to live in a city they regarded as nothing less than Sodom, with skyscrapers. When Mary Perot Nichols told her Philadelphia Main Line mother she wanted to live in New York after graduating from college, her mother, like any God-fearing parent, went to the minister for help. "My mother told our minister to talk me out of it," Mary says. "She warned me that if I moved there I'd be 'kept' by somebody. Later, when I was living and working in New York I used to wonder why I didn't get kept like my mother said I would be."

At least some parents would have been reassured to know that much of our early New York life was heavy with romance and light on sex, as Ned O'Gorman remembers: "In those days there was still a radical innocence, not endless sex, not endless lovemaking. There was an enthusiasm that bubbled up through all that life. I remember going to mass on Saturday nights with some of the Catholic Worker girls, and then to the San Remo. We'd be running around at four in the morning. Nobody had a TV, everybody read books, there was a kind of serious gaiety — we all knew we had to grow up and do the work the Lord decided us to do."

Even many of us who were recent converts to collegiate atheism still believed, if not the Lord, then Frank Sinatra when he told us in his 1955 hit song that love and marriage go together like a horse and carriage. We, of course, would have amended it to say that love and at least the *intention* of marriage went together if both boy and girl consented (or were mutually swept away) to the ultimate act, what we had called in high school the Big Deed, the Dirty Deed, or going all the way.

This early postcollegiate atmosphere of romantic innocence prevailed the first year or so out of college, when we were still sharing the big communal apartments of boys and girls that functioned like makeshift, miniature sororities and fraternities — this being the era of impromptu but proper pajama parties with "the boys upstairs" of the kind where Ann Montgomery met Howie Hayes.

It was in 1955 that I met my first great love in New York. Like the new, "mature" Sinatra (as he was christened in a *Time* cover story), I was no longer a callow youth but a college graduate and published writer with a bylined article in *The Nation*. Though I was yet shy and nervous around women, I believed — and was told — that my professional achievements should impress those sophisticated Manhattan beauties whom Irwin Shaw described in his *New Yorker* short story that my friends and I so admired, "The Girls in Their Summer Dresses" — a story so ingrained in my generation's consciousness that a mention of it forty years later to Brock Brower prompts him spontaneously to recite the last line: "What a pretty girl, what nice legs."

I met Emily Lamson when I went to see an editor of a women's magazine in hopes of getting an assignment; their rates of payment for articles were roughly ten times that of *The Nation* and other "little magazines" I was writing for. I didn't get the assignment, but better still got a date with Emily, the bright, attractive Wellesley graduate who worked as the editor's assistant.

When I fell in love with Emily I thought she was Jewish, an assumption I based on the fact that she had dark hair and was highly intelligent. Being Jewish made her seem more sexy to me. Like most men, I believed that women of ethnic backgrounds different from my own were more exotic than those of my cultural tribe, and perhaps this was another manifestation of rebellion against family and home. Some of my Jewish friends had similar lustful reactions to preppy WASP women, a Brazilian novelist I knew went only for

Nordic blondes, while an Irish friend was equally mad for Italian girls, and I'm sure the Italians thought nothing more enticing than a freckle-faced colleen.

I was pleased at the thought that Emily was Jewish not only because of the added sex appeal it gave her in my eyes, but also because I would, paradoxically, have no religious conflict in marrying her. As a newly minted intellectual atheist, I was adamant in my rejection of the religion I grew up with, and had stopped dating a lovely southern girl I met in New York because she admitted to being a churchgoing Christian. When I rudely told her I could not "get serious" with someone who harbored such beliefs — the same ones that had served as the basis of my life until a few years before — she said with a sadness that haunts my memory of her gentle voice, "I'm sorry we didn't have more a meeting of the minds." Beyond all this, I was proud of being recently made an "honorary Jew" by Sam Astrachan, and it seemed only fitting I should now have a Jewish girlfriend.

Emily turned out to be of Anglo-Irish descent, from Dayton, Ohio. By the time I learned this disillusioning news, however, I was already crazy about her. She reminded me of Leslie Caron in *Daddy Longlegs,* and along with her winsome, wistful quality, Emily had a sharp, resilient mind that caught me up if I tried to pass off second-hand ideas. She challenged me when I lapsed into sloppy thinking, keeping me alert and alive. Her eyes and nose suddenly crinkled when she laughed, and she would surprise me, walking along MacDougal Street or hanging by the strap on a downtown local, with spontaneous bursts of Millay: "What lips my lips have kissed / and where and why / I have forgotten."

Too bad she was only a WASP like me, but I consoled myself with the idea that Sam Astrachan could "christen" her (as I thought of it, in a theological malapropism) as an honorary Jew. The disappointment in her ethnic heritage was softened by the news that she also was an intellectual atheist, one who was far more matter-of-fact about it than I was in my impassioned rebellion against religion.

We embarked on a postcollegiate courtship typical of the time, often double-dating with one of my 92nd Street roommates, Bill Chapman, who was going out with the girl he would marry, Christine Patton. She was the bright, peppy Wells College grad Bill had met when our apartmentful of guys met the apartmentful of girls on West End Avenue.

My friends were all impressed that Chris, in her first year out of college, wrote *Scholastic* magazine's teenage advice column under the running byline "Gay Head," named for the cliffs on Martha's Vineyard. The name was used as a *nom de plume* for the succession of young women college grads who did their best to dispense words of wisdom, at a salary of $50 a week, to troubled high school students throughout the land. This was before the days when the likes of Ann Landers — much less Dr. Ruth — could convey factual information about sex on the printed page (the word "pregnant" was banned on television), and Chris was disturbed and frustrated by not having the freedom to deal with real issues.

Chris's already big brown eyes grew larger as she told us of a letter she'd gotten that was scrawled on notebook paper from a teenage girl who said her boyfriend did funny things to her and now her stomach was getting bigger even though she was on a diet. What should she do? These kids who wrote to a magazine columnist were too afraid to ask the adults in their lives, and their own peers didn't know much more than they did.

"But I can't write about it," Chris lamented. "The 'big problems' I get to give advice about are questions like, Should I serve pretzels or potato chips when I have the gang over to my house after school?" (Chris also expressed her genuine concern years later, as a much-loved teacher at the Sidwell Friends School in Washington, D.C., and in the book she wrote based on her counseling experience, *America's Runaways*.)

Over beers at Louis' or late night coffee at a Rikers on Broadway, Bill, Emily and I, and our friends moaned and sympathized with Chris, but in truth we were hardly experts on sexual matters ourselves. Our "sentimental educations" prepared us for romance but not sex, the mood but not the mechanics of love. Ours was the last generation for whom foreplay was accepted as an end in itself. Bruce Jay Friedman recalls with amused wonder that at the University of Missouri "we dated the girls at Stephens College. You'd hear someone was a hot kisser, and you'd go out with her and kiss endlessly to no purpose. It was one long second act."

Emily and I were groping our way into act three but hadn't reached the climax. We were going at it hot and heavy on her living room couch after dates (panting, humping, groaning, and pumping until sometimes I even came in my pants), but the restless warning coughs of her roommate, Jeannie, from bed in the next room stopped us short of going all the way, or perhaps gave us the excuse we somehow wanted or needed not to try what we both in some way feared.

Ardor built to a crescendo the night Emily and I and Bill and Chris went to see *Red Roses for Me,* the play by Sean O'Casey that was running on Broadway. Everything Irish seemed romantic, especially the lilting language of O'Casey, and when he spoke of red roses, the very symbol of love, we were carried away. We took the mood on down to the Village, where we went to our favorite night spot, Marie's Crisis Café, where you could drink and hear good music without cover or minimum, just the price of the drinks (we always had beer, which was cheapest and lasted the longest).

Marie's was in the basement of a townhouse where Thomas Paine had lived on Grove Street, near Sheridan Square, and supposedly it was there he wrote his series of revolutionary pamphlets *The Crisis.* That accounted for part of the nightclub's name, the other part coming from the owner, a large and rather shy Frenchwoman named Marie Dumont. By chance, the popular piano player also had the same first name. Marie Blake was a magnetic Negro woman with a sandpaper voice who sang and joked with the young patrons as she banged out love songs with alternate moods of passion, humor, romance, and lust, from "Love for Sale" to our gang's favorite, "Down in the Depths on the Ninetieth Floor."

Sometimes late, when there wasn't a crowd and only the loyal regulars were present, Marie Dumont, who planted herself at a table in the back, would consent to sing by popular demand "Two Loves Have I" or "Just Plain Bill" with her marvelous accent and a few chanteuse-like gestures. On other good nights, when the place felt intimate and no loud out-of-towners were clowning it up or demanding that Marie Blake sing "Deep in the Heart of Texas," a slim blonde in her late thirties who always wore a plain black dress and a string of pearls would perch on the piano and half sing, half talk "Miss Otis Regrets." It was so sophisticated and ruefully charming it made us brand-new, wet-behind-the-ears New Yorkers feel jaded and knowing and worldly-wise.

Tangled on the living room couch that night, full of beer and spaghetti and desire, I asked Emily to marry me, which seemed a necessary step leading to sexual intercourse, as crucial as taking off your pants or making sure the roommate was away for the weekend, which luckily was the case. I meant it, of course: this was not just a fast-talking ploy from a slow-moving boy, but a declaration of commitment and intent, even though I'd wrestled with the wisdom of getting married, since I wanted more than anything else in the world to be a writer. "Settling down" didn't seem the way to reach that goal, especially if the usual American accompaniments to matrimony came with it, like a house and car and kids. All that could be worked out, though; it was certainly nothing that had to be decided at that moment as I struggled on top of Emily on the couch.

Emily said yes to my proposal of marriage and also, by her actions, to the more urgent request, yet my own body shrank from it. The stiff rod softened, or in the words of Dylan Thomas, which I couldn't help feel came from painful personal experience, it slunk pouting out from its foul mouse hole. Ugh. We tried another weekend when the roommate was away, and Emily blamed herself for being a virgin and inexperienced. I was just about as inexperienced but not technically a virgin, since I'd managed to somehow wrangle on a Trojan and get myself inside a girl from home in my last year at Columbia. When I told this to Emily, thinking it would give us hope, she burst into tears.

"What's wrong?" I asked in my innocent desperation.

"You must have liked her better than me."

"No, not near as much. Listen, you're the only girl I ever asked to marry me."

"She must have been sexier, then."

"No! I swear to God."

"But you can't —"

"I can't help it!"

Our arguments got more hysterical and our efforts more frenzied and blighted. This was hell. After a few more episodes of such agony, as I drank more to numb the pain, switching from beer to bourbon, Emily announced she was leaving. Not just me, the country. She was going to take a job her boss at the magazine told her about in Europe, scouting for a publisher. To make it worse, she told me she loved me and always would.

Nothing had prepared me for this chaos that came from the failure to be doing what supposedly comes naturally. A friend from Indianapolis had hinted at a similar problem when he went to bed with his college girlfriend, saying only "something went wrong." A guy I knew at Columbia told me, over beers at the West End Bar & Grill, a veiled story that was so metaphorical the only thing I could gather for sure was that he'd encountered difficulties trying to make out with a girl he'd just met. In each case, I was too afraid of betraying my own inexperience and ignorance to inquire further.

I thought of Chris Patton and our talks about the lack of knowledge of those poor teenage kids. But what about graduates of the best colleges? If we were so smart, why weren't we able to satisfy our most basic needs? At least those pregnant high schoolers could "do it" even when they weren't sure what they'd done. I knew guys and girls from my own high school who claimed to enjoy fabulous sex — especially some of the jocks and their cheerleader girlfriends. So what was wrong with me and my tortured buddies and frustrated girlfriends, all of whom had good grades and high IQs?

From novels, movies, plays, and magazines we understood all about candlelight and wine, kisses and love songs, and from the street and the Army most guys knew you were supposed to use rubbers to prevent pregnancy and venereal disease, but beyond that lay a vast sea of ignorance and mountains of misinformation. What little I knew about sex was inadequate or incorrect. Most of it I had learned in high school and college.

"Don't read *The New York Times Magazine*," our professor told us. "Those full-page advertisements for women's bras, undergarments, and stockings can be very arousing. They may lead you to masturbation."

I sneaked a look around me, not only to see how the other students were reacting to this information, but also to make sure I was in the right place. The lesson sounded eerily like one I might have heard in my Sunday school class at the Baptist church I attended as a boy in Indianapolis, except the word "masturbation" would not have been uttered in such a holy setting. But I was sitting in a class-room in Hamilton Hall, at Columbia College in New York City, in 1952.

The course was called Personal Living, and it was taught by a well-meaning fellow who also served as an assistant wrestling coach of the Columbia Lions. The information he conveyed was supposed to prepare young men for life and marriage in the largest and most sophisticated city in the United States of America in the 1950s.

The only other nugget of information I remember from the course concerned the frequency of sex during marriage. Coach said that if you put a bean in a jar for every time you had sex during your first year of marriage, and you took a bean out of the jar for every time you had sex during the remaining years of your entire married life (and this presumed a lifelong marital union), you would never get all the beans out of the jar. He also showed us a documentary film of a baby being born. I got an A-minus in the course.

Some desperate instinct told me there must be another way of understanding all this disturbing stuff, which was still so shrouded in mystery and whispers and taboos, and I suppose I had hoped that such enlightenment would be among the many blessings pro-vided by a Columbia education. When it came to literature, after all, we received the best possible instruction from renowned professors like Van Doren and Trilling. When it came to sex, however, we got Victorian folk wisdom from an assistant wrestling coach.

I suppose I had hoped for some kind of Lionel Trilling of sex education, an urbane and learned man who would explain and il-luminate, guide and instruct us out of the darkness of our sexual fears into an understanding of the driving force of our lives, the life force itself. Trilling, of course, taught no such class, but I was im-pressed and encouraged to find that at least he had written on the subject, in one of the essays in his highly regarded collection, *The Liberal Imagination*.

My hopes soared, for trying to understand the mysteries of sex was a continuous subtext to everything I did (which hardly set me apart from the other young men I knew), looking for clues in nov-els, poetry, sociology, psychology, plays, movies, even literary criti-cism. If Trilling could make clear the convolutions and intricacies of Henry James's *The Princess Casamassima,* might he not be able to provide some helpful insight about sex? I turned eagerly to his essay on the first Kinsey report, *Sexual Behavior in the Human Male.*

The very name Kinsey had become a source of titillation when I heard it as a sophomore in high school in 1948, the year the report was issued following research done at — of all unlikely places — the University of Indiana. It was self-described as simply "an accumulation of scientific fact" (as Jack Webb would say on "Dragnet," the popular TV cop show of the fifties, "Just the facts, ma'am"), complete with charts, graphs, and tables of data. The foreword said the report was intended primarily for a professional audience of "teachers, social workers, personnel officers, law enforcement groups, and others concerned with the direction of human behavior" (no leering lay people out for excitement, please). The very use of the still-taboo word "sexual" in the title was surely part of the reason it exploded into the country's consciousness like a psychic A-bomb and became a national best seller. The intellectual significance of the report and its reception was signaled by *Partisan Review*'s publication of a commentary on it by Trilling, who deemed its appearance "an event of great importance in our culture."

I was happy to read that Trilling thought the report was therapeutic because of the "permissive effect" it was likely to have by establishing what he called "the community of sexuality." That meant, in my own interpretation, that the report let people know that not only birds do it, bees do it, but even respectable people do it — and not only in a variety of positions and body orifices with humans of both sexes but also with, yes, animals. Right there in the charts and tables was statistical proof of those seemingly exotic farmland fables involving sheep, goats, cows, and horses we had heard since childhood. As a matter of fact, Trilling noted, the chapter on human-animal relations was the only part of the book "which hints that sex may be touched with tenderness."

In addition to its therapeutic value, Trilling thought the Kinsey report was also a symptom of our society's need: "Nothing shows more clearly the extent to which modern society has atomized itself than the isolation in sexual ignorance which exists among us." I was not bold enough to tell Professor Trilling he could find an example of this atomization if he walked down the hall from the office in which he wrote his essay and monitored the Personal Living class, which the students of his literature courses were required to take.

I was left fascinated but puzzled by Trilling's jocular comment that "American popular culture has surely been made the richer by The Report's gift of a new folk hero — he already is clearly the hero of The Report — the 'scholarly and skilled lawyer' who for thirty years has had an orgasmic frequency of thirty times a week." This sounded like admiration for a kind of athletic record, something our assistant wrestling coach, rather than a sensitive literary critic, might approve of. It seemed the sexual equivalent of someone scoring an average of thirty points a game during his entire varsity basketball career, yet the coach had led us to believe such "scoring," when it came to sex, was limited to the first year of marriage.

Was this sexual hero of the report a married man, or was he like one of the underworld characters Kinsey said engaged in intercourse with many hundreds of partners but "cannot endure relations with the same girl more than once"? Why was the criminal able to "score" with hundreds of women, while most college men I knew were having a hard time making it with one? Would my luck increase if I engaged in armed robbery?

I was relieved when Trilling told us the report concluded that masturbation did no physical harm, nor even mental harm ("if there are no conflicts over it"), yet found that adult masturbation was due to "insufficient outlet through heterosexual coitus" and so was an "escape from reality, and the effect upon the ultimate personality of the individual is something that needs consideration." So even in this enlightened study, conducted by a team of scientific researchers led by a zoologist who wanted only "the facts," were they telling us masturbation might be "bad" after all? I tried to ascertain the opinion of such an enlightened critic as Trilling, but was left with his observation, based on accepted Freudian theory, that "masturbation in children may be and often is the expression not of sexuality only but of anxiety." If this held true through adolescence, the student body of Columbia College in the fifties was beset by high anxiety indeed.

One warm spring night as I pored over texts in my dorm room, trying to ignore the distracting fragrance of the season, which clouded the mind with lyrics of love songs and restless daydreams, I heard a hum and buzz of voices in the quad below, a rising and gathering of excitement, something like the sound of a group assembling for a pep rally prelude to a big game. But this was the week of final exams, and there were no games or social events. I wondered for what purpose the milling group of students was forming when I heard the electrifying cry: "Panty raid!"

These demonstrations of postadolescent frustration were my college generation's version of the orgy, in which male students stormed women's dormitories and demanded not sex but the symbol of it, in the form of panties, bras, and other assorted female undergarments, which the damsels were supposed to drop from the windows of their walled fortresses. Forty such raids — labeled in the press as "lace riots" and "silk sorties" — took place around the country in the spring of 1952 and broke out again the following spring, turning into riots in Columbia, Missouri, where the National Guard was called, and Knoxville, Tennessee, where street lights were shot out. *U.S. News and World Report* informed us that "co-eds sometimes incited the rioters, sometimes fought them off with brooms and water bombs."

We were, of course, supposed to be more sophisticated in the East, and especially at Columbia and Barnard. Noting the fad at other campuses, the *Spectator* ran an editorial, "Cherchez La Bras," asking, "Could it happen here?"

It was happening!

I hurried downstairs and followed the crowd that was growing and massing as it moved toward Barnard, growling and whooping, whistling and cheering, stopping traffic on Broadway as the sex-starved students chanted their demand for — women's underwear! Barnard girls came to the windows of the dorms, some of them tossing down tokens of intimate apparel, like morsels of meat to a pack of baying hounds. As the *Spectator* later reported, "The lingerie-longing throng saw three pairs of freshly-laundered white nylon panties floating gracefully from the open windows of the graduate women's dormitory." When police came to disperse the mob, the Barnard lovelies laughed and called down taunts to the boys, and one was dutifully reported in the pages of the *Spectator:* "What's the matter, did you lose your virility?"

So retreated the motley mob that the *New York Daily Mirror* described the next day as "2,000 roaring lion men." All the New York papers covered the event, with the *Post* calling the undergraduates "cavemen," and reporting their "furious assault on the trembling women students in three dorms. . . . The raiders never did get what they wanted (whatever that was)."

Columbia's dean threatened disciplinary action: the worst threat was loss of student deferment from the military draft. Adults had been more disturbed than amused by the panty raid craze of 1952 and 1953, claiming such frivolous nonsense was an affront to the many young men who were fighting in Korea. *U.S. News and World Report* bluntly asked of the panty raiders: "Why aren't they in the Army if they have so little to do?" College authorities warned that deferments went only to students in good standing, and those leading raids were in "uncertain standing."

The biggest scandal in the dorms during my years at Columbia took place in my own room, when I was paired for one semester with a notorious wild man for a roommate. This devil-may-care cad once smuggled into the sanctity of our male dormitory room a Barnard girl. She was dressed in men's dungarees and work shirt, and her longish brown hair was tucked up into a workingman's cap. The wild man had sneaked her up in an elevator, and everyone on our floor came to peek in the room and see the incredible sight: a fully clothed girl sitting on the top bunk, swinging her legs back and forth and smiling. That was it. Then the adventurer hustled her back down the elevator and safely to her own dorm.

The only men I heard of who "made out" when I was at Columbia were veterans and/or graduate students, men of experience and maturity who had obviously learned secrets as yet unrevealed to me and my still-innocent cohorts. It was not until forty years later that I actually met one of these legendary cocksmen. The novelist David Markson had graduated from Union College in Schenectady and served his time in the Army before enrolling at Columbia on the GI Bill in 1951. Recounting his access to willing young ladies he met at the West End, Markson says, "I thought there was no need for the sexual revolution in the sixties. As far as I was concerned, we had it in the fifties." Evidently, grad student veterans were as skillful at making out on Morningside Heights as those gangsters whose exploits were described in the Kinsey report.

I knew of only two of my fellow undergraduates at Columbia who claimed to have had sex with a woman during our time in college. One was a guy from New York who said he made out with a girl he knew from high school, at her parents' apartment when they were out of town. The other was a student from out west who said he knew a Negro prostitute who took him to a room she had around Morningside Heights. He said her name was Honey. I never saw her. One of my friends told me about a middle-aged woman who "took on" college boys for sex and had a reputation for being kind to them (translated, that meant she did not make fun of their ineptitude). This woman, too, lived not far from campus, near Riverside Drive, and one day I set out to see her. First I had five or six beers at the West End, to get up my courage, then walked to her address, tapped lightly on the door, and was greeted by a rather weary if kindly voice speaking from the other side of a peephole. "I'm busy now, dear," she said, "but come back in half an hour." I pictured a washed-out blonde in tattered underwear and a worn robe. I fled and never returned.

My only sex during college came when I finally got rid of my virginity (which had come to seem like a giant albatross), with the help of an understanding girl I knew from home who had come to New York on a spring break visit. I took her to dinner at the V & T Pizzeria on Amsterdam Avenue and then to a dank and dusty hotel room on Broadway where, after struggling with a condom, I officially entered the promised land of sexual completion — if not what either my partner or I could by any stretch of the imagination call fulfillment.

The other thing I learned about sex while going to college was the most crucial piece of information for a young person coming of age in the fifties: there was now a way to discover the hidden factors from the past that caused sexual problems, and in so discovering their causes, cure them. The name of this seemingly magical, but certifiably scientific, process was psychoanalysis.

The sky above New York City in the 1950s was crowded with dreams. To the naked eye there were only flocks of clouds and spires of skyscrapers, but sometimes I got a glimpse of the dreams, not just the old ordinary kind that people had always had above this island — dreams of roses and diamonds and bubbling champagne, of starring on Broadway or singing at the Met, making a fortune on Wall Street or becoming an advertising mogul on Madison Avenue. Now there was a popular new variety of dreams that featured long hallways and sinister figures, mountain peaks and rising towers, limbs and faces juxtaposed and jumbled like Picasso's paintings at the Museum of Modern Art. Nothing was what it first seemed in these dreams, for they were Freudian dreams, filled with symbols, and they had to be interpreted by an expert.

The interpreters of dreams (like Joseph in the Old Testament, except with medical degrees) all had their offices on Madison or Park or Fifth Avenue between 60th and 90th streets, on the Upper East Side of Manhattan, and the sky above that area was like a whole traffic jam of dreams. It was there people lay on long black couches, telling their dreams to the experts who sat behind them in leather chairs, and I imagined the dreams then drifted into the air above those buildings and bumped into all the other dreams emanating from the analysts' offices as thick as factory smoke until they were crowded off into space and finally disappeared because the earth's atmosphere over the Upper East Side of Manhattan simply could hold no more dreams.

I dreamed of snakes.

Weren't they supposed to be sexual symbols? Wasn't the fact that a snake slithered into my dreams a sign I was making progress? The analyst wouldn't tell me. He sat in an easy chair behind the black leather couch I lay on and said only, "Yes, go on." A hard-core Freudian, a member of the New York Psychoanalytic Association, the real thing.

I dreamed of my mother.

"Is that good?" I asked.

"What?"

"That I dreamed of my mother."

"What do *you* think?"

"You're supposed to be the expert."

No response. Only heavy breathing. Was he having a dream of

his own? Did he ever dream of his mother anymore, after being analyzed himself?

"Are you still there?" I asked.

"Yes, go on."

I did. I even dreamed I had sex with my mother. (Surely *that* would get his attention!) The dream was curiously unemotional and bland, like something constructed for the occasion, invented to display in class. I was a good boy, a good student, and I wanted my dreams to get good grades. No grades were issued, though, nor was much of anything said by the expert behind my head except "Yes, go on," and at the end of the fifty-minute hour, "We have to stop now."

Since the analyst rarely, if ever, commented on anything the patient said, including the fabulous, fascinating (to the patient) dreams he or she dutifully reported, the patients felt the need to tell their dreams to others, so at least someone would appreciate them. The unconscious had gone to all the trouble to concoct terrific dreams full of symbols laden with meaning — like the hidden-picture puzzles of seemingly ordinary landscapes that revealed faces and figures in the branches of trees if you looked closely enough — and you wanted the damn things to get their due, wanted some other sensitive, perceptive person to acknowledge the cleverness and complexity of the mind that dreamed it. So people exchanged their dreams. They told them to friends and lovers over dry martinis in the Oak Room of the Plaza Hotel or over draft beers in the back room of the White Horse Tavern. While dining on steak tartare at "21" or stew from the steam table at the West End, in taxis and subway trains, in bed and in the office, young New Yorkers in psychoanalysis traded their dreams like some wampum of the psyche that had inherent value when understood by the person who gave his own similar currency back.

There was no use telling your dreams to your parents from Indianapolis when they came to town, or to your old high school buddy from Sheboygan. Such unenlightened people would simply stare at you blankly and think you must have really run out of things to talk about if you had to resort to boring them with some damn dream you remembered that didn't even make sense. It took other analysands, who were also dreaming for a purpose, to appreciate the value of your dreams. Really good dreams were passed on to others and made the rounds of New York like good jokes or literary gossip. One of the favorites was a dream dreamed by a woman someone had pointed out to me at a party. She wore a plain black dress and no makeup and was said to be a Barnard graduate — good preparation for complex, interesting dreams. After seven years of being in analysis, she dreamed she was swimming toward a shore. As she reached forward with her last stroke, just before the dream was over, her hand touched the sand of the beach, the dry land. It meant she was coming to the end of her analysis. Of course.

That dream was so damn good I wanted to have it myself, but I knew it was way out of reach, since I was only in my third month of analysis. In the kind of Freudian ("real," I thought of it) analysis I was in, you went four or five days a week for a minimum of four years, but there were people I met all over New York who had gone for ten, twelve, even fifteen years. I heard from a man a long time later who told me, "I was in analysis twenty-five years, and then my doctor up and died on me. That's how I got out." So I wasn't even in sight of the shore — I mean, I had hardly left the place you dive in to start the long swim to that promised land of freedom on the other side of the psychic ocean, where monsters of the deep lay in wait, and you had to pass Scylla and Charybdis just for starters. Three months in analysis was only like dipping your toes in the water.

After this short length of time on the couch, Emily called to say she was back from Europe and couldn't wait to see me. It had been a little more than six months. I'd had one letter from her, mostly about scenery, and wrote one back, mostly about literature, matching her friendly, noncommittal tone. I hadn't reported that I'd started analysis and moved to the Village to share an apartment with Ted the Horse, my Indiana buddy. I felt that on the whole — with results of the analysis still pending — I had put my life back together after the breakup with her and the sexual failure that caused it. I was going out with a nice, bookish girl whose shyness matched my caution, and thought I had pretty much gotten over Emily.

Now here she was again, more attractive than ever, sitting across from me in the Menemsha Bar, a place we'd gone in the old days (six months ago), even though we knew it was corny. It was in the Allerton House, a residential hotel where girls just off the train to New York could stay and be protected while they learned how to fend off the evils of the big city. Behind the bar was a kind of diorama of the town of Menemsha, on Martha's Vineyard, and at regular intervals a "storm" was produced, with dark clouds, muted thunder, and miniature lightning, followed by the fall of rain; then the storm ended and the sun came out again. Very popular with college girls and their dates. Not the place for a Village writer, but what the hell, she invited me.

A light streak in her dark hair and a hint of eye shadow (something she'd learned in Italy?) made Emily look sexier. She loved her time abroad but was glad to be back. The only thing she regretted was that she hadn't given us a chance. She realized she still loved me, she said, and wished we'd gotten married. She was staying at the apartment of a former college friend who had gone back to visit her family in Texas for a week. Would I like to come up and have a drink?

Emily started kissing me as soon as we got in the door of the apartment. On the way to the bedroom, when I told her I had only just begun psychoanalysis, she said not to worry about sex, she was no longer a virgin. An Italian guy had initiated her, and evidently gave her tremendous confidence. (His name was Giorgio. By the end of the decade, it seemed that every woman I knew in New York had gone to Italy at some time or other and had a masterly Italian lover named Giorgio. I wondered if it was the same guy, waiting at docks and airports for American girls to arrive.) I wasn't upset or jealous. I was relieved. I caught some of her confidence and simply stopped worrying about the results.

"It was fabulous," I reported to the doctor next day as I lay on the couch. "We did it in the bed, and then we took a bath, and we actually did it in the bathtub. Under water. Did you know you could do it under water? Then we dried off and did it again. I was so completely satisfied and slaked I didn't have a single dream. I woke up the next morning and found my penis standing at attention, ready for a new day. It was glorious. We did it again before breakfast, and then went back to bed and did it

after breakfast again. We had French toast — I mean for breakfast."

I waited for the doctor's response to the miracle.

"Yes, go on," he said.

"I intend to," I said.

Emily and I made up for all the time we'd lost, all the anguish
we'd gone through when we simply hadn't been experienced
enough and patient enough. No one had even told us to hang in
there, to give each other a chance to get comfortable when we undertook this enterprise for the first time in our lives. She said we
should write an advice column for fumbling, fearful new lovers. I
said we should write a book. Whenever we tried new positions and
styles and settings, we said we were only doing research. We made
love in every room of her apartment — even in a broom closet,
standing up. Emily said it was a good time of the month, right after
her period, so we didn't have to worry; she had timed getting in
touch with me so it would be safe to do it.

I could hardly lie still on the analyst's couch, I was so excited with
my new sexual prowess, my miracle cure. I was happy to give the
doctor credit, though I felt he had to share it a bit with Giorgio. I
figured the doctor would at last express an emotion. After all, how
many patients undergo a complete recovery in three months? If
only Freud were alive to accept his rightful share of the glory! I
would be right up there with his other famous cases, like the Wolf-
man. The doctor said nothing, though, so I asked him, "What do
you think?"

"What do *you* think?" he responded.

"I think I'm cured," I said. "I guess I just needed a short analysis.
Maybe the dream about my mother did it."

The doctor explained patiently that my sexual difficulty was
merely a symptom, a small part of the overall work of analysis,
which seemed to be (from what I could gather, though the doctor,
of course, couldn't come right out and say it) nothing less than the
full flowering of the human personality, free from anxiety, from
self-destructive impulses and patterns, from blockages of creativity,
free to live up to its full and glorious potential. Who wouldn't want
to reach such a goal, to realize such a complete functioning of all
one's powers?

Emily was in favor of my pressing ahead with it. Maybe it would unlock my creative potential — not only get me writing better magazine articles but provide the key to the great novel that was locked away in my head. The important thing now for me and Emily was to take up where we'd left off and get married. We didn't want to do it in Dayton or Indianapolis but right here in New York City, where we met and where we planned to live our exciting, fulfilling, creative lives, at the very center of the universe.

We nuzzled and giggled as we fantasized our ideal New York wedding, with the ceremony at the Circle in the Square Theatre, directed by José Quintero. Afterward, all our friends would be taken by horse and carriage uptown to the Plaza, where we'd dive into the fountain like Scott and Zelda before going inside to guzzle champagne in the Edwardian Room, and then on to a fabulous dinner of coq au vin and French-style green beans at the Café Brittany, followed by a party at the Museum of Modern Art, with Marie Blake of Marie's Crisis Café playing the piano and for the finale Mabel Mercer appearing beneath a single spotlight to do her plaintive rendition of "My Funny Valentine."

The doctor didn't approve — not of the plans (in reality they were considerably more modest) but the marriage itself. In fact, he said no. I had roused him at last. He asked me to sit up on the couch while he told me the rules again, reminding me that I had agreed to them when we began. The rules were the same ones Mary McCarthy later described in her novel *The Group*, about Vassar graduates who lived in New York City in the 1930s: "The psychoanalyst said it was a principle of analysis that the patient should not change his life situation while undergoing treatment; this would upset the analytic relation." In the case of Gus LeRoy, the editor in *The Group* who had just begun his analysis when he met and fell for Polly Andrews, the restriction against a "change in his life situation" meant he could not get divorced; in my case, it meant I could not get married. Not until the analysis was over. How many years that might be, the doctor couldn't say.

Emily didn't understand. Not only did she fail to understand the necessity of this analytic "agreement"; more important, she didn't understand, or accept, my willingness to put it above my love for her and my desire to get married, especially now that we had solved our sexual problems. We argued. We drank. We cried. We made up. We made love. We argued again. I poured it out to my analyst — the anguish, the pain, the loss of someone I loved. She was leaving me. She was leaving New York again too, but this time for good. She was going to San Francisco. She went. I got drunk.

"Yes, go on," the doctor said.

And I did.

On and on, to new girls, new breakups, new relationships that lasted from a night to three or four dates to three or four months. Again and again and again.

Marriage was *verboten*. The doctor decreed no change in my life situation, so I put my life on hold. Commitment, except to the analysis, wasn't necessary — in fact, it wasn't allowed. This might have been a cause of conflict with the women I became involved with were it not for the convenient fact that most of the young women I met in New York during those years were also in analysis, so they too were committed to the same kind of impermanent relationships.

Perhaps because of our middle-class backgrounds, most of us did not believe in promiscuity, or think that we were being promiscuous. In other words, we didn't screw around with other partners while "seeing" someone. The name of the game that analysis spawned was serial monogamy: when you tired of one partner or the relationship got difficult, you simply moved on to the next one. It was like musical beds, with the latest cool jazz as accompaniment to the mood. Of course, we didn't call it serial monogamy. We called it love.

THE BED AND THE COUCH

Being a committed analysand made me a part of my time the way that being a member of the Young Communist League had made Murray Kempton part of the legend of his own generation of the Great Depression. The Communist dream, which offered to idealistic youth of the thirties a road to salvation through politics, was already seen as what Arthur Koestler called "the God that failed" by the time my own generation came of age. The new hope of salvation, this time of a personal rather than a societal kind, was psychoanalysis.

Richard Lingeman feels that analysis was "a preoccupation, not necessarily with sex, but in the sense of what people called 'finding yourself.' It was the Silent Generation turned inward, rather than expressing itself through political action. It seemed like the alternatives were going into the corporate world or going 'on the road.' "

"Finding yourself" was the overall hope, the grand purpose of Freud's method of treatment for the human condition, and those of us who entered it thought of the process as noble and ennobling, a search for the truth through painful dark passages of the past, a delving into the heart of the matter, whatever the psychic pain. The idea that the truth was buried, that the nub of our very angst and disorientation was hidden like some precious stone in the tar pits of our earliest childhood memories, spoke to us in literature and art. The concept seemed to blaze forth from the screen in Orson Welles's *Citizen Kane,* with the dying man's utterance of "Rosebud" surely the key to the riddle of Kane's whole life. The idea was even more eloquently stated in T. S. Eliot's "Little Gidding," which we so often quoted as analogous to our therapy: "We shall not cease from exploration / And the end of all our exploring / Will be to arrive where we started / And know the place for the first time." Yes, wasn't that the exact summing up of the course of our sacred journey into the unconscious?

The dream of wholeness was what drew me and other analysands into the expensive journey we undertook in committing ourselves to years on the couch in a free-association, stream-of-consciousness monologue punctuated only by the doctor's inscrutable "Yes, go on." Wasn't this the real American dream, the key to life, liberty, and the pursuit of happiness as proclaimed in the Declaration of Independence? No wonder Freud's treatment had caught on in hopeful America far more sweepingly than in gloomy Europe, where the notion of happiness wasn't even written into the law of the land.

For many of us, though, the less lofty, more urgent and specific promise of psychoanalysis was that it offered the cure for what ailed you sexually. If we'd stayed back home in Indiana or Kansas or Alabama, we'd probably have taken our troubles to our minister, priest, or rabbi, but our parents' religion was part of what we'd left behind when we came to New York. As Helen Weaver explains: "We didn't go to church with our problems because that's where we came from, and that might have been what fucked us up anyway with sexual guilt. It wasn't happening in bed, and it drove us all to the couch."

Helen went into analysis around the time she had her affair with Kerouac, who, she says, recommended another method: "Jack used to say, 'Go to confession, it's free.' "

But the priest didn't offer sexual salvation and the analyst did. He became our priest, garbed in his vestments of three-piece dark flannel suit, and his orthodoxy became our religion. Whether one partook of it or not, this communion on the couch was part of the dialogue and texture of our time and place. Donald Cook, a young psychology instructor at Columbia, walked out of the West End after lunch with his colleagues one day and hailed a cab on Broadway. One of his friends asked why he was in such a hurry that he had to take a taxi, and Donald said, "I'm going to have a synapse pinched."

They all laughed, knowing what he meant.

"That was the first time," Cook says, "I revealed to my colleagues that I was in analysis, but eventually it turned out all of us were. We later had the daring idea of going to the same analyst, getting him to come uptown to see us so we wouldn't have to travel so far — though we never actually pulled it off. I knew a lot of people in analysis then, not just in the psychology department, and we all talked about it, traded labels, like 'I'm an ego neurotic.' " Cook remembers seeing Lionel Trilling on campus one afternoon and telling him he'd had a dream about him. Trilling immediately smiled and said, "I hope you had it analyzed."

Cook also believes that "talking about psychoanalysis was a way of legitimizing talking about sex."

We all talked about both, with friends, mentors, and lovers, in bed and in bars, wherever we met and gathered and conversed. "Everyone went to a shrink," Meg Greenfield recalls. "Everyone said at parties, 'He said such-and-such today,' and we all knew who 'he' was. None of us had money but we all went to shrinks."

We got the money from our parents, who then felt guilty because they must have done, or failed to do, something or other to their children to screw them up to such an extent that they needed to see a psychiatrist. Like all good parents, they wanted the best for their children, and this latest new path promised the sort of personal salvation that had somehow eluded them, but perhaps was now available to their sons and daughters.

The word spread from the hot center of psychiatry in New York through the popular press, informing and enlightening the masses, making the name of Freud known in every educated household. "Magazines helped popularize psychiatry," says Walter Goodman, a veteran journalist who worked on the staff of *Redbook* in the fifties. "This was before television was widespread, and magazines were the main teachers of popular opinion — they made new ideas manageable. *Redbook* was that kind of conduit. Like at the other big magazines in New York, as an editor you could easily get an expert to write an article or be interviewed. We had a lot about sex — we were always for openness, but we were very family-oriented. Adultery was viewed as a serious problem, so we'd bring in a psychiatrist to answer a question like, Why would a married man want to sleep with someone else? It was rather touching, really."

As more and more people across the country were reading about psychiatry in the fifties, more and more people in New York City were entering psychoanalysis. In fact, if you weren't on the couch, there was a danger of feeling that something was wrong with you. My healthy, happy, bright friend Ted the Horse once confessed that he was ashamed of being one of the only people he knew in New York who wasn't in analysis or some other therapy. Did it mean he was square, or insensitive, or just a dumb jock? I tried to assure him that he might be envied the fact that he didn't need a shrink, since he seemed to be alone in having no complaints about his sex life.

Dawn Cook, Donald's wife, says so many people were in analysis that "there was a component of peer pressure — my boyfriend wanted me to go into therapy, everybody was in therapy, yet no one seemed to be very well or getting better. I had the feeling that to get better was not the program. People talked about it in a certain way that wasn't sincere."

The jazz musician David Amram is one of those who thinks the whole business was insincere at best: "Freud was in his heyday — he peaked in the fifties. If you were really a big success, a smash, one of the first things you were supposed to do was psychoanalysis. It was a real sign of success. I felt that people who'd been in it for years became heartless, lost compassion for others. They were taught they had no reason to feel guilty."

Unlike the literary crowd of the time, "very few musicians I knew did psychoanalysis," Amram says. "The ones who needed it couldn't afford it. Most of us functioned as each other's therapists. You talked through your problems with your friends, and the older masters made themselves available — people like Varèse, the composer, and, among the painters, Kline and de Kooning. They always reminded us how lucky we were to be around in the fifties — not selling apples, like in the Depression, or making money painting apartments or selling sketches for a dollar."

Even those people who resisted the lure of the couch, who were skeptical, or who didn't believe in it at all, still talked about it, for it was a pervading part of the talk of the time. "Psychoanalysis was the dominant influence on the fifties," Norman Mailer says. "I used to feel I was getting caught in plastic wrap talking about it, engaged in the most tiresome arguments about analysis. It was more of a religion then than now, and like all religions it had its way of dealing with all problems and criticisms. When you attacked or questioned its believers, they got pious — there was no argument you could present because they'd give ground here and get around you on both flanks."

This concept of psychoanalysis as a religion in the fifties was not just a radical notion of Mailer's. An *Atlantic Monthly* special supplement in 1961, "Psychiatry in American Life," stated in its introduction that "psychoanalysis, by force of circumstance, has in effect become a secular religion."

Mailer even feels analysis had a *bad* influence on our sex life. "When you went to bed with a girl who was in analysis," Mailer says, "you'd be in a bloodless argument — the three of you — the girl, the analyst, and you. It was a bad way to make love, and a bad way to live."

People like myself who were in analysis tended, as I did, to welcome the news that a new lover was also in analysis. It was like meeting up with someone who believed in the same God, followed the same path to faith, adhered to the same rituals. You felt immediately an ally; there was so much you didn't have to explain, justify, or defend.

It was often possible to determine in advance if a person you were to meet was in analysis. "I imagined then that girls of a certain background were in psychoanalysis," Calvin Trillin says, "just as in China girls of a certain background bound their feet. I figured eastern college graduate girls who'd gone to Dalton [a private prep school in Manhattan] all saw analysts. I tried to explain it once to Fats Goldberg, the pizza king of Kansas City. He was worried about people doing it — he thought it meant there was something wrong. I said, 'It's just cultural, Fats.' "

The ongoing, growing debate about psychoanalysis and its effects on our sex life was not just limited to talk but became a subject of controversy in intellectual magazines. What I thought of as the Great Orgasm Debate began with Norman Mailer's bombshell essay "The White Negro," in the summer 1957 issue of *Dissent,* an independent left-wing quarterly edited by Irving Howe. The piece caused more excited talk among people I knew than anything published in a magazine since Salinger's short story "Franny" came out in *The New Yorker* a few years before. The debate over Salinger's story had involved what seemed then the daring question of whether a sensitive college girl on a date during an Ivy League weekend was having a nervous breakdown because of her resistance to a phony society or because she was pregnant.

How innocent that was compared with the debate over Mailer's impassioned argument that, for the new avant-garde rebel he called a "hipster" or "White Negro" (with whom he obviously identified), the best therapy was not the search for self on the analyst's couch, nor even the search for a mate, but rather the quest for the "apocalyptic orgasm." The hipster, the new American existentialist (by Mailer's definition a male), needed no psychiatrist at all but only a woman, to serve as what sounded like a sort of sexual receptacle, for "orgasm is his therapy . . . good orgasm opens his possibilities and bad orgasm imprisons him."

I got a copy of *Dissent* hot off the press because Irving Howe had asked me to contribute an essay to the same issue, with the overall title "American Notebook." My own piece, "In Defense of the Full-back," was a mild and, in the context of the other articles, even culturally reactionary essay that tried to make a case for the athletes I grew up writing about and befriending (like Ted the Horse) as cultural heroes instead of the dull automatons that intellectuals thought them to be. To make it seem even more gauche, this sentimental treatise about the glories of football had to appear alongside Mailer's breakthrough declaration of freedom to find the best orgasm!

In the psychic revolution Mailer now proclaimed, the interior trail to freedom being blazed by the White Negro or hipster or — and he used this term interchangeably — the psychopath (with his marijuana and his existential action "in the theatre of the present") was replacing confession of desire "in the safety of a doctor's room." While evidently timid souls like myself were content to lie on the analyst's couch, Mailer was exploring far out on the fringes of experience, speaking on behalf of those who shared "a disbelief in the socially monolithic ideas of the single mate, the solid family and the respectable love life." Mailer was like some intrepid sexual Columbus looking for the "apocalyptic orgasm," while I was just trying to have any kind of orgasm at all.

I was frankly relieved and pleased when Mailer's anti-psychoanalytic orgasm theory was challenged in a subsequent issue of *Dissent* by Ned Polsky, a Village writer I knew from the White Horse Tavern who was certainly no square. Polsky admitted that psychoanalysis, which was once the property of the European rebels who had pioneered it, had now fallen into the hands of bourgeois American M.D.s, and this posed the danger of bringing a patient "adjustment" to "the present social structure" — that monolith symbolized by the organization man and the lonely crowd.

Nevertheless, Polsky maintained that "it is equally undeniable that psychoanalysis — whatever the brand — still provides greater sexual benefits than does the dreary alternative that Mailer glorifies." Polsky even charged that many hipsters "are so narcissistic that inevitably their orgasms are premature and puny." Was he accusing Mailer, who had grabbed the macho torch from the aging Hemingway, of having "premature" and "puny" orgasms? Was he questioning the virility of the very Mailer who, in his *Advertisements for Myself,* had written with convincing authority of a man who gave a woman "the time of her time" by bringing her to the best orgasm of her entire experience? Those were fighting words, and Mailer was not known to shirk a fight, whether with fists or phrases.

Polsky remembers that after his rebuttal appeared he got a call from Mailer. "I thought maybe he wanted to fight, but he just wanted to talk. We had lunch, and he was very friendly." Instead of challenging Polsky to a duel or a boxing match (as he did on another occasion to Harold Hayes, the editor of *Esquire*), Mailer defended the honor of his own orgasms in a printed reply in *Dissent* (this was now the third installment of the Great Orgasm Debate), arguing that ultimately "one cannot enter another being's orgasm and measure its scope."

Mailer got in another dig at psychoanalysis in his reply to Polsky when he coined the term "ball shrinker" to describe the analyst. Nothing so annoyed my dedicated brother and sister analysands and me as the common designation of the analyst as a "head shrinker," for we believed the job of the doctor was to expand our consciousness. It was also to increase our sexual performance and pleasure, so Mailer's term of genital shrinkage was especially offensive — he knew where to hit you where it hurt!

Whatever the final judgment on whether hipsters or analysands had the best orgasms, the debate was a manifestation of the mood of the time, in its serious fascination with both sex and psychoanalysis. Most of my friends and I who took the couch route naturally agreed with Polsky that psychoanalysis offered the best means of achieving what he called "sexual benefits."

Looking back on the overall benefits of psychoanalysis, Mailer says now, "There are always people who desperately-need-help — that's always said as one word, you know — and for them analysis serves a function, and people can be helped. But others are in it ten, twelve, fourteen years and are exactly the same as when they started. And then they realize that all that time they had to pay someone to be their friend — they hadn't been in a nice relationship."

Of course, many people who tried the couch decided to rise from it early. "After being in psychoanalysis for a year I picked myself up and left," Mary Perot Nichols says. "That's why I'm normal now. It was straight Freudian. I lay on the couch and all he said was 'Yes, go on.'

"A friend of mine went to the same analyst. We used to leave notes for each other on the pillow on the couch. She went for ten years trying to cure her anxiety, then later found out she had undulant fever, which she got from drinking unpasteurized milk as a child, and it caused extreme anxiety. When she was cured of the undulant fever, she was cured of the anxiety."

Others who were dissatisfied with their original analysts switched and found better results. "My first two analysts were terrible," Helen Weaver recalls. "The one I had when I was with Kerouac never opened his mouth. He even fell asleep during sessions. How are you supposed to choose a good one anyway? It's a Catch-22 situation. You're neurotic, you haven't learned to trust your instincts, and yet you're supposed to find someone to make you healthy.

"Nothing worked until '62, when I went to Europe and hit bottom. I had always picked neurotic boyfriends. The one I met in Italy was physically violent, and yet I stayed with him. When I came back to the city, I knew it was a problem and I really wanted to get to the bottom of it. I was ready to change and found a great analyst. He was human, he laughed at my jokes, and actually talked — in fact, nowadays he even goes on TV talk shows."

One of the most prevalent criticisms of psychiatry in the fifties was that it somehow led to conformity, that its goal was to "shrink" the patient to fit the mold of middle-class society. I knew several writers who feared they would lose their creative powers, that the muse would be analyzed right out of them, along with their hangups. Donald Cook says he knew a man in the late forties, a Communist, who was afraid that if he went into psychoanalysis he would lose his political beliefs. Some homosexuals who saw psychiatrists feared becoming heterosexual as a result, and many went into analysis — or were sent by disapproving parents — to be "cured" of their homosexuality.

All the more surprising, then, that one of the most positive evaluations of psychiatry and its effects on the life and career of a creative person comes from Allen Ginsberg: "In 1950 I got out of a psychiatric institution and I started going to a lady psychiatrist," he explains now. "She called up my father and told him my parents must accept the fact that I like men, they should accept it if I was having a man over for supper, or to stay the night. Later, in San Francisco, I told a psychiatrist I wanted to quit my job and write poetry, and he said, 'Why don't you?' I was dubious, so I said, 'What would the American Psychiatric Association say about that?' and he said, 'There's no party line.'

"Of course there were, and still are, psychiatrists who say to a gay man, 'Just hook up with some pussy and you'll be cured.' Now it's just the right wingers of the profession saying that. Back in the fifties one psychiatrist was famous for it — Burroughs satirized him in *Naked Lunch*.

"I like psychiatry. I went for four or five years a long time ago, and now I'm finishing another five years, an examination of the family nexus, looking at the balance of forces, of mother and father. It's very useful."

I lay down on the couch of Freudian psychoanalysis in the fifties and rose up six years later in anger and disillusionment. For me the most accurate diagnosis of the treatment was made by Norman Mailer in "The White Negro" when he called it "a psychic bloodletting" — one in which, like the bloodletting of the Middle Ages, some patients got better, some got worse, and some were almost killed in the process. Like many other former Freudian couch potatoes, I would find aid, comfort, and insight in briefer, more interactive interludes of psychotherapy in years to come. There is little doubt, though, that Freudian psychoanalysis of the five-year, three-to-five-times-a-week-on-the-couch variety had its heyday, for better or worse, in New York in the fifties.

By the late seventies, *Newsweek* was reporting, in an article called "Psychiatry on the Couch," that "throughout the 1940s and 1950s, psychoanalytic chic ran high, generating optimism about its potential that far outran Freud's. . . . Freudian psychoanalysts in particular, who account for only 10% of the nation's psychiatrists, have felt the common unhappiness of post-Freudian deflation."

That deflation, by the late eighties, had made psychoanalysis "The Incredible Shrinking Business," as examined in a remarkable article with that title in the magazine *Boston Business* by Caroline Knapp, the daughter of one of Boston's most prominent psychoanalysts. Knapp reported that "classical analysis . . . the long-term probing process developed by Freud at the turn of the century" has become one of the least-practiced forms of treatment: "Only 2 percent of the estimated 5 million Americans who seek psychotherapy each year turn to the couch for help. The average analyst has only three patients in analysis at a time, and in the past decade, the practice has declined nationally by 36 percent." Dr. Bernard Bandler, past president of the American Psychoanalytic Association, said the forties began the "fat years" of psychoanalysis, and by the fifties "we were *it.* Anybody who was anybody was an analyst." Dr. Julius Silverberger, a psychoanalyst, summed up the current status of his profession: "The days of glory are over. . . . In the world of modern psychiatry, we're really just a pimple."

In its prime, psychoanalysis seemed the best route to the American dream, especially the newly acknowledged dream of sexual fulfillment. We believed that insight on the analyst's couch would translate into ecstasy in the lover's bed, or at least lead to some kind of mutual satisfaction, if not "apocalyptic orgasm."

If Allen Ginsberg finds fresh insights from further therapy in the nineties, most of us fifties veterans of the couch may identify more readily with a poem of Allen's old Columbia friend Donald Cook, which ends with this verse:

> *These days I don't see my therapist.*
> *But I remember everything*
> *And I think I'm changing, slowly.*
> *Soon now I'll take a patient.*

OFF TO THE RACES

We were spooning up prune whip Lacto yogurt for breakfast out of the purple and white cardboard containers while we sat on the dusty floor of my crumble-down apartment on Jones Street in the Village. This was the life. Yogurt was still considered an exotic food, something you would never eat in Indianapolis or Dubuque, just as you would never in places like that be able to have a beautiful, doe-eyed Barnard graduate spend the night in your bed, and lounge around the next morning with her wearing only underpants and one of your old button-down shirts in lieu of pajamas. In these intimate circumstances, a woman I'll call Sandy was telling me about the time she got her diaphragm a year or so before, just after she graduated from college.

There was no birth control pill on the market, and the diaphragm was considered the most effective means of preventing pregnancy. Condoms were known to break, or come off inside the woman after the man had ejaculated and was withdrawing; or in the clumsy effort of the man to wrestle one on, the rubber was sometimes abandoned in the heat of a passionate moment. In any case, a diaphragm was considered the best protection against pregnancy, and most of the unmarried women I knew in New York had one.

Sandy said she had gone to a gynecologist on the Upper East Side whom a friend recommended. She told the doctor she wasn't married, but she wanted to be able to make love with her boyfriend, and she didn't want to get pregnant. The doctor, a distinguished-looking man in his mid-forties, didn't say anything, but he fitted her for the diaphragm, told her how to use it, and she thanked him and got up to leave. He walked her to the door of his office and uttered a line she would always remember. "Well," he said, "you're off to the races."

Sandy laughed when she told me the story, amused rather than angered by the doctor's presumption of her promiscuity. She and I both took it as an indication of the jealousy of an older man for a beautiful, intelligent, "nice" young woman who could have sex with whom she chose, with a freedom that was not available in his own generation.

In a sense, most of us who came to New York after college in the fifties were, as the doctor put it, off to the races of sexual experience and experimentation. At least that was true of those who stayed on and lived in the city for more than a year or so. The big communal apartments with multiple roommates of the same sex which many of us joined after college began to break up after the first year or two at the most, with traditional marriages and moves back home or to other cities, and that early era of relative innocence and sexually pure pajama parties ended then too. Those of us who remained in New York as singles got our own apartments, alone or shared with only one other person, who was usually a close enough friend to allow overnights with someone of the opposite sex and who would vacate the place for an important evening or weekend, which allowed the romantically involved roommate to use the place as a temporary love nest. Armed with cigarettes, booze, and our own psychoanalysts, we lit out for what Huck Finn called "the territory ahead," which for us was not geographical but sexual, lying not to the west but in the bed, the new American frontier of the fifties.

We were still discreet about our affairs, though, unlike the following generation, which blatantly celebrated its sexual freedom as a sort of political triumph. In this as in other realms, if we were silent, it was not out of apathy or inaction but adherence to a code of privacy. We also were still respectful of our parents, who seemed to be looking over our shoulders and who made periodic visits from home. At least in part for their sake, we kept up appearances of the old propriety.

"You weren't supposed to just go out and 'do it,' " Helen Weaver remembers. "I didn't even allow myself to have a double bed until I'd moved into my third Village apartment. In the first two apartments, I slept on these little bitty single beds so no one would think anything was happening. But they were inconvenient, to say the least, so first I bought one of those hideaway jobs, where one twin bed slides out from under the other and makes a sort of double alongside the top one. The trouble with those is that just when things get interesting, somebody falls in the space between.

"After I got my first real double bed, my parents came to visit from Connecticut. Of course, I had to hide all Tommy's clothes and shaving stuff in the closet. I'm giving them the tour of my apartment. My mother pins the double bed, which takes up most of the tiny bedroom, and announces, 'I don't understand why Helen has to have such a *large* bed.' She really didn't know, and I didn't enlighten her. What could I say — the better to get laid in?"

When my own parents came to the city from Indianapolis or my girlfriend's parents visited from out of town, we hid each other's belongings or took them back to our own places, making sure especially to rid our respective bathrooms of intimate items like toothbrushes — not to speak of diaphragms — so the folks wouldn't think we had sunk to the sin of living together without being married. At least we could all keep up the pretense that we were not engaged in what seemed then the ultimate flouting of society's values, even in New York, even in Greenwich Village.

Meg Greenfield recalls that "when parents came to visit, we kicked out the boyfriend, defended the kind of life we lived, and got some good dinners at a restaurant we liked but couldn't afford to eat in too often ourselves, like Peter's Backyard. They'd go back to Seattle or Indianapolis and say, 'How long is this going to go on for?' But we tried to protect them from knowing that 'this' — our single, bohemian lifestyle — even included overnight guests of the opposite sex, in a kind of undercover living arrangement."

Calvin Trillin says, "Very few unmarried people lived together then. I know I would have thought it was quite an unusual arrangement to be living with someone. It was awkward, complicated. I'd have been unable to explain it to my parents."

No one I knew then "lived together" in the way that became commonplace for couples from the sixties onward — not even people in the Village, who considered themselves liberated from all middle-class phoniness. The only exception to lovers living together were those of the same sex. Harvey Shapiro remembers, "You and I knew homosexual couples, but you didn't think of them that way. You just thought of them as couples, two men or two women who lived together, who shared their lives together like a heterosexual couple would do if they were married."

We never questioned the morals of our homosexual friends, whom we thought of as the writers or artists they were, ones who could find a greater freedom and acceptance in New York than they would in the provinces from which they and we came. We were enjoying greater freedom for our own lifestyle that wouldn't have been approved of back home, and so we were sympathetic to others seeking the same liberty. We had liberated ourselves from our parents' views and customs, but not from their visits, and we heterosexuals kept up the pretense of a kind of cultural virginity in our separate living arrangements.

"This was the era before the double nameplate on the door," Gay Talese says. "A girl who was staying at your apartment overnight or for the weekend never picked up the phone. Nan and I always had separate apartments before we were married. Even if you were living together most of the time, you still had separate mail drops and phone numbers."

Once when I used the apartment of a former girlfriend to work on a book, her mother asked her to tell me not to answer the phone, since people who heard a man answer in her unmarried daughter's apartment "would think it 'more than strange.' "

But it was not only parents we were trying to hide our liaisons from, but also the neighbors. "When I was living with Tommy in my walk-up on West 13th Street," Helen Weaver remembers, "there was a snoopy woman on the second floor who watched us. We always left the apartment separately — he'd go down the stairs first. One morning we were feeling great and we walked down together. The woman flew out her door as we passed and said, 'That's better — less furtive!' "

Gay Talese: "You didn't have women in your apartment and feel comfortable about it. I remember trying to slip in and out when the super wasn't there. Or if he saw you, the super then had something on you. You might have to buy him off."

Hostility of apartment supers was especially strong in the Village, where the landlords tended to be from the older Italian generation and considered us college grads from the provinces to be wild bohemians. The super of the building where my girlfriend Sandy lived had been very friendly and helpful to her when she moved in, but after he saw her leaving the apartment with me one morning, he never spoke to her again, and did no more repairs he had been so happy to do in the beginning.

Dan Wolf, the original editor of the *Village Voice,* tells me that by the sixties, when the hippies were moving in, the old Italians were telling him how much they missed "you bohemians." We were Chamber of Commerce types compared with the pot-smoking youth who came after us. But compared with the folks and the friends back home, we unmarried young men and women were living it up in the sexual capital of the country.

"It wasn't just that there was more sex in New York," Calvin Trillin says. "There were lots more single people here our age. It wasn't unusual to be single in New York, while everyone at home in Kansas City was married. The big difference was you could be twenty-six or twenty-seven in New York and be single and it was considered perfectly normal. You did have to get married by your thirties to be normal. Thirty was the pressure time."

I remember feeling the pressure myself as I neared that landmark age, which seemed the end of youth. You were considered a bit odd or out of it in Indianapolis if you hadn't married in your early twenties; in New York the stigma began to appear at thirty, when people started to become suspicious in the same ways folks were back home at an earlier age. Were you normal? Were you unattractive, unbalanced, or sexually screwed up? Men were suspected of homosexuality, while women were rarely imagined to be lesbian, but more often "frigid" or "neurotic."

The thirty stigma hit home one night when I was having drinks at the San Remo with a former girlfriend who'd become a pal, and we were both lamenting a temporary lack of love interest in our lives. I mentioned a man I had recently met whom I could fix her up with, and told her he was a lawyer in his mid-thirties. She asked if he'd ever been married, and I said no. She said thanks but no thanks, and I asked why not. She said, "I'd rather go out with a man who's been divorced by then than a man much past thirty who's never been married at all." I asked why, and she said, "He's likely to have mother problems, some kind of weird mother problems." I quickly finished my drink and ordered another; I was twenty-nine at the time. (I was married for the first time just before my thirty-second birthday.)

Regardless of age, New York provided one of the greatest assets for illicit, or at least unmarried, love affairs. It was so big and there were so many people, the very size and scale of it gave you privacy. When my beautiful cousin Coo from Kentucky came to visit New York as part of "Mr. Boyd Martin's Theatre Tour," an annual cultural trip for the citizens of Louisville led by the drama critic of the *Courier-Journal*, she said, "Why, Danny, ah just love New York, ah just love the anonymity of it. Ah hardly know which crime to commit first!"

Calvin Trillin says, "You could do what you wanted in New York because you weren't going to run into your aunt Martha. If I was in Kansas City, there was no way I wouldn't run into someone I went to school with, dozens of people I knew every week. There were only fifteen restaurants where you might possibly go in the whole city. The anonymity part of New York doesn't exist in any other city."

But evidently this anonymity so prized by lovers was threatened for employees of *Time* magazine by Trillin's good friend John Gregory Dunne. "When I worked at *Time* there was a lot of underground romantic stuff," Trillin says. "I wrote about it in a novel called *Floater* [the term for a staff writer who went from one department to another within the magazine]. Many novels have disclaimers that the characters are all fictional and bear no resemblance to any real person, but I had a *claimer* saying the character named Andy Wolfersham was based on my friend John Gregory Dunne — though I said my portrait in the book tended to flatter.

"John Dunne was always discovering two people who worked for *Time* necking in some place you'd never go, like Washington Heights. His typical sentence would begin, 'I just *happened* to be going through the lingerie department of Bloomingdale's yesterday, when who should I see but . . .' John and I tried to figure out how many romantic couplings were going on. You didn't know people were involved until there was some awful scene in the hall or you got an invitation to a wedding.

"Working at *Time,* you had to be in close quarters with fifty people through the week. There were late closings, time spent with feet up on the desk waiting for editor's initials on a piece. There were lots of girls — or young women, as we say now — working as researchers. All the writers were male, all the researchers female. It was a totally sexually divided magazine — based on a researcher crying at the end of the week, arguing with a writer over what he should or shouldn't change. There was lots of screaming in the halls, tearful confrontations."

Those of us who didn't have the social advantages offered by working for the Luce empire mainly met one another at parties. There were always parties, and any gathering of more than two people with a bottle of wine was considered a party. All you had to do to organize a party was get on the phone and tell people you knew to bring friends and booze.

"We all went out hustling to parties," Meg Greenfield recalls. "We had a sort of base of good pals — all of us had been boyfriends and girlfriends at one point or another, and when the romance cooled we became friends. We always watched one another trying to meet new people, and there was a whole lot of searching. We all smoked heavily and drank. We really drank a lot of the time. Being drunk was considered a source of amusement. There was lots of conversation about it, and everybody drank to get drunk."

John Dunne says, "I'm amazed at how much more we all drank then. When we left New York to go to California, Joan said, 'You know, I think I've had a low-grade hangover for eight years.' "

Joan Didion agrees, adding, "With all those drinks at lunch, and drinking all night, I think we all did. Can you imagine having another drink when the sun came up?"

But we did. It was thought of as romantic, as living to the hilt, carrying on the great traditions of the twenties, of Edna St. Vincent Millay's burning the candle at both ends. Our candle burning did not include pot smoking, and the only people I knew about who did dope in the fifties (except for the legal uppers and downers dispensed by our psychiatrists and analysts on request) were Ginsberg and the beats — and Norman Mailer, who wrote about it in *Advertisements for Myself*. I knew only one friend who kept marijuana on hand, and that made her, in my mind, incredibly exotic (even more so than eating prune whip yogurt), but I didn't care to indulge. I attempted it once but choked trying to inhale the stuff, and didn't pursue it. Pot was part of being beat, and I was loyal to my own addiction to alcohol.

The booze we drank certainly lowered our inhibitions, as well as our awareness, at the parties we staged. I was reminiscing with Donald and Dawn Cook about those parties at their apartment in the Village, and they were talking about how everyone danced. I said I didn't dance at all — I had never been able to dance and felt very shy about it.

"But you used to dance at our parties," Dawn said.

"I can't believe it," I said. "Are you sure?"

"Yes," said Donald, "you even danced with *me*."

"Get yourself a pessary."

When the Barnard girl said it to a table of college students at the West End, I laughed with the others, pretending I knew what it meant. The line turned out to be from a Mary McCarthy short story everyone was talking about that had just appeared in *Partisan Review* for January-February 1954, called "Dottie Makes an Honest Woman of Herself" (later it was included in her novel *The Group*).

I was relieved to learn that the heroine of the story, a twenty-four-year-old Vassar graduate who worked in New York as a reader for publishers, didn't know what the word meant either. At first she thought her new lover said, "Get yourself a peccary," which was a "pig-like mammal they had studied in zoology." The command reminded her of Hamlet telling Ophelia, "Get thee to a nunnery." Seeing her confusion, Dottie's lover explained he was talking about "a female contraceptive, a plug," and she learned it was also called a diaphragm.

The ignorance of Dottie Renfrew could be excused on the grounds that she was living in the thirties, when such things were brand-new, even in New York. My excuse in 1954 was that "pessary" was by then an old-fashioned term from a bygone era, but more important, I'd been in New York for only two years, at college, and in Indianapolis I'd never even heard of a diaphragm.

The only forms of birth control I'd known about before I came to New York in 1952 were abstinence, aided by the cold showers and "hip baths" recommended in the Boy Scout manual of the forties; condoms, more commonly known as rubbers, which men found awkward and constricting; the rhythm method, whose calculations were always a risk; and "pulling out," which was the most widespread practice among my friends back in Indianapolis, as well as the least reliable. A new kind of attitude was required for an unmarried woman to use a birth control device, and it was still revolutionary in the fifties, and extremely rare outside New York City and its environs.

I was amazed, and impressed, that a famous author had written a story about an unmarried girl getting a diaphragm (described in frank and sometimes humorous detail), and that it was published in the most highbrow literary journal of the known (to me) world, the periodical whose pages carried the words of such luminaries as Lionel Trilling, Irving Howe, Philip Rahv, and William Phillips, high priests of intellectual life in New York. (In fact, the magazine looked to me like some kind of holy missal, the list of titles and authors on the cover seeming to give it the weight and authority of a prayerbook.)

The story became so well known that Philip Roth's characters could refer to it in the first story of our fifties generation whose plot hinged on a girl getting a diaphragm, "Goodbye, Columbus," which was first published in *The Paris Review* in 1959. When Roth's young librarian suggests that his Radcliffe student girlfriend go to the Margaret Sanger clinic in New York to get a diaphragm, he denies that he's sent a girl there before, but knows what to do because he's read Mary McCarthy. So has his girlfriend Brenda, who complains, "That's just what I'd feel like, somebody out of *her*." Somebody out of Mary McCarthy meant somebody jaded and sophisticated to Brenda; but she was still in college, and she got the diaphragm anyway.

J. D. Salinger's "Franny," which appeared in *The New Yorker* in 1956, was without a doubt the most widely discussed and debated short story in New York in the fifties. Nor have I known of another time or place in which short stories were taken so seriously as to have the impact "Franny" did in its time. The story tells of an Ivy League weekend that Franny Glass spends with a phony named Lane Coutell. At the end of the weekend she faints, and the story closes as she is reciting the "Jesus prayer." The question readers are left with, and which was so hotly debated all over Manhattan in the weeks that followed, was whether Franny was pregnant, or having a nervous breakdown, or both.

If, in fact, Franny was pregnant and wasn't about to marry Lane, what did she do? That's a story Salinger never told us. It's not the sort of thing we think of as a "Salinger story." If Franny had lived in Indianapolis and was going to college in the Midwest, the odds are if she was pregnant she would marry the guy — even a phony like Lane Coutell. But if Franny was like most of the young women of her age and background who went to college in the East or lived in New York at that time, and she found herself pregnant with the child of a man she didn't want to marry, she would most likely get an abortion.

Abortion was illegal, dangerous, expensive, and commonplace in New York in the fifties. It was the nightmare threat, the dark cloud of death that shadowed the freedom of sexual liberation in the days of its first dawn, not just for wild young people who were out for kicks, but starry-eyed romantics who believed they were truly in love and dared to bring their passion to physical completion without the sanction of marriage. It was not just pot-smoking beatnik girls who got pregnant when they weren't married; it was "nice girls" who graduated from Vassar and Smith, girls as bright, sensitive, and serious as Salinger's much-beloved Franny Glass.

If, indeed, as many readers guessed, Franny was having a nervous breakdown, then she might have been able to get a legal abortion for psychiatric reasons in the safety of a hospital. Only if a woman's life was threatened by her pregnancy could she get a "therapeutic abortion." In the fifties the proportion of legal abortions sanctioned by recommendation of psychiatrists began to rise, and one out of every three abortions performed at New York City's Mount Sinai Hospital in 1956 was "for reasons of mental health." This led to a crackdown by conservative elements of the medical profession who anyway were hostile to psychiatrists, and some hospitals set requirements so severe that a patient had to have demonstrated "a convincing intention of suicide" to qualify for an abortion on grounds of mental health. In order not to risk her life with an illegal abortion in some tenement kitchen, a woman had to convince a hospital board of M.D.s that she would take her life by her own hand, making the threat credible with details of specific plans: a leap from the Triborough Bridge, an overdose of sleeping pills chased with Scotch, a slice of the wrist with a razor blade.

I sat in the Limelight coffeehouse off Sheridan Square one night, advising the girlfriend of a guy I knew how to convince a psychiatrist she would really kill herself if she didn't get a legal abortion. Because I was in analysis, I supposedly knew how and what psychiatrists thought (had I known, I wouldn't have been in analysis), and how to make them believe your story. Actually, the girl seemed so terrified of going the black-market route of backstairs abortions, I suggested that all she had to do was tell the truth. The trouble was, so many other young women were telling similar stories to psychiatrists all over the city, it was hard to make your own story sound more truly desperate than the others, since psychiatrists couldn't write too many such recommendations or they'd get a reputation for it and face the possible loss of their license. Getting a psychiatrist's letter advising a therapeutic abortion in New York then was about as difficult as getting a visa to leave Casablanca in the days when Humphrey Bogart was running Rick's Café.

According to an article called "Important Facts About Abortion," in the February 1956 issue of *Reader's Digest* (hardly the voice of radicalism), "If there is any class of patients who do not get a fair hearing when they seek legal abortion — no matter what reasons they may have — it is unmarried women whose lives and health may be endangered by pregnancy. Doctors often take a moralistic attitude in these cases, as shown by the remarks of one doctor on a hospital abortion committee: 'She has had her fun, and she can sweat this one out.' "

The article reported that many doctors feared persecution from their own colleagues in approving a therapeutic abortion. A "conservative estimate" by *Reader's Digest* of the number of illegal abortions performed in the United States every year at that time was 330,000. A "conservative estimate" by *Newsweek* in the following decade reported that 5,000 women were killed each year "from such complications as bleeding and infections" caused by illegal abortions.

"All abortion was illegal then," Meg Greenfield says, "and that engendered a whole lot of anxiety. It wasn't about coat hangers, but it had a lot of imponderables and danger and fear of the law and of infection and fear of pain, and they didn't like to give anesthesia."

Women I knew experienced horrors at the hands of illegal abortionists who were not M.D.s, people who, as *Newsweek* put it, "practiced furtively in dingy walk-ups and sleazy hotel rooms," charging as much as $1,500 for "hastily performed and often botched services." One woman I knew who had an abortion in a hotel room on lower Fifth Avenue was shoved out the door when she started to bleed profusely. She fainted on the sidewalk, was helped by a passerby who got her into a cab, and after getting back to her apartment called a friend who helped her to a hospital. Now that she had been injured and her life was in danger, she could legally receive medical treatment.

Such stories abounded, true stories of physical and psychic damage, and sometimes death. A grapevine of rumors, warnings, and advice gave out phone numbers and addresses that were sometimes reliable, sometimes not. A highly touted "clinic" in Puerto Rico might turn out to be a back room tenement in old San Juan; a retired doctor in Passaic, New Jersey, could be a twenty-five-year-old Romanian immigrant who barely spoke English; a nurse who let her patients sleep in a quiet bedroom in her Vermont cottage had left the place three days before.

The best hope was a doctor in the small town of Ashland in the drab coal region of eastern Pennsylvania, where there really was a building that served as a clinic with overnight facilities run by a kindly, efficient M.D. named Robert Douglas Spencer, who usually charged $50 and never more than $100 for the operation. Patients received an anesthetic before Spencer did a D and C (dilation and curettage), then were given 600,000 units of penicillin to protect against infection, and a day's rest in bed. The facts of Spencer's underground career were reported by *Newsweek* when he died at age seventy-nine in February 1969, a legend to the thirty thousand women who had come to him over the years.

Spencer was trusted and admired by the townspeople because he had come there after World War I as a pathologist in the miners' hospital and risked his own safety to go down shafts for them after accidents. They protected him even though he was breaking a state law in performing abortions. Still, there were times he had to temporarily shut down his clinic, and cryptic messages were sent to the hapless women who had planned to come to that safe haven, saying the doctor would not be able to see them, he would be unavailable until further notice.

In an anonymous paper describing his cases that was read by a sociologist at a conference on abortion, Spencer said most of the women he saw in the early years of his practice were married, but since World War II "fully half" his patients had been single women in their late teens and early twenties. One in ten were referred by a college guidance counselor or psychologist, most others by women who had gone to his clinic and told their friends that there was at least this one safe place, this one good doctor who would take you in when all the others shut you out.

A young woman went during one of those winters to the small town in Pennsylvania to see Dr. Spencer, and spent the night — as many young women before and after her must have done — in a room in an old hotel, reading a Gideon Bible and talking on the phone to the man who had made her pregnant. The woman, who grew up Hettie Cohen in Brooklyn, describes in her memoir, *How I Became Hettie Jones* (wife of the poet LeRoi Jones), how she stood at the side of the road the next afternoon, "still a bit drugged," waiting for the bus that would take her back to New York, when a car came by, slowed down, and a man shouted, "Oh, you must have been a *bad girl!*"

The Vassar graduates living in New York in the thirties whom Mary McCarthy wrote about in her landmark short story of 1954 realized that birth control, now available for use by women with diaphragms and by men with condoms, was "just one facet, of course, of a tremendous revolution in American society." That revolution, which began after World War I with the loosening of moral strictures in the Roaring Twenties, was part of the whole women's movement for full equality that really took off in the sixties and has permanently changed the way we live.

Jane Richmond looks back on the fifties as a preliberation period of oppression and unquestioned male dominance. "My whole life then was bound up in pleasing men," she says. "Camille Paglia said recently that women know when they're women because they get their period. Women who went to school in the fifties felt they knew they were women when men made them feel they were. Camille is writing from ten years later. I think of the fifties as a time of 'waiting for him to call' — organizing my life around different men.

"Men I was involved with made it clear that it was more important for them to write than for me to write. I believed their lives were more important. During a time when I was seeing a man who was a writer, we were both sending in stories to magazines, and I had a story taken by *The New Yorker*. When my story came out, he made it clear it should have been his story that was published. The message was I shouldn't even continue writing." So Jane actually lived the Zelda role in more ways than as the flamboyant and glamorous flapper at Barnard who got her nickname from the boys at Columbia.

Her story reminded me of my surprise at receiving in the seventies a book written by a woman who had been an important girlfriend of mine in the fifties. She had done me the enormous favor of voluntarily typing up the entire manuscript of my first book. I had no idea she wanted to be a writer herself, though she worked for a publisher. I wrote back a letter of thanks and appreciation of her book, and said, "Why is it the boys of the fifties didn't know the girls wanted to write their own books, instead of just typing the boys' manuscripts?" The only answer I offered in defense of my own obtuseness was another question: "Why didn't the girls *tell* the boys?"

Some of them did, of course, and some of them wrote and published and were duly honored, as their female predecessors had been — Edith Wharton, Millay, Dorothy Parker, Mary McCarthy, and Carson McCullers, to name a few. Women friends of mine were writing articles, fiction, poetry, and criticism I admired as much as any being done, including Meg Greenfield, Marion Magid, Joan Didion, May Swenson, and Jane Mayhall. From the twenties generation we so admired there were talented and accomplished women who served as mentors and friends to many of us coming up in the fifties, especially Josephine Herbst and Kay Boyle.

I honestly didn't know any men who professed, as Norman Mailer did in *Advertisements for Myself* when evaluating his competition, that he couldn't read the talented women who were writing then. He found their work "fey, old-hat, Quaintsy-Goysy, tiny, too dykily psychotic, crippled, creepish, fashionable, frigid, outer-Baroque, *maquille* in mannequin's whimsy, or else bright and still-born" (in a footnote he admitted "with a sorry reluctance" that the early work of Mary McCarthy, Jean Stafford, and Carson McCullers gave him pleasure). He doubted there would be "a really exciting woman writer until the first whore becomes a call girl and tells her tale." In true Hemingway tradition, he concluded that a good novelist can do without everything "but the remnant of his balls," and to top things off, said what little he had read of Herbert Gold "reminds me of nothing so much as a woman writer," which was obviously his worst damnation.

As unaware of women's issues as most men were in those days, such blatant gender hostility was rare and shocking. Us guys were trapped in the same system as the girls, and the social rituals we followed were part of an inherited order we took for granted and even imagined was chivalrous. Remembering some of those unspoken rules of the fifties, Jane Richmond says, "If a girl ordered veal parmigiana at a restaurant, it didn't become a fact till the man said, 'The young lady will have the veal parmigiana.' It was mythic until the man said it — the waiter became deaf when the woman talked, and the woman thought she was invisible. Later, in the sixties, a man I was having lunch with said, 'If you don't order when you're with me, you'll starve,' so I started giving my own order."

Other women friends from that era regard it differently. As Marion Magid puts it, "When I read pieces by women my age, I don't recognize the experience of oppression they describe. I had a career, marriage, a child. I think the fifties had a very bad rap. I was supposedly growing up in a conformist world, but I didn't get married until my thirties. My parents were immigrant Russian Jews, but they didn't tell me to marry a doctor. In fact, I was never told that anywhere, at Barnard or anywhere else."

Marion doesn't envy the more liberated generations that came of age after us, saying, "I think a sense of sin is a very erotic thing. Now young people start by going to bed with each other and then trying to see if they get along or even like each other. We had more discovery, more a sense of being special. Everything now is in quotes — 'He wouldn't commit,' or 'He hasn't explored his own sexuality yet.' The options have been numbered and tagged."

What now seem like indications of changes in the balance of sexual power, or breakthroughs in communication between the sexes, seemed at the time completely personal discoveries between me and a particular girlfriend. I think the kind of education I was getting from women I met in New York was different from what was going on in Indiana.

I found that a woman with a diaphragm not only had control over her sexual fate, but this control gave her, in a natural way, the freedom to have a say in the proceedings. By tradition, the man ran the show in bed; he was the director of the movie, and the woman was to play her role and act as if everything was just fine, the way he liked it. That scenario changed the first time I went to bed with a woman who had a diaphragm.

After my breakup with Emily Lamson, my first great love in New

York, I met at a party a gorgeous, self-assured Brazilian woman who worked for a literary agency. You might think her Latin American background was responsible for her forthright attitude, but I found the same approach in American women from Nebraska as well if they, too, had diaphragms. At the advanced age of twenty-nine, Carlotta was an Older Woman to me, and I think one of my appeals for her was my youth, not only in age but in innocence.

Innocence in bed was no plus, however, and after the first time we made love — I came in about a minute — Carlotta sat up in bed, brushed back her long black hair, and complained. "You're supposed to stay longer," she said, "to make the woman happy. Don't you know about that?"

I learned. I learned many other ways to satisfy a woman, even when I was not able to stay inside her as long as she would like. I discovered my tongue had a function as well as my penis. In Indiana, I had only heard about oral sex as administered by a woman to a man. I learned in New York that it works both ways. Years later, a man I had gone to high school with told me of his lovemaking with his wife, which was limited to his quick release in the missionary position. "I'm one of those in-and-out kind of guys," he explained.

You should have met Carlotta, I thought. You should have lived in New York in the fifties.

We talked frankly about intimate sexual practices and reactions that would have been unmentionable to Evan Connell's characters Mr. and Mrs. Bridge in Kansas City (prototypes of our own parents), or probably my own generation of young men and women outside New York.

The Great Orgasm Debate was carried on not only in the pages of *Dissent* but in beds all over New York. "We talked about women and orgasm problems," Donald Cook says. "There was a belief in Freud's theory, the shifting of true orgasm from clitoris to vagina. If you were helping your girlfriend have clitoral orgasm, were you really doing her a disservice, holding her back from the greater fulfillment? It was something you and she discussed together."

Just as I had forgotten about strontium 90, one of the hot issues of atomic testing in the Stevenson-Eisenhower campaign of 1956, I had forgotten, until Donald brought it up, the great debate over whether clitoral orgasms were "immature" and only vaginal orgasms were "the real kind."

A man worried that if a woman didn't have an orgasm while they were having intercourse, he had failed to please her, while a woman worried that if she failed to have an orgasm, she had failed to please the man. Sometimes we reassured each other that not having any kind of orgasm was all right. After I went to bed with Helen the first time, she confessed that up to that point in her life, she had never had an orgasm. (That was before her great analyst, I learned later.) She tells me now she still remembers my response to her confession because it was such a relief to her: "You laughed and said, 'Don't worry, nobody has *those.*'"

Helen taught me the excitement of sharing my sexual fantasies and discovering the woman's fantasies too. And even, oh God, acting them out, "making your dreams come true." She had a rich imagination, filled with humor as well as eroticism. After hearing Helen's dreams, I wasn't so embarrassed about revealing mine. With Helen I learned the intimacy of speaking to a girlfriend more frankly than I had ever spoken to any man.

One summer morning, we sat at her kitchen table without any clothes on and wrote down all the possible ways people could give pleasure to each other, all the openings and all the things that were possible to put in the openings that made you feel good, excited, aroused, satisfied. This was before *The Joy of Sex,* when the only sex manuals seemed to have been written for squares in Topeka and Dubuque. The *Kama Sutra* was the only instructional manual people I knew referred to, and Helen and I found its innumerable descriptions of positions dry and pedantic, like a series of yoga lessons. So we made up our own sex manual, a do-it-yourself project.

Helen was my own age but seemed a lifetime older in terms of knowledge, experience, and overall understanding of the world. I bought groceries and she cooked. She introduced me to the joys of chicken livers for dinner and bagels for breakfast with hot black freshly ground coffee. I spent most of my time at her apartment, writing there during the day and sleeping with her there at night, but we never completely moved in together.

Like most such couples, Helen and I were both in analysis and thus not "ready" for such a commitment, so from the start we had only a temporary relationship. We didn't even use the word "relationship" then. We called our arrangement an affair, like an event that had a beginning and an end, which is how we approached it, and how we ended it when it seemed to have run its course.

"Yes, go on," as the analyst said. And both of us did, as our other friends did, beginning the same process with other partners, coupling and holding together for a while and then coming undone when things got rough or just stale, moving on to the next, and the next, and the next.

Little did we know we were setting a trend for a future in which noncommitment was a way of life, even for the middle class in middle America, where divorce rates followed the soaring marital crack-ups of the coasts, boosting a national average of 50 percent as the norm. Even steven. Half and half. You pays your money and takes your chances.

Who knows if back then we were riding the wave of freedom or being catapulted into a future of chaos, tossed helter-skelter like so many random surfboards whose riders are lost in the sea? Whatever mistakes we made, whatever illusions we nurtured — and there were many of both — we did it all with conviction and passion, with love of the time and place and the people who appeared in our lives like marvelous characters in a great play, lovers and companions.

I think back to those days with Helen in the cozy apartment she had near Hudson Street, convenient to the White Horse, near the river and the docks, where you could hear in the night the low horns of steamships coming in. One winter I wrote there with my typewriter set on a table by the window. I'd put on the Miles Davis album *Sketches of Spain* and watch the snow come down past the faces of small brick houses on the quiet, winding street, so far from Indianapolis. The plaintive music mixed with the hissing sound of the radiators and made it seem like another dimension, a world that was mysterious, yet safe and warm. In the fading light of five o'clock, with a lamp turned on above my table, Helen would appear in the doorway, stamping the snow from her feet, shaking out her long brown hair. There was no other place I wanted to be.

NINE

From Joe McCarthy to Jean-Paul Sartre

POLITICS

In our time the destiny of man presents its
meaning in political terms.
— Thomas Mann

How can I, that girl standing there
My attention fix
On Roman or on Russian
Or on Spanish politics?
Yet there's a travelled man that knows
What he talks about,
And there's a politician
That has read and thought,
And maybe what they say is true
Of war and war's alarms,
But O that I were young again
And held her in my arms!

RUEFULLY recited that Yeats poem to myself just before my thir-
tieth birthday, blaming my blind pursuit of a girl for landing me
in the "subversive" political soup for the first time since leaving Indiana. Damn! It was spring, it was 1960, dawn of a whole new decade. I was wooing an uptown beauty who was also pursued by a

number of men of considerable affluence, and I was trying to think of ways to impress her that didn't involve great outlays of cash. Just then the phone rang with an invitation to a cocktail party where I would meet Jean-Paul Sartre and Simone de Beauvoir. Fate.

It wasn't to be a cozy affair in someone's living room, but a midtown hotel soirée to listen to the two great French intellectuals tell about their recent trip to Castro's Cuba. Not surprisingly, they'd had a wonderful time — but why not go and hear them? I casually called the object of my affections and dropped the names of the Parisian dynamic duo. Would she like to meet them over cocktails? You bet.

We pushed our way into the crowd pressing around Beauvoir, but even standing on tiptoes we couldn't spot Sartre, at least not until we got to the very center of the gathering. Then, in a flash, I understood existentialism. Sartre was short, about the size of Napoleon, or Jimmy Hoffa. Talk about compensation — this guy had created a whole philosophy, one that explained the angst of the human condition, including being too short.

Both Sartre and Beauvoir spoke glowingly of what they had seen on their trip and warmly endorsed Castro and his regime. Not exactly a social or literary tête-à-tête, but we could always say we'd met them. Good enough. The hitch was that on the way out, one of our hosts said the guests of honor, as well as a number of American writers and intellectuals, wanted to publish a statement in an ad calling for "fair play" for Cuba. He said he'd send along the statement and hoped I would sign it. I said to send it on.

The envelope came but I didn't open it. I had never signed anything for a political cause, and I wasn't inclined to start, though I did think Castro was getting a raw deal from the American press and politicians. I forgot about the whole thing until the phone rang a few days later, and the host who sent me the statement asked again if I'd sign. I said I hadn't yet read it, but he said he needed an answer right away because they were going to press with a full-page ad in the *New York Times*. So far, he said, the statement had been signed by James Baldwin, Norman Mailer, and even Truman Capote. I knew I agreed with Baldwin on most things, and I felt I owed something to this guy on the phone — I mean, I had taken a date to the party and we'd drunk their liquor and munched their hors d'oeuvres, hadn't we? Signing his ad seemed a bit like picking up the tab, so I said yes, then hung up feeling queasy. I couldn't even find the letter with the statement I'd just "signed" — I'd already tossed it.

When I saw the full-page ad with my name on it, I felt even queasier. It was full of flaming rhetoric of the kind that makes me cringe, even though I agreed with the basic idea of "fair play." My stomach gurgled at the phrase "dollar diplomacy," which was straight out of stale, stock leftist rhetoric. I put down the ad and tried to put it out of my mind.

I had never been ashamed of anything I'd written and published on political topics — most of which were reportage rather than interpretation — but those pieces were, for better or worse, expressed in my own words. I could stand by them and for them. Affixing my name to somebody else's rhetoric, though, made me feel like a parrot. I tried to console myself that I wasn't alone, but part of a distinguished chorus. After all, Truman Capote was right there with me on the barricades.

When the bearded Castro and his young revolutionaries came down out of the mountains and took Havana on New Year's Day of 1959, ousting the longtime dictator Batista, I regarded Fidel as my friends — and I think most other Americans at the time — did, as a hero of the people, a liberator rather like Marlon Brando in *Viva Zapata*. (Perhaps to transpose that image onto its invasion force, the Kennedy administration gave the code name Operation Zapata to the Bay of Pigs mission two years later.)

Castro came to the United States in April 1959 on what seemed a triumphal visit, winning further sympathy when he left his hotel in midtown Manhattan and quartered himself and his people at the Hotel Theresa in Harlem. There were stories of his hardy band cooking chickens over open fires in Central Park — *viva la revolución!* Castro was a hero on many college campuses, and though Princeton limited his audience to 150, a crowd of 6,000 turned out at Harvard when he spoke at Dillon Field House.

If Castro raised the suspicions of conservatives, who thought him a Communist right off the bat, he won the hearts and imaginations of liberal and left-wing intellectuals, who saw in his revolution a hopeful, non-Communist, non-Soviet, socialist answer to the downtrodden countries of the world. Besides that, Castro himself had credentials as a true intellectual: while he was hiding out in the Sierra Maestra he was reading *White Collar* and the other works of my former professor and boss, C. Wright Mills.

By the time I signed the "Fair Play for Cuba" ad a year later, a lot of people were already disillusioned with Castro, calling him a Communist and a menace to the security of the United States. But that seemed panicky and reactionary — certainly it wasn't fair play. So what was I worried about?

What I feared came to pass: some of the people who signed the ad were called before the Senate Internal Security Committee of Mississippi's James O. Eastland and grilled in public testimony; others (including me, I was told) were subjected to investigation by the FBI. I sat down and wrote a long letter resigning from the Fair Play for Cuba Committee (it seemed superfluous, in a way, to resign from something I didn't think I'd joined), stating all kinds of valid political disagreements and questions — though I knew I was really motivated by the fear of what I'd dreaded ever since Columbia, the witness I saw who seemed to foreshadow my own possible fate.

No one I knew had a television set in college. It was considered an expensive and frivolous luxury for a student, and it seemed beneath one's dignity. A TV set was called an idiot box, and we were intellectuals. If we wanted to watch anything on television — most likely a sporting event or some national disaster or spectacle — we went to a bar. (Most of my friends and I continued this practice until I took an apartment in 1961 and had to buy the furniture, which included an old, boxlike TV.) At Columbia we went to the West End, and it was there, with friends from the *Spectator,* that I watched several sessions of one of the landmark political events of my time, which was both disaster and spectacle: Senator Joseph McCarthy's first nationally televised hearings on subversion, with his investigations of alleged Communist influence in the Voice of America. The reason my friends and I went to see these particular three days of testimony in March 1953 was that one of our own alumni who had been an editor of *Spectator* and now worked for the Voice of America was the subject of investigation.

In some eerie, quite scary way, watching this man Reed Harris was like watching us, *ourselves,* as we might be put on some stand twenty years in the future and asked to explain, justify, and perhaps recant things we had written in college, words and ideas we were thinking and writing *now,* in the same *Spectator* that was being quoted back at this alum in an effort to discredit him, strip him of his good name, his job and career.

Reed Harris had worked for the Office of War Information, which waged psychological warfare against the Axis forces during World War II. The office was re-formed by President Truman in 1952 as the International Information Administration, which included the Voice of America. Senator McCarthy, in his new role as chairman of the Senate's Permanent Subcommittee on Investigations (in the past it had studied such dangerous matters as "employment of homosexuals and other sex perverts in government"), announced he was going to investigate the Voice of America, which, he darkly told reporters, employed people who were "sabotaging" the foreign policy of the United States.

We got a hint of the nature of McCarthy's tactics in February 1953, when he charged that there were thirty thousand books in our government's overseas libraries by "Communist" authors. The number was compiled by listing copies of books by more than four hundred writers, including Edna Ferber, Arthur Schlesinger, Jr., W. H. Auden, Stephen Vincent Benét, and Dashiell Hammett. Columbia's former president, now president of the United States, at least spoke out for intellectual freedom by defending the works of one author whom he wanted to remain on the shelves: Ike himself asked that the mystery stories of Hammett not be purged.

As my friends and I from *Spec* sat around the horseshoe bar at the West End, nervously sipping beers, munching peanuts, and smoking cigarettes, we watched with a combination of disbelief, amusement, anger, and foreboding the appearance of Reed Harris before McCarthy and his committee. It was the first time many of us had actually seen the Red-hunting senator live on television. He glowered, droned, badgered, and bullied in a malicious monotone that seemed immune to nuance or contradiction — you were either friend or enemy, supporter or target, one or the other.

McCarthy "exposed" the former student editor from the thirties for having written editorials in our college newspaper, more than

twenty years before, attacking such sacred institutions as intercolle-
giate football, the American Legion, and, literally, apple pie. Reed
Harris had been given two favorable "full field investigations" by
the FBI and clearance from the Civil Service Commission, but he
was still accused by McCarthy of harboring disloyal thoughts and
opinions, and was ordered to produce documentary evidence of
having had a change of heart.

Evidently, Mr. Harris had not recanted his subversive belief that
college football had assumed too much importance in American
life. While still a student at Columbia he had written, in addition to
those subversive editorials denouncing apple pie, a book called *King
Football* in which he went so far as to defend the idea of academic
freedom, even upholding the right of Communists to teach in colleges. This position had been endorsed by Republican stalwart Senator Robert Taft, but was regarded in the political atmosphere of
the fifties to be proof of disloyalty and — that most scurrilous new
designation, one for which there was not only a name but a committee of the U.S. House of Representatives to investigate it — un-
Americanism.

What I still clearly remember from those hearings of nearly forty
years ago is not just the droning voice of McCarthy accusing Reed
Harris of writing those satirical, youthfully exuberant editorials and
demanding demonstration of a change of heart. The line that
comes back the loudest and still raises goose pimples along my arms
is the angry, frustrated, bitter voice of Harris objecting to the senator's unrelenting efforts over three days of testimony "to wring my
public neck."

How far did I want to stick out my own neck? That was the inevitable question that came to my mind, as it naturally must have come
to all the other guys from *Spectator* sitting around me at the West
End as we watched one of our own — an obviously bright, talented,
spirited man who seemed pretty much like ourselves but twenty or
so years older — being pilloried for words he had written and
thoughts he had expressed as a college undergraduate.

Harris resigned his post on April 14, 1953, and McCarthy commented, "I only hope a lot of his close friends will follow him out."
That spring hundreds of employees were fired from the International Information Administration (later reorganized as the U.S.

Information Agency), and the hearings dragged on until July, though no evidence of treason or conspiracy was found. (Reed Harris was later rehired under the John F. Kennedy administration.)

More than jobs and reputations as loyal Americans were lost in the wake of McCarthy's televised investigations. Raymond Kaplan, a forty-two-year-old Voice of America engineer, committed suicide by jumping in front of a truck, leaving a letter to his wife and son that said, "You see, once the dogs are set on you everything you have done since the beginning of time is suspect. . . . I have never done anything that I consider wrong but I can't take the pressure upon my shoulders any more." After Kaplan's death, McCarthy said blandly that he had no evidence of wrongdoing against the man.

It would hardly be surprising if young people listening to those hearings became cautious about what they did and said, both in print and in conversation, in public and even in private — perhaps intimate — situations. A former girlfriend testified against Roger Lyons, who was director of religious programming for the Voice of America, saying that he was, or had once been, a nonbeliever. Lyons denied that he was an atheist or even an agnostic, and testified before the Senate subcommittee and the nation: "I believe in God." No doubt to prove his credentials in religious and spiritual matters, Lyons said he had studied psychology with Carl Jung. McCarthy asked if Jung attended a church or synagogue.

My friends and I on *Spectator* didn't get to see our most famous alumni editor grilled by McCarthy that spring, for the two times that *New York Post* editor James Wechsler was brought before the committee the sessions were closed — though later, transcripts were released at Wechsler's own request. No doubt he wanted the press and the world to know that the senator from Wisconsin had charged that the *Post*, New York's leading liberal newspaper and a constant critic of McCarthy, was "next to and almost paralleling the *Daily Worker*."

Wechsler had been a member of the Young Communist League from age eighteen until twenty-one, yet he'd been a staunch anti-Communist ever since, attacking both internal subversion and Soviet foreign policy, but McCarthy accused him of a "phony break" with the Reds: "I feel you have not broken with Communist ideals.

I feel that you are serving them very, very actively. Whether you are doing it knowingly or not, that is in your own mind. I have no knowledge as to whether you have a card in the party."

Though the term "McCarthyism" came to be the name of this type of witch-hunting mentality and procedure, McCarthy in 1952 had to elbow his way onto the already crowded field of anti-Communist snipers. "Tail Gunner Joe" had to agree not to compete with the investigations of the House Un-American Activities Committee, which was going after the Hollywood community, and the Senate Internal Security Subcommittee, headed by William Jenner of Indiana, which had taken for its own Red-hunting grounds the United Nations, as well as public and private schools. This was the Cold War, and as my Village neighbor David Amram now reflects, "The fifties was a repressive time too, in spite of all the creative things going on. McCarthy got as far as he did because of the nature of the times. He wasn't just the cause, he was part of the whole picture. Miles Davis used to say, 'Only the strong survive in jazz.' But he meant in general terms, too."

Young people were bound to be affected by the witch-hunts that were rife at the time, and wonder how our own futures would be influenced by what we said, wrote, joined, and signed while in college. Max Frankel, who was the editor of *Spectator* that spring of 1953 when McCarthy grilled Reed Harris on television, says, "There was an anxiety with which we came through the Red-baiting period. Those of us who wanted mainstream careers felt we were walking on eggshells — in what we signed, what political organizations we joined."

Though we indeed were cautious about joining and signing, we did not stifle our opinions, nor were we cowed into the fearful silence for which we were unjustly famous. The little known, often denied fact — the truth that is lost because it doesn't fit our generational image — is this: we did stick our necks out!

The harassment of Reed Harris for opinions he had expressed in *Spectator* editorials did not silence Max Frankel or his successor on the paper, Jerry Landauer; it did not prevent them from writing outspoken editorials defending academic freedom, opposing congressional inquiries of colleges, and protesting Columbia's own administration for banning controversial speakers, like Howard Fast, from campus. Nor did the atmosphere of the times prevent me from expressing my own new liberalism the following year in the place most likely to cause controversy, my own hometown.

The great Robin Hood controversy began on May 21 that year, my birthday, while I innocently munched a French cruller and sipped my coffee at Mr. Zipper's drugstore on Amsterdam Avenue while reading the *New York Times*. My eye was caught by an editorial titled "Liberty in Indianapolis." It cited an earlier story about a member of the Indianapolis school board who wanted the story of Robin Hood banned from the public schools on the grounds that his habit of taking from the rich and giving to the poor was a sign of communism. My hometown had also gained notoriety the previous year when the War Memorial banned from its premises the initial meeting of the Indiana chapter of the American Civil Liberties Union. Edward R. Murrow had come to Indianapolis and filmed a documentary on the War Memorial banning, showing that the ACLU was finally allowed to assemble in a local Catholic church whose priest believed in the principles of free speech.

"Now the issue has arisen again," the *Times* editorial went on, "in connection with a meeting of the Indiana chapter of the ACLU at which Paul Hoffman, one of Indiana's most distinguished citizens [he was a liberal Republican businessman, chairman of the board of the Studebaker Corporation], is scheduled to speak on the Bill of Rights. Again the use of the War Memorial has been refused this group. . . . It seems to us that the guardians of the War Memorial made themselves ridiculous. Certainly, they have failed once again to honor the purpose to which their building is dedicated."

I finished my cruller and coffee and hurried back to my room in the dorm to write an impassioned letter to the *Indianapolis News*. I mailed it the same day, then forgot about it when I took the train back home for the summer break, arriving just in time to see my letter published as the lead of the Letters to the Editor column of May 25, under the headline "University Student Mourns Loss of His Home City's Prized Prestige."

I looked at the page and took a deep breath. Uh-oh, I thought. Now I've done it. Back home in Indiana, my words sounded more inflammatory as I read them in the pages of the *Indianapolis News*, drinking a Coke in the den of my parents' mock-colonial home with all the amenities of fifties living, including a small, screened-in hall-way connecting house and garage called a breezeway. How can you oppose the status quo from your parents' breezeway? Such discomforting thoughts needled me as I reread my letter.

Lamenting with heavy irony that my hometown used to be famous for the 500-mile auto race, I said it was now becoming better known as the place where Robin Hood was thought to be a Communist and a civil liberties group was banned from the War Memorial. Showing my patriotism as well as my liberalism (thank God I'd put *that* part in), after quoting from the *Times* editorial I said,

> The saddest and most shameful aspect of the situation is that people in every communistic country will read this just as they read reports of the Robin Hood incident which the Russian press so gleefully gobbled up and dispatched. Here we have provided them with a blatant example of American hypocrisy. This is the nation, founded on the principle of free speech and free assembly, now denying those basic rights. . . .

My poor parents were barraged by phone calls offering condolences for having sent their son east to college, especially to a hotbed of pinkos like Columbia. Weren't the worst fears of Uncle Clayton and Aunt Mary proved true? After all, when I left home my only political affiliation was as a founding member of the Young Republicans of Indianapolis; only two years later, I was defending Robin Hood and the ACLU!

The prevailing local opinion of my radical new outlook was expressed eloquently in a letter the *News* featured four days later in answer to mine, under the headline "Reader Says It's Up to ACLU to Prove Its Pro-Americanism." That reader, who identified him- or herself only by the initials J.G.T., wrote:

> It is regrettable that the young people today have had so much sensational and left wing propaganda thrown at them the last 20 years that they cannot possibly get a true picture or judge correctly the situation of today. . . . They

do not have a firm belief in Christian principles, in logic and in facts. . . .

Why do not Dan Wakefield, et al. get down to the real meaning of the Robin Hood story and appreciate and approve our independent stand on federal aid to education, federal welfare, federal hospital grants and even PTA board dictatorship?

Indiana has proved to be a pro-American state and we are mighty tired of the liberties allowed subversive groups and see no reason why their detrimental endeavors should be encouraged in our tax-supported public buildings. There have been no facts but only opinions on whether the ACLU is a left wing organization. . . . When it is proved that the ACLU is thoroughly pro-American and not leftish, then it is time to weep for Indianapolis and not before.

Other letters followed, as well as other phone calls. My parents, though disturbed, never once berated me or asked that I keep my new opinions to myself. My letter could have hurt them in their respective businesses, for my father had a drugstore at that time under his own name, and my mother was selling real estate. Patriotic customers could well have shunned them, which was not unheard-of, and perhaps some did. My mother and father would never have told me if it happened. My impression was, though, that they received more sympathy than condemnation. After all, you couldn't control young people, not even in those days. That sourpuss young actor with a bad attitude, that James Dean fellow, was a hero to lots of young people, and with a cigarette dangling from his mouth, he summed up the disrespectful mood that lots of kids seemed to be in around that time.

Another letter to the *News* asked pointedly, What other newspapers did I read besides the *New York Times*? The implication was clear — I'd been brainwashed. Most readers seemed to understand that my parents weren't to blame. It was New York, and the *Times,* and going east to college, especially Columbia. The I-told-you-so doomsayers who believed that east was the direction of hell and the George Washington Bridge the gateway to it were no doubt as confused as I was delighted by the next letter in the ongoing controversy.

My friend Richard T. "Fuzzy" Stout, with whom in high school I'd written words to unpublished — and unpublishable — musical comedies (e.g., "Alaska — Or, The Old Folks at Nome"), had written to the *News* in my defense. It was a true act of friendship and political conviction. The letter from Stout, a talented journalist who was later to become a staff writer for *Newsweek* and a popular college journalism teacher, was all the more powerful — and all the more gutsy — because he had not gone east to school but was a student at DePauw, right there in Indiana. His letter was featured on the editorial page of June 3: "Local 'Youngster' Rallies to the Defense of His Generation."

Stout defended my views on Robin Hood and the ACLU, identified himself as one of the "et al.'s" referred to by my attacker J.G.T., and said that critic's letter would have been more meaningful if its author had signed his or her name. He ended by quoting a noted "son of Indiana," the famous radio commentator Elmer Davis, who had said, "This nation was not established by cowards, nor will it be preserved by cowards." Hurray for Elmer Davis, and hurray for stout-hearted Fuzzy Stout.

We were hardly silent. Not even in Indianapolis, where views such as Richard Stout and I expressed were definitely in the minority.

"All right we are two nations" was a cry from John Dos Passos's trilogy *U.S.A.*, which I'd read the previous autumn while lying in the hospital after my automobile accident. The sentence took on a physical, geographical specificity for me when I still lived in Indianapolis with my parents during summer and Christmas vacations from college and spent the rest of the time in New York as a student. It was like commuting between two countries with the same language (though different accents) that held opposing values, customs, manners, and politics.

Fuzzy Stout was one of the few Democrats I knew from high school. Most of us grew up accepting the political and religious faith of our fathers and mothers, most of whom were God-fearing, Christian, middle-class, middle-of-the-road, middle-aged, conservative Republican, all-American believers in the values (or their symbols) that Reed Harris satirized when he was a student at Columbia.

I never had a Communist professor at Columbia, nor did I ever hear any teacher or student defend or uphold communism or the Communist Party. I'm sure some of the faculty had once been members — as had been the student editor James Wechsler — of the Young Communist League in the thirties, or maybe even the Party, but by the fifties the idealism that drove such zeal had turned to disillusionment, and some of the strongest anti-Communists were those who felt they'd been duped by the Party.

I did, of course, meet many liberals, Democrats, and maybe even Socialists, and certainly left-wing views were as prevalent on Morningside Heights as Republicanism was the norm in Indianapolis. So was I simply falling in line, taking on the coloration of my landscape — red white and blue in Indiana turning to pink at Columbia? That may be partly the case, but I know there was more to it. One emotional factor was that after my rejection at fraternity rush at Northwestern, I identified for the first time with the underdogs, the have-nots instead of the haves, the Outs instead of the Ins. (Later I learned that C. Wright Mills told his friend Harvey Swados he believed the severe hazing he underwent as a college freshman at Texas A & M before transferring to the University of Texas "had made him into a rebel and outsider.")

After striving so hard to be a "big dog" (we literally called it that) in high school and succeeding, when I failed to achieve the same high status at Northwestern, I suddenly knew what it felt like to be Out. I realized that people who were Out (out of jobs, out of the right fraternities or country clubs) might be good guys just like me, and that their low circumstance, whatever it happened to be, *might not be their own fault!*

I argued this with my old Boy Scout friend Johnny when he came to New York my last semester at Columbia, while I lived in my wondrous basement apartment on West 77th Street and cooked up frozen tuna pot pies (still icy in the center but ameliorated by Chianti). I had taken history courses that dealt with the Depression, I was taking C. Wright Mills's seminar in liberalism, and I had come to see, for the first time in my life, that sometimes world, national, and local economics determined the circumstances of individuals, whose futures were often beyond their own control. This was a revelation!

Growing up in Indiana, we were so imbued with rugged self-reliance that we believed every unfortunate turn of events was the fault of the individual. Now, as I explained to Johnny, you can see, can't you, that in the Depression, when millions of people were out of work, it wasn't their fault.

No, he didn't see that at all.

"I mean, it wasn't that millions of Americans in the course of a few weeks suddenly just got lazy, was it?" I asked.

"Yes," Johnny said, "that must have been it."

There was no other explanation he could accept. In light of my new belief that there were forces beyond the control of these individuals that forced them out of work and onto bread lines, I was — in Johnny's terms — a left winger and a liberal, if not a pinko or a Red.

At Columbia I heard, for the first time, real left wingers spoken of with respect and I listened to their stirring words and was moved by them. I remember the force of the eloquence of Eugene V. Debs, the declaration of his faith, which I read in history class and then in Dos Passos's *U.S.A.*: "While there is a lower class I am in it, while there is a criminal element I am of it; while there is a soul in prison, I am not free."

Those words had all the more power for me because they were not uttered by Karl Marx, V. I. Lenin, or any such foreign thinker or enemy of my country, but by one of its own, one who, in the words Dick Stout had used to describe Elmer Davis, was a "son of Indiana." Eugene V. Debs was a guy from Terre Haute!

But was he, in the lingo of McCarthy and Jenner and the Cold Warriors of the fifties, un-American?

Such questions filled the pages of the *Indianapolis News* in the late spring and summer of 1954, when the biggest headlines of all, and the biggest TV spectacle, were the Army-McCarthy hearings. I had watched them at the West End near Columbia, and I continued to watch them back home in Indiana in my parents' den, just off the breezeway. By the time they were over, so was McCarthy's power: a Gallup poll rated McCarthy's popularity at only 34 percent, with 45 percent expressing disapproval. The Senate's condemnation (not "censure") of McCarthy came that December.

Millions of Americans watched the televised hearings, and everyone who watched has memories of them and their impact. "I recall watching the Army-McCarthy hearings," Marion Magid says, "and my father was terrified. He was an anti-Stalinist, very much aware — and rightfully so — of the Communist Party as a threat, but he also hated McCarthy. He wanted America to vindicate itself, and when Joe Welch stood up and did that, when Welch finally embarrassed McCarthy and stood up to him, my father saw it as proof that Golden America had triumphed again."

Richard Lingeman, from Crawfordsville, Indiana, says, "I went into the Counter-Intelligence Corps of the Army in 1954, when the Army-McCarthy hearings were on TV. I went to Washington, and everyone was arguing about McCarthy. A friend and I had enlisted together, and my friend's father was considered a security risk, so my friend was bumped out of the CIC — it had a chilling effect.

"There was a guy in my college class whose parents were kicked out of teaching jobs, a sociology professor who got in trouble because of McCarthy. It kept filtering in — but there I was in the CIC, scared that I'd be dropped out, and we were investigating people who needed security clearance. I was against McCarthy, but like many people in the fifties, I felt sort of politically schizophrenic. Luckily, when I was sent to Japan, my field was ultra-right-wing nationalists who wanted to bring back the emperor."

Sometimes fear of the Red menace became so ludicrous it brought a few laughs. Calvin Trillin was stationed on Governors Island in New York when he was in the Army. "I wrote for the base newspaper," he recalls. "The editor of the paper was Rudy Wurlitzer [a former Columbia student and future novelist and screenwriter], and when he wrote an editorial supporting National Library Week, they took his security clearance away. After that, we called him Red Rudy."

Norman Mailer thinks the McCarthy period "increased the inner tension with which I lived, but it didn't have a hell of a lot of effect on my work. When *The Deer Park* came out [1955], one reviewer did a snide review in *Time*, and said I must be suffering from 'subpoena envy' — he must have been the hero of the office for the next week."

According to the journalist and editor Walter Goodman, "A very small number of people were really hurt by McCarthy. You had to be in Hollywood or TV, though some of the academics were also hurt. I don't mean to downplay it — for those who really were injured by it, it must have been awful. But I was working at the CIA when McCarthy was riding high, and no one I knew there liked him. I covered the McCarthy hearings for *The New Republic,* and we used to knock him all the time, but we weren't concerned or fearful. I feel there's been a rewriting of history from people like Lillian Hellman, that the liberals took a dive during the McCarthy period, and it's not true. They were split on how to deal with him, but plenty of criticism came from the liberals, sharp stuff."

The split over how to deal with McCarthy left many deep divisions, and one of the deepest and most basic was over the issue of "naming names." Most of the people called before the McCarthy committee were willing to tell about their own past political histories but didn't want to give names of friends from the past who might also have belonged to or attended meetings of Communist or Communist front organizations.

One of the leading liberals who vigorously opposed McCarthy and yet did name names was our former *Spectator* editor James Wechsler. McCarthy demanded that Wechsler give his committee a list of people he remembered from his youth who had been in the Communist Party or the Young Communist League. Wechsler complied, and one of the names he gave was that of his own colleague at the *Post,* Murray Kempton.

I didn't know at the time that Wechsler had given Kempton's name to the committee. I simply wasn't following the hearings that closely, but would tune in and out as exams and studies permitted. Though I've known Kempton since 1955, I never heard him mention this. When I ask him about it now, he simply explains Wechsler's point of view: "When Jimmy gave names to the McCarthy committee, he felt he would discredit the *Post* if he didn't cooperate."

When I once criticized Wechsler over something I'd read in the *Post* (I never met the man, so it probably was criticism of what I considered the clichéd nature of the *Post*'s liberal editorials, like their use of the phrase "he happens to be a Negro"), Murray defended him. He made that kind of squint he has that expresses discomfort and disagreement, and said, "Jimmy is a man who's been badly served." There was no suggestion that Jimmy had badly served anyone else.

Kempton had told the McCarthy committee's chief counsel that if called to testify, he would not give names. Murray says, "When Roy Cohn said he might subpoena me, I told him, 'I'm not giving you any names.' I said, 'I could give you a lot of high-minded reasons for it, but I'll give you a low-minded reason — I can't afford it commercially.'"

Murray is disturbed that this was misinterpreted by a writer who thought that when he said he couldn't afford it commercially, he meant he just didn't want to offend his liberal friends. "I wasn't just talking about liberals," Murray explains. "I wouldn't give names because Bill Buckley would have had no respect for me. Everyone whose opinion I value would have had no more use for me. So at any rate, Cohn never called me."

I had always assumed that Murray wasn't called before the McCarthy committee because there wasn't anything to expose about him, since he spoke and wrote freely about his past, including having been a member of the Young Communist League when he was a student at Johns Hopkins.

"I dined out on having been in the Young Communist League." Murray says. "But aside from that, my curse and blessing is I am incapable of being taken seriously."

I don't believe it. I spent too many evenings on West 92nd Street with my friends, fresh out of college, reading and reciting passages from *Part of Our Time* or poring over his columns in the *Post*. I continue to look for them in *Newsday* whenever I take the shuttle down from Boston, and sometimes search them out when they're reprinted in *The New York Review of Books*.

Besides, Murray's use of "serious," like that of most of his words and ideas, has many nuances. I'm reminded of this when he speaks of his good friend William F. Buckley, Jr. "I've never thought of Bill as a serious man, which is a sort of compliment. There's a wonderful letter Whittaker Chambers wrote to Bill, and in a review of their correspondence someone said something like, 'In Buckley, Chambers found what he was looking for all his life — the friend

James Baldwin gave generously of his advice and his bourbon to young writers who gathered at his apartment on Horatio Street in the Village. (*Dave Hollander/Archive Photos*)

David Markson met Jack Kerouac for the first time at a neighbor's apartment, but the famous author of *On the Road* had already done too much partying for the night. (*Elaine Markson*)

Helen Weaver met Kerouac when he came back to New York from San Francisco in 1956, and felt he "had endless imagination, and that gorgeous Massachusetts accent—and his sweetness." (*Courtesy Helen Weaver*) *Left:* William F. Buckley, Jr., provided youth, eloquence, charm, and a new magazine, *The National Review*, to the conservative cause. (*Gert Berliner*)

Seymour Krim was creating a free-flowing, personal, jazzy style of critical/confessional writing a decade before the New Journalism was christened. (*Fred W. McDarrah*)

Murray Kempton's column in the *New York Post* seemed to his fans like Proust working as a city desk reporter. (*Henry Grossman/Courtesy Life Picture Sales*)

Nat Hentoff (*right*) didn't want to be typecast as a jazz critic, and started his column in the *Village Voice* to write about education, civil rights, books, and politics. (*Fred W. McDarrah*)

As a young *New York Times* reporter, Gay Talese (*second from left*) recorded the homespun wisdom of Harry Truman during the ex-President's morning constitutionals along Park Avenue. (*Courtesy Gay Talese*)

As a precocious young critic and editor, Norman Podhoretz wrote that the Beat Generation was "a conspiracy to overthrow civilization" and replace it with "the world of the adolescent street gang." (*Gert Berliner*)

Joan Didion got a facial as part of her duties as a college guest editor of *Mademoiselle*. Later she worked for *Vogue*, where she broke into print with an essay on jealousy. (*Mademoiselle/Condé Nast Publications*)

Allen Ginsberg made writers and rebels welcome at his Lower East Side pad, where he lived with his poet companion Peter Orlovsky. (*Fred W. McDarrah*)

Village Voice editor Dan Wolf got Norman Mailer to invest in the new paper and also to write a column that became (of course) its most controversial feature. (*Fred W. McDarrah*)

Charlie Mingus was one of the star jazz musicians whose innovative music drew hip crowds of painters, poets, and musicians to the Five Spot. (*Fred W. McDarrah*)

Billie Holiday was banned from singing in New York nightclubs for more than a decade because of her arrest for heroin possession, but she gave a concert at the Loew's Sheridan theater that packed the house in 1957. (*Frank Driggs Collection/Magnum*)

who didn't understand.' Wechsler was 'serious,' and it was his un-
doing."

The friendship of Kempton and Buckley is now legendary, and
when it began in the fifties it was almost a scandal, the ultimate
definition of "politically incorrect" for its era. If Kempton was, as
Buckley described him in a column, the "pinup boy of the bohemian left" in New York at the time, Buckley played much the same
role for the conservative right. Joan Didion says that when she was
writing for Buckley's *National Review,* she thought of him not so
much as an editor (she worked on her pieces with Frank Meyer, the
back-of-the book editor) but as "a very glamorous presence."

Buckley and Kempton, the two bright stars from opposite ends
of the political firmament, both armed with literary grace, acerbic
wit, and political acumen, were supposed to be opponents, if not
downright enemies, like medieval knights crossing lances in furious
battle on behalf of their respective camps. How shocking and con-
fusing it was to see them prance forward, smile, do a bit of gentle-
manly tilting, and ride off in absorbing conversation, a dialogue
that continues today.

Back at the White Horse Tavern with some of my left-wing liberal
friends, I was called upon (or seized by the lapels of my corduroy
jacket) to defend Murray for being a friend of Buckley's. Raging
arguments over ethics, politics, responsibility, credibility, and other
issues personal and political foamed over the pints of arf 'n' arf in
the great debate. Should they be friends? How could they be
friends? How *dare* they be friends?

Similar internecine wars were waged, I am sure, over sherry in
the inner sanctums of the Yale Club and the New York Yacht Club,
wherever supporters of Buckley tried to defend his friendship with
Kempton of the high-liberal *New York Post,* his pal the former Red
who left the Communist cause but didn't turn right, refusing to
follow the course of so many from the thirties — Frank Meyer,
James Burnham, Whittaker Chambers, John Dos Passos — who
found a conservative home at *National Review* in the fifties.

So how did this ideologically surprising friendship come about?

Murray Kempton: "I met Bill Buckley when I did a radio program with him about McCarthy. Buckley's different from most con-

servatives — the ex-Communists on the far right who feel guilty, desperate for the good opinion of their fellow conservatives. Bill's to the manor born, and he has no political past he feels guilty about.

"The important thing about Buckley is he's incredibly decent. He's the only man I'd call for a loan, long distance, and be sure I'd get it. There was a young woman who wanted to be married in church, but she couldn't get anyone to stand up with her, and she asked Bill if he'd do her a favor. He said 'Anything,' and went to the church with her. This generosity is automatic with him, you could see that a mile off, so I always liked him."

Bill Buckley: "Murray covered right-wing activities, like protests against Khrushchev coming to America. I thought of him as the guy who walked around with a steno pad and a pipe. He invited me to Princeton, and Pat and I went for dinner there with his family one night. When I ran for mayor, Murray was there two or three days a week, doing pieces on my campaign."

Buckley says friendships between figures of the left and right in New York were difficult, if not impossible, during the McCarthy period, and though he met Kempton at the end of that era, Murray was a rare exception to that, or almost any other, rule: "Murray's a bird of paradise. I don't know anyone who doesn't like him. But don't tell him that — he wouldn't like it. He's always defending the underdog. I remember him saying once, 'God help me, but I'm defending Roy Cohn. He always helped anyone who was down.' Nixon always liked Murray."

Despite that exception, however, Buckley feels that "those kinds of friendships, between people on the left and people on the right, were only possible post-McCarthy. Dwight Macdonald and I were friends — I admired his journalism — but after my book on McCarthy came out [*McCarthy and His Enemies,* written with L. Brent Bozell], Macdonald said, 'Anyone who can tolerate that guy, I can't tolerate.' I asked Dwight to help me with the title of the book, and he said, 'Why should I give a title to a terrible book?' He took out his fury by writing a review for *Commentary* on *National Review*'s first issue, and he said I had no sense of humor, I lacked intelligence.

"I wrote around that time how in England there was a different spirit among people of conflicting political views. There, the editor of *Time and Tide,* which was conservative, could be godfather to the son of the editor of the liberal *New Statesman.* But that couldn't happen in the United States. I don't think there was that much intercourse between right and left until after McCarthy passed from the scene. I don't mean when he died — he was really out of it by '54. A few years later, there was an easing of tensions, room for more interchange of a friendly nature. But McCarthy was such a fighting word. A leading liberal tried to keep me out of the Century Club because of McCarthy. Vietnam came close to being that divisive an issue, but McCarthy was such a *personal* issue."

In that window in time, from the end of McCarthy's power to the beginning of the Vietnam War protests, the last years of the fifties and the first few years of the sixties, young people of right and left lay down together like the lion and the lamb — sometimes more like the boy and the girl. I can testify to its happening. I was there, in the back room of the White Horse, stronghold of Mike Harrington and the Young Socialist League, haven of the Clancy Brothers and their songs of Irish rebellion, watering hole of the Catholic Worker and the *Commonweal* staff and the *Village Voice* — when who marched in to join us but the Young Americans for Freedom, the leaders of the New York's Youth for Goldwater movement.

The socializing and friendships that came about between right and left were possible in part because we of the fifties generation had no political pasts to live down. By the time I got out of Columbia in 1955, McCarthy was on the decline and there were only scattered hangovers of the effects of his reign, as in a piece I did for *The Nation,* "The Case of the Outdated Victim," about a Queens College English professor who was fired because of "evidence" of a photograph showing him in a May Day parade twenty years before.

I never actually knew a card-carrying Communist, nor saw such a card. The only real live American Communist I ever knowingly laid eyes on was the correspondent for the *Daily Worker* who covered the Emmet Till murder trial in Mississippi. He was about the last person there I would have identified as such. I remember him wearing a blue suit and white shirt with a rep tie and smoking a pipe, looking like somebody's kindly uncle, no red tail peeking out of his trousers or pointed ears sticking up through his gray hair.

The politics of my friends in New York, supporters who worked and voted "madly for Adlai" in 1956, is best summed up by Meg

Greenfield: "We were part of a community of people who objected to the Republican philosophy of government — ours was the politics of objection. We all had a shared sense of being fugitives from the provinces and from the values of our parents and former high school friends.

"The Hungarian revolution was a big thing," she says. "I went with my boyfriend to the UN, and we were sitting in the gallery when the debate went on. That event had a whole lot of importance in our lives — seeing the tanks, seeing people on TV hollering, 'Help me.' "

If there was any vestigial sympathy for Soviet Russia and its brand of communism, or any need to see its totalitarian nature in our own time, the tanks in Hungary gave us a graphic jolt on television — perhaps the first time the terror of tanks and guns and bloodshed was brought into people's living rooms. With the demise of McCarthy, politics in the early sixties had become more like a spectator sport for us journalists, and though most of my friends and I backed Kennedy against Nixon, the young JFK didn't stir the passion in us that Adlai had raised, and seemed a smooth lightweight compared to the eloquent Stevenson.

The level of passion during the 1960 campaign is summed up for me in a scene I remember at a hotel ballroom in New York — a rally, Republican or Democratic (it could have been either; they haunted the same ballrooms), with the now familiar crowd of journalists who gathered at such places, as if someone had been ordered to round up the usual suspects. Murray Kempton was prowling around with his pipe and steno pad, and there was Joan Didion, whom Murray referred to as "the correspondent from *Vogue*," huddled in a raincoat and colorful scarf (since few of us read *Vogue*, we were not yet aware of the original and brilliant essays she was writing amid the fashion pages). Joan often wore sunglasses, not common in New York then, and at one cocktail party we went to, a noted liberal lawyer asked her, "Why do you wear those intriguing dark glasses?" I broke out laughing and told him, "I think you've answered your own question."

Noel E. Parmentel, Jr., the tall, shambling New Orleans freelance pundit, was there too, and Meg Greenfield of *The Reporter*, looking sharp in a Peck & Peck blouse and circle pin, ready to skewer the rhetoric of some platitudinous politician — I thought of Meg as our political Dorothy Parker. And, of course, Bill Buckley, tall and elegant, surveying the scene with a happily jaundiced eye and those large, knowing winks for everyone, his casual greetings rolling out like oratorical gems. When I greeted Buckley he bent down toward me, peering at a small badge on my lapel that said *JFK,* then uttered "Ah!" and rose up smiling, his teeth alight with the famous grin. He gave me the big wink and said, "I see you're *engagé.*"

That summed up the level of my passion: *engagé* for JFK.

Kennedy was young, handsome, and hip. (We didn't know *how* hip until he said in an interview that his favorite book by Norman Mailer was *The Deer Park,* the sexually suggestive novel that was called "the most controversial" of 1955, which showed Kennedy had taste and really read books, otherwise he'd have cited the best seller whose name everybody knew, *The Naked and the Dead.*) He showed his respect for intellectuals by having Robert Frost read a poem at his inauguration and inviting Pablo Casals to play cello at the White House (though everyone said that was Jackie's doing). He gave idealistic college grads a way to see the world and serve their country without joining the military when he created the Peace Corps, everybody's favorite government program and avenue of escape. Many young people told themselves, "If this job (or book, or magazine assignment, or marriage) doesn't work out, to hell with it, I'm joining the Peace Corps!"

It was chic and fun to go to Washington now, especially if you got to meet the great-looking girls who worked at the White House, with cute preppy nicknames like Fiddle and Faddle. Best of all was if you wangled an invitation to one of Bobby's parties at Hickory Hill, where you could become really In by getting pushed into the pool with all your clothes on. Harold Hayes sent me on assignment to "do" Bobby for *Esquire,* with special orders to make the pool party scene, but the best I could manage was a touch football game with Bobby, Ethel, and the kids on the White House lawn, and I dropped a pass.

An unexpected new aggregation of young conservatives began to form around Barry Goldwater at the 1960 Republican convention in Chicago. That fall, more than a hundred of them from forty-four states encamped at the Buckley family estate in Sharon, Connecticut, to draft the Sharon Statement, which endorsed "eternal truths" like the law of supply and demand — and the Young Americans for Freedom was born.

Rally!

American flags, an explosion of confetti, then red white and blue balloons and a brass band filled the air as more than eighteen thousand young conservatives packed Madison Square Garden to overflowing on a spring night in 1962, where the Young Americans for Freedom showed their strength and support for Senator Barry Goldwater and his right-wing principles. Fresh-faced usherettes with good teeth and clean hair (what a refreshing respite for the press after the beatniks!) cradled copies of Goldwater's *The Conscience of a Conservative* the way my friends and I used to hold *Franny and Zooey,* and welcomed the faithful who carried signs that said "Better Dead Than Red," "Let's Bury Khrushchev," and "Stamp Out ADA."

The crowd chanted "We want Barry!" and Goldwater took the podium as the band played "The Battle Hymn of the Republic." As each speaker was introduced, music blared forth to match his image: "Dixie" was played for Senator Strom Thurmond, "Boola Boola" for L. Brent Bozell, a fellow graduate of Yale with Bill Buckley. Perhaps most depressing was the appearance of John Dos Passos, in a kind of symbolic culmination of his journey from left to right, from the twenties through the early sixties. Before he took the stage, a roll call was read of the famous authors of his generation of flappers and flaming youth — only F. Scott Fitzgerald got a hand from the young conservatives — and then "Dos" was introduced as our only remaining literary giant, and the band struck up "When the Saints Go Marching In."

All this made good copy for me and Murray, Joan and Meg, Noel and Bill, and the other members of the press who were eager for something new and colorful to come along. YAF was good at providing it, with rallies and efforts to outdo the traditional appeal of the left to youth, like composing its own folk music and running an article in the YAF magazine, *The New Guard,* posing the question that surely has plagued generations of conservatives: "Must the Devil Have All the Best Songs?"

These card-carrying, flag-waving members of YAF were suddenly appearing with greater frequency in the press, and now they were showing up at the White Horse. Just like Bill Buckley, they turned out to be perfectly pleasant, witty, intelligent people, and we lefty liberals and right-wing conservatives found we had more common ground of conversation and interest with one another than with all those people who didn't give a hoot about politics, the great yawning masses of the middle.

Added to the social life and political repartee in the back room of the Horse were fresh young righties like Myrna Bain, a bright Negro student who started a YAF chapter at Hunter College, and Bob Schuchmann, a law student at Yale who was master of ceremonies of the big YAF rally at Madison Square Garden. Most noticeable was Rosemary McGrath, a tall beauty who was president of the YAF chapter in Greenwich Village. When asked who in the Village joined a young conservative group, Rosemary listed "civil libertarians, free-market economists, anti-Communists, Ayn Rand followers, longshoremen, students, one Teamster, and a couple of anarchists." With her long black hair, bright red lips, soulful dark eyes, and Goldwater rhetoric, Rosemary soon became known as "La Pasionaria of the Right," giving conservatives a heroine to match the legendary Communist orator of the Spanish civil war.

Rosemary once told me the story of her finest hour before making her dramatic entry into Greenwich Village political circles. She attended a Catholic girl's school north of the city, on the Hudson River, she said, and was often asked on dates by the dashing cadets of West Point. So magic was her name among them that when the Army crew rowed past her school, a chant rose up, a call from the Hudson, to the classroom where Rosemary studied dry mathematics, a chant of longing and homage that sang out in plaintive tones, "Ro-o-o-ose-mar-y . . . Ro-o-o-ose-mar-y . . ."

The unflagging energy of Rosemary's political activism came not so much from the inspiration of Barry Goldwater, I suspected, as from F. Scott Fitzgerald — the Fitzgerald of "Winter Dreams," "Absolution," and "The Diamond as Big as the Ritz." My judgment was not one of dismissal but, rather, affection; I knew the appeal of those stories myself.

Future historians of the White Horse will probably find that the young conservatives found their way to the back room courtesy of Noel Parmentel, who had satirized their movement in *Esquire* in a piece called "The Acne and the Ecstasy." Like most of the targets of Noel's pen, the YAFs laughed and became part of his fan club, or at least if not fans, then among those who knew about him, and anyone who knew anything about New York then knew Noel.

I can no more remember how and when I met Noel than I can remember living in New York in the fifties without knowing him. He was as much a part of the scene as Moon Dog, the blind street musician and poet who wore a robe and what looked like a Viking headpiece with horns sticking out. Moon Dog stationed himself in the doorways from Times Square to the Village. Jaded New Yorkers automatically gave him coins, listened to his odd music that seemed to come from another sphere, greeted him by name, and later reported in passing to a roommate or friend, "I saw Moon Dog today," as if mentioning a cousin whose business took him to various parts of the city.

Noel was not offbeat in appearance, but his big frame, easily spotted lumbering along Fifth Avenue or MacDougal Street, decked out in white suits and other Rhett Butler–type menswear, with a shock of light brown hair falling over his wide brow, was considered the ultimate in masculine charm by many of the girls who succumbed to his southern charms, which were spiced with put-downs that seemed to engage as well as enrage the ladies.

Even for his time, Noel was the most politically incorrect person imaginable. He made a fine art of the ethnic insult, and dined out on his reputation for outrageousness. In print, he savaged the right in the pages of *The Nation*, would turn around and do the same to the left in *National Review*, and blasted both sides in *Esquire* — and everyone loved it. The mention of his name brought a smile to the face of Carey McWilliams, editor of *The Nation*, just as it did (and still does) to Bill Buckley of *National Review*, and Harold Hayes of *Esquire* would break into a broad grin when he told you "I got a piece in from Noel."

Noel always had a number of projects going, including his famous option for the movie rights to Robert Penn Warren's novel *Night Rider*. The movie never got made, but some of the best parties in New York were given to celebrate each stage in the movie option's progress. I doubt that anyone has gotten more fun out of a project that never got off the ground.

I didn't see the LP he was going to do, *Folk Songs of the Right,* but I did hear him sing new lyrics to "Bill Bailey": "Won't you come home, Bill Buckley." He was always threatening to write his autobiography and call it *Uptown Local,* which for all I know may be in the works at last. I hope so, for Noel was able to make us laugh at our own pretensions, especially the political ones.

My principal image of Noel is of him pacing my small, cluttered apartment on Jones Street, rattling the ice cubes in his glass of bourbon, clearing his throat with a series of harrumphs, and pronouncing who was a phony and who was not, like some hulking, middle-aged Holden Caulfield with a New Orleans accent. Most people, in Noel's harsh opinion, were phonies but he delighted in discovering the few who were not, like C. Wright Mills. "Mills is no phony," Noel would say. "He means it when he pounds his fist on the desk and says 'Pow-ah!'" Noel would stop and pound his fist on whatever surface he could find and shout "Pow-ah!" and give out his hearty, deep laugh, rattling the ice cubes madly. Joan Didion was no phony either, and Noel championed her as a writer when she was still known mainly as "the correspondent from *Vogue.*" He took half the manuscript of her first novel around to publishers and editors, pressing it on them, arguing her case as the brightest young literary star on the horizon, cajoling Ivan Obolensky to read it and cheer-leading the publication of *Run River* by McDowell, Obolensky, bringing me and other writers he knew galleys of the book and urging me to read it, guaranteeing I would love it (and he was right, I did).

Perhaps the high point of Noel's own celebrity among the In political-literary journalism crowd was his one-man show, *An Evening with Noel E. Parmentel, Jr.,* hosted by the Greenwich Village chapter of the Young Americans for Freedom at the rather seedy old Hotel Earle, off Washington Square, in a room "conveniently adjacent to the bar," as Stephanie Gervis (future wife of Mike Harrington) reported in her account of the performance in the *Village Voice.* Noel identified himself politically as a "reactionary individualist," and came up with his trademark quips: when asked about the UN he said, "I want to give Red China a seat in the UN — ours" (getting the United States to pull out of the UN was a popular notion of the right wing). Concerning the House Un-American Activities Committee he declared, "That isn't my America that needs creeps like that. . . . They're a bunch of cheap, tacky, self-serving politicians" (this opinion dear to the hearts of liberals). He then switched directions again by opposing public libraries as "an extension of socialism." With his audience already dizzy from these pronouncements, Noel was asked what he thought about YAF activists who were going into food stores and putting tags on products such as Polish hams to show they came from a Communist country: "If I were a grocer and any of those creeps came into my store, I'd give 'em warning and then give 'em grapeshot."

In New York, more than the rest of the nation, we journalists tended to see the world not so much as black and white but as left and right, which led us sometimes to overreact to trends, predicting — as most magazines and newspapers did as late as 1963 — that the conservative boomlet on campuses was a rising tide that would define the sixties generation. The term "hippie" had not yet been heard, the summer of love was still in the future, and Haight-Ashbury was just another district gone to seed in San Francisco. This was still a year or so before the voice of the Beatles was heard in the land, via "The Ed Sullivan Show."

"We must assume that the conservative revival is *the* youth movement of the sixties," Murray Kempton wrote after the big YAF rally in Madison Square Garden in 1962. He tempered the prediction by saying that the conservative youth movement "may even be as important to its epoch as the Young Communist League was to the thirties, which was not very." Still, the YCL was one of the symbols of the thirties, and it looked as if YAF would make the vest the youth symbol of the sixties. I thought so myself, in a piece I did for *Mademoiselle* in 1963.

It was not until that fall, as I drove to Rockland County with Harvey Swados, that he asked if I'd seen some pieces in the *New York Times* by a young guy named David Halberstam, telling about this ridiculous war we were backing in some little country in Southeast Asia — it was called Vietnam. I couldn't remember hearing the name before.

■　　■　　■

I'd continued my friendship with C. Wright Mills after I did research for him when I got out of college, and found him always
inspiring, witty, and concerned, not only about the world but about
what I was up to, and whatever personal or professional problems
I might have. Others have spoken of Mills's egotism and selfishness,
but with me he was generous, kind, and solicitous. His interest and
confidence in me was a source of real strength — or what Mills
called "Pow-ah!" Of all my mentors and friends, Mills was one who
never let me down.

In the midst of my own angst and troubles — a frustrating psychoanalysis, broken love affairs, and too much drinking — Mills
gave me a model for going on with my work no matter what the
personal difficulties. I went to visit him when he came home from
Europe in 1957. With his family life in turmoil, he was living alone
in one of those dingy university apartments near Columbia, which
he'd managed to make bright and cheerful, and where he "set up
his files" — his metaphor for surviving, moving on.

After a fabulous lunch Mills cooked (this was his gourmet period), and after he questioned me about my own life and work, he
asked me what my plans were — and then told me what they should
be.

"China," he said.

"China?"

"A third of the earth's population," he proclaimed with hushed
drama, "and we know nothing about it."

"But I —"

"You'll be the reporter. We'll also have a photographer, an econ-
omist, perhaps a full-time cook, so we won't have to fool with that.
I'll be the sociologist and head up the expedition. We'll fit it out
with a Volkswagen bus or two and tour Red China — getting real
stuff. It has to be done. We'll worry about the State Department
when we get back."

Until then I knew almost nothing about China and had little interest in learning more, but by the time Mills finished his spiel, I
could hear the mysterious tinkle of bells in ancient temples and feel
the immense weight and drama of the massive landscape. I was
ready to pack for Peking. The great project never came off, but like
everything else Mills went in for, he could make you believe it was

the most exciting and important thing in the world. He could have done the same for Labrador.

Three years later, Mills made such an expedition on his own, to Castro's Cuba, at the invitation of his fan Fidel. He worked furiously to prepare himself for the trip during the summer of 1960 and set off equipped with every historical fact he'd been able to unearth and also his latest gadget, something still new at the time — a tape recorder. He could no more imagine someone without a tape recorder now than he could imagine someone who didn't bake his own bread.

When he came back, Mills worked with furious energy, writing *Listen, Yankee* in six weeks' time. The book was widely read and attacked in the American press. Its aim — clearly stated and seldom acknowledged — was to present the viewpoint of the Cuban revolutionary about the revolution, and for all the faults of the frankly polemical text, it was the first and I think the last time such an attempt was made by a leading American intellectual. (Mills, of course, was hardly the only American writer to pin great hopes on Fidel. Just after the Bay of Pigs invasion in April 1961, the *Village Voice* published an "Open Letter to Castro" by Norman Mailer, who wrote: "You were the first and greatest hero to appear in the world since the Second World War. . . . I think you must be given credit for some part of a new and better mood that is coming to America.")

After the enormous effort of finishing *Listen, Yankee* on that breakneck schedule, Mills drove himself back into high gear to prepare for a nationwide TV debate with A. A. Berle on U.S. foreign policy in Latin America. I saw Mills once while he was immersed in this preparation and he was terribly worried, alternately unsure of himself and brashly confident. He seemed to take it as a crucial test that he would either pass or flunk with profound results, as if it were a matter of life and death, which in an odd way it turned out to be. The night before the broadcast, Mills had his first heart attack.

Walter Klink, another of Mills's former research assistants and friends, drove me out to visit him in January 1961. It was a shock to see Mills in a sickbed, and yet his old fire and enthusiasm hadn't deserted him. He was pleased and proud of the sales, if not the reception, of *Listen, Yankee,* and above his bed was an advertising poster proclaiming that the paperback edition had 400,000 copies in print. Mills delightedly explained that such posters were carried on the side of newspaper delivery trucks in Philadelphia. He was reaching a greater public now than he ever had — "mass circulation stuff," he happily called it.

He lectured us on publishing, among other things, that day, and emphasized that paperbacks were now the important thing. He also told us how much more intelligently he felt all types of publishing were done in England, and reported that after seeing the English setup, he had told one of the older, more conservative American publishers, "You gentlemen do not understand what publishing means. You think the verb 'to publish' means 'to print,' but that is not so. It means 'to make public.'"

Flat on his back, he kept us entertained and laughing, joking about his pills, praising his doctor (his qualifications included having read some of Mills's work), talking of books and of the world, and even then, in that weakened condition, he spoke of "taking it big." There was one thing, though, that frightened me. He had, in a drawer by a bedside table, a pistol. He took it out and showed it to us, explaining it was for protection. He feared now the political consequences of his pro-Castro position.

When he was on his feet again, Mills went on a frustrating journey to the Soviet Union and Europe, not finding the answer to his heart problem he had hoped a Russian clinic and specialist might offer, and grappling with unfinished work. When he came home exhausted early in 1962, there were many projects left hanging, including the book I had helped him research, on intellectuals; a political book proposing and hoping to create what he called the New Left; an imaginary dialogue between a Russian and an American intellectual called "Contacting the Enemy"; and plans for a giant, or Mills-sized, "World Sociology."

I picked up the *Times* one rainy morning that March, and while sipping coffee in Sheridan Square saw two stark lines on the obit page that numbed me:

C. WRIGHT MILLS;

A SOCIOLOGIST

It was the first time I cried for the death of a friend. He was forty-five years old.

Noel Parmentel called and asked if I'd like a ride up to Rockland County for the funeral. He wanted to pay homage to one of the few people he didn't think was a phony, and he'd borrowed a car from a girlfriend to make the trip. Mills proudly considered himself a pagan, but his widow, Yara, had arranged for the one sort of service he might have approved, a simple Quaker meeting at which we sat in silence and anyone could speak from the heart if so moved.

I couldn't say a word, and only years later put something on paper that expressed some of my feelings. I quoted Mills himself when he wrote of James Agee's *Let Us Now Praise Famous Men,* commending the author for "taking it big" in writing about the sharecroppers. He said the important thing about the book was "the enormity of the self-chosen task; the effort recorded here should not be judged according to its success or failure, or even degree of success; rather we should speak of the appropriateness and rarity of the objective."

In that same spirit, I speak of Mills.

His friend Harvey Swados wrote in a personal memoir that Mills was "as combatively exhilarating as any man has ever been, he worked with the contagious wild passion of an inventor or a driven idealist, and when he was really dauntless he was the bravest man I ever knew."

With his premature passing a part of my youth passed, and part of the New York I loved was gone.

TEN

The New Word, The Old Dream

IN THE FIFTIES was the word. The word was everywhere. The image was yet to predominate. For my friends and me in New York, television was still an oddity, of little interest except for a few distinguished live drama series like "Playhouse Ninety" and the local interview program "Night Beat," hosted by a tough-minded interrogator we admired, Mike Wallace. We would sometimes seek out one of the few TV owners we knew or go to a bar with television to watch Wallace, but owning your own set was considered gauche for writers and intellectuals, a sign of decadence and mental sloth.

The only person besides Mike Wallace who drew me to watch a particular TV show was Charles Van Doren, the handsome, charming son of the great Columbia professor. My pal Ted the Horse and I went to Aldo's, a bar on the corner of 10th and Bleecker, to cheer on Charles, then a young Columbia instructor, as he sweated out the right answer in the isolation booth of the quiz show "Twenty-one," where he became a national idol, symbol of intellectual youth. Enshrined on the cover of *Time*, Charles was hailed by press and parents as the clean-cut alternative to Elvis the Pelvis. Then the scandal broke and we learned that the quiz shows were fixed — that star contestants were given answers. Charles's eventual confession of complicity was a great disillusionment. To my friends and I, it was proof of the inherent danger of the new mass medium —- television had corrupted the son of Mark Van Doren, the Lincoln of academia, the man whose very name stood for integrity.

Movies were entertainment rather than art, occasions for popcorn and dates. Movies were somewhat useful, in a crude way, for bringing some good novels to the screen, like James Jones's *From Here to Eternity* and John O'Hara's *Ten North Frederick* and *From the Terrace*. But movies didn't seem to translate the work of the finest writers, the Hemingways and Fitzgeralds and Faulkners. Their artistry was in language and defied successful rendering in big pictures, with laughably mistaken attempts at replacing a powerful fictional image with a deadly wrong face, no matter how attractive, like Ava Gardner as Lady Brett, Alan Ladd as Jay Gatsby.

A few real writers took movies seriously: Mark Van Doren had in his *Nation* reviews, and James Agee in *The Nation* too, and in *Time*. Agee even went to Hollywood in 1950 and wrote the script for *The African Queen,* and again in 1954 to write *Night of the Hunter*. He was the intellectual who made movies respectable in the fifties as a serious topic of conversation. For most of us they were a way to blank out the mind or cool off in summer: theaters hung out blue and silver flags in hot weather, with pictures of a polar bear and promises of "Cool Inside."

An exception was beginning to grow with the idea of foreign films as art, especially with the advent of the French and Italian directors in the early sixties. Helen Weaver made me go to a double bill at the Greenwich Theatre, Truffaut's *Shoot the Piano Player* and *Jules and Jim,* and I came away breathless, with a feeling of illumination and transcendence — almost the kind of artistic high I got after reading a good novel. As we walked out onto Greenwich Avenue afterward, on our way to get shish-kebab at McGowan's, Helen stopped and recited spontaneously: "Federico Fellini may come, Antonioni may go, But I'm in love with you, François Truffaut."

But that moment was like a recognition of the future. Except for the work of these foreign directors, whose impact and influence we were just beginning to absorb, movies were mundane. The theater, however — Broadway and now, in the fifties, off-Broadway — was magic. It was based on words rather than pictures, on the language and lines of the play. Directors and actors were supposed to serve the purposes of the playwrights, who were *literary* people, like Arthur Miller and Carson McCullers.

Kurt Vonnegut recalls of that era, "I went to the theater whenever I could. I was thrilled by Tennessee Williams and William Inge the way a later generation was thrilled by the Beatles. Their plays were my Beatles albums."

Vonnegut worked in public relations for General Electric in Schenectady from 1948 to 1951. "I made trips down to New York to try to get features about the company sold to *Life* magazine and King Features Syndicate. I'd do what I could to lead the literary life, like going to plays and staying at the Algonquin because it was the writers' hotel. The first time I had lunch there I saw George Jean Nathan talking to this little girl who turned out to be Julie Harris."

We went to the theater, and we read novels and poems, and discussed them in bars, in night classes, in the apartments of friends. "Even if you didn't write, you read," Harvey Shapiro says. "My wife and I were members of a reading club. We read Trilling's novel *The Middle of the Journey,* and the English writers Joyce Cary and Henry Green. I remember there was a couple who had a meeting of the reading club at their apartment and afterward announced they were getting a divorce, but they decided to host the meeting before they split up — that was the most important thing."

In New York the word was most honored, most powerful, most brilliantly imagined, created, and produced, by the writers and editors and literary agents, the newspapers, magazines, and publishers of books, gathered on one single island, which made us love it and believe in it all the more. Here was the place where more writers lived than anywhere else on earth, more even than in Paris. A few exiles remained abroad, like Irwin Shaw, but many young expatriates (Shaw called them "the Tall Young Men") returned to New York, as George Plimpton, who founded *Paris Review,* did in 1956.

Though some of the giants preferred to live in literary isolation, like Faulkner in Mississippi or Hemingway in Key West or Cuba, even they came here to pay obeisance, to see their editor or agent or a critic — even if only to punch one in the nose, as Hemingway did to Max Eastman. New York was where the word, in most cases, was made and, just as important, made *known.* Vance Bourjaily was once asked, after he'd left New York to teach in Iowa, "If you want to be a writer, do you have to live in New York?" He thought for a moment and said, "At least for a while."

The writers who produced the words that moved us were our heroes and heroines, our stars and guides, their works our texts for study and debate not just of literature but for life, the very meaning and understanding of it, in fact the conduct of it. These gods and goddesses walked among us, living next door and down the street, drank in the same bars, showed up at the same parties, or made appearances to read or speak their wisdom, and we sat at their feet and listened, rapt, as young people through the ages had come to learn the secrets of prophets and seers, for these were ours. And where else would you have the chance of seeing and hearing so many of them if not in New York in the fifties?

Carson McCullers was coming to Columbia.

She had left Georgia for New York City as a teenager, knowing that's where writers went, and now she lived in Rockland County but came into the city sometimes to give readings or talks. Word spread like a drumbeat, because her novel *The Heart Is a Lonely Hunter* was one of the sacred texts of my generation, a coming-of-age evocation as powerful to many of us as *The Catcher in the Rye*. The heroine, Mick Kelley, was a female version of Holden Caulfield, a sensitive girl attuned especially to music, who thought the symphonies of Beethoven sounded "like God striding in the night."

Responding to this novel was a sign of sensitivity; Marlon Brando claimed he'd read it nine times! It was first published in 1940, but all of McCullers's works were still read and discussed in the fifties, when her novel *The Member of the Wedding* became a hit play starring Julie Harris, Ethel Waters, and Brandon de Wilde; only the musical *South Pacific* had a longer concurrent run on Broadway.

The author up on the stage of a Columbia lecture hall looked more like her teenage heroine than the distinguished novelist and playwright who was thirty-seven when I saw her that afternoon in 1954. She was small and frail looking, with her brown hair in bangs, and for me she had a tremendous magnetism, perhaps based on my knowing who she was and loving her writing, yet it was more than that. There was a wistful charm, a kind of sadness and yet a power, not of force but more like magic. I thought she was absolutely beautiful, and I was immediately, madly in love with her, even before she spoke. By the end of that afternoon, I thought she was the most beguiling and brilliant woman in the world.

The beginning of her talk was not auspicious. In fact, it seemed headed for disaster. She started by reading — or trying to read — from a prepared text that lay on the table before her in what looked like a black loose-leaf notebook. Her voice trembled, and so did her hands, as she tried to turn the page, and she was aided in that effort by a man who sat beside her and seemed to be an assistant, or perhaps a relative, an uncle or older brother. He was a handsome, dark-skinned man with a mustache, and he was obviously devoted to her. She called him by a name that sounded like Ten or Tin and at some point introduced him as Tennessee Williams, her friend and fellow southerner.

Despite McCullers's efforts to steady herself and read what sounded like a rather dry academic paper on current literature, she suddenly closed the notebook and put her head in her hands. I think everyone in the audience wanted, as I did, to rush to the stage and comfort her, tell her it didn't matter, she didn't have to say anything further. Writing a book like *The Heart Is a Lonely Hunter* was quite enough; she need not offer more of herself. But we waited, hushed, and then, with her hands still covering her eyes, she said in a different voice, more calm and steady, though still soft, yet clearly audible, "I think I'll say a poem now."

With her eyes closed, she recited one of her own poems, "The Ransomed Heart," from which I have always remembered the words "malignant winter afternoons / and empty clocks," an image she later used in *Clock Without Hands*. It was like a liturgy, the recitation of a sacred text, and it affected the audience that way, as if a priestess had delivered a deep truth of the spirit, an articulation of our own unexpressed inner emotion, a kind of contemporary psalm, and it must have soothed her as well as us to say it.

McCullers opened her eyes when she finished the poem and, in a lighter tone, relieved and almost playful, she said she thought she'd just talk a little bit about writing *The Heart Is a Lonely Hunter*. This was mainly a graduate school audience, and there was a scholarly rustle and rush as notebooks and pens and pencils were whipped out, ready to trap the words, capture the secret.

I sat transfixed as McCullers told how she was writing the novel while living at home with her parents (she was nineteen years old at the time). She said there was a point at which she had written a number of pages, had all the characters, even had constructed some scenes, yet she didn't see the story yet. She wrote in her own room, but when she came to a stopping place, or felt stuck, she would go out to the living room.

"We had a checked rug on the living room floor," she said in her soft drawl, "and I used to hop from one check to the next, like you do on a checked rug, while I was trying to think. Well, one day I hopped to this check, and I suddenly thought, My main character, his name isn't Minowitz, his name is Singer. And he is deaf, and that's why all these people are talkin' to him." McCullers smiled and said, "And then I just wrote the book."

Goose bumps went up my arms. It was like hearing magic explained that can't be explained, but nonetheless the magician has told you as much as she knows, the way she knows it. During the question period, I cringed as a young man in the grad school uniform of horn-rims and corduroy jacket with elbow patches stood up and said something like, "Mrs. McCullers, in your discussion of the creative process in regard to your novel, you referred to the point of illumination at which you perceived the plot or structure of the work while you were in your parents' living room. Would you please expand on that, in regard to the illuminative experience and its role in the creative process?"

There was a slight pause, and then McCullers smiled and said, "Well, like I said, I just hopped to that check!"

A burst of laughter broke over the room, followed by applause. The "lecture" was over. I floated out of the hall.

I never got to see J. D. Salinger — hardly anyone else did either, after *The Catcher in the Rye* made him a cult hero, guru, and seer for the youth of America, which included my friends and me in the fifties. The literary agent Knox Burger, who as fiction editor of *Collier's* bought one of Salinger's short stories, knew him as "Jerry" in those days. "I bought 'The Ocean Full of Bowling Balls' in about

'51, before *Catcher* was published. It had been turned down else-where because it was downbeat — one of the Glass kids got killed. The story was sad but it was terrific, and I was very excited we were getting it. I corresponded with Salinger and he even suggested an illustrator for it — I liked him and commissioned him to do things for us. But our publisher read the story and said we couldn't do it, it was too downbeat, and then I think Jerry turned against the story and said it shouldn't be published. It was a terrific piece, though, and I was very disappointed.

"After that, I met him at a poker game with the agent Don Cong-don. Jerry was living in Connecticut then but he came down for this game, and afterward we went out for pizza, which was still a novelty then, and Jerry told us in detail about the kind of cheese in it. He knew all about it because his family was in the cheese business."

When *Time* did a cover story on Salinger in 1961, they sent Mar-tha Duffy to Cornish, New Hampshire, to try to get him to talk. When she spotted him on the steps of the town post office and sim-ply said, "Excuse me, Mr. Salinger," he turned, ran, jumped in his jeep, made a U-turn, and fled.

The only person I know who actually met and talked with Salin-ger after *Catcher* came out is Jane Richmond, who was working at *Partisan Review* when Salinger walked in one day unannounced, wanting to speak to the editor, William Phillips. Phillips was home with a cold, and Jane got to take the famous guest to the editor's apartment in a cab. Salinger was her greatest idol. "I'd been disap-pointed in so many writers when I met them," Jane says, "but he was exactly like the person I expected. He was extraordinarily nor-mal — a wonderful man who was anxious to get back to Cornish and be with his new baby. He was not some literary Howard Hughes — his normalcy and gentlemanliness were what struck me. In the cab to William's house we talked about old movies."

Salinger's popularity and mystique only increased with the pub-lication of "Franny" and "Zooey" and the rest of the Glass family stories that succeeded the novel, and continued even after he be-came a virtual recluse. Still, his presence was almost tangible in New York when I was there, and all my friends remember his influence. Kitty Sprague, who went to Barnard in the fifties, says, "I knew a woman at college who was in analysis because she said she had a reading block. She couldn't read any books except *Catcher in the Rye* — she kept reading that over and over." Less extreme fans read other books but kept going back to Holden Caulfield. "I used to read *Catcher* once a year," Murray Kempton says. "It was wonderful. I loved Salinger."

When I lived on West 92nd Street, I got a phone call from a friend telling me Salinger had a story in *The New Yorker* that just came out, and I grabbed my coat and rushed to the nearest newsstand on Broadway to buy the magazine. Calvin Trillin recalls that "in those days the appearance of a Salinger story was an exciting event," and to Richard Lingeman, "those stories in *The New Yorker* really meant something. People discussed Salinger avidly, asking, What did it mean?"

As Meg Greenfield puts it, "We were all 'Zooey' people."

Well, not quite all of us. Seymour Krim thought Salinger a snob, a "way-up-in-the-penthouse Manhattanite." Joan Didion was even more scathing, putting down *Franny and Zooey* as "self-help copy," writing in *National Review* that the Glass family saga "emerges finally as *Positive Thinking* for the upper middle classes, as *Double Your Energy and Live Without Fatigue* for Sarah Lawrence girls."

Joan complained that Salinger's work gave his readers "instructions for living," but that's what a lot of us found in novels, and was one of the reasons we read them so avidly. Richard Lingeman remembers reading Vance Bourjaily's *The End of My Life* in his senior year in college, "and I adopted the nihilism and despair of the main character. This was the novel that spoke to us. In the Army I read *From Here to Eternity*. James Jones gave me a way of seeing my own condition, that I really felt at bottom, 'Don't trust officers,' and 'It's your duty to go out and get drunk.' I identified with all that in basic training."

Though Joan Didion was not a "Zooey" person, she anyway was a Peyton fan. The beautiful and doomed Peyton Loftis was the heroine of William Styron's lyric first novel, *Lie Down in Darkness*, which he finished in a writing class at the New School taught by the noted Random House editor Hiram Hayden. Looking back, Joan Didion says, "*Lie Down in Darkness* was a stunning event, especially the last pages, where Peyton is in New York. The stuff in New York was exactly the period we were living."

Styron, I thought, was the true successor to F. Scott Fitzgerald, and I was delighted to meet him at a party at Bill Cole's apartment, where I met more writers than at any other place besides the White Horse Tavern. Bill worked in publicity for Knopf, but he had the same kind of influence and knowledge of books and writers that a good editor had, and in fact he was responsible for getting James Baldwin's first novel published. He lived (and still does) in a comfortably funky apartment spilling over with books in the nonresidential area a little uptown from Times Square. The place was in no way fancy, any more than the food, which was mainly peanuts and potato chips, or the drinks, just bottles of booze set nakedly out on a table with mixers, but Bill's natural amiability drew people to him and his parties.

There were always writers there you knew or wanted to know, and the booze ran freely and the talk was always funny, sharp, knowing, dealing with what we cared about most — books, magazines, and stories, the words and the people who wrote them. Nobody talked of advances or royalties or how much money any book or writer made. That was the sort of thing business people talked about, the organization men, the ones in the gray flannel suits — or the girls who married them and joined what Mary Nichols and her mother's friends in Washington Square called the Lamb Chop Set.

Writers talked about writing and asked one another what they were working on now. When I introduced myself to Styron, he said he had read a recent piece of mine in *Esquire,* and told me he was writing for the magazine himself. We started talking about the editors we knew there, Rust Hills and Harold Hayes, when a pretty girl came over and introduced herself to Styron. He immediately introduced her to me, saying, "Dan and I are colleagues at *Esquire.*"

Colleagues! With the author of *Lie Down in Darkness*! I felt I had just been elevated to the literary heights, and I knew then that Styron was a true gentleman as well as a great writer.

The writers I admired were almost always as good as their books when I met them, and sometimes uncannily *like* their books, as if they were one of their own characters coming off the page. Isaac Bashevis Singer, a rather slight, bald man with eyes that glinted mischievously behind his glasses, was as warm, sly, witty, and entertaining as the people in his stories and novels. I'd become a fan when I read *The Magician of Lublin,* which was set in the *shtetls* of Poland but conveyed more understanding of the relationship between men and women right then than any other book I knew.

Jane Mayhall, the novelist friend I'd met at the Bread Loaf Writers' Conference, knew of my admiration for Singer and introduced me to him at a dinner of the Poetry Club of New York. Afterward we went out to a Jewish deli in midtown with Singer, his wife, and a few other writers, including Cecil Hemley, who translated some of Singer's work and also was his editor at Farrar, Straus. Cecil was about to have his own first novel published, and he jokingly said to Singer, "Isaac, since I translated your novel from Yiddish to English, why don't you translate mine from English to Yiddish and see if we can get it published in the *Daily Forward?*"

Everyone laughed but Singer, who shrugged, deadpan, raised his hands with palms up, and said, "It's not impossible. We'll take out the sex, put in some socialism . . ."

I'd recently written an essay on Salinger's work for *New World Writing,* and when an editor of *American Heritage* asked me if I'd do a similar piece on some other contemporary writer, I enthusiastically proposed Singer but was told his work was too limited in appeal. That was a long time before Singer won the Nobel Prize in literature.

I wrote the author a fan letter when *Enemies: A Love Story* came out a decade or so later, saying how unfair I thought it was that he was still being pigeonholed as an ethnic writer and politely dismissed. "I am from darkest Indiana," I said, "and your characters from nineteenth-century Poland seem to me basically just like the people I grew up with." I reminded him we'd met once in New York, though I doubted he'd remember. Almost at once I got back an air mail letter of thanks from Singer, postmarked Monaco. He said of course he remembered me, that my kind words made his day, and added, "I'm in Monte Carlo — not gambling!"

My friends and I weren't shy about our literary enthusiasms or our efforts to meet our favorite authors. Brock and Ann Brower loved *The Young Lions,* one of the influential novels of our time, as well as Irwin Shaw's short stories coming out in *The New Yorker,* especially "The Girls in Their Summer Dresses." "When Ann and I were in Paris in '56," Brock says, "we went looking for Shaw, going to the bars and cafés where he was supposed to hang out, but we never found him. We felt his stories were about *us* and people we knew."

Gay Talese had better luck: "I'd written fan letters to Shaw, and when I went to Rome to do a piece on the Via Veneto for *The New York Times Magazine,* Bernard Kalb of the *Times* introduced me. Shaw knew me from my letters. He was generous — he knew the Italian bureaucracy and helped me and Nan get married in Rome on June 10, 1959. He thought of us as these kids from New York and thought our marriage was a terrific idea. He even rounded out the evening with a party at the Excelsior, and Merle Oberon was there."

Our literary idols almost invariably turned out to be generous, both personally and professionally, to us younger aspiring writers. Like most everyone I knew, Leslie Katz was an admirer of James Agee's, and he recalls, "I sent a story to *Partisan Review* — that was the reigning glory we all looked to — and they turned it down, but it led to my meeting Agee. I got a phone call from him, saying he and Dwight Macdonald had liked the story and wanted to publish it, but Philip Rahv was negative. Agee said to come have a drink with him and Macdonald. They were at the Blarney Stone on 14th Street, and I went over and met them. Evidently, the argument about the story was part of a growing disagreement that led to Macdonald leaving *Partisan.*

"Meeting Agee changed a lot for me," Katz adds. "He befriended me and helped me get free-lance magazine work. The story that *Partisan* turned down was then published by *New Directions* magazine. That was a real thrill. I saw Agee for a considerable period in the early fifties, and we would have lunch frequently. He was at *Time,* and I'd meet him at a little restaurant he liked in Rockefeller Center that was very comfortable. We had an affinity. Agee's *Let Us Now Praise Famous Men* had been a failure commercially, but it wasn't a failure to any people who knew Agee. He was already legendary."

Most of these heroes and heroines of ours were novelists, and most of my friends in New York dreamed of writing a novel. Some of us did, with greater or lesser degrees of success, and almost all of us tried at some point. Meg Greenfield speaks of working on a novel in Rome after college as "the kid thing to do," before she turned to the factual writing she mastered at *The Reporter* and went on to practice with distinction as editorial page editor and editorial writer at the *Washington Post* and as a columnist for *Newsweek*.

Walter Goodman recalls the fifties as "quite an exciting time for novels — Saul Bellow and Bernard Malamud were big, and made a big impression on me." It was an earlier novelist, though, whom Walter tried to emulate as a young man: "When I worked for the BBC in Europe in '51 I was trying to write a novel, under the influence of Thomas Wolfe — he was an awful influence on young writers — but I didn't have the knack." Walter discovered he did have a knack for editing and writing first-class journalism and nonfiction, for magazines ranging from *The New Republic* to *Redbook* and *Playboy* in the fifties and later for the *New York Times*, where he now serves as a cultural commentator and TV columnist.

After my first book, the nonfiction *Island in the City,* was published, I decided it was time to try writing my own novel. I was still supporting myself by free-lance writing for magazines and had to steal time from these assignments to pound away at my fictional creation. I was granted a month at Yaddo, and I sat there through August 1959, staring out the window at the lovely manicured lawns, waiting for my lunch to come in the workman's black lunch pail that was left outside the door of each artist. I was also waiting for inspiration, and nipping from a pint of bourbon in a desperate effort to help it along. I ate the enormous dinners and breakfasts with my fellows every day and left the place eight or ten pounds heavier but with only a handful of pages, not a single one of them worth preserving.

Like a sculptor hacking at the rock of Gibraltar, I banged away at the stubborn subject of youthful love and angst in Indiana when I got back to the Village. I carried on the battle in between magazine assignments, late at night, managing finally to accumulate some fifty pages, which *seemed* like a promising beginning.

My publishers disagreed. They were as kind and gentle about it as possible, bringing me up to lunch at the swanky Locke-Ober Café, Boston's finest restaurant, but leaving me, after the lobster Savannah, with the clear message that they considered me a fine young journalist but not a novelist. I was shattered, defeated, disillusioned — and of course that night I got drunk, my reaction to any news, good or bad (and sometimes just for the hell of it, with no news at all). I tossed the fifty pages but determined to try again. I wasn't giving up.

Disappointed as I was about the novel, I enjoyed the kind of journalism I was doing to make a living. I sensed a growing interest among writers, editors, and even literary critics in the way nonfiction was opening up, becoming more artful. As early as 1950, Lionel Trilling had said in *The Liberal Imagination* that some of the new sociology, like David Riesman's *The Lonely Crowd,* was telling us more about our world in a more interesting way than current novels.

The excitement about experimenting with new forms of nonfiction — the sort of excitement stirred among writers by Agee's work — and the possibility of trying these approaches were expressed by C. Wright Mills in a letter he wrote me from Europe in November 1956, after I had written to tell him my idea for a book about Spanish Harlem. "We've got to work out a new form of writing — using some fictional techniques and some reportage tricks and some sociological stuff," Mills wrote. "Of course all that's nothing without some really big view into which all the little stuff fits and makes sense. . . . No matter what you're writing about, you're also writing about the whole goddamned world. Huizinga does that [in *The Waning of the Middle Ages,* one of Mills's favorite books] — it's easier to do it for the past, less risky. Agee touched it on those sharecroppers. Dos Passos did in *U.S.A.* The trouble is when you try it, you can fall so very, very hard. It's easier not to try. Go detailed scholarly. Go clean journalist. Disguise it . . . in fiction. No fiction nowadays is 'about the world' in this sense."

Besides the kind of books Mills was talking about, and writing — *The Power Elite* had just come out — I was getting a dose of an experimental, brilliant kind of writing when I read Murray Kempton in the *New York Post.*

What distinguished his column from every other one I had ever seen was not only the literary excellence and complexity of the prose, but the fact that Murray was not content to sit in his office and reflect on the news; he went out to cover events as a reporter (he regarded the term "journalist" as pretentious, and it made him wince).

Each column came out like a short story, with scenes and dialogue — real dialogue — and ended with a kind of epiphany. He wrote a tragic piece on a Communist who committed suicide after being hunted down by the government, about a union boss betraying his men, and about Richard Nixon introducing Eisenhower at the Republican convention of 1956 ("at last he ceased his looting of the collected works of Jane Addams, and fell back to the shadows, and the real pro came on"). He described the birthday party the producer Mike Todd threw for himself at Madison Square Garden in 1957, when Sinatra didn't show up and the host left early: "How awful it must be to have scored a triumph and still to remember that you held a party for the kind of people who steal eight-month-old domestic champagne."

A lot of new things were happening to encourage writers to use their best talents writing nonfiction, like the appearance of the *Village Voice* in 1955. The cofounder and original publisher, Ed Fancher, says, "We had a lot to do with the New Journalism, though we never really knew it. Our approach was that journalism should be *writing* instead of just news reporting. Dan Wolf gave young writers who came here an opening when they couldn't get a foot in the door elsewhere."

Jane Kramer, Jack Newfield, and Bill Manville were among the many who got their start at the *Voice,* while some who had already published elsewhere found a natural audience and home in its pages, like Nat Hentoff and Seymour Krim.

"We felt guilty we were unable to pay our writers, and in the beginning we were flabbergasted because so many writers loved us," Fancher recalls. "It took us a long time to realize how badly writers were treated by editors. They liked us because we treated them with dignity and their stuff wasn't tampered with, without their approval."

"The Article as Art" was a shocking idea when Norman Podhoretz wrote an essay about it in 1958. Podhoretz noted the irony that "we call everything that is not fiction or poetry 'non-fiction,' as though whole ranges of human thought had only a negative existence," and observed that "the novel is to us what drama was to the

Elizabethans and lyric poetry to the Romantics. . . . The aura of sanctity that used to attach to the idea of a poet has now floated over to rest on the head of the novelist."

Yet Podhoretz found the essays of many novelists, like James Baldwin and Isaac Rosenfeld, more interesting than their fiction. (The same was said of Harvey Swados, which made him angry, as it did most novelists; they took it as a put-down.) He argued that imagination hadn't died in our time — it was chic then to claim that the novel was dead — but that it was channeled into, of all unlikely forms, the magazine article. He saw that many writers were finding it possible "to move around more freely and creatively within [that form] than within fiction or poetry."

Podhoretz remembers being attacked for what he said: "Styron, Bellow, other novelists got pissed off. I took a lot of flack but never got credit. I really think it was revolutionary at the time — the term and talk of the New Journalism came later."

Walter Goodman, who wrote for *The New Republic* and worked as an editor for *Redbook* and then *Playboy*, says, "Journalism was becoming hotter in the fifties. It had the appeal of fiction. The popular magazines had always been big fiction magazines, but suddenly people began reading magazines for nonfiction pieces. Goodman thinks *Redbook*'s editors, himself included, were too conservative. "We were afraid our readers wouldn't get it, but *Esquire* readers were Hemingway readers, so they could understand this new kind of journalism. They responded to it, then everyone picked it up."

"It's what everybody was doing," Joan Didion says. "It started with James Agee, really." Brock Brower, who was "doing it" in *Esquire* in 1960, tells me, "The idea was in the air and everyone I know was thinking this way too." Norman Mailer was thinking this way when he wrote "The White Negro" in 1957 and the personal running commentary in *Advertisements for Myself* in 1959, around the time Seymour Krim wrote his gut-wrenching piece "The Insanity Bit," for a little magazine called *Exodus*.

Whether it started with Agee or the columns of Murray Kempton, or was given a new orgasmic pump by Norman Mailer's "The White Negro," or was unleashed in the pages of the *Village Voice*, this whole trend of quality writing, which was negatively known as nonfiction and later got promoted to the more hip category of the New

Journalism, came to full bloom around a particular editor and magazine in the late fifties and early sixties: Harold Hayes of *Esquire*.

Harold came from Winston-Salem, North Carolina, went to college at Wake Forest, and never lost his southern accent in New York, but there was nothing slow or drawly about his way of working. He spoke — drawl and all — with a snappy quickness and force that conveyed an infectious enthusiasm. You automatically did your best and hardest work for Harold, and he always made it seem like fun.

Harold was having fun himself as he tossed ideas at you, listened to yours, told you what terrific writer he had just assigned to which unexpected story, tamped or lit or puffed or knocked ashes from his pipe, stood up and paced around his desk to show you a piece of innovative art work for the cover of the next issue.

Harold went to *Esquire* from *Coronet* in 1956 to be articles editor of the magazine when he was twenty-nine years old. He was named managing editor four years later, and editor in 1964. He had a boyish charm and exuberance, but it was anchored in a sense of authority and purpose. Gay Talese, one of the principal stars he developed, thought of Harold as an older brother, and so did we all, those of us five or so years his junior who did our first "big magazine" pieces for him, the group Talese was thinking of when he said of Harold, "He nurtured a whole generation of writers."

Harold liked to wear bow ties and suspenders, and always looked sharp, though never a fashion plate. He was more like a natty newsman out of *The Front Page*, and he brought that air of old-fashioned daily newspaper excitement to the monthly magazine business.

I went to his office at eleven one morning to ask if he had an assignment for me. "Can you be on a plane for Dallas at four o'clock this afternoon?" he shot back. My blood began to race at the very question, picking up speed as I quickly computed how long it would take to throw a couple of shirts in a bag, grab my portable typewriter, cancel a date, and hail a cab to La Guardia or Idlewild.

"Damn right!" I said, watching his grin spread, and then I asked what the assignment was, what fast-breaking big story he was sending me to cover. "The Miss Teenage America contest," he said, and we both broke out laughing because he had made it sound like the equivalent of the *Hindenburg* disaster or the Hungarian revolution.

But what the hell, it would be a blast, a great piece of cultural satire of the kind *Esquire* loved, and I hurried on my way.

I first wanted to write for *Esquire* when I saw some unconventional profiles by Thomas B. Morgan, and wrote the first of my own such pieces on Adam Clayton Powell in November 1959, followed by others on William Buckley, Robert Kennedy, John Dos Passos, and Billie Jean King, as well as a variety of Harold-like assignments on everything from "The Sophisticated Woman" to the latest in civil rights activism. I felt the freedom to experiment, go far out, do my best stuff, the brasher the better.

Brock Brower walked into the editor's office one morning and said, "Harold, I need work." Without skipping a beat, Hayes asked him, "Can you get on a plane to Los Angeles this afternoon?" The assignment that day was an interview with Peter Lorre, which not only turned into an *Esquire* profile of the actor, but served as the seed of inspiration for a marvelously funny, incisive novel Brock later wrote about a horror movie star, *The Late, Great Creature.*

"Harold and I hit it off right away," Brock says, "maybe because he was from North Carolina and I'd been stationed there and knew about the place." Brock had been at Fort Bragg writing guerrilla warfare manuals for the Special Forces — the Green Berets — and found time to write two pieces that he sent on spec to *Esquire:* a parody of a *Paris Review* interview with Shakespeare, and "A Lament for Old-Time Radio." They were bought by Rust Hills, the magazine's fiction and literary editor. When Brock got out of the Army and went to New York in 1958, Hills said, "You should meet Harold Hayes. He knows your wife." It was Ann Montgomery Brower's friend Howie, one of the boys upstairs, who had come down to Ann's apartment for the pristine pajama parties back in the early days after college.

"I went in to see Harold," Brock recalls, "and he said, 'We have to get you a real good assignment.' He offered me a chance to do a major piece they wanted to commission on Alger Hiss. Harold said, 'We're not going to solve the Hiss case. We don't care if he's innocent or guilty, but we want to know what's happening to him now.'

"I did the first draft and Harold said, 'There's a year missing here. Who paid Hiss till he got his first job after he left jail?' The suspicion of readers might be that he was being financed by Commies. I called Hiss's lawyer, and Hiss called back and said, 'I was living on unemployment.' Harold made me be specific — every year of Hiss's life had to be covered. And Harold was dead right. I talked to Hiss, to his son Tony, to the lawyers, to men he had been in government with and men he had been in prison with.

"I talked to Hiss at the Players Club, which I'd just joined, and when I took him there for lunch everyone wanted to know who *I* was. The place was buzzing with a kind of undertone of 'Guess who's here?' Everyone was looking at us and Hiss was enjoying it — he liked being the villainous celebrity. He said I couldn't quote him on anything, so I couldn't take notes, but afterward I rushed back to the Players' library and wrote down everything I could remember. I used it, but not in direct quotes in the piece. All of us learned to do that — we had no tape recorders then, and it put you into a kind of double or bifurcating mind-set. You had to ask the best question and also remember what he answered. I did it with indirect quotes like, 'Hiss feels today . . .' I think I came out with about seventy-five percent of what he said. I was plenty proud of it, and Hiss didn't challenge anything I said. He was surprised I was able to remember it all, and I said, 'I went to law school too.'

"It took me three months to write the piece, during which we were very broke. I was paid $1,000 for it, their top price. I was freelancing then, but after that piece they hired me as a part-time editor."

The article, "Hiss Without the Case," came out in the December 1960 issue, and is still talked about today among writers who read it at the time. All the writers I knew were reading *Esquire* in those days, and I was especially drawn to the piece on Hiss because I'd met Brower in college. When my high school friend John Sigler came down from Dartmouth one weekend while I was at Columbia, I took him for beers at the West End. I told him I was working on the *Spectator* and taking courses with Van Doren, Trilling, and C. Wright Mills, and he said, "You've got to come to Dartmouth and meet my roommate. He's interested in all the same stuff."

Sigler's roommate was a strong-jawed, all-American-looking intellectual named Brock Brower, a future Rhodes scholar who was editor of the *Daily Dartmouth* and, like me, a rabid fan of Scott Fitzgerald. We sat up all night drinking beer and talking about the relative merits of *Tender Is the Night* and *The Great Gatsby,* the *New York Times* and the *Herald Tribune.* Now here we both were, writing profiles for *Esquire.*

When I read "Hiss Without the Case," I was surprised to learn that Alger Hiss, this once powerful Ivy League, New Deal aristocrat, now worked as "a salesman for a small line of stationery," and I felt I had come to understand his odd situation, as Brock Brower left him at the end of the piece: "He shook hands and went off across lower Fifth Avenue — a tall man in a summer straw, with certainly no mince [a description from Whittaker Chambers] to his energetic walk — going after that most mundane of American goals, and the last one that anybody would think that Alger Hiss would end up in pursuit of: a customer."

I ask Brock how he approached writing that piece, and he says, "I cared more about what was going on in the real world, but I wanted to write with the techniques of journalism and novels working together. I'd justify everything in a profile like the one on Hiss in two ways — that it was factual, and that it would evoke a character the way fiction does. I was very influenced by Dickens."

Brock says Harold Hayes didn't actually teach him any of these techniques but simply gave him the opportunity and the impetus to use them, and, most important, "There was a huge sense that I did it for this man. I stayed up all night in the office once to finish a piece for a deadline and forgot to call my family. My wife called my father, and he got the night watchman of the building to come and find me and have me call home."

Gay Talese says of Hayes, "He was demanding and I had a strong desire to please him. He was a Marine, a southern minister's son, and he had very severe standards. Harold had a way of making me feel at once that he was supportive, but there was a little fear in the relationship, and threat — he had to be satisfied, standards had to be met. He was only a couple of years older, but he was like a severe older brother. If I wrote fiction, he'd be the older brother in my story.

"Harold gave me the opportunity to be published the way I wrote it. At the *New York Times* then you didn't own what you wrote, the copy desk did. I'd wait for the first edition to come out, leave at nine o'clock, buy a paper, and if they had mangled my copy, I'd call the desk from a phone booth around Times Square and say, 'I want my name off it,' and we'd have a big argument. At *Esquire,* what you wrote got printed the way you wrote it and was read the way you wrote it. I loved Harold more than any editor I ever had. I greatly missed his presence when he left *Esquire,* and I said I'd always work for him. I even did a piece for some tennis magazine when he was running CBS magazines."

Hayes was vice president of CBS Publications from 1981 to 1984, having left *Esquire* in 1973 after a dispute with the owners. Harold became a magazine consultant and one of the originators and producers of the ABC News show "20/20," and hired his *Esquire* writer Brock Brower to help him start the program. He wrote two books on ecology, *The Last Place on Earth* and *Three Levels of Time,* moved to Los Angeles to be editor of *California* magazine from 1984 to 1987, and was working on a new book when he died of a brain tumor in 1989 at age sixty-two.

Talese didn't learn writing techniques from Hayes. His role models were writers he read in high school. "I wanted to be a writer more than a news reporter. I loved short stories, especially Maupassant. I wanted to write about real people the way a short story writer did, showing the person's character. I clipped out of a collection a story called 'The Jockey,' by Carson McCullers, and I saved it. A jockey walks into a restaurant to have dinner, and his trainer and the owner of the horse berate him for eating too much, and the jockey walks away. I thought, I'd like to write that way, but why can't I write that way about a real jockey? I wanted to write in the style of fiction but I didn't want to change the names. I wanted to write short stories for newspapers.

"In '59 the *Times* assessed me as a good writer who needed more experience with hard news. If there was anything I had no interest in doing, it was hard news. They sent me to Albany to cover the state assembly and senate. I had to write about what bills were introduced. I hated it. I didn't know how to write it. It was formula journalism and I did it, but I didn't want my name on that stuff. I learned there was a rule that if your story wasn't longer than seven or eight paragraphs, you didn't get a byline. So I never wrote more than seven paragraphs.

"It only lasted a month. Before that I was a young star getting bylines in my mid-twenties, after that I was out of favor. They sent me to purgatory, dayside obit, but I didn't write the big obits. Mine were of people like an executive at Gimbel's who died of a heart attack and was worth three paragraphs. There were twenty or thirty a day, and you had to call the funeral director and get the information and write.

"That's when I started writing for *Esquire*. I had plenty of time, and I could use the *Times* morgue and files for research. I even wrote a piece on Alden Whitman, the chief obit writer for the *Times*.

"My piece on Floyd Patterson in '62 was a turning point. I'd written about twenty-five pieces on him in the past for the *Times*, so I was free to fictionalize — not make things up but use fictional techniques — since I knew him so well. I saw how essential it is to know people you're writing about, have a feeling of their character."

It was Talese's piece on Joe Louis that got Tom Wolfe to read *Esquire* and ask himself, What the hell is going on in magazine journalism that an article could sound almost like a short story?

When I first met Talese, at a party at Bill Cole's, he had already read my profile of Adam Clayton Powell in *Esquire* and I had read his Josh Logan and Floyd Patterson pieces, and toward the end of the party he asked if I'd like to join him and his wife, Nan, who was a rising young book editor, for a hamburger and beer at P. J. Clarke's. I was impressed not only with Talese's sharp mind and conversation but by the marvelously tailored suit and highly polished shoes he wore, a sartorial excellence of style that was a legacy of being the son of a tailor. He was a perfectionist, in his clothes and in his work.

Talese looked straight into your eyes, his own eyes like powerful x-ray instruments boring into your thoughts, recording everything you said and the gestures you made. Set below his eyes was a mouth in a sort of half smile, which I wasn't sure suggested reassurance, or maybe just amusement, or curiosity, or more likely all the above.

"How old are you?" he asked me, his eyes boring in, and when I told him he seemed to relax, moving back in his seat. "We're almost the same age," he said. "I was afraid you were going to be younger — and doing the kind of pieces you're doing for *Esquire*."

Talese wrote an article for *Esquire* about the *New York Times* that he turned into the best-selling book *The Kingdom and the Power,* enabling him to leave the newspaper and give full time to his nonfiction articles and books. "It started with Harold's idea," he said.

Harold Hayes wanted to devote a whole issue of *Esquire* to sports. "He called and wanted me to write the introduction," Bill Buckley recalls. "Harold said, 'You're my second choice. Mailer was my first but he turned it down, and I just want you to know that.' I said I knew nothing about sports, and he said, 'That's why we want you.' I said I'd have to read all of the issue before I wrote the introduction, and he said that was impossible, since he wouldn't get the galleys until the night before he had to go to press with what I wrote. I said I'd stay up all night and read the galleys and then write the piece, that's the only way I'd do it, and he said O.K. It took guts for him to say yes, but he did.

"Later I wrote a piece called 'The Politics of Truman Capote,' and Harold said, 'You can't say he has no politics if politics is in the title.' With two or three pieces I wrote, he'd say, 'This is what's missing,' and he'd put his finger on it."

Norman Mailer tells of his own experience with Hayes as editorial diagnostician: "He could put his finger on what was wrong. He was a very good editor. He was like a doctor poking his finger in a part of your body, like poking very unhealthy tissue, and he did it so it hurt, the place where he poked really hurt." Mailer is the only one of Hayes's frequent contributors I talked with who looks back with any negative reflection: "He was very cold, at least to me. You wrote a wonderful piece and he barely acknowledged it. If he thought he could make a good cover by making fun of you, he'd do it — like when he put a picture of me on Germaine Greer's lap on the cover of *Esquire.* I invited him to a fistfight with me over that. He wrote back and said, 'I don't box, how about tennis?'" Mailer didn't take up that challenge.

The magazine work that Norman Podhoretz recognized as art in the fifties came to its full flowering as a new genre in *Esquire* with the work of Tom Wolfe, beginning with his classic breakthrough piece on custom cars in 1963, "The Kandy-Kolored Tangerine-Flake Streamline Baby." The literary phenomenon known as the New Journalism was dubbed "para-journalism" by Dwight Macdonald, but no such criticism could stop its spreading, into the signature magazine of the sixties, *Rolling Stone,* and eventually into all magazines (Joan Didion even broke the moldy style of *The Saturday Evening Post* with such pieces as "Slouching Towards Bethlehem"). The practice even moved into newspapers, those bastions of what Wolfe calls "totem journalism," with writers like Jimmy Breslin and Pete Hamill bringing their own talents to the kind of artful reporting Murray Kempton began.

Wolfe, who became the spokesman and the star practitioner of the method, said when Harold Hayes died in 1989: "He was one of the great editors. Under him, *Esquire* was the red-hot center of magazine journalism. There was such an excitement about experimenting in nonfiction, it made people want to extend themselves for Harold."

All these writers extended the limits of the nonfiction medium, making it more expansive, exciting, entertaining, and fulfilling, both for writer and reader. The New Journalism was part of a confluence of historic forces, a growing trend that probably would have sprung up sooner or later, but if it got its name and fame in the sixties, like so many other movements that shaped our time, it started in the fifties.

I loved writing journalistic pieces and profiles for Harold Hayes and *Esquire,* but I hadn't given up on fiction. One night I had a dream in the form of a novel. It began with a title page, and then a story unfolded, not as words on a page but as characters moving and talking as they would in a novel. The story had a rather simple but convincing plot, with a beginning, middle, and end, and when it was finished, a page appeared that said "The End" and the book was closed, the dream was over.

I woke up exhilarated, hurriedly got dressed, and went out and sat on a bench in Sheridan Square as the dawn came. I felt refreshed and affirmed, confident I would write my novel, though I didn't know when. I knew the story I dreamed was not the one I would write, but was rather a sign or symbol of it, as if my own unconscious — or spirit, I might now say — were telling me, "I have it in me." I knew, in a deeper way than anyone else's words or opinions could persuade me, I would do it.

ELEVEN

Graduating to the Five Spot

EXCEPT FOR a few hip girls I knew, who admitted to a strange, aberrational passion for a greasy-haired guy who shimmied his hips on stage while he sang, we thought Elvis Presley was for hoods. Elvis the Pelvis in his blue suede shoes — a joke, a crude idol for guys who gunned the motors of souped-up cars and their girls with beehive hairdos and toreador pants so tight they seemed to be painted on the skin. We were too cool and smart for that. We listened to real love songs: Frank Sinatra's "In the Wee Small Hours," Joni James doing "Let There Be Love," and June Christy's "Something Cool." Our serious music was jazz. That was the music we listened to for inspiration, meditation, nurturing the soul. New York was, of course, its capital.

We started out listening to Dixieland in high school, and when I first came to Columbia my friends from back home who were going to college in the East would meet me in New York and we'd go out to hear the music. Sally Green would commute down from Vassar, and Pete "Esty" Estabrook would train it up from Penn and Tommy Evans from Princeton (a few times the adventurous Joe "the Fox" Hartley would even make it all the way from Purdue in his ancient Buick, which looked like a gangster's getaway car). We'd go to Jimmy Ryan's on 52nd Street, or the Metropole on Broadway near Times Square, where I heard Philly Joe Jones play drums and Red

Allen on trumpet, the music blasting out to the street. We'd go downtown to the Stuyvesant Casino, where you got big pitchers of beer and watched the musicians play in front of a full-length mirror, the whole place bright, or to the Central Plaza, and at Nick's in the Village there was Phil Napoleon and Miff Mole, and best of all, way down on West 3rd Street, a small, dim club that was Eddie Condon's.

Eddie himself circulated around the room, his dark hair slicked back, immaculate, sporting a neat bow tie, a sharp guy out of some George Raft movie of the thirties, and on stage was Pee Wee Russell, fondling the clarinet and looking as gentle as Wild Bill Davison looked tough, the way he blew a cornet out of the side of his mouth when they did the Dixieland classics and sometimes Eddie would join them on guitar. One night Esty Estabrook had enough whiskey sours in him to have the guts to summon Mr. Condon himself to our table ("Hey Eddie!"), but Eddie simply looked at us — a couple of whiskey-soured college kids — and moved on.

Rousing as it was, how many times could you listen to the Dixieland repertoire? How many times could the saints come marching in, and the muskrat ramble, and Bill Bailey be summoned home? As Bruce Jay Friedman said of the made-up World War II battles in the adventure magazines he edited in the fifties, you can't keep storming Anzio every month. It was fun, it stirred the blood, and created immediate festivity, party time, forget your troubles, come on get happy! But after four years of high school and four more of college, the Dixieland standards began to take on the familiarity of "On, Wisconsin" and "High Above Cayuga's Waters."

It began to seem old-fashioned, which had once been part of its charm, but then these cool sounds began blowing in from the West Coast. There was a brand-new shrine I made a pilgrimage to during the summer of 1953, the Lighthouse in Hermosa Beach, California, where this guy who reminded me of a jazz version of James Dean was playing a soft, sexy trumpet and whispering love songs like "My Funny Valentine." His name was Chet Baker, and suddenly all my friends and I had his records and played them to our prospective girlfriends, hoping they would be as stirred as we were by the sexiness of this cool new sound. After the girl had yawned and gone home, successfully resisting not only your charms but Chet's, you had another drink and played Baker again, imagining the next girl, the real one who'd fulfill all your fantasies, the kind of girl Chet himself must have played and sung to when he did those amazingly muted (and all the more lustful for being so) numbers like "Love Letters."

But there was a sound that was even more hip than Chet's right here in New York, more adventurous and surprising and just as romantic — so poignant, in fact, that it inspired the British theater critic Kenneth Tynan (one of the first literary appreciators of J. D. Salinger) to call the man who made it, Miles Davis, a "musical lonely hearts club."

I went to hear — and *see,* for his presence was as cool and impressive as his music — Miles Davis at Birdland, that anonymous-looking cellar downstairs on Broadway where Charlie Parker himself played, and where Bud Powell, J. J. Johnson, Count Basie, Dizzy Gillespie, and jazz buffs from Europe went first when they came to New York. I got to hear Miles Davis down in my own neighborhood too, at the Village Vanguard, and I bought and played his records late into innumerable nights, on Jones Street and West 13th and East 12th and practically wore out his album *Sketches of Spain.*

Everyone I knew had bullfight posters on their walls at some time during the decade, and went through a phase of heavy listening to flamenco music (the *cante hondo,* the "deep song," surely was the wail of our own desire). We were preparing for the obligatory pilgrimage to Spain — I made mine with Ivan Gold in 1958 — under the influence of our generation's papa, Hemingway. We wanted to see, if not the running of the bulls at Pamplona, at least a *corrida* or so. We wanted to take in the other hallowed sights of that land as well, cities I thought of as being the literary property of certain writers and artists: Orwell's Barcelona, Lorca's Seville, El Greco's Toledo. One of our bibles was Hemingway's youthful handbook *Death in the Afternoon,* which gave us literary advice ("write when there is something that you know; and not before; and not too damned much after") and also the legends of the ghosts of the twenties ("we never will ride back from Toledo in the dark, washing the dust out with Fundador, nor will there be that week of what happened in the night that July in Madrid"). To translate the essence of all that mythology — so central to our generation's imagination — into modern jazz, our own time's music, was simply an act of instinctive genius that Miles Davis performed in *Sketches of Spain*.

The new sounds of Miles, Charlie Mingus, Lester Young, and Ornette Coleman were coming out of the New York jazz clubs, and then there was the incredible ultimate cool synthesis of classical music with fugue-like jazz, the Modern Jazz Quartet, who liked to perform in concert halls rather than in clubs. "The quartet does much better . . . in places where people can listen attentively," the piano player and musical director of the group, John Lewis, explained to Nat Hentoff. Lewis said on another occasion that he was proud of being an American Negro and wanted to "enhance the dignity of that position."

I played the MJQ's LPs like litanies, especially the album John Lewis wrote as the musical score for a movie, *No Sun in Venice,* which combined our generation's dream of Europe with the native American medium of jazz, or, as it was put more elegantly by Lewis in the liner notes, speaking of his composition "Cortege": "This is *my* Venice. . . . I know Venice's history, the music it has produced, I love its *commedia dell'arte* and in my *Fontessa* gave it musical expression. In seeing a colorful funeral procession on the Grand Canal, however, I can't help but think of funerals in New Orleans, which are happy as well as sad, and that double image in my mind is undoubtedly reflected in my music." The MJQ's music reflected a mood of our time by one of the most successful groups of the fifties.

Because he knew John Lewis was one of my idols, Leslie Katz arranged for me to meet him (Leslie's brother Dick Katz is a jazz piano player and a friend of Lewis's), and Leslie, Jane Mayhall, John Lewis, and I had lunch one day at the Russian Tea Room. It was one thing to meet a literary idol; at least then I would have a few comments to make that I knew didn't sound too dumb. But with a musician I felt completely inadequate and tongue-tied. My technical experience is limited to three years as last-chair clarinet in the School #80 orchestra, so my mumbles of tribute must have sounded like Thelonious Monk speaking to the press. Lewis was quiet, gracious, and dignified, and if nothing else I had the pleasure of saying I had once lunched with the man, like a Giants fan having downed a beer with Sal Maglie or Willie Mays.

Murray Kempton, the most knowledgeable jazz buff I know, tells me that Margot Hentoff (Nat's wife, and herself a fine writer) claimed that "the MJQ *was* the fifties." She was right, as she usually is — they were listenable, and they were also extraordinarily good.

"One of the great changes in pop culture occurred in the fifties," Kempton explains, "in jazz, art, everything else. It was the same thing Henry James describes, how the Venetian painters are ultimately unsatisfying because the light there is too good — it's what he called 'the demoralizing effect of lavish opportunity.' The LP gave jazz musicians the opportunity of stretching out, and it was demoralizing. If you listen to an old Ellington recording of 'I'm Beginning to See the Light' — what he does in eight bars is unbelievable. It was compression, you had to get on and off. But the Modern Jazz Quartet was very compact. Of course, there are exceptions to Henry James's rule — Michelangelo had a huge ceiling and it didn't ruin him."

There were cool new saints marching in, and innovative sounds in the air, which seemed to express the confusion, heartache, and excitement of a more complex time, so it was harder to get worked up over another rendition of "Muskrat Ramble." Kempton had told me in 1955 about an old friend of his from college who had looked him up in New York and wanted to go hear some Dixieland. Murray shook his head, raised his eyebrows behind his horn-rims and said, "I wanted to tell him, 'He don't live here anymore.'"

Back in his Dixieland days, Kempton recalls, "We all used to go downtown and listen to Bunk Johnson at the Stuyvesant Casino." Johnson, a New Orleans trumpet player, was discovered working in a rice field near New Iberia, Louisiana, and brought to New York in 1945 with his own band. He was promoted as the last of the "pure" or "true" jazz players, delivering the music as it was done a generation before. "I used to go to Minton's and listen to Charlie Parker too," Murray says. "I thought he was just terrible. I didn't like him till after he was dead."

I am certain Murray is the only New York intellectual courageous enough to make that confession, but he also can state, "I was the only reporter at Charlie Parker's funeral." (When I mentioned that to Nat Hentoff he said, "There were *two*. I was even asked to say a few words about the deceased.")

It was Murray who in the mid-fifties told me, "Nat Hentoff is the only one writing about jazz" — meaning the only one who was worth reading on the subject. Soon Nat was not only writing about jazz in *Down Beat* and reviewing books about jazz in *The Nation* and other magazines, he was also writing a column on civil rights, education, and whatever injustice caught his attention, in the *Village Voice.* I got to know this gentle bearded man with a pipe perpetually stuck in his mouth as a neighbor and fellow writer in the Village, which meant I had the pleasure of drinking with him at the White Horse. Though he accomplished his aim of breaking out of the pigeonhole of jazz by writing on every subject under the sun, not only in the *Voice* but later in *The New Yorker,* Nat remains the premier jazz interpreter and critic of our time.

Nat still lives in the Village, where I met him recently in Bradley's bar. "The fifties was a continuously stirring time in New York," he says. "Every night there was exciting music somewhere. Coleman Hawkins used to say, 'You ain't nothing till you come to New York.' He used to say that when he met some trumpet player in Topeka who was supposed to be the best. And they all came."

One who came in the fifties was David Amram, a jazz musician, composer, and, as Nat Hentoff describes him, "a ubiquitous deliverer of good cheer." He knew more painters than writers, and he acted as "a link between different groups — music, art, and writing."

"At my first Town Hall concert there were sculptors, artists, writers," Amram says proudly. "There was a cohesiveness in the arts, an attempt to make the connections seem natural. We did the first jazz poetry reading at the Gallery, and I have a poster of one we did at the Circle in the Square with Howard Hart, Philip Lamantia, and Jack Kerouac. I was backup, I played piano — those guys would go out drinking between shows and not come back for an hour or two and I had to entertain. This was in '57. Jack played bongos, he was a great improviser of words, and he loved music. After listening to a jazz piece I played, he said, 'That's what I'd like to do with words but I can't quite do that.'"

Amram plays French horn, piano, guitar, plus the flutes, whistles, drums, and other assorted folk instruments of twenty-five countries. In the fifties he played in the hot Village clubs like Café Bohemia and the Five Spot with Dizzy Gillespie, Sonny Rollins, Cecil

Taylor, Charles Mingus, and many other jazz greats of the era, went on to become the first composer-in-residence with the New York Philharmonic, and wrote musical scores for movies, including *The Manchurian Candidate* and *Splendor in the Grass*. Now he conducts and performs as a soloist with symphony orchestras from Kansas City to Toronto, and is called by the *Boston Globe* "the Renaissance man of American music." Amram, at sixty, lives on a farm in New York State with his wife and children, cows and chickens, and still keeps his old loft apartment in the Village, whose door is decorated with stickers proclaiming "Dizzy Gillespie for President" and "Shalom, Y'all."

In the apartment, Amram stretches out on a cot below the skylight, tucks his hands behind his head, and speaks from memory. "I first went to New York to hear music when I was a kid in college in D.C. It was a big thing for musicians to go to the Big Apple — they started calling it that in the forties. We'd drive to New York and sleep in my car. I had a '32 Plymouth — it couldn't go over forty-two miles an hour, so the trip took eight hours. We'd go and listen to the big bands.

"I came back from Paris in '55 and went to the Manhattan School of Music to study composition. The first night back, I went to Café Bohemia to hear the alto sax man Jackie McLean, and five weeks later I was playing there with Charles Mingus. Going to hear Mingus play was one of the great experiences of the fifties. His audience wasn't just intellectuals — it was pimps, pushers, pickpockets — but they all had a bond of appreciation. They all knew something really valuable was going on.

"Jackie McLean was one of Charlie Parker's protégés. Jackie felt that jazz as it came to be in our time was a quintessential New York expression, because from all parts of the country the best musicians came here."

Jazz was *the* music of New York in the fifties, at least of literary and artistic New York (as well as those "pimps, pushers, and pickpockets"), and many of us later pretended, or imagined, that we dug the more advanced sounds, like those of Charlie Parker, all along. Pretending sometimes led to pretentiousness about jazz, as Bruce Jay Friedman testifies: "Jazz lovers are the most arrogant people. I never dared venture an opinion around real jazz buffs. If

I said I liked the way a guy blew horn, they would always know a guy named Pee Wee or Junior who wiped my guy away. I didn't like the church feeling while a guy was doing a riff — I was scared to tinkle a glass, I was scared out of my wits. I wasn't a jazz guy."

Friedman did become friends with a jazz musician whose music he liked, who in turn was an admirer of Friedman's fiction. Paul Desmond, the most literary of jazz men, played in the Dave Brubeck Quartet. "Paul loved a story of mine in a collection called *When You're Excused, You're Excused*," Friedman says. "It's about a Jew on Yom Kippur who keeps doing darker and darker things. Paul was the only one who mentioned the story. Of course, our friendship didn't qualify me as a true jazz buff — liking Paul Desmond was about the same as liking Rick Barry in the NBA."

Desmond used to say, "I was unfashionable before anyone knew who I was," and "I'm not hostile enough to be currently acceptable." He said being white made him part of "the real underground."

Despite his unfashionableness with the critics — he was very melodic, and his music was easy to follow — Desmond won the *Down Beat* readers' poll as best saxophone player eleven times (only once did he win the critics' poll). Joe Goldberg wrote that the Dave Brubeck Quartet, with its popularity on college campuses, was "the most maligned, and possibly the most affluent" small group in jazz in the fifties. Brubeck made the cover of *Time* in 1954, but by the early sixties, Desmond said, "most jazz fans wouldn't be caught dead listening to us anymore." Still, the group has "picked up a whole new audience. Just people."

He meant people like Bruce Jay Friedman who made no claim to being jazz buffs. Desmond had many literary fans and friends, for he had once thought of being a writer, studied writing at San Francisco State, and was an avid reader who kept up with everything and everyone in contemporary literature. I met him at a party at Bill Cole's in 1959. He was standing in a group where a chic woman was holding forth on "Goodbye, Columbus" when she noticed Desmond, no doubt knew he was a saxophone player, and unnecessarily explained, "It's a story by a young writer named Philip Roth." Desmond nodded politely, not bothering to mention he had read everything Roth had written.

Desmond was genuinely unassuming, shy, and good-natured,

and I was delighted to spend an evening with him in New York a decade after I'd moved up to Boston. I'd come down to promote my novel *Starting Over,* which was just published, and Abbey Hirsch, the ultimate publicist, was working on the tour for me. She had a dinner date with Desmond and asked me to join them, I think as consolation for having survived a horrendous radio call-in show she had booked me on, and we went to the French Shack, and after dinner we went to Desmond's apartment, which was close by, at 55th and Sixth. We drank brandy and Paul entertained us, talking of the autobiography he was writing, *How Many of You Are There in the Quartet?* (He swore it was the question most commonly asked him.) He wondered if we knew it was possible to play music by pressing the buttons of a telephone; each button made a different note, he explained. Paul picked up his Touch-Tone phone and, nodding his head to the rhythm, played "My Funny Valentine" on the buttons. Full of brandy and a good meal, listening to Paul Desmond play the telephone, I knew I was back in New York, and I loved it.

Even my friends who made no claim to being real buffs had some acquaintance with jazz, some favorite place they went to hear it, and sometimes the style they liked naturally reflected their inclinations in politics and literature.

"I've always loved jazz," Bill Buckley says, "and I went to Nick's now and then to hear Dixieland — I wasn't interested in innovative jazz, I wasn't able to catch up with them. I used to go to Hanratty's bar to hear a graduate of Columbia named Dick Wellstood. He became a leading jazz piano player, in the opinion of Nat Hentoff."

Sometimes proximity or style of music determined a person's jazz hangout, and Gay Talese found both to his taste at the Hickory House, on 52nd Street, when he worked at the *Times*. "I used to go sit at the oval bar to hear Marian McPartland, or to impress a date I sat at a table and ordered drinks," Talese says. "When I worked at night, I left the paper at eight or nine, or at one or two if I was on rewrite, and I'd go to hear jazz. I loved McPartland, George Shearing and Don Shirley. They were wonderful stylists."

A stylist himself in journalism, Talese admired stylists of jazz.

My own progression in amateur jazz appreciation, and that of many of my friends, is expressed by the journey Richard Lingeman describes: "I started on 52nd Street to hear Dixieland, went down to Eddie Condon's, then graduated to the Five Spot." In my own pilgrimage, I stopped along the way at Birdland, the Village Vanguard, the Village Gate, and the Half Note, but I knew the Five Spot was special, and marked one's graduation to the new jazz of the era.

"The Five Spot," Nat Hentoff says, "was the most significant jazz club since the clubs of Chicago in the twenties where Louis Armstrong played. The house group was Thelonious Monk with John Coltrane. Musicians and lay people lined up three and four deep to get in. The Half Note was just a mainstream jazz club like the Village Vanguard — it had Zoot Sims, Jimmy Rushing, Al Cohn. They had good groups, but not the new exciting thing, like Monk and Coltrane. The Five Spot was different. Monk gave the club an aura. I went there three or four nights a week just getting into it. I remember one night Coltrane came off the stand and was looking destitute. I asked what's wrong, and he said, 'I missed the turn with Monk and it was like stepping into an empty elevator shaft.' And of course Charlie Mingus played there too."

The Five Spot figures in almost everyone's memories of the time. During a conversation with Helen Tworkov about her book *Zen in America,* I happen to mention that the day before I was talking to Nat Hentoff about a jazz club I used to go to called the Five Spot.

"Oh, I know it well," Helen says. "I used to work there."

"Were you a jazz musician?" I ask.

"No, I was the hatcheck girl."

Helen explains that her father, the painter Jack Tworkov, had a studio on the Bowery across from the Five Spot. He was one of the group of abstract expressionists, along with de Kooning, Kline, Rothko, and others, who rented lofts in the area. "My father and other painters went to the Five Spot after finishing work in the afternoon." It was the painters who encouraged the owners, Joe and Iggy Termini, to bring in jazz musicians to play. "The Terminis didn't know who the artists or musicians were — the scene was self-made. It wasn't like some entrepreneur said, 'Let's start a jazz club.' It was all underground word of mouth."

Later Helen sends me copies of entries from her father's diary that mention trips to the Five Spot:

> Monday/Feb/10 . . . Went to Five Spot at ten — to hear Kenneth Koch read poetry — to jazz accompaniment. Also to music by Marty. Marty was a flop. Koch amusing in an intelligent way. All the old club there. Always amusing to see each other in a public place, as a crowd, a group.
>
> Monday/Feb/24 . . . Later in the evening — the Five Spot. Guston — Rothko, Motherwell and others. Arnold Weinstein and to jazz.

Helen grew up in Manhattan and went to the Dalton School, where, she says, "I read 'Howl' illegally in the auditorium. I didn't think *On the Road* was a great novel, but more like an avatar of liberation." In search of her own liberation, she hung out in Washington Square.

"After Dalton I went to the University of Cincinnati, but I fled after a year and came back to New York, and my parents said I had to be on my own and have my own apartment. I got one on West 14th Street for $42 a month. I worked as the hatcheck girl at the Five Spot and made $50 for a Sunday night. The Terminis didn't take a cut, so I was following the formula of a quarter of your wages for rent. Maybe the Terminis gave me a deal, no kickback on what I made in tips, because of knowing my parents."

Some of the painters who frequented the Five Spot with Jack Tworkov were the friends who first introduced David Amram to the club. Amram thinks part of the affinity of painters and jazz musicians in the fifties was that they shared a common experience: "The struggle painters had was like that of jazz musicians. People still thought that if art wasn't from Europe it was worthless. Jazz was an accepted art form in Europe in the fifties, but only a small group of people recognized it here. Miles and Bird were playing an incredibly sophisticated kind of music, like spontaneous chamber music at the best level.

"When Kline and de Kooning and that bunch of painters took me to the Five Spot in the fall of '56, the piano player was Don Shoemaker, a merchant seaman who played piano awhile and then shipped out. There was a bass player and a young piano player named Cecil Taylor. Cecil was strong — he once broke the piano keys and Joe Termini flipped out. He said, 'Cecil Taylor will never play here again.' I said I wouldn't either. All the painters got together and told Joe Termini that if Shoemaker shipped out, he should hire Cecil Taylor and Amram.

"Cecil and I played for five weeks, then I came with my quartet and stayed eleven weeks. They still had pitchers of beer for seventy-five cents. The 'Tonight' show came with Jack Lescoulie, and we had monthly jam sessions. The painters had decided it was a great place. Franz Kline said of me, 'That's Wagner playing bebop.' "

Amram played there later with Charlie Mingus, and remembers, "Mingus said to his musicians when they played the Five Spot, 'Look man, I don't care how raggedy this place is. When you're with me and playing this music, every night is Carnegie Hall.' "

Mingus insisted that not only the musicians regard it that way, but also the audience. "One time at the Five Spot," Richard Lingeman says, "I remember Mingus stopped playing, and he wouldn't go on because people were talking. It was kind of a shock, the way he stopped and lectured people — he said he wasn't going to play unless they shut up. He thought of himself as a serious artist, and he was really angry. He walked off for a while. He was famous for doing that. Mingus was great, a figure."

Mingus was a figure all right, and could be as dramatic and surprising off stage as on. The novelist and screenwriter Rudy Wurlitzer will never forget the time he took a beautiful girl to the Five Spot when he was nineteen years old. "I wanted to impress her," he says. "Mingus was playing, and I could tell he noticed the girl — everyone noticed her. When the last set was over, Mingus came up to our table and took out a pair of handcuffs. He didn't say a word, just clamped one of the handcuffs on his own wrist and then clamped the other on the wrist of my date. She didn't say anything, and he pulled up her arm, so she stood up, and then they walked out the door together, neither of them saying anything. That was my first and last date with that girl."

Mingus was not the only colorful character who played the Five Spot. Thelonious Monk was already a jazz legend when he brought a quartet, which included John Coltrane, there in 1957. A proud and private man, known as an eccentric even in the jazz world, Monk was given to wearing capes, an assortment of hats and caps from silk to fur, and sunglasses with bamboo rims. Nat Hentoff said in *The Jazz Life* that it seemed as if behind Monk's controversial music was "mostly vapor in dark glasses and a goatee." One night Joe Goldberg, who would later write *Jazz Masters of the Fifties*, was at the Five Spot when Monk was playing his solo set of the evening and some yahoo in the audience yelled out, "We wanna hear Coltrane!" Monk said, "Coltrane bust up his horn." After the intermission, when Monk came out alone again the exchange was repeated. The heckler then got more hostile and asked Monk what he meant when he said Coltrane "bust up his horn." Monk stood up at the piano and delivered the following dissertation: "Mr. Coltrane plays a wind instrument. The sound is produced by blowing into it and opening different holes to let air out. Over some of these holes is a felt pad. One of Mr. Coltrane's felt pads has fallen off, and in order for him to get the sound he wants, so that we can make better music for you, he is in the back making a new one . . . *you dig?*"

Sometimes when Monk let Coltrane go on a long riff with only the bass and drum for accompaniment, he would rise from the piano and dance, keeping time by moving his elbows along with his feet, "rhyming" with his body, as one of the jazzmen put it. Monk had played at Minton's with Charlie Parker, who said, "The Monk runs deep." Monk was called the master of the new sound that was emerging there, and was crowned "the high priest of bebop," even though he said the word was mispronounced: "I was calling it bip-bop, but the others must have heard me wrong." The mistake is understandable if you see the superb documentary Charlotte Zwerin made of Monk called *Straight, No Chaser*, as he mumbles his way through New York and Europe but sits down at the piano and plays familiar tunes like "Just a Gigolo" and "I Should Care" with an innovative eloquence that is nothing short of breathtaking (and you get to see a shot of the Five Spot too).

Norman Mailer remembers going often to see Monk at the Five Spot: "The place was incredibly small, and you could sit about five feet away from Monk's hands on the keyboard. I'd be looking forward to the weekend — it was a special time there, getting high and listening to music. I felt that jazz and marijuana were one. I never thought of one without the other. I've never since had mental rides like I had then."

Allen Ginsberg also went to hear Monk at the Five Spot. "I got closer to jazz, listening to Monk," he says. He also remembers the time he went to hear Lester Young ("the Prez") and went back to the kitchen to read the saxophone player some poetry of Hart Crane, which he thought would help Young with his music, just as jazz had helped and inspired Ginsberg's poetry. "I read it to him for the sound, for the rhythm," Ginsberg says. "I don't think he especially got it. He said, 'Man, if an A-bomb came now, I'd go downtown to Tiffany's and smash the windows and take what I wanted — I'd get mine!'

"I got to know Mingus when he played at the Five Spot, and later I sang at his wedding in Millbrook, New York. I'd just come back from India and I knew monochromatic chanting — there were a lot of musicians interested in that mode, like Coltrane. I did a recording of it with Coltrane's drummer. At Mingus's wedding I was chanting mantras to Shiva, to Buddha."

Though Ginsberg's reading of Hart Crane didn't seem to do much for Lester Young, and though the jazz-and-poetry business never really took off except as a novelty, the jazz buffs who frequented the Five Spot were also poetry buffs, and they turned out in full force when Ginsberg gave a reading of his own work. "The Terminis called to ask me to come and wait tables that night," Helen Tworkov remembers. "The place was packed, and I made a fortune."

Ray Grist, my painter friend from East Harlem, used to carry a copy of *Howl* around in his hip pocket when he was a high school student, and though he didn't catch Ginsberg's reading at the Five Spot, he heard most of the musicians who played there. "I started going when I was sixteen. They let me sit in a telephone booth and just listen to music, without ordering any booze. I went every night. After a while I had this route I'd take, beginning at Romero's, where Bernie Hamilton, the actor, was the bartender. Romero's was the hippest place in town. Then I'd hit Café Bohemia — Miles played there, and Art Blakey. From there I'd go to the Half Note, then across town to the Five Spot."

Ray shows me a recent issue of his magazine *Jump,* which contains the artist Charles Mingus III's "Vignettes at the Five Spot":

I was about 20 yrs old, and I had just quit my other job and started working at The Five Spot as a bus boy and waiter. I wanted to work there because of Monk.

You had to have a special talent, and mine was picking up broken glass with my bare hands — that was my talent. I could pick up broken champagne glasses in the dark, and people used to say "You are going to cut yourself, you know."

The Five Spot used to be on St. Marks Place, but it's a pizza joint now. It was a unique club because sometimes Monk would stay for a whole year, playing by himself, or with the whole band. Or sometimes the club would have, like, an Elvin Jones month. As long as the musicians were drawing a crowd, and the bars were making money, they would extend the engagement.

Down the street you could see some musicians hanging out at the cleaners, standing in front of the exhaust fan, smelling the fumes of the dry cleaning fluid, getting stoned. You could tell after a while that some of these people were just getting high to get high 'cause that's what was happening. Some were getting high because it was cold and they wanted to stay warm enough to listen to the music. They were learning something when Monk was there.

The Five Spot was one of those small places that exerted a big influence, a magnet that drew poets and painters as well as musicians. In her memoir of her life with the poet and playwright LeRoi Jones, Hettie Jones remembers when they lived in the same building with the jazz musician Archie Shepp on Cooper Square, across from the Five Spot: "The acoustics of Cooper Square augmented every music; if it was warm weather when Archie's groups played, they'd open up his studio windows and let the sound ricochet off the factories and repeat a millisecond later on the tenement wall on Fifth Street. The Five Spot was only a stone's throw away. Roi was always hanging out the window. The casual proximity to his life of his chosen frame of reference made him deeply happy."

•   •   •

I also heard Mingus and Coltrane at another spot that became a fixture of the Village in the fifties, not only for jazz but for folk music, hip popular singers like Nina Simone, and even stand-up comics. It was Art d'Lugoff's Village Gate. "I felt I had to run the place like a store," Art explains. "You couldn't just depend on one item."

Art began his midnight folk concerts at the Circle in the Square Theatre in 1955. "I was one of the first folk impresarios in the U.S.," Art says. "I personally liked the music, and I thought it would be good commercially. I first heard it at political rallies, and hootenannies at people's houses. I felt the public was looking for some alternative to the bland music of the time. Jazz had become cool — there was no dancing with it, the melody had gone out of it."

When he opened the Village Gate in 1958, d'Lugoff wanted to feature folk music, but he couldn't afford it: "The Weavers I couldn't buy, or the Kingston Trio, and I couldn't afford Joan Baez, so I turned to jazz. I had Coltrane, Mingus — all of them worked for me."

I tell Art that I remember hearing some stand-up comedians there, like a scrawny little guy with horn-rims named Woody Allen.

"That's right," Art says. "Woody Allen played the Gate, but he never was a big draw. He doesn't want to be reminded now he once was a comic. Even then he was on his way, though. I had Dick Cavett, Mort Sahl, Jackie Mason, Redd Foxx. I mixed 'em up, and mixed up the kinds of music too — I had the Clancy Brothers, Leon Bibb, Erroll Garner."

Art wanted Billie Holiday, but he couldn't have her at the Gate because, like many jazz musicians of the day, she had had her police ID card, commonly called a cabaret card, taken away. No one could work at a nightclub or cabaret — a place of entertainment where liquor is served — without such a card, issued by the New York City Police Department, and no one could have a card "who has been convicted of a felony or of any misdemeanor or offense, or is or pretends to be a homosexual or lesbian." Leaving aside the constitutional rights of homosexuals and lesbians (essentially they had no rights then), the main effect was to bar people who had been convicted or even simply arrested for possession of narcotics, as many jazz musicians had been. Thelonious Monk was unable to work in New York from 1951 to 1957 because his cabaret card was taken away.

For *The Nation*, I covered a test case on the issue, brought by J. J. Johnson, who in the five previous years, from 1954 to 1959, had led both critics' and readers' polls as the outstanding trombone player in the country. In 1946 he'd been given a suspended sentence on a narcotics charge, and because of that the police took away his cabaret card. Despite his clean record after that, the police would issue him only temporary cards, forcing him to reapply every time he got a club date.

Johnson, a most solid citizen, was able to prove he had been married since 1946, was the father of two children, owned his own home, and was a member in good standing of national fraternal organizations — a real sign of respectability in the fifties. He still hadn't been granted a permanent ID card, and the attorney Maxwell Cohen, who represented other jazz musicians on this issue as well, went to court in behalf of Johnson. In covering the court proceedings, I got to meet Johnson, another of my jazz idols, who held the extra fascination for me of being from Indianapolis (he composed and recorded a piece called "Naptown, USA"). I introduced myself to him and his wife, another Indianapolis native, who told me her sister was now attending my old high school, Shortridge, and I proudly wrote to my parents of how I had met and talked with this famous couple from Naptown.

Club owners later joined musicians in the battle to end cabaret card regulations. "We finally fought the ordinance," Art d'Lugoff says, "and got the police to end the fingerprinting of nightclub performers in New York." But that was not until after Art had tried to bring Billie Holiday to town in the summer of 1957.

For the previous ten years she had been banned from singing at any New York club by denial of her police ID card, based on previous narcotics arrests. But there was another way Art d'Lugoff could bring Billie Holiday to the Village: no edict prevented her from performing in a theater.

"I couldn't have her at the Gate," d'Lugoff explains, "So I put her at the Loew's Sheridan." He hands me a yellow leaflet announcing Billie Holiday's appearance at the 2,500-seat movie theater in the

Village. The concert was cosponsored by d'Lugoff and the *Village Voice*.

The afternoon before the night of the concert, Art called Jerry Tallmer, the theater critic of the *Voice*, and asked if he could pick up Billie in Philadelphia and drive her to the evening's event. Art explained she was working in a nightclub in Philly and the show wouldn't be over until eleven. Tallmer would have to get her to the Sheridan between one and two A.M. in order to beat a three A.M. entertainment curfew in New York.

The only car the *Voice* owned was a 1949 Olds that Tallmer doubted could make it to New York from Philadelphia in two hours. Tallmer was a great Billie Holiday fan who'd gone to hear her on 52nd Street when he and she were both twenty years old (compared to her, Tallmer felt as if he were ten), and he managed to commandeer a new, "powder-blue, push-button Chrysler" for the trip. Tallmer packed Billie, her husband and manager Louis McKay, her accompanist Mal Waldron, Waldron's girlfriend and future wife, Billie's evening dresses and portfolios of music, and assorted other bags into the car at about a quarter to twelve, with Billie holding her Chihuahua in one hand and a drink in the other, and they sped north. Billie insisted on stopping at a bar on the way, but they made it to the theater just before three for her first major appearance in New York City in over a decade.

She wouldn't have been allowed to sing after the three o'clock curfew, but the police had been greased, and Billie started on the dot of three. She sang to a wildly enthusiastic full house, and afterward went to a party at Tallmer's apartment on Christopher Street, and then he took her to the hotel where she was staying on Columbus Circle. Two years later, Tallmer wrote an account of the adventure as part of an impassioned tribute in *Evergreen Review* ("Bye Bye Blackbird") after he heard on the radio that Billie Holiday was in Metropolitan Hospital with a guard posted in her room. She had been booked on a charge of possession of heroin, which the police found in her purse.

Early on a Saturday evening that summer of 1959, when I was at my typewriter trying to finish a piece that was due the following Monday at *Harper's Magazine*, I got a call from Billie Holiday's friend Maely Dufty. I had met Maely through the narcotics committee of the East Harlem Protestant Parish, where she was one of a number of people from around the city who came to help addicts who were trying to get off heroin.

Maely asked if I would help her in an emergency. Billie Holiday was in the hospital, dying, and the police were stationed in her room. Maely and Louis McKay had written a petition asking the city to remove the police from her bedside and allow Billie to die in peace, without police harassment in her final days and hours. They wanted to get as many signatures as possible and present the petition the following day, while there was still time.

I said of course I would help. I took the subway uptown to Maely's, and she introduced me to McKay and gave me the petitions. Then I set out on Saturday night to get signatures. I thought it would be easy. I figured people would be lining up to sign for one of the great singers of our time.

I was wrong. The old McCarthyite fear of signing your name to anything was still alive in the land, even in New York. The attitude of many people I asked was summed up by a young man I encountered at a party at Ted the Horse's apartment who nervously refused on the grounds that "I'm not a signer."

I figured my only hope was to find some politically aware citizens, so I hurried over to a meeting of the Young Socialist League and asked Mike Harrington if I could make an appeal for the petition. Mike sympathized at once. He signed it himself, then interrupted the debate going on at his meeting, introduced me, explained the petition, and urged everyone to sign it. Out of a crowd of about forty people, I got eight or nine signatures.

I hit the White Horse, the San Remo, Louis', and found more suspicious people unwilling to help. And this was the Village! Finally, around one o'clock in the morning I wearily took the IRT back uptown and handed over a sheet with about twenty names on it to Maely and Louis, and explained it was the best I could do. They thanked me.

Maely was doing everything she could think of to ease the pain of Billie's last days, and as part of that effort she called Reverend Norm Eddy of the East Harlem Protestant Parish. "Maely took me up to see her," Norm recalls. "She was under guard, which was ridiculous — there was no way she could leap out of that hospital bed and escape. Maely and I were among the few friends who came to visit. Maely asked me to come because she recognized that Billie had a deep faith. A priest had visited her, and Maely wanted to bring a minister. I felt different because I didn't know Billie Holiday, but I went.

"The first time I visited, Billie was fully conscious and we talked, but when she signed a paperback copy of her book for me, *Lady Sings the Blues,* she was so weak and out of it she couldn't spell her name [it is signed "Billie Holday"]. The next day she was in an oxygen tent, and she breathed in and out saying, 'Oh God, oh God.' Three or four days later, people were lined up for three blocks at the funeral parlor, but she died alone."

Frank O'Hara wrote a poem called "The Day Lady Died" that not only paid tribute to Billie Holiday but beautifully captured a feeling of those times.

> *It is 12:20 in New York a Friday*
> *three days after Bastille day, yes*
> *it is 1959 and I go get a shoeshine*
> *because I will get off the 4:19 in Easthampton*
> *at 7:15 and then go straight to dinner*
> *and I don't know the people who will feed me*
>
> *I walk up the muggy street beginning to sun*
> *and have a hamburger and a malted and buy*
> *an ugly NEW WORLD WRITING to see what the poets*
> *in Ghana are doing these days*
>   *I go on to the bank*
> *and Miss Stillwagon (first name Linda I once heard)*
> *doesn't even look up my balance for once in her life*
> *and in THE GOLDEN GRIFFIN I get a little Verlaine*
> *for Patsy with drawings by Bonnard although I do*
> *think of Hesiod, trans. Richard Lattimore or*
> *Brendan Behan's new play or* Le Balcon *or* Les Negres
> *of Genet, but I don't, I stick with Verlaine*
> *after practically going to sleep with quandarines*

> *and for Mike I just stroll into the PARK LANE*
> *Liquor Store and ask for a bottle of Strega and*
> *then I go back where I came from to 6th Avenue*
> *and the tobacconist in the Ziegfeld Theatre and*
> *casually ask for a carton of Gauloises and a carton*
> *of Picayunes and a NEW YORK POST with her face on it*
>
> *and I am sweating a lot by now and thinking of*
> *leaning on the john door in the 5 SPOT*
> *while she whispered a song along the keyboard*
> *to Mal Waldron and everyone and I stopped breathing*

In the summer of 1962 the Five Spot moved three blocks north. As Hettie Jones, who lived across the street, explained, "To push out the poor it barely acknowledged, the city had condemned certain 'slum areas.' One began just south of us, across Fifth Street, and included the Five Spot." In *How I Became Hettie Jones* she remembered that summer also as the time Marilyn Monroe died and Martin Luther King was jailed in Albany, Georgia — and Jamaica and Trinidad and Tobago became free nations.

Helen Tworkov recalls the following summer of 1963 as the last big time at the Five Spot, and by that fall "people weren't crowding in like they used to, and everyone seemed to be going to Gerde's Folk City."

Ray Grist, who had worked as a bartender at the Five Spot, says of the new era, "The folk singers took over MacDougal Street. Cosby was the comedian at Gerde's Folk City, and Bob Dylan, Richie Havens, and Odetta were there, then the Beatles came, and after that it was all disco."

David Amram played the Five Spot for the last time when it moved to St. Marks Place. "They were having a hard time, doing their best to hang in there," he says. "Joe Termini was so generous, so bighearted, but he didn't really have a business sense. I played a benefit to help the Five Spot stay open, but finally it closed in the seventies. It couldn't survive the changing times in New York."

TWELVE

In Exile Till We Come Again

ONE MORNING I awoke in my high-ceilinged, floor-through apartment on East 12th Street — the best apartment I'd ever had, wangled by getting a copy of the *Village Voice* classified ads before the paper hit the newsstand — and the high steel scream of garbage trucks devouring the city's waste like menacing mechanical dinosaurs crawling through the street below my third-floor window pierced my habitual hangover like a rusty kitchen knife thrust into the tenderest part of my brain, reaching even deeper, to something that seemed like my very soul. Feeling hot and in need of fresh air, I reeled to the living room and opened the window to one of those gray, anonymous days that could have been any season, since the smog was heavy and soot seemed to clog the nostrils. I blinked and saw small buds like dabs of pale green paint on the otherwise bare, scraggly tree whose skinny limbs reached awkwardly upward like pleading arms. It was spring of 1962, May, almost my birthday. *Thirty.*

The same scene would have looked different to me, more pleasing, less menacing, even a year before (in my twenties). Then the sight that would have secretly cheered me was of the office across the street — Fairchild Publications, home of *Women's Wear Daily* — where I could look down and see through its windows men and women in suits and ties, dresses and heels, moving efficiently be-

tween desks like bees in a hive, regimented to a nine-to-five life. I'd
managed to escape that life by virtue of living by the pen, no matter
how hard or precarious it was to patch together the rent with checks
from magazines and modest advances for books and maybe a
grant — if not from Guggenheim, as Ivan Gold had gotten, then
one from another foundation, the Ingram-Merrill perhaps, which
bestowed something on my worthiest literary friend, Robert Phelps.
Our highly irregular (in terms of timing) checks that were always
"in the mail" from magazine and publisher were supplemented
sometimes with a temporary research job for a good cause: Mike
Harrington had once worked for the Fund for the Republic, on a
study of blacklisting in movies and television. From time to time
Seymour Krim did stints as an editor, lending literary class to the
new girlie mags, where he could assign work to free-lance friends
(like me) for a good fee — up to $500 a shot, enough to live on for
a month.

I remembered walking down Perry Street with Mike Harrington
one fresh fall afternoon in the late fifties when he said with a smile,
"Once you free-lance, I can't imagine ever going back to a regular
job." I agreed, though later, when Mike had a wife and children, he
would sensibly take a teaching position at Queens College and still
have time to write and carry on his lifelong work as a socialist
leader. Free-lance meant freedom, and so did New York, especially
Greenwich Village, until that not so fine morning when the garbage
trucks really got to me and all of it seemed like a trap, a smog-bound
prison.

I've got to get out of here.

I told it to two different people that day. One was the second of
the Freudian psychoanalysts I'd seen every weekday, except during
August, for five years, and he responded just as his almost identical
predecessor had: "Yes, go on." I said I would, for one more year. I
was going to stick to the analysis that much longer because I'd already invested so much time in it (that and my parents' money,
which I'd pledged to pay them back, and finally did, more than ten
years later). When I started I was told five years was about the minimum for the treatment to be successful — the patient free, golden,
glowing. But no end seemed in sight, and I'd begun to meet people

around New York who'd been in analysis twelve years, even fifteen or twenty, and I said to my inscrutable doctor, "I'm not going to spend my life at this." It was already slipping away, maybe half had already gone, more if I died dramatically young, like Dylan Thomas at thirty-nine, whose ghost I toasted when I lifted my glass in the White Horse. Hell, I was almost thirty.

"Yes, go on."

I did. I went to Harold Hayes at *Esquire,* who was always able to dispatch me on assignment when I felt stir crazy and needed to get out of town. But this was different, this was a longer, more permanent respite and change I sought, yet if anyone would know, Harold would know, and I considered him a friend now as well as my editor. He took me to a lunch of fat hamburgers and frosty mugs of beer at some new spot around the corner from his office at 488 Madison, a place where you sat in one of those long-armed wooden school chairs, balancing your mug and plate on the extended arm. We joked as we usually did of my ritual request to do a piece on a luxury cruise, giving as my journalistic rationale for a freebie vacation the fact that the legendary Agee had written such a story for *Fortune.* It was no go again and Harold laughed, then took a swig of his brew and said, "O.K., what is it you really want, Wakefield?"

Without hesitation, the response came: "Harold, I've got to get out of here."

"New York?"

"Yes. For at least a year. I need a break. How do I do it?"

"Apply for a Nieman fellowship in journalism. Gives you a year at Harvard. You take some classes, write, do what you want."

"I thought that was only for daily newspaper people."

"It used to be. They're broadening it out. I got one as a magazine editor — why shouldn't you get one as a magazine journalist? I'll write you a recommendation."

At that moment I saw what came to be popularly known, during the Vietnam War, as "the light at the end of the tunnel." The city I'd loved so much had become the tunnel, maybe because the city had come to seem so much the same as my psychoanalysis, that passage that kept getting longer and darker, without any end in sight. New York, the enlightened place of liberty that held among its hopes the freedom offered by probing the psyche through lying on the couch, somehow was merging with the couch in my conception of it — long and black and cold.

The light was not just the hope of the Nieman but New England itself: open spaces, the North, nature, fresh air, silence, all those elements I had once scorned as boring now seemed like succor. I'd discovered the country by visiting Norman Thomas di Giovanni, the writer I'd met through *The Nation* when he was doing pieces for the magazine from Boston, where he'd lived in a loft in the North End, the city's Little Italy, and worked in a neighborhood grocery while researching a book about Sacco and Vanzetti and translating poetry from Spanish.

Norman had moved to a cabin by a pond in New Hampshire with his lovely and brilliant companion Priscilla Hudson, and invited me to visit. Walking the pond, eating pasta and pesto, made from fresh basil leaves Priscilla grew in the garden, as well as Norman's proudly planted corn, tomatoes, and beans, I had a taste of that other promise of the good life. Maybe I was coming to the part of that life Malcolm Cowley wrote about in *Exile's Return* when his friends from the twenties came back from Europe and fled New York in "a great exodus toward Connecticut, the Catskills, northern New Jersey and Bucks County, Pennsylvania."

I took a deep breath of the fresh, smogless, soot-free air of New Hampshire and arranged to rent, for $40 a month, one half of a converted ice house near Norman in the town of Hudson when I ended the analysis the following summer of 1963. Whether I got the Nieman or not, I planned to hole up and finally realize the dream, the writing of the Novel, living on pasta and pesto, corn and beans — and air. I'd be living by a pond, just like you know which great writer, who also sought solitude and peace and advised us to "simplify, simplify," which meant to anyone weary of scrambling through the maze of Manhattan — leave.

The knowledge that I was going to be leaving at the end of the next year's worth of analysis gave me a goal, got me organized, tugged me out of the torpor of looking down open-ended years on the couch. (The couch began to look like a slide, tilting, aimed for dumping me down to the dark nothing, Hemingway's *nada*.) I followed C. Wright Mills's advice for dealing with crisis, beginning again: "Set up a new file!" The determined courage of his voice came back in memory, stabbing with the realization of his recent and premature death, which was also the death of part of what I previously meant when I said "New York."

To shoulder more of the financial burden of my own analysis, which was said to be part of the trick of having it work, I sold the idea for collecting, editing, and writing the introduction to what I felt was a much-needed anthology of fiction and factual work on drug addiction. I first learned about the problem in Spanish Harlem, and continued to write and learn about it and work as a volunteer for the narcotics committee, drawn to the subject with a mixture of fear and fascination. As the addict author said in *The Fantastic Lodge,* I "had eyes," and I included that part of her pseudonymous book in my prospectus.

I presented the idea — we didn't say "pitch" then — to an editor at Fawcett with a reputation for no-nonsense fairness and honesty, Knox Burger, the guy who first found a story of Vonnegut's in the slush pile at *Collier's* and published it, and later brought out Kurt's early novels in paperback. Already balding and wittily acerbic (the term "crusty" is used with affection by those who know him), Knox listened attentively, fired some pertinent questions at me, then said with the decisiveness and clarity one always hopes and dreams of hearing and seldom does: "We'll do the book."

I divided my working time among that project, my magazine pieces, and my newly resumed attack on the magic novel. Every afternoon I'd leave my own apartment, with the file cabinet and factual material from which I was hammering out my "living by the pen" (the money for rent, food, booze, and a greater share of the monthly analytic bill, the biggest cut of all), and go to a corner I was given in a sunny part of my dear friend Jane Wylie's living room on Perry Street. The room overlooked one of those small Village gardens, which always made me think of a poem by May Swenson, "The Garden at St. John's in the City" ("this garden / of succulent green in the broil of the city"), and of May herself, who lived only a few blocks away and whose head-on, solid, gum-chewing confidence in my writing was part of my hope and inspiration and nourishment of soul.

That last year my already considerable consumption of bourbon increased, causing blackouts a couple of times, when I didn't know how I'd gotten back home or where I'd been, and those scared me enough to stop drinking for a few days and try to cut down, but no one else I knew was cutting down, and continual drinking seemed to be part of what it took to live in New York.

This was not just an individual excuse but a recognized phenomenon of New York in that era. Norman Podhoretz wrote, in *Breaking Ranks*, "Of course everyone, including me in those days, drank too much; for literary people it went with the territory. A writer was expected to drink and suspected if he didn't; and far from being frowned on, drinking heavily was admired as a sign of manliness, and of that refusal of respectability that seemed necessary to creative work."

A writer friend of mine came back from lunch with his editor to celebrate a new book contract and complained bitterly that the editor had so many martinis so fast that the writer had to pour him into a cab to go home. My friend pointed out that it was the *writer* who was supposed to get drunk at lunch, and the editor's job to see that *he* got home. He felt cheated.

When Joan Didion spoke of feeling she'd had a low-grade hangover for eight years when she left New York, she was speaking for all of us. I justified the hard drinking as part of the life I chose to lead (an occupational hazard, like black lung for coal miners), but it was increasingly turning sour, creating scenes of conflict and pain rather than the early exhilaration that came from toasting the dawn with bourbon on Village rooftops.

One night in my last year in New York I went to dinner with Baldwin at his friend Mary Painter's apartment, and the bourbon Jimmy and I sloshed down fueled a terrible misunderstanding and argument. Mary was a gentle, quiet women who was like a big sister to Jimmy (he dedicated *Another Country* to her, and she was the friend he had in mind when he met with Muslim leader Elijah Muhammad and felt he had to defend his friendships with whites). Jimmy invited us to a fashion show in Harlem the following week being staged by his sixteen-year-old sister. He told of his fears for her because she was talented and ambitious and a Negro, and felt she was in pain now because of all that.

A Frenchwoman who was visiting Mary tried to console Baldwin by saying that *all* sixteen-year-old girls are in pain, and I jumped in to add, thinking of myself, that all sixteen-year-old boys suffer too, no matter what their color. Baldwin's enormous eyes grew wide as he turned on me and said in accusation, "*You don't understand.*" Mary wisely kept silent, but I kept pressing my point — that each person's private pain was as great as any other's, since each of us could only suffer to the limit of our own capacity. All this got more tangled the more we drank, and Jimmy receded into silent fury.

I remember thunder and lightning and summer rain, and the evening ended in a painful haze. I don't remember getting home but only recall waking with a hangover, made more severe by the pounding memory of breaking the trust of a friendship I treasured. (We later picked up the pieces, but it never was whole again.) I couldn't help thinking with irony the next morning that the pain of my hangover could not have been greater no matter what my race.

The city that once was bright with promise seemed to be growing dark with anxiety and trouble as I used more bourbon to numb the pain. Different, dire images of New York began to accumulate, adhere to my consciousness, words that defined the place in this bleak new mood. I salted some away as prospective epigraphs for the novel I would write, my favorite being the opening line of Stephen Crane's short story "The Open Boat," which seemed to sum up not only the plight of those people bent over oars while rowing for their lives in a stormy sea, but also our striving to survive and even struggle upward in the densest concrete jungle of them all: "None of them knew the color of the sky."

Before Norman Podhoretz wrote his much-maligned autobiographical book *Making It,* speaking aloud of "the dirty little secret" of success in literary New York, Seymour Krim wrote an essay about the even dirtier secret of *not* making it. In "Ubiquitous Mailer vs. Monolithic Me" he confessed his frustration and sense of failure at being what someone known as the Celebrity Checker called a "semi-name," and spoke of the emotional wringer of "living your 40s inside the heightened Manhattan crucible." I'm sure that is what Ted the Horse had in mind when he asked me, "Are you going to talk about 'the New York crucible'?"

Part of that ordeal is getting your first bad review in the *Times,* as I did with my second book, *Revolt in the South,* a collection of my pieces on civil rights stories in *The Nation,* stitched together for a Grove Press paperback original. It was blasted by a reporter, a transplanted southerner, who took the occasion to bash me and the book and northern liberals in general, especially those who go below the Mason-Dixon line to write about civil rights. James Baldwin and Bayard Rustin wrote eloquent letters to the *Times* in my defense, and Ralph McGill gave the book a fine notice in *The Saturday Review,* but nothing seemed to stick but the blot in the *Times,* which in literary matters is truly the newspaper of record. It hurt. I learned then how public are writers' defeats, how unlike the lawyer who loses a case or the doctor who loses a patient, for nobody outside the office or medical center knows, while the writer's defeat is read about by neighbors, bartenders, friends, enemies — everyone who reads the paper over morning coffee, which in New York is everyone who reads, and that is *everyone.*

I didn't feel jealous of writers my age whose work I liked getting published and acknowledged; I just wanted to do my *own.* I felt *Rabbit, Run* by John Updike was the first real novel that spoke for people my age, and when my old sportswriter friend from the *Indianapolis Star,* Bob Collins, came to New York, I dragged him into a bookstore and made him buy it. The stories in *Goodbye, Columbus* caught the tone and feel of people of my generation, and I met Roth when it was published by Houghton Mifflin, the same house that did my own *Island in the City* the same season, as well as a marvelous book of short stories called *The Poison Tree* by Walter Clemons, another of our generation.

Whatever frustration I felt about not yet doing my novel when I lived in New York was erased seven years after I left, when Gay Talese invited me for drinks to celebrate the publication of *Going All the Way* when it was named as a book club selection and hit *Time*'s best-seller list (it eventually sold more than a million copies in all editions). Talese poured us both big gin and tonics, turned his x-ray eyes on me with full force, and said, "Congratulations. You've really done it." And I knew he meant it and was genuinely pleased.

In the meantime, back in the midst of my bourbon-brown mood of that last year in New York, I plunged for salvation into my work, and though the novel I still plugged away at came chokingly slow, if at all, I managed to write magazine pieces of which I was proud.

The most monumentally researched and meaningful to me was an *Esquire* article called "Dos, Which Side Are You On?" which followed John Dos Passos's path from 1920s rebel to 1960s conservative, written in the style of *U.S.A.* In preparation I read every book he had written — it was well over thirty volumes by then — and was moved again by the mass and power of *U.S.A.*, and freshly taken with his early mastery, in *Manhattan Transfer,* of a new, kaleidoscopic form that captured the hardest place of all to pin down in its shifting modes and moods.

I also interviewed James T. Farrell, the author of *Studs Lonigan,* for the *Esquire* article while he paced his studio bedroom at the Beaux Arts Hotel in his pajamas. He suddenly stopped and crawled under the bed to search for some old papers and letters. With his bare feet sticking out the side of the bed, I heard him say, "Don't you see, Dos has lived a world so different from these contemporary writers. His interest isn't just himself, it's the world." I admired Farrell's respect and loyalty but cringed when he showed me a map of the world with marks on various countries indicating support for his own candidacy for the Nobel Prize. (He was running for laureate!) Then he pointed out other countries and said, "Dos has a lot more backing there than I do."

My God, I thought, will it come to this? Will my friends and I, twenty or thirty years later, be scrambling under hotel beds for evidence of our standing in the world literary market? Show me the way to Walden Pond!

Dos himself — in the carriage house on the slope of a hill in Baltimore where he worked during the week, spending weekends at the country estate that had been his father's in Westmoreland, Virginia — seemed subdued and patient, politely doing his duty with the interview, reflecting, I guessed, the disillusionment and exhaustion expressed in one of his later novels, *Midcentury.* There he plumbed depths lower than I had yet struck; I wondered if this view, too, awaited me with the winding down of the years:

> *Musing midnight and the*
> *century's decline*
> *man walks with dog . . .*
> *The hate remains*

> *to choke out good, to strangle the*
> *still small private voice that is*
> *God's spark in man. Man drowns in his own scum.*
> *These nights are dark.*

He had come a long way from the Jazz Age, the literary Roaring Twenties of his friends Fitzgerald and Hemingway.

I used those quoted words to end my piece, perhaps because they mirrored my own dark mood, one that sank to the pit of an April evening when, for the first time since the early years of the analysis, I drunkenly cut my wrist, and later woke not only with the pain, guilt, and anguish of that self-destructive act but the horrible realization that this was the day I was scheduled to have my interview with the Nieman committee at the Harvard Club of New York.

"It's over," I wailed, "it's all over." But I had enough will to live to wail my lament to the right friend, Jane Wylie, who came to the rescue from Perry Street with bandages and aspirin and soup and juice, sticking me in the shower, getting me dressed, cajoling me up to the favorite spot where we used to go and play F. Scott in brighter days, the very Plaza where he jumped into the fountain. Just before the interview Jane fed me two frozen daiquiris and secured the sleeve of my left arm with a safety pin so the cuff wouldn't slip and show the bandage on my wrist. Sailing out on a safety pin and a smile, I appeared before that august body and calmly presented my credentials as a serious journalist, posing as a sane and upstanding citizen, speaking of my work on the racial conflict in the South, my variety of reportage for *The Nation, Esquire,* and other worthy journals, and proudly mentioning my book *Island in the City: The World of Spanish Harlem.* I exited into the brisk afternoon feeling like a winner, but not taking any bets.

I got my mind off my worries when *The Saturday Evening Post* sent me to cover a coal mining strike in Hazard, Kentucky, but the piece I produced wasn't as "colorful" as they wanted. I went with what I knew was a meaningful story of American working-class life (including a threatened leader of the striking miners who kept an ax beside him in the seat of his car whenever he left home) to Norman Podhoretz at *Commentary*. He nodded, got the picture precisely, said to redo it, and helped me clear away the rhetoric and hit the story's bone. I wrote out of my angry weariness, which matched the mood of the striking miners: "I would just as soon forget about Hazard, Kentucky . . ."

A letter arrived in the mail in late May that said I got the Nieman. I yelped for joy and relief and called everyone I knew. My agent and friend, the courtly and gracious James Oliver Brown, took me to a fabulous dinner at Peter's Backyard — the Village steak house that Meg Greenfield says we always got our parents to take us to when they came to town. When "In Hazard" was published in *Commentary,* I was asked to lunch by Harrison Salisbury and A. M. Rosenthal, who said that was the kind of reporting they wanted to have in the *New York Times,* and offered me a job. I was flattered but not tempted, for I had the Nieman in my pocket, lots of time ahead to write the Novel, and the ease of not having to worry about the rent for a whole year — I had "lived by the pen" in New York for eight years, and I was all scratched out.

I wrote that piece for *Mademoiselle* on the new young conservative movement, and the magazine invited me to a cocktail party for their new crop of guest editors fresh out of college. I was drawn to a lively young editorial aspirant of abundant beauty and charm, whose enthusiasm about being in New York (she had just arrived from Dubuque or Des Moines, or maybe it was De Kalb) reminded me of how I had felt when I got off the train from Indianapolis more than a decade before. Time had evaporated.

Caught up in the magic of her Manhattan excitement, the first flush of it, I got excited again myself, like the contact high jazz musicians sometimes experienced, and when she said, "Being here, it's like being on fire," I remembered that kind of burning passion for New York I used to have, and a tingle went through me. I was on the verge of asking her to dinner, of pursuing an evening of New York youthful romance — "Dancing on the Ceiling," "My Funny Valentine" — and then I stopped before the words came out, for I suddenly sensed the enormous gap between her experience of the moment and mine. It was clear that I would only be trying to get some of what she had to rub off on me, and it seemed unfair, like theft. I felt old and grubby. I finished my drink, wished her luck, went back down to the Village, and called up an old girlfriend of roughly my own vintage and had a quiet, desultory dinner, realizing something was over.

Maybe that's when the fifties ended for me, or maybe it was just the end of my New York, or my youth — or maybe they all were the same. What came to me then was the line from *The Crack-Up*, when Fitzgerald wrote in "Echoes of the Jazz Age" about the twenties: "It all seems rosy and romantic to us who were young then, because we will never feel quite so intensely about our surroundings any more."

There were other endings too, other demarcations of the era, for me and for everyone I know, and sometimes we look back on them, identify them, in personal experience and in public events and issues, and sometimes the two converge in a single memory. For Norman Mailer, the shift in the zeitgeist of the decade came in political terms.

"I can tell you when the fifties ended," he says. "It was 1959 in Chicago, and I was on 'Kup's Show' [Irv Kupcinet was a Chicago newspaper columnist who hosted his own TV talk show]. He got whatever visiting firemen were in town, this odd mix of people, from an executive of the UJA to the mayor of Dublin, the police chief of Ghana, and Hazel Scott — whoever was in town. There were about twelve people that night, and the show went on for hours, from midnight to three or four in the morning. I got into a debate with some pro-Ike person and it was terribly dull, so finally, to get something going, I said, 'In my opinion, J. Edgar Hoover has done more to harm this country than Stalin.' Well, that got the ball rolling. Hazel Scott was the only one who joined forces with me, the rest were all out to get me. After saying that, I didn't know how long I had to live — I was as paranoid as the next guy in those days. I thought there would be a horrible response from the FBI. It turned out later, when I saw my FBI file, there were about three hundred pages on me, and about eighty pages were devoted to that one program!

"A friend of mine was out in the control booth and he said calls started coming in, and there were twenty-eight opposed to what I said and twenty in favor. I felt it meant there was something in the air, some dissatisfaction with the Ike era that I didn't know existed.

I'd have thought the response would be something like fifty to five against me."

For many people the fifties ended with either the hope brought about by the inauguration of John F. Kennedy in 1961 or the despair and disillusionment that came when he was assassinated in 1963. Looking back, however, William F. Buckley, Jr., argues that "it's not accurate to think the election of JFK established the sixties. There was nothing innovative about JFK, though one has to say that now while wearing a safety vest. The civil rights movement was innovative, but he didn't kindle it. The difference he brought to the office was his persona — he was very glamorous. People forget he was not all that popular before he was killed. The issue of *Time* before the assassination said JFK was going to Texas because he thought the Texas vote might decide the presidential election. The fifties weren't really over till Vietnam, in '64 or '65."

For many people, the Vietnam War became the defining event between eras, and for some it came not just as headlines but in terms of personal and professional decisions. Even those of us too old to face issues of college deferment or the draft were faced with moral dilemmas brought home by Vietnam.

John Gregory Dunne recalls: "In '62 I was writing this stuff for *Time* about Indochina and I didn't even know where the countries were, so I asked *Time* if they'd send me there. I was a bachelor, so I said I'd take my vacation there for three weeks if they'd pay my air fare, and they said O.K. I went to Tokyo, Hong Kong, Saigon, Bangkok. I met David Halberstam, Neil Sheehan, and Peter Arnett, and I got to know Charlie Mohr, who was the *Time* correspondent over there. I respected these guys, and by the early fall of '63 they were all saying things are not like the Pentagon says they are.

"One day I got a long story on the war to work on, a report from Charlie Mohr. I can remember his first sentence as if it's in big block letters in my mind: 'The war in Vietnam is being lost.' That night I had a date with Joan [Didion] for dinner, and we went to the Chalet Suisse on West 52nd Street and had fondue, and I said, 'There's no way *Time* is going to print this story from Charlie Mohr and I'm not going to change it. I'm going to call in sick.' Joan said, 'No, write it the way he sent it.' The procedure at *Time* was you took these report files and worked on them like a carpenter, and that's what I did. I went back that night and worked till two or three in the morning and got it done as Mohr had reported it. The next morning I got in around eleven. I saw the edited version of the story and Otto Fuerbringer had written 'Nice' across my copy — but instead of the war being lost, he had edited it into 'There's light at the end of the tunnel.' I told the editor I wouldn't continue to work on the story and I wouldn't write any more Vietnam stuff. That was the end of my career at *Time*. I stayed on, but I was reassigned to the Benelux countries. I knew my days were numbered, and I didn't get a raise when the time came around. Joan and I were married in January of '64, and that April I went to work one morning and called Joan and said, 'Do you mind if I quit?' and she said no. I asked for a leave of absence — I knew I wasn't coming back, but I wanted to keep my health benefits as long as I could. I left in May and we went to California."

Some of us who were adolescents in the age of Ike found the signal of change in the new sexual attitudes. For Bruce Jay Friedman, who first etched some of the male's sexual fears and hang-ups in his black humor novel *Stern*, the fifties ended at a party in the Village: "My wife and I had a son, so we had moved to Glen Cove, Long Island, and we just came into the city at night for musicals in the late fifties and early sixties. One night in 1961 I saw another life. I went to a party given by a woman who lived in a brownstone in the Village. She was a one-woman sexual revolution. It was the beginning of the bossa nova craze. Paul Krassner, who published *The Realist*, and John Wilcock, who wrote 'The Village Square' column for the *Voice*, were there, and the jazz musician David Amram, and my friend Arthur Frommer, who later did the guidebooks to Europe on five dollars a day. I was there with my wife, and I had on a tweed suit. That night was the first time I ever smelled pot. Instantly, the world tilted. It was the smell of pot in concert with seeing this woman who was giving the party — this tall woman with black hair to the floor and a perfect body, dancing to one of those bossa nova songs. It was a magical vision, smoking dope and seeing this fabulous woman, and in the john there were nude pictures of her from floor to ceiling! This woman almost single-handedly ushered in the sixties. When I was ready to leave the party, I couldn't find my raincoat, and this incredible woman who was the hostess said, 'Your raincoat will be here tomorrow.' I didn't even catch on, I was so dumb. I sent my friend Frommer over the next day to get the raincoat! But I knew after that party there was a wonderful craziness out there to be had."

In his next book jacket photograph, Friedman had lost the tweed suit and grown a beard.

Clothing and style signaled deeper changes for women, too. Jane Wylie says the fifties ended when "suddenly you had to have two wardrobes. One was the classic stuff, like the sleeveless linen sheath and the dresses you bought at Bendel's and Bloomingdale's, the other was short and laced up the side and was supposed to look really sexy, and also there were pantsuits and low-slung trousers with vests. You got those things at a store called Paraphernalia, in the East 60s. You had to think where you were going before you decided what to wear. You could get kicked out of someplace 'nice' if you had on pants that weren't elegant.

"It was around this time that women started talking — I mean to each other. It was a huge thing. Suddenly there was a lot of talk about masturbation — whether, where, when, how — and everyone was reading *The Joy of Sex*. Women began to say they didn't like the stuff about being perfect, as in 'the perfect housewife.' I knew a woman who was married to a graduate student whose apartment was always filled with empty coffee cups and piles of books, and she stopped worrying that people would think her a bad housewife. Now you were allowed to have that kind of place and you weren't judged on your housewifeliness. That was a new kind of freedom.

"Now the girls I teach who are thirteen think about what they want to be — they have an idea about being something besides a wife. They can have a real career. In the fifties it was like women could have a career but then they were going to get married, and after that it was sort of a haze."

For Helen Weaver, the fifties were over when ballroom dancing gave way to the twist: "Instead of having to know steps or follow your partner's lead, you could just stand there and wiggle. A woman didn't have to be a partner at all — a revolutionary concept! She could dance with herself, or the whole room.

"Literary parties in the fifties were still dominated by alcohol and ambition, but at parties in artists' lofts there was a friendly haze over everything that seemed to emanate from the bathroom, where people stood around looking conspiratorial and reverent while blowing their minds.

"The fifties really ended on November 22, 1963, when it became clear, as John Lindsay said, two assassinations later, 'The country's lost its way.' That day marked the beginning of the end of our innocence. In the fifties we were still innocent enough to feel guilty. In the sixties, guilt went out of style."

For David Amram, a pioneer of racial and musical freedom in the fifties, the coming of the Beatles — and with them a revolution in pop music that rang changes through the whole culture — was not the sound of liberation that it seemed to many. "When the Beatles came to America, suddenly music took on a whole different picture. There were no black people, not just in the Beatles but in the new imitative groups throughout the country. All the time all of us spent in integrated bands, even in the South, risking our lives, and then suddenly with the Beatles came these all-white groups. It was almost as if the music industry and media gave a totalitarian answer to the miracle of the fifties. The whole fifties coming together of poetry, music, and arts looked as if it might be squashed. A lot of us were told we were passé. There was a high level of recording techniques — sound reproduction and amplification became arts. The counterculture of the sixties hooked in with the music industry, a colossal amount of money could be earned by musicians in their twenties. It began a new era — a decade of greed and narcissism."

A lot of things were changing by 1964, and I wasn't the only one who was leaving New York around that time. On April 24 of that year, when I was at Harvard, I got a letter from Joan Didion;

> Dear Dan,
>   Mainly I'm writing to ask if you (or anyone you know up there) need an apartment. We rather suddenly decided to go to Los Angeles for 6 or 7 months, starting June 1, and want to sublet this place to somebody we know and leave furniture, china, linens, silver, everything. . . .
>   For six months I am going to have a tan and a Thunder-

bird and work very hard at talking to people and not being my own creepy self. Suspecting accurately that my entire image of our life in Los Angeles is based vaguely upon "A Star Is Born," John has vetoed a house at Malibu, but I am holding fast on a pool. I don't know exactly how we'll like it there, actually, but he was sick of *Time* and I was sick of New York, so he just took this leave of absence until Christmas. I am supposed to finish a novel and he is supposed to finish some diverse projects and we are both supposed to Think Things Over. An unsubsidized Neiman is what we had in mind. (That is probably not the way Neiman is spelled. It looks suspiciously as if it should be followed not by "Fellowship" but by "Marcus.")

> Love
> From
> Joan

In her classic essay on leaving New York, "Goodbye to All That," Joan wrote that on her first trip there she spent the first three days talking long distance to her boyfriend, whom she told she could see the Brooklyn Bridge from her window, and was going to stay for only six months, then she adds, "As it turned out, the bridge was the Triborough, and I stayed eight years."

In the letter she wrote me, she said John had vetoed a house in Malibu, and they'd planned to stay for six months. As it turned out, they later bought a house in Malibu, and stayed in L.A. for twenty years. Oh yes, and they wrote the original script that became the new version of the movie *A Star Is Born*, with Barbra Streisand and Kris Kristofferson.

"For the first three years in L.A. we kept our apartment on East 75th Street," Joan tells me now, "even though it was a great irritation — the subletters never paid the rent."

Other friends of mine kept their apartments when they first left the city, which enabled them to still think of themselves as New Yorkers and believe their move away from it could only be temporary. "*The Reporter* sent me to Washington in '61," Meg Greenfield says, "and I thought I'd just be gone for a couple of months. I flew to New York on the shuttle every Friday afternoon — it cost $16 then — and went back on Monday morning. I found it wasn't so easy to leave. When I first got to Washington, I was part of a little group of displaced New Yorkers, and we all bitched about Washington. After three years, I finally gave up my New York apartment, in '64, and rented a house. I went to the *Post* in '68 when *The Reporter* closed down."

I didn't try to keep my own apartment in New York, but turned it over to Robert Phelps, who magically transformed it from a bare, dusty, cluttered Village pad to a warm, bright, book-lined haven that surely would have pleased Henry James. When I went back to visit, I envied the way he'd made it the kind of place I'd always wanted to live in, but I didn't yearn to move back. I had rented half of that converted ice house by di Giovanni's pond in New Hampshire before I got the Nieman, and decided I could use it on weekends, then move in permanently when the fellowship year was over.

My "back to the land" dreams lasted only a year, but on the Nieman I discovered Boston, especially Beacon Hill, and I also made a connection with the new editor of *The Atlantic Monthly,* Robert Manning, who soon became a friend. The *Atlantic* under Manning gave me a pleasant and stimulating journalistic and literary base (with an office of my own in the beautiful old building at 8 Arlington Street), and I became an official part of the magazine as a contributing editor from 1967 until it changed ownership in 1980.

The extra good fortune of connecting with Seymour Lawrence at his independent publishing office on Beacon Street gave me the right publisher for the novel I finally finished in 1969 (*Going All the Way* came out the following year), and I signed up with Sam for the next three novels, completing the solid and congenial professional home I found in Boston and on the Hill. Except for two temporary displacements in Hollywood, Boston has served as headquarters and seemed like home ever since.

I made occasional trips to New York on the train and the shuttle, but they became less frequent. I'd go there for only two or three days, so I didn't have time to keep up with all my old friends. I started losing touch and even losing track of some. Sometimes I had the feeling that Joan Didion expressed in "Goodbye to All That," when she went back to New York and found "many of the people I used to know had moved to Dallas or had gone on Antabuse or had bought a farm in New Hampshire." I was the one she was talking about in New Hampshire, but I didn't buy the place by the pond, I only rented, and by then I had left and moved to Beacon Hill.

The cultural shift to the West had drawn the English writer Sarel Eimerl to San Francisco, though he was later to join our free-lance philosopher friend from the Village, Art "the Rug" Bernstein, in the new urban mecca of the hip, Seattle. Meg Greenfield was in Washington, the Dunnes had defected to L.A., Sam Astrachan had gone to live in the south of France, Ivan Gold and his wife and child came up to settle in Boston, and so did another novelist from the Village days, Richard Yates. Even before I got there, Cambridge had claimed Justin Kaplan, whom I met through C. Wright Mills when Kaplan was a young editor at Simon & Schuster, before becoming a Pulitzer Prize–winning biographer of *Mr. Clemens and Mark Twain*. He and his novelist wife, Ann Bernays, made their Cambridge living room the most active literary salon north of Elaine's, starring John Updike and sometimes, up from Connecticut, the surprisingly social Annie Dillard, who seemed as much at home at a cocktail party as at Tinker Creek.

When I went to New York, I usually stayed at the Village apartment of Ted "the Horse" Steeg, who had camped out on the floor of my basement apartment on West 77th Street when he arrived fresh from Indianapolis in 1955. I hung around with Ted in the Village or went uptown for business or editorial meetings with Harvey Shapiro at *The New York Times Magazine* or Art Cooper at *GQ,* or for tea at the Plaza with Jane Wylie (I had switched from the daiquiris that got me through the Nieman interview).

When I came back to stay at Lynne Sharon Schwartz's studio to do the intensive round of interviewing for this book in the early months of 1991, it was the first time in twenty-eight years that I had the experience of living again in Manhattan. I joined the Paris Health Club on West End Avenue, went to Sunday services at All Angels on West 80th Street — an Episcopal church with the best rock music for hymns I have ever heard — and became a regular browser at the Shakespeare & Company bookstore on Broadway and 81st Street. I learned to take the subway again instead of depending on taxis, and developed my on-guard alert for the homeless people pushing Styrofoam cups at you for change when you buy your tokens. The first time a tattered man appeared in my subway car shouting "Attention!" I thought it was a holdup or hijacking until I learned this was the sales pitch for the *Homeless News*. I loved being back, got a definite rush of the old excitement, yet I felt how much physically harder it was to live here than what seems by comparison the bucolic landscape of Boston and Beacon Hill.

When I asked my friends and acquaintances from the fifties who still live in New York what it's like for them now, I got a powerful sense of the change from the city we knew forty years ago. "I've been watching the city fall apart for the last forty years," Norman Mailer says. "No question it's been falling apart since '69. In '69 I felt it was important to run for mayor. I had the conceit that I could do something, that I could help the city, improve it. Now I wouldn't begin to know what you could do. I also ran because I thought it was a way to pay for my sins because I thought I'd get elected — that's how ignorant I was."

William Buckley has always commuted from Connecticut, but like Mailer he once ran for mayor, and says he would never do it again: "New York is a mess. The poor are having a harder and harder time. A lot of it stems from drugs — I believe in legalization, you know. I ran for mayor in '65, but I wouldn't dream of doing it now."

Nat Hentoff and his wife, the writer Margot Hentoff, talk about leaving. Speaking of the contrast with the old days, Nat says simply, "New York seems more consciously show biz now than it used to be, and I'm not attracted to that." Margot is more vehement on the subject: "New York is horrible now. We're all talking about leaving. The city we came to doesn't exist anymore. It was safe and glamorous and rich. Now, if you want to live in a Third World country that's poor but exciting, you come to New York. I never wanted to go to Calcutta. I remember jazz musicians used to come back from Calcutta in the fifties and with shock tell us there were people sleeping in the streets, and we couldn't believe such a thing. Now it's all around us."

Ed Fancher, cofounder and former publisher of the *Village Voice*, and a therapist who practices in the Village, came to New York in 1949 and has lived in the city ever since, but now is considering moving. "Crack has really made everything worse," Ed says. "We're thinking about leaving when our youngest son gets out of high school. He's thinking about going to college in Boston. Maybe we'll come up there too."

The only friends I know from the New York of the fifties who left for any length of time and came back again to live in the city are Joan Didion and John Dunne. In "Goodbye to All That," Joan wrote that New York is "at least for those of us who came there from somewhere else, a city for only the very young." How does it feel to return after one's youth? "I don't think of it as the same place. It's not the same people and I'm not the same person. It's just different. I don't have a sense of that infinite romantic yearning. I like living here. It's irritating, but I do like being here. When I say it's different now, it's not objectively different, it's *us*. But it's a better place to be than London or Paris."

And in spite of all the hazards and handicaps of New York in the nineties, look at all the people still here who never left, who couldn't imagine life in another realm: Harvey Shapiro, Marion Magid, Norman Podhoretz, Allen Ginsberg, Murray Kempton, Knox Burger, Kitty Sprague, Lynne Sharon Schwartz, Norman Mailer, Ned O'Gorman, Norm Eddy, Ray Grist, Walter Goodman . . . When all is said and done, more are still here from my time than have left.

Jane Richmond stayed in New York but moved from the Village to the East 60s. For her, going back to the Village now is like stepping into her old life: "I hadn't been there for something like ten years. The presence of the past was so great it was like having a coat on. I felt like I was invisible at the deli, the newsstand. It was like *Our Town*, when Emily goes back and sees everything but the people can't see her. The sense of the past was so strong it almost took the breath out of me."

"Everyone is dispersed," Meg Greenfield says. "We were transients and we had our community — we had solidarity and stability. Now I go back and it's like a sandstorm had blown over and buried the place, like it never happened. That life and community we knew are not there."

I tell her of Helen Weaver's theory about the "real" Village being buried underneath the current "stage set" we see now, and Meg laughs and says, "Yes, and if you did that excavation to unearth the real Village, we'd all be down there. We'd be going to Balducci's grocery on Sixth Avenue, and the women from the house of detention would be hollering down at us like they always did, and at night we'd go to that place on MacDougal Street, the San Remo, and then to the Portofino . . ."

When she says this I get tears in my eyes, fantasizing for a moment that it's possible, like Alice going through the looking glass, and I think, *I'd do it in a second*. I don't want to recapture the pain, of course, the drunken nights and hangovers and the dark mornings on the analyst's couch, but I'd like to get back the excitement, and most of all the people, the friends. Talking to them again, wherever they are, I feel an old camaraderie. I'm comfortable with them in a way I'd forgotten, as if I'm with my own people again — the refugees from the provinces or boroughs, the dreamers, the misfits like me, the ones with talent and problems, the daring ones, the witty and understanding, the loyal ones. I know I'm romanticizing now, but New York still does that to me — maybe just because I don't live there anymore.

Going to Seymour Krim's memorial service at the Village Gate a few years ago brought back many of the friends from those days whom I hadn't seen for many years — Art d'Lugoff, Ned Polsky, Jim Finn, and other habitués of the back room of the White Horse. We took to the stage and told good stories about our friend Sy, and David Amram, with his usual verve, played French horn as he led a group in a composition he wrote in honor of Krim.

Yet none of that brought back the spirit of the times as much as a postcard I got a week or so later, written by Krim himself just before his death, and sent on to me by his lawyer and friend Bruce Ricker. Since Krim had chosen in full consciousness to end his own life, on instructions he asked for from the Hemlock Society (because he didn't want to live on physically incapable of taking care of himself), he knew the time of his passing, and just before it he wrote to some friends.

In the old days he used to send postcards just like this to fellow writers when he saw a piece of theirs he admired, cheering them on (Nat Hentoff and Walter Goodman mentioned with gratitude such messages, which I myself had received from Krim), and the tone of this card was equally generous and uplifting. He explained that he had been quite ill — "heart failure and circulation turbulence" — but that "I wouldn't want to check out without expressing affection at an unshakeable level. . . . I always had good times with you, my friend." He spoke about my book *Returning: A Spiritual Journey,* which he'd reviewed favorably in the *Chicago Tribune,* but he wished that in chronicling my own troubles with psychoanalysis I had mentioned his piece "The Insanity Bit." Krim was a writer to the end. He forgave me, though: "But what the hell. You've forged an unexpected path for yourself, I take my hat off to you even though it is not for moi." Then he corrected a line I had misquoted from O'Neill's *Strange Interlude,* and ended by saying, "Just wanted to make touch, wish you the happiness that's possible. And the Work!"

His fifties code of ethics prevailed to the last.

Renewing bonds with friends who remain when I spent those few months in New York in the early part of 1991 turned out to be more enriching than I'd expected. I never even had a fantasy of living in New York again, but such wild ideas really came to me then, in spite of the grime and the crime, the sense of danger and drugs and the homeless, the dilapidation and the sky-high expense and what Nat Hentoff calls the show-business aspect of current New York. There were times, though, and people, and places: walking through Washington Square, hearing the political gossip in the jacuzzi at the Paris Health Club, laughing with Jane Richmond, reminiscing with Norm Eddy in East Harlem, and going to dinner at the Blue Mill with Ted the Horse. I don't think I'd have the guts and courage — and money — to really go back, but at such times, with such old friends, I was thinking, well, maybe I could just go back for a little while. Then the lines came back to me that we used to recite on West 92nd Street, or on the roof at 10th and Bleecker, John Reed's ode to New York that we said with the requisite sophisticated satire but also an eerie, exciting sort of chill:

> *Who that has known thee but shall burn*
> *In exile till he come again*
> *To do thy bitter will, O stern*
> *Moon of the tides of men!*

Index